SOCIAL WORLDS

WORLDS

PERSONAL LIVES

An Introduction to Social Psychology

SOCIAL WORLDS

PERSONAL LIVES

An Introduction to Social Psychology

EDWARD E. SAMPSON

California State University, Northridge

HARCOURT BRACE JOVANOVICH, PUBLISHERS

San Diego   New York   Chicago   Austin
London   Sydney   Tokyo   Toronto

Requests for permission to make copies of any part of the work should be mailed to:
Permissions Department, Harcourt Brace Jovanovich, Inc., 8th Floor, Orlando,
Florida 32887.

ISBN: 0-15-581805-8
Library of Congress Catalog Card Number: 90-84204
Printed in the United States of America

Preface

AS AN INTRODUCTION to social psychology, *Social Worlds, Personal Lives* has a twofold purpose. First, it covers the major current topics, theories, and research findings in the field, giving students a taste for a discipline that has continued to excite and challenge me for more than thirty years. Second, it highlights some of the serious problems and shortcomings in the existing research, presenting both a reasoned critique of social psychology today and what I believe to be a sensible alternative vision for the future.

While it would seem that presenting the existing field and, at the same time, questioning the thinking that underlies it are contradictory goals, I have come to believe that the two approaches are complementary. The central theme of this book is that the insights that drive social psychological work need to be understood in a new and provocative context. By arguing that the times in which we live and the places we inhabit are central in shaping the kinds of beings that we are and that we become, I hope to return the *social* to social psychology. A clear recognition of the intimate and complex interplay between our social worlds and our personal lives can enrich our understanding by integrating old and new thinking.

Part One introduces the student to the two basic approaches of social psychologists today: the dominant conventionalist view, which continues to drive most research in the field, and the sociohistorical alternative, which both challenges the conventional approach and offers some pointedly different ways of understanding the outcomes of conventionalist work. It is within the sociohistorical context that the book's focus on historical, cross-cultural, and European work emerges as a reminder of the truly *social* quality of social psychology.

Part Two uses several key case examples to contrast the conventionalist and sociohistorical views of cognition. It examines several aspects of social cognition traditionally dominated by conventionalist thinking—for example, attribution and accuracy—and suggests alternative interpretations implied by the sociohistorical approach—for example, how a cross-cultural understanding of the person affects the meaning of the person–situation split that is the basis of most attributional analyses.

Social influence is the focus of Part Three, where the contrast between the majority- and minority-influence models illustrates the different ways conventionalists and sociohistoricists approach such topics as conformity, obedience, and attitudes.

Part Four, on the self, shows how conventionalist and sociohistorical accounts can complement each other. Cross-cultural and historical analyses of self and identity as well as work on impression management, self-schema, and gender all reveal how the insights of a conventionalist approach are enriched by the sociohistorical framework.

Finally, Part Five examines the currently relevant topics of altruism and aggression. It once again considers the existing work in the field and presents a sociohistorical view that suggests how we might rethink some of the understandings we have achieved.

E. E. S.

Contents

PART TWO

. . . .

PART THREE

· ·

PART FOUR

· ·

The Self in Social Psychology

PART FIVE

· · · · · · · · · · · · · · · · · ·

Helping and Harming: The Social Psychology of Altruism and Aggression

PART ONE

A Perspective on Social Psychology

1

The Science
of Social
Psychology

OST INTRODUCTORY TEXTBOOKS define social psychology as a discipline devoted to the scientific study of how the individual's thoughts, feelings, and behaviors are affected by other people. In adopting this definition, authors are following the lead of one of the pioneers in the field, Gordon Allport (1954). Describing social psychology as *scientific* suggests that it falls within the web of today's more familiar sciences. As a science, then, social psychology seeks to discover the fundamental laws that govern how thoughts, feelings, and behaviors of people are affected by others.

This definition would be satisfactory if there were a single understanding of what we mean by scientific. A closer examination of current thought, however, reveals two contrasting views of science: the *conventional* and the *sociohistorical*. In this chapter, we will describe these two views in detail and see why the sociohistorical approach is the more persuasive of the two. We will begin by examining the distinction between these two approaches regarding the primary goals of social psychology.

. . . .

Primary Goals

The conventional view argues that the primary goal of the science of social psychology is to describe the world as it really is and as it really functions. This approach should not sound surprising. The conventional view has been the dominant one, and has been most influential in shaping our own understanding of science. The definition of social psychology introduced earlier reflects this conventional approach. In contrast, the sociohistorical view argues that because there is no way to describe things as they really are but only as they are framed by particular social and historical factors, the primary goal of the science of social psychology is to describe the various accounts of reality developed by different groups of people and to understand both their social and historical bases as well as the role these accounts play in the people's lives.

Given that there are two different views of science, those textbooks that define social psychology as a discipline dedicated to scientific study have said very little unless they indicate just which of these two contrasting views of science they have adopted. Most texts either consider only the conventional view to be truly scientific, or are unaware of the sociohistorical alternative. Although it is deeply rooted in the western tradition, the sociohistorical view of science has only recently seriously challenged the conventional view, beginning around 1960 with the publication of several major works in the philosophy of science (for example, see Gadamer, 1960/1975; Kuhn, 1962; Winch, 1958). Also, although a growing number of both philosophers and social psychologists have further developed this perspective (for example, see Bernstein, 1983; Gergen, 1982, 1985; Harré, 1984; MacIntyre, 1988; Rorty, 1979, 1989; Sampson, 1983; Shotter, 1984), it has not yet achieved the widespread acceptance in social psychology of the tried and true conventional point of view.

. . . .

Governing Beliefs

Before we can examine the implications of these two views of science for social psychology, we must develop a better understanding of their governing beliefs. Consider, for example, a current argument between two different ideas or theories on what constitutes a family. An argument is an especially useful starting point; we can usually assume that each side wants to win—that is, have its view of the situation prevail—and tries to persuade its opponent by appealing to well-grounded, often factual arguments.

When most of us are asked to define a family, we are likely to refer to a group of people related by marriage or blood; for example, parents and their children. This is what we usually imagine when we think of the idea of family, and it is what we would be likely to study if we were interested in learning more about how families function.

Recently, however, especially in response to the appeals of gay and lesbian couples in several major U.S. cities, efforts have been made to introduce a new conception of the family. These efforts are motivated by the need to overcome some of the unique problems that homosexual couples confront. Because homosexual couples are currently not permitted to have their relationship defined as a legal marriage, they are not defined as a family for a wide variety of important social functions. Consider these examples:

- ❏ The lesbian partner of a dying woman does not have family-member visiting rights in the hospital; this means that they cannot spend their final moments together.

- ❏ The male partner of a man whose father dies cannot receive paid leave benefits to attend the funeral because he is not considered to have a family relationship to his partner; on the other hand, the spouse can receive paid leave if he must attend the funeral of his wife's father.

- ❏ A case in New York involved the continued availability of a rent-controlled apartment to the male partner of a man who had just died and in whose name it was leased. Current law dictates that when the renter of a rent-controlled apartment dies, it is no longer subject to rent control unless a family member living there wishes to remain. Since the deceased's male partner was not legally considered a family member, he was asked to vacate the apartment.

Some efforts to change the legal definition of a family have recommended that a family be defined as any couple, regardless of sex, who have made a formal commitment and have recorded this fact in City Hall. It is assumed that such a change will provide homosexuals with the kind of legal protection and guarantees they currently lack. Needless to say, these efforts have not been met with indifference on the part of the dominant community. Many argue that a homosexual couple is not a family, and to consider it as such degrades the meaning of family and further erodes an already beleaguered social institution.

In the majority's view, a family narrowly signifies those persons joined by marriage or blood—meaning a man, a woman, and their offspring, but not two men or two women. The opposing minority view presents a different theory about what a family is, or at least what it should be. How might we resolve this disagreement? What objective facts could each side call on to support its definition of the family?

Is there a real object, "family," that exists in the world independently of the different ideas and theories used to describe it? In other words, is there a *place*, outside all social and historical contexts, from which to impartially determine just what a family is? If there were such a neutral place then, of course, we could resolve the argument between these two contrasting theories of the family by judging one to be clearly incorrect: the incorrect theory does not match the reality of the family as determined from our independent standpoint.

On the other hand, if there is no neutral observation point—because wherever we stand represents a particular social or historical perspective on the family—then there is no independent body of facts to which we can turn to declare one view correct and the other incorrect. In this case, therefore, our standpoint would necessarily bias the judgment in favor of one side or the other.

To return to the debate between the conventional and the sociohistorical views of science: we can say that the conventionalists would argue the case of what defines a family by appealing to the facts, seeking a theory of the family that best fits the traditional definition; the sociohistoricists would insist that because there is no real object ("family") that exists independently of any theory used to describe it, the debate is a struggle over which definition will prevail and be accepted by future generations.

We have so far considered two differences between the conventional and the sociohistorical views of science: their primary goals and governing beliefs. The primary goal of the conventional view is to describe the world as it really is, guided by the governing belief that there is a place from which to observe reality independent of that reality. The idea of a *nonpositioned* scientist-observer is central to the conventional definition of science. Observers are nonpositioned insofar as they can grasp reality without occupying any particular position or standpoint that would bias their ability to observe things as they really are.

The primary goal of the sociohistorical view is to describe various accounts of reality, and to understand both their social and historical bases as well as their respective roles in our lives. The governing belief that guides the sociohistorical approach is that we can only encounter reality from some standpoint or position. Scientist-observers are therefore necessarily *positioned*; that is, they are always occupying a place in some historical and social context. Where they observe affects what they perceive and what they understand.

At this point, it should be noted that there is no easy way to choose between these two contrasting views of science. To what neutral view could we turn to help direct our choice? We must rest as comfortably as we can with the unnerving possibility that the view of science we choose to follow is not in itself grounded in "the facts," but is a socially and historically driven choice.

Let us now sharpen our understanding of these contrasting images of science by examining a third distinction—the different metaphors that guide these two views.

Guiding Metaphors

Two metaphors demonstrate the fundamental difference between the conventional and the sociohistorical points of view: the conventional view regards science to be a *mirror* of nature, an accurate reflection of reality; the sociohistorical view considers science to be a *story*, a proposal about reality.

Science as a Mirror of Nature: The Conventional Perspective

The philosopher Richard Rorty (1979) refers to conventional science as a *mirror* of nature, while the sociologist Joseph Gusfield (1976) uses a parallel metaphor of conventional science as a *windowpane* of clear glass giving an undistorted view of nature as it really is.

Reality is considered to lie somewhere "out there," to be a factual world existing independently of our perception and ways of thinking about it. In the conventional view, the goal of scientific inquiry is to describe that reality as accurately as possible. Scientific knowledge therefore tries to mirror reality; hence the metaphor of conventional science as a mirror or windowpane.

Science must also be as free as possible from the particular biases that stem from any one point of view or position, so that its view is of reality, not of the viewer who happens to be looking at reality. Because scientific inquiry tends to be objective in representing nature as it really is, we can confidently appeal to science whenever we are faced with a dispute over matters of fact. Science offers a neutral, objective arbiter to resolve disagreements and distinguish what is true and correct from what is not.

This conventional understanding of science helps us to choose among competing theories: we select the theory that provides us with the most accurate representation of the way nature works; an inferior theory offers us a cloudy mirror or a dirty windowpane. Even if at any given time we cannot make a rational choice among competing theories because all the facts have not emerged, we nevertheless feel secure that eventually the facts will reveal nature's true story.

According to the conventional image of science, there are hidden truths awaiting our eventual discovery. Our personal preferences do not matter; what we wish to be true is not the issue. Scientific inquiry tests its ideas about reality against the facts, and so ultimately resolves any existing conflicts by discovering the actual nature of reality. The truth will eventually be revealed and will be as pure as we imagine the truth to be—a picture that accurately describes nature and that transcends mere preferences, tastes, opinions, and social or historical biases.

It should now be apparent why the conventional view is so appealing, especially for the science of social psychology. The planets in our solar system are indifferent to the laws that govern their motion, but people have a definite interest in the laws that influence their own behavior. By the very nature of its subject, social psychology needs to be objective, to be free from bias, to let the facts speak loudly for themselves regardless of our own personal preferences or opinions on what is or is not true.

Science as a Story: The Sociohistorical Perspective

Those who take comfort in the belief that science will someday so closely approximate the truth that almost all of our questions about nature, including human nature, will be correctly answered, will find the sociohistorical view of science unsettling. In this view we are no longer explorers trying to discover reality, devising theories that reflect its real nature. We are transformed instead into storytellers whose theories are like *stories* giving an account or version of reality. If the conventional view perceives reality as independent of the theories used to describe it, the sociohistorical view argues that reality can be known only by means of the stories we tell about it. Our stories *propose* a version of reality rather than independently seek to discover its actual nature.

It is important to realize that storytellers do not deny the existence of a reality independent of their theories about the nature of that reality. They do not see themselves as gods who create reality out of their stories. As Rorty puts it, "most things in space and time are the effects of causes which do not include human mental states" (1989, p. 5). In other words, the world exists whether or not our minds tell stories about it. But there is no way to know what is true about that reality without our intervention: "The world is out there, but descriptions of the world are not" (Rorty, 1989, p. 5).

How, then, do we choose among competing theories? It is clear that in the sociohistorical view discrimination cannot be based on any neutral description of reality. Because every description of reality is in some way influenced by the observer's own standpoint there is no alternative than to appeal to various accounts or stories to get what is at best a version of the truth. There is no account that categorically fits reality better than any other: there can be no one "true" story. To claim to have discovered the one true story, we would need an objective description of reality to base a judgement on competing theories, but, according to the sociohistorical view, *all* descriptions of reality are necessarily biased by the observer's own standpoint.

Methodological Priorities

We have thus far considered three major differences between the two images of science: their primary goals, governing beliefs, and guiding metaphors. A fourth difference between the conventional and the sociohistorical views of science involves their methodological priorities. A recent analysis reported by David Sears (1986) gives us a good sense of the conventional view. Sears examined the major research publications in social psychology, finding that (a) over 75% used college undergraduates as its subjects while (b) over 70% of the work was based on laboratory experiments. Both of these reflect the conventional view's methodological priorities.

When social psychology continues to rely on the college undergraduate as the primary source of information, what does this tell us about its understanding of science? If there is a basic reality of human social behavior, and the task is to discover the laws by which this reality functions, then there is little reason not to use college undergraduates in research. If the goal is to study something fundamental about all people—and this study includes college undergraduates—why not use them as research subjects?

Sears gives us some fairly good reasons to be wary about this kind of dependency on college undergraduates, noting that there are several important differences between this age group and older adults.

For example, undergraduates' beliefs are often less well formed and their concerns rather different than those of older adults. He recommends broadening our sample in order to give our findings greater validity, maintaining the conventional belief, however, that those enlarged samples will still lead us to discover the fundamental laws of human social behavior.

The use of the laboratory, with its controlled conditions and possibilities for identifying true causal relationships, also reflects the conventional view; as Sears' data suggest, laboratory research continues to be the method of choice among social psychologists.

While it is indeed reasonable to insist that the controls available in the laboratory—usually missing elsewhere—permit investigators to feel more certain about the claims they make for their research findings, those who advocate the sociohistorical view insist that the bias that stems from the broad social and historical factors operating at the time and in the cultural fabric in which the research is conducted are still at work. Even the laboratory cannot eliminate all kinds of bias.

While these broader social and historical biases cannot be eliminated, we can become cognizant of their effects by seeking diverse frameworks within which to conduct our work. Thus, the methodological priorities for those adopting the sociohistorical view urge us to engage in more cross-cultural research. This would align social psychology with a kind of ethnopsychology, examining the various cultural and subcultural theories that different communities have formed about their lives and that guide their experience and behavior. Throughout this text we will see many illustrations of this view, and have opportunities to examine some of its implications for the kinds of understanding that we achieve.

Table 1.1 summarizes the four points we have examined in this chapter distinguishing the conventional from the sociohistorical views of science.

Objectivity and Relativism

From the standpoint of its conventionalist critics, the sociohistorical approach appears to have given up objectivity and plunged into the abyss of relativism, leaving no objective standards grounded in reality to guide us in our choices. According to the conventional view, to be objective one must perceive reality without the biases that stem from one's personal, historical, or social point of view. It is to

TABLE 1.1
Two Views of the Science of Social Psychology

	Conventional	Sociohistorical
1. Primary Goal	To describe the world of human social experience and activity as it really is and as it really functions	To describe the various accounts of human social experience and activity; to understand both their social and historical bases and the role they play in human life
2. Governing Belief	There is a place from which to see reality that is independent of that reality; thus, there can be a nonpositioned observer who can grasp reality as it is without occupying any particular biasing standpoint.	We can only encounter reality from some standpoint; thus, the observer is always standing somewhere and is thereby necessarily a positioned observer.
3. Guiding Metaphor	Science is like a mirror designed to reflect things as they really are.	Science is like a storyteller proposing accounts and versions of reality.
4. Methodological Priorities	Methods are designed to control those factors that would weaken the investigator's ability to discern the true shape of reality.	Broad social and historical factors always frame the investigator's understanding; the best we can achieve is a richer and deeper understanding based on encountering the historically and culturally diverse accounts that people use in making their lives sensible.

see things as they really are, not as they are said to be from any particular standpoint.

The Japanese film *Rashomon* (see Richie, 1984) provides a useful illustration of the conventionalist's concerns. The film unveils the testimonies of seven different people about what is purportedly the *same* event—the murder of a raped woman's husband. For example, the woman tells of her being raped in the woods by a passing bandit, subsequently spurned by her husband and, in her grief, killing her husband. The bandit's story tells of tying up the husband, raping her, and then accepting her appeal that he and the husband duel for her honor, killing the husband in the duel. The dead husband, speaking through a medium, has yet another version of what happened: after the bandit raped his wife and she prepared to go off with the bandit, she insisted that the bandit kill her husband; this so upset the bandit that he left, and the despairing husband took his own life.

Because each version of the husband's death is given from a different point of view, there is no way to objectively ascertain what really happened. Objectivity, at least in the conventionalists' sense of the term, would require having seen the "murder" as it really took place. But what does this mean? Is there a place from which to observe events independent of any one person's view? Do we search for commonalities in the several accounts and then conclude that, because all three versions speak of a rape, a rape must have actually occurred? Was it murder or suicide?

It is apparent that if we accept a conventional definition of objectivity, there is absolutely no way to adopt a sociohistorical argument and be objective. Of course, there is no reason to believe that the conventional account is the only version of objectivity available for us to consider. Indeed, the sociohistorical version has a view of objectivity more fitting with its understandings.

Since there is no place from which to observe events independent of some point of view—every observation point is *somewhere*—we simply accept that feature of our lives and consider objectivity to mean the prevailing agreements among members of a given community about the nature of truth and reality (Bernstein, 1983; MacIntyre, 1988; Rorty, 1979, 1989). Therefore, objective truth is not a truth that exists somewhere "out there" beyond any human standpoints. Rather, objective truth refers to those statements about the world that we currently can justify and defend using the standards of argument and proof employed within the community to which we belong—for example, the community of scientists. In this sociohistorical view, truth is open and modifiable, not firm, solid, and fixed in place for all time and all people.

Many critics argue that without some objectively grounded realm of truth, anything goes: saints and devils are free to cavort through our civilization, and there is no basis for right and wrong. People always make choices, however, including choosing what acts to consider to be saintly and what to consider devilish. These are not choices based on contact with the unvarnished truth, but on particular human interests and values plus the balance of power among competing versions. As those values and interests change, and as the power balance shifts, new stories may successfully compete with the older versions. The best we can hope for is a society that encourages free debate on equal terms among proponents of various versions of truth and reality, so that any one version that may support one group's advantages at another's expense will not continue to dominate in the guise of being objectively true.

The concern with relativism is based entirely on the conventional view of science. If there is an objectively grounded truth, then it provides the touchstone by which everything else can be measured and correct choices made. If we argue that there is no such thing as an objectively grounded truth that has a privileged contact with reality as it actually is, we are haunted by the ogre of relativism only if we continue to be captive to the myth of an objective truth. If we agree that truth is inescapably rooted in social and historical conditions, we are no longer concerned with the grounding of truth but rather with the social functions served by proclaiming that something is or is not true. To worry that society will collapse if there is nothing objective on which to ground our beliefs misses the real point: who stands to gain and who stands to lose from the currently prevailing versions and stories that parade around as objective truths?

2

Implications for Social Psychology

GIVEN THE CONTRASTS between the conventional and the sociohistorical views of science, it should not be surprising to learn that they introduce us to two rather different versions of social psychology. In this chapter we will examine how the conventionalists and sociohistoricists respond to three major questions: (1) How is the object of social psychological investigation to be understood? (2) What is the proper role of social psychology in society? (3) What role does power play in social psychology's understanding?

How Is the Object of Social Psychological Investigation to Be Understood?

As we noted in Chapter 1, most definitions of social psychology indicate that the object to be studied is the individual human being, and that the properties of particular interest are the individual's thoughts, feelings, and actions. But what exactly is "the individual"? For most of us, the answer is self-evident: we are all individuals and, as we look around us, see more of the same. Surely, then, there can be no disagreement about the object of social psychological investigation. The individual is a *naturally* occurring thing, a part of nature that social psychologists study even as rocks are natural things that other types of scientists study.

While this conception of the individual seems to be common sense, on closer inspection this is conventional reasoning. According to sociohistoricists, both the individual and its properties—thoughts, feelings, behaviors, and so on—are not naturally occurring objects, but rather are social and historical constructions designed to serve certain purposes.

Let us turn to some of the ideas introduced in Chapter 1 to clarify what is meant by the individual being a social and historical construction rather than a naturally occurring object. Remember that the argument was people do not create reality; our only understanding of reality, however, occurs by means of the descriptions of it that people formulate. Thus, it is not possible to see reality as it really is; our contact is always mediated through some particular position, standpoint, or framework from which we describe it. Now let us apply this way of thinking to the concept of the individual.

On the one hand, we do not doubt that individual persons actually really exist as objects "out there." Let us refer to the individual in this sense as *the real object*. On the other hand, according to the sociohistorical view, we would also have to maintain that we cannot know this real object except by means of some particular framework that tells us what it is and what its characteristics are. In other words, although individuals have a reality independent of any theory, we only know of individuals by means of these particular theories. Furthermore, these theories are developed in different cultural and historical contexts, serving particular functions in the time and place for which they were constructed.

At this point, we can begin to see the consequences for social psychology of whether we adopt the conventional or the sociohistorical perspective. Most people reared in the culturally dominant conventional view are undoubtedly somewhat puzzled that reasonable people disagree over what an individual is. There is nothing more obvious to all of us than what an "individual" is and, furthermore, that individuals have thoughts and feelings. So what is all the fuss about? Let us look again at the idea of "naturally occurring object" in order to broaden our understanding of the differences between the conventional and the sociohistorical view.

Natural Versus Social and Historical Objects

If we say that something is "a naturally occurring object," we mean that it is a part of nature rather than a human construction based on some theory about nature. Some scientists study animals, others study flowers, still others, atomic substructures—all things supposedly occurring in nature, in reality, in the world "out there." To say that that the very thing social psychologists study—the individual—is not naturally occurring, but is a socially constructed object, seems to fly in the face of what is clearly self-evident to anyone who looks. Or is it?

As noted earlier, although the individual as real object may be naturally occurring, the *idea* of the individual is just that, an idea. And, as we have already seen from the sociohistorical perspective, ideas about the world—our only vehicle for knowing the world—are not fixed somewhere "out there" in the world but vary in historical and social contexts. This suggests that if we examined things more closely, we might very well find that both the concept of the individual and of the individual's characteristics change over time and across different cultural milieus.

Although we will examine some of this historical and cross-cultural evidence in more detail in Chapter 12, it will be helpful to introduce a few thoughts on this matter in the present context. Careful historical study of the western world, combined with anthropological examination of different cultures, teaches us that the western concept of the individual is (a) a relatively recent creation, gaining prominence around the sixteenth and seventeenth centuries; and (b) is very differently understood in other cultures.

Several historical works examining early European life provide numerous illustrations of the extent to which the modern concept of individual was not understood in quite the same way. For example, historical evidence suggests that the household, not the individual, dominated the western world's everyday experience until about the sixteenth century. This is not to suggest that the real object—the individual—did not exist until some four centuries ago, but that to-day's idea of the individual only began to take shape at that time. Recall that, according to the sociohistorical view, the idea we have is the reality we have: our social and historical beliefs and descriptions about things establish their reality for us.

If we compare our current idea of the individual with the pre–sixteenth century idea, we discover two competing theories. But how do we determine which one is "correct"? Is there a standard for se-lecting a theory of the individual that transcends historical and cul-tural limitations? The answer must be no: *every* theory of the individual is a product of some place and some time. Anthropological studies add further to this picture of competing theories of the individual, one going so far as to suggest that the western world's current concep-tion of the individual is a rather *peculiar* idea (Geertz, 1973). To refer to our current conception of the individual as "peculiar" is hardly to describe a naturally occurring object.

Based on their research in India, for example, Miller (1984) and Shweder and Bourne (1982) suggest that most people in the western world have an *egocentric* idea of the individual, whereas the Indian conception is more *sociocentric*. The egocentric formulation sees the individual as someone who has sharp boundaries separating self from nonself and who strives to maintain those boundaries. The sociocen-tric formulation, while distinguishing between self and other, has more fluid boundaries: self is defined in and through others, not by virtue of how distinctly different self can be from others. We will encounter many similar cross-cultural examples that illustrate different under-standings both of the individual and of the presumed characteristics of individuals as we move further into the text.

It seems, then, that the very object of social psychological in-vestigation is understood differently within the conventional and so-ciohistorical frameworks. The conventional perspective adopts the western world's prevailing idea about the individual and accordingly conducts its research on what is believed to be a naturally occurring object. Given this way of thinking, it makes sense for proponents of the conventional view to believe that their research findings describe characteristics of the real object—that is, qualities that individuals really have—and that they are thereby able to discover the fundamen-tal laws about human nature.

In contrast, proponents of the sociohistorical view assume that the individuals they study and the properties they discover about them all refer to a socially and historically constructed character. We cannot discover general laws about how individuals as such function, as though these individuals are naturally occurring objects; we can only discover laws that operate at a given time and place (Gergen, 1973). We cannot assume that our understandings are objective in the sense of referring to something "out there" entirely independent of the very theories used to describe the individual. From a sociohistorical perspective, there is no theory-independent individual to be studied, and no way to find "the real person" who exists outside all historically and culturally based theories.

Some Further Illustrations from Ethnopsychology

To better grasp these ideas, let us consider some examples contrasting the conventional with the sociohistorical approach to cross-cultural work in the area of *ethnopsychology*. The conventional approach tends to assume that because there is such a thing as a basic human nature, research on other cultures only improves our ability to generalize the findings obtained within our own culture and so discover a truly fundamental law of human social behavior. For example, we know that many people in our own culture are quick to get angry and aggressive when they are frustrated. We may even formulate a general principle of human nature arguing that one of the central causes of human anger and aggression is frustration (see Part Five for more on this topic). Are people in other cultures likewise quick to express anger and aggression when frustrated? Suppose that we find a culture in which there are very few expressions of anger and aggression under any conditions?

Would this failure to find anger and aggression lead us to abandon our principles about a basic human nature? Probably not. Rather, we would typically assume that anger and aggression are present somewhere and so look for alternate expressions: we notice, for example, that the myths of this nonaggressive culture are filled with anger, aggression, and violence (for example, see Lutz, 1988).

In contrast to the conventional approach, which takes our own culture's concepts and seeks to generalize them in other cultures, the sociohistorical view of the ethnopsychologists insists on trying to understand each culture *in its own terms* (Lutz, 1988; Rosaldo, 1989; White & Kirkpatrick, 1985). That is, rather than assuming that all people become angry and aggressive when frustrated, an ethnopsychologist would make two different assumptions: first, that cultures have formulated different theories of human nature; second, that current western theory (that frustration produces aggression) may or may not be the same as another culture's theory. Indeed, another culture might not only offer a different array of events said to be frustrating, but might also set forth a very different array of reactions to frustration learned within that culture.

Lutz's work with the Ifaluk, a small cultural group living on an atoll in the Pacific, offers an instructive lesson in a different enthnopsychology of anger than that conveyed by our own frustration-aggression view. Lutz comments how our own cultural view tends to adopt a very individualistic perspective: when I am frustrated in my personal efforts to achieve a goal I have set for myself, it is considered proper for me to experience and perhaps even express anger. For us, frustration tends to refer to an infringement on our individual rights; and the emotional experience of anger is justifiable whenever our individual rights have been restricted.

In contrast, among the Ifaluk it is the community rather than the individual who has rights: anger arises, therefore, in collective settings when a threat to the well-being of the group is at issue. Lutz notes, for example, how one can be justifiably angry if someone who is smoking *fails* to share the cigarette with others. The offense is to the community's concern with sharing things understood to be the possessions of the entire community. In this case, cigarettes are not owned by individuals, but rather are a communal property to be freely shared with others. Thus, the failure to share can justifiably arouse anger designed to induce sharing by, but not harm to, the person who has failed to share.

Another illustration stems from the work on the Baining of New Guinea, as reported by Jane Fajans (1985). Our own culture has a rather rich set of terms to describe the inner world of the individual, and we use these terms quite freely in our efforts to make sense out of our own and other's behavior—for example, "the reason that I did poorly on that exam was because I was depressed over breaking up with my lover." In contrast, Fajans noted that the Baining are "reluctant to speculate about the personal motivations, actions, and feelings either of themselves or others. They do not offer interpretations of the meanings of the behavior and events around them in these terms" (p. 57).

In effect, it is Fajan's contention that both we and the Baining are interested in living in a world that makes sense. But whereas we achieve this sense by using a set of beliefs about the rich internal endowment of motives, needs, and so forth that people have, the Baining eschew this kind of internal analysis in favor of focusing "on external behaviors and relationships" (p. 371).

Therefore, when viewing other cultures, ethnopsychologists do not search for western beliefs about the individual or about the characteristics individuals presumably possess. Rather, they attempt to see how different cultures have formulated different systems of belief in making their social world sensible. This does not mean that an ethnopsychologist would reject the possibility of ever finding universal ideas about human social behavior. It does mean, however, that the local context in which various ideas about individuals and their "psychology" have been generated must always be considered to be paramount. The context of the typically western investigator must not be taken as any more privileged, correct, or true than the local context of the particular culture being studied.

Admittedly, these several points can be difficult to grasp. We are captives of the particular theory with which our own culture constructs the world we inhabit. We have learned to believe that such terms as "mind," "thought," "feeling," and "idea" all refer to real things taking place inside each individual. We must now consider the idea that these terms refer to a social theory. As with all theories, this particular modern western theory does not describe a discovery about the state of reality; rather, it proposes a theory about reality, in this case, the reality of the individual: individuals are the kind of creatures that we currently find it useful to assume have richly furnished interiors (Dreyfus & Rabinow, 1982). Or, as Rorty has stated it, "To say that a given organism . . . has a mind is just to say that, for some purposes, it will pay to think of it as having beliefs and desires . . . [it proves to be] a useful tactic in predicting and controlling its future behavior" (1989, p. 15).

. . . .

What Is the Proper Role of Social Psychology in Society?

A reasonable argument based on the conventional view of social psychology would say that the discoveries of science are simply about nature itself, to be used by societal decision-makers for whatever purposes they deem important. In this view, the science of social psychology itself is neutral: it seeks truth for its own sake, independent of how it may be used in public policy. For example, Kimble (1989) recently noted that although the facts we discover might be relevant to a wide variety of social issues—for example, pornography, violence, privacy, insanity, abortion—we undermine the scientific basis of our discipline if we attempt to use our facts as authority for making social policy. Social policy is to be left up to the people and politicians; those engaging in scientific discovery should simply provide the facts of human nature, nothing more.

Proponents of the conventional framework clearly recognize that their personal biases may enter into the kinds of research problems they study and may even help shape the kinds of hypotheses they test. Their personal biases should not influence their findings, however, because their use of the scientific method will guarantee that their results mirror reality as it is rather than reality as their prejudices may wish it to be.

What do the proponents of the sociohistorical version of social psychology see as their relationship to society? They obviously cannot claim the same impartiality of their conventionalist colleagues, because they maintain that their theories do not mirror a reality independent of those very theories. Thus, facts are facts by virtue of the particular theory that proposes them as facts, not because they are real features of the world as it is.

When a given theory dominates a culture's understanding of human behavior, that theory does not simply describe the facts of human existence in a neutral way, but rather confirms one version of reality over another. We will later see instances of this process at work, but as a brief and informal illustration of this point, let us consider the current concern among some feminist scholars that the male theory of human behavior has dominated and, in their view, distorted our understanding.

Suppose there is a theory of human behavior in which females are defined as incomplete males because they lack the instrument of male potency, namely the penis. Now suppose further that this theory suggests how in recognition of this deficiency, females feel inferior to males—so-called "penis envy"—and that respectable research has indeed empirically found a degree of penis envy on the part of many women studied by the investigators.

Does our theory describe the essential quality of human nature in which women "naturally" envy men because of their penis? Or has our theory proposed a version of reality which, if widely accepted, might prove useful to one group (men) in their efforts to dominate another group (women)? According to the sociohistorical view, the latter is clearly the case. There are no "facts of nature," only human proposals about nature which often have the consequence of affirming one group's interests at another's expense.

What Role Does Power Play in Social Psychology's Understanding?

As we have seen, according to the sociohistorical view of social psychology power is the ability to have one's own version of reality dominate other versions. One potent form of power is the ability to control people by governing the ways in which they understand the world they live in, including themselves and their places in it. Power comes from being able to define the rules of the game that people play in their daily lives.

When we commonly think of one person's or group's power over another, we usually believe that it is founded on brute force rather than reason. Force usually involves the ability to compel another to comply with what we want through the threat of violence. Certainly, we also recognize other bases of power that seem to involve less coercive means, but the potential to inflict harm on another provides a baseline of last resort when all else fails. The sociohistorical framework adds another dimension to our understanding of power and, in so doing, suggests that even the social psychological theories we hold about people may participate in wielding power over them.

This understanding of power has led proponents of the sociohistorical view to be interested in the ways that social psychological theories might participate in one group's domination over another. For the most part, proponents of the conventional framework have either been reluctant to see power as central to their work in social psychology or have insisted that if power is a part of their work, it is the power of scientific knowledge to free the rational mind from the domination of superstition and irrational thought. Thus, their concern is with how knowledge developed by social psychology can be used to increase human rationality and, through this process, to challenge those who would try to dominate others.

According to sociohistoricists, the only problem with pinning all of our hopes on scientific rationality is that reason itself is a socially defined idea that may be used to dominate others in its name. Conventionalists see reason and rationality to be fundamental properties of the human mind. Reason seems to stand apart from the momentary biases of history and culture, and thereby holds out the hope of fending off irrational uses of power. But, argue the sociohistoricists, there is no theory of reason that can be evaluated independently of the particular society that has proposed that theory; even reason has a history and a cultural framework to define it.

According to the sociohistorical view, to claim that social psychological knowledge can serve as a foundation for human reason, and that this is the only real power it has or should have (a conventional argument), is to commit a serious error. Dominant groups in a society use the appeal to reason, as *they* have defined it, as a way to keep other groups from having a voice in determining social policies. For example, it is not surprising to learn that at one time it was claimed that women, among several other social groups—for example, children, savages, and those not owning property—did not have the same capacity as adult white propertied men to think and act rationally. It was believed that because women were naturally driven by irrational passions, they could not properly participate in the affairs of their society. Does not this theory of reason sound like yet another way to justify the advantages certain members of a society have over others?

Sociohistoricists suspect that even as theories of reason have been used as powerful weapons of social control, almost any social psychological theory can likewise be exploited. When social psychologists develop a theory about human behavior and report findings that confirm that theory, therefore, they need to ask some serious questions about the possible role of those ideas in the struggles for power and domination among various groups in society.

It is not an exaggeration to say that, whereas the conventionalists do not see power as really relevant to their brand of social psychology, sociohistoricists see power and the struggle for power almost everywhere.

. . . .

Conclusions

We have seen that the conventional and sociohistorical views of science give us two versions of social psychology. In this chapter we have examined three implications of these two very different approaches involving the understanding of the individual, the role of social psychology in society, and power and its implications for social psychological theories and research findings.

In each case, the conventional view emphasizes social psychology's role in discovering the fundamental laws about how individuals' thoughts, feelings, and actions are influenced by other people. The role of social psychology is to simply report the facts it discovers to policy makers. In the conventional view, power is seen either to be irrelevant to what social psychologists do or relevant in the same way that any scientific knowledge is, providing human reason with the knowledge needed to battle superstition and unreason.

For those adopting the sociohistorical view of social psychology, the idea of the individual is not a feature of nature, but rather is an idea with historical and social dimensions. Because social psychology is itself a product of the society it studies, its theories are inseparable from the theories underlying the society's own foundation; social psychology cannot consider itself a neutral discoverer of facts, but must always be sensitive to its role in potentially confirming or challenging prevailing societal theories. Social psychologists must therefore be sensitive to their participation in the various struggles for power that exist in their societies. Their theories and research findings are not just stories about nature, but about culture and history and so may be utilized to benefit one group at the expense of others.

Given the recent dramatic changes in Eastern Europe and the Soviet Union, it should be emphasized that democratization is central to the notion that "reality" is a contended turf to be continually negotiated rather than something "out there" waiting to be discovered. Because there is no special position from which to impartially proclaim truth, the sociohistorical perspective insistently demands that a diversity of voices is heard. To still *any* voice is to diminish the possibility of encountering a way instructive in our search for a deeper understanding of the human condition.

This is not to suggest that conventionalists are displeased with the collapse of totalitarian regimes brought about by mass uprisings for freedom, democracy, and political reform. It is rather to point out that the sociohistorical view, unlike the conventional view, has built-in requirements for widespread democratization as part of its framework. Although they have insistently sought the one "true" version of reality, however, the conventionalists' allegiance to a scientific ethic of openness and progress has fortunately aligned them with the democratization of societies in a manner less evident among those non-scientists who similarly have sought a single "true" account. Both the conventionalists and the sociohistoricists, therefore, share a common belief in democratic ideals and can join together in applauding the movements sweeping away totalitarian regimes in recent years.

PART TWO

The Cognitive Perspective in Social Psychology

3

· ·

Cognition and Context: Locating the Mind

I N CONTEMPORARY SOCIAL psychology, the cognitive perspective has dominated as a way to understand human social behavior. According to this view, the world we experience is reasonably organized, structured, and coherent rather than chaotic or random; the cognitive perspective seeks to discover the principles that underlay this orderliness.

In the late nineteenth century, a school of psychology known as Gestalt suggested that the human mind has certain built-in structures that organize the ways we see and experience the world. In their view, stimuli are not organized in themselves; their organization occurs centrally in the mind of the individual. This suggests that in order to understand why people behave as they do, we need to examine those central processing systems in the mind that organize stimuli. For example, the same glass of water is seen as half-full or half-empty by different people. The stimulus—the glass containing the water—is experienced very differently as a function of differences in people's own internal organizing structures and principles.

The two versions of social psychology we encountered in Part One clearly have contrasting views of the primary "location" of the organizing structures and principles of interest to cognitive social psychology: conventionalists seek them *within* the individual, whereas sociohistoricists look to society and history to better understand how human experience is structured and organized.

. . . .

The Conventionalist View of Cognition

The conventionalist approach invites us to examine the inner workings of the human mind in order to understand how individuals act upon information: what they attend to and select from the rich array of possibilities the world presents; what kinds of cognitive operations they perform on the information to which they have attended; how they store and retrieve information; and so on. This approach also invites us to consider the exciting possibility that all persons have a central processing system that functions according to a set of universal principles, and that it is possible to systematically study such systems in order to discover just what these universal cognitive structures and operations are.

This is not to say that everyone thinks alike; we are well aware of the many differences that exist among individuals' thought processes. It is to suggest, rather, that even though John has extreme right-wing political beliefs while Barbara holds extreme left-wing beliefs, for example, the structures and operations of their central processing systems may be highly similar: both are simplistic and tend to make narrow, categorical judgments leading to extremist political views. The attractive feature of this understanding is that it permits a cognitive science to develop on the basis of our ability to discover universal laws of mental functioning.

Consider the central processing system as a kind of computer program. The same program permits us to write in a variety of different formats—letters, essays, novels, poetry—and solve any number of different problems. Once we understand how the program itself is structured and how it operates, however, we can build our science upon the universality of its basic features rather than upon the variability of the products it can create. Many psychologists have been interested not only in how these mental programs function but how they are learned and become part of the individual's mental machinery in the first place. One of the distinguishing features of different programs is their *developmental level:* some may reflect earlier and less sophisticated ways of processing information when compared with more developmentally mature programs. We will consider these and related issues later in this chapter.

The Sociohistorical View of Cognition

The sociohistorical approach to cognition, in contrast, argues that cognitive dynamics are better seen as processes located in the social world rather than in the individual. If we continue with the computer program analogy, we would argue that rather than looking for programs inside the head of the individual we would search within the social world that creates the various programs that people learn. In effect, the argument is that sociohistorists claim that to understand how human experience is structured and organized, we should examine the social mechanisms that provide this organization rather than self-contained mental events or processes.

Because each social and historical period operates by a program determined by the particular issues of its time and place, it is unlikely that we will find universal programs that all people use in dealing with their world. Therefore, rather than try to ground human knowledge in something eternal—that is, universal and fundamental—about the way the human mind works, we should examine the various ways social groups have structured and organized understandings of their particular world at different times in history.

At first glance, this may seem a bit puzzling. Is it not obvious that *the who* that does the thinking is the individual person? The way that people collectively think and process information may, however, tell us even more about how information is organized. Therefore, although the cognitive processing of information is performed by the individual, the dynamics of processing reflect something about how different social groups and cultures organize information.

It is no coincidence that two prominent figures of the sociohistorical school of cognitive social psychology are the Soviet psychologists, Vygotsky (1978) and Luria (1976). Within the Marxian tradition, the social world plays a central role in establishing the terms of human existence. Adopting an understanding of human cognition consistent with the Marxian perspective would mean that we would look at the social world in which the person lived rather than the individual's inner world to understand how cognitive structures and operations develop and function. Let us first examine Vygotsky's analysis of the social basis of cognitive processes.

Vygotsky offers the example of a little child whose arm and fingers are extended, apparently "pointing" towards an object in the room. The word "pointing" has meaning for the adults, but not yet for the child. In seeing the child's outstretched finger, the mother concludes that the child is trying to point towards an object that the child wants. In other words, the mother transforms the situation by imposing her understanding on the child's desires. It is the social world—the world of other people—that establishes the meaning of the situation for the child. *"The grasping movement changes to an act of pointing"* (p. 56). Over time, these and other behaviors whose origin lies in the child's social world become internalized:

> **Every function in the child's cultural development appears twice: first, on the social level, and later, on the individual level; first, be-tween people (interpsychological) and then inside the child (intra-psychological). This applies equally to voluntary attention, to logical memory, and to the formation of concepts. All the higher functions originate as actual relations between human individuals   (p. 57).**

Luria's own work, built on Vygotsky's ideas, demonstrates that "the most important forms of cognitive processes—perception, generalization, deduction, reasoning, imagination, and analysis of one's own inner life—vary as the conditions of social life change" (p. 161). His research examined changes in the mental life of Soviet citizens of Uzbekistan corresponding to the transformation of the entire socioeconomic system and culture after the Russian Revolution.

With growing literacy and a change in the daily activities required of them, they not only created new concepts of motivation for their behavior but, in addition, radically changed the very forms by which they thought and reasoned. Their thinking, for example, which had been more concrete and centered around specific details of their village life, became increasingly abstract as life became more technically advanced.

In the conventional view, as people develop from infancy through adulthood, they pass through various stages of cognitive growth, moving from the concrete to the abstract. These stages are thought to represent a universal sequence of human cognitive development. The course of development is a property of the individual's mind as it grows. For both Vygotsky and Luria, in contrast, the movement from concrete to more abstract ways of thinking describes a historical change in the way the social world functions; individuals, including adults, learn to operate in these changed ways. There is nothing universal or inevitable about this; nor is the developmental sequence descriptive of something about the way that the human mind works. It demonstrates, rather, how different kinds of social life and social organization create different systems of cognition.

For a social psychologist interested in understanding the relationship between the individual and the social world, then, the sociohistorical approach to cognition is very appealing: cognition is defined not only as how individuals think but, more importantly, as about how social life gives rise to different forms of thinking:

> . . . sociohistorical shifts not only introduce new content into the mental world of human beings; they also create new forms of activity and new structures of cognitive functioning. They advance human consciousness to new levels   *(Luria, 1976, p. 163).*

This focus on the social foundations of cognition is not only a Soviet concern; a growing cadre of social psychologists in the United States and Europe have described a process they term "psychological symbiosis" (Shotter & Newson, as reported by Harré, 1984). This process describes how one person supplements the psychology of another; for example, how a mature person—(the mother or parent) actually supplies the immature person—(the child or novice) with a host of internal cognitive and psychological mental states—wishes, intentions, desires, thoughts, and so on—by dealing with them as though they possessed these qualities.

In other words, the reason why children brought up today in the western world "have" certain kinds of motives, intentions, and ways of structuring and organizing their world is because adults (who are experienced in the ways of western culture) treat them *as though* they possessed these inner qualities. In time, as Vygotsky has noted, children internalize the ways of their culture and so come to operate in the same terms. In this view, children reared in another culture would clearly be treated by adults very differently, acquiring a very different set of terms by which to organize their experiences and account for their own and others' behavior.

To summarize this view, Harré, among others (Harré, 1984; Shotter & Gergen, 1989), suggests the general principle that there is nothing in the mind that did not first exist in some conversation between people, especially conversations between experienced members of the culture and novices.

A valuable cross-cultural study comparing several middle-class western—American, English, Scottish, Dutch, Australian—caretaker–child interactions with two nonwestern cultures—the Kaluli of New Guinea and Western Samoans—reported by Ochs and Schieffelin (1984) offers us some important insights into this process. Ochs and Schieffelin observed how caretakers (mothers) engaged in conversations with their young children. They noted how the western caretakers treated their young children as though they were partners in a conversational exchange, treating them as social beings with certain qualities that would permit them to hold a conversation together: they sat face-to-face with the child; they spoke directly to them; they modified their own speech so that they could adopt the child's perspective. In these and other ways, they sought to accommodate themselves to the child. Confirming the concept of psychological symbiosis, Ochs and Schieffelin also noted the frequency with which the caretakers helped the children complete stories, fill in missing details in their accounts of their experience, and interpret unintelligible utterances to make them meaningful. In other words, caretakers supplied the child with the qualities of thought and understanding considered relevant in their culture.

In contrast, a very different pattern of caretaker–child interaction appeared among the nonwestern cultures. Rather than relating to their young children as though they were conversational partners, these caretakers assumed that their children were lacking in understanding. They did not, for example, hold them face-to-face as if a meaningful conversation was being held. The caretakers tended to direct the child's attention outward "so that they can see, and be seen by, other members of the social group" (p. 289). Unlike western caretakers, who adjusted their behavior to the child, the nonwestern caretakers followed a "pattern of fitting (or pushing) the child into the situation rather than changing the situation to meet the interests or abilities of the child" (p. 293).

This last feature was central to Ochs and Schieffelin's tentative, but important conclusion: "In contrast to the white middle-class tendencies to accommodate situations to the child, the Samoans encourage the child to meet the needs of the situation, that is, to notice others, listen to them, and adapt one's own speech to their particular status and needs" (p. 298). In effect, these early caretaker–child interactions helped to socialize the child to become the kind of adult the culture valued.

Consider for a moment the thrust of this view of human cognition. The repertoire of mental qualities whose common existence we take for granted—motives, intentions, ways of thinking and reasoning, and so on—are supplied by the adult members of a culture to the novices by treating the novices *as if* they possessed these characteristics. These "inner" characteristics are a given culture's proposal about how behavior is to be understood; they are not "real" in the sense of being things naturally occurring within a person that we can discover by looking inside that person. They do not refer to things that exist in the world of the mind independently of a cultural theory that proposes their existence. In this literal sense, then, they are not real. Of course, they are very real, meaningful, and significant for all members of that culture.

This way of thinking about thinking and cognitive activity not only departs from our usual ways of understanding, but provides a truly *social* cast to cognitive science, making the study of cognition an appropriately central feature of social psychology.

In summary, the sociohistorical school of social psychology views cognitive activity as a process rooted in society and in interactions between persons rather than as a personal, private activity occurring entirely within the individual (the conventional view). As such, the sociohistorical perspective marks a radical departure from our usual ways of thinking about thinking. It also provides an essential social understanding of cognitive science by arguing that there is no way to understand human cognitive activity without examining the social contexts in which such activity occurs. This approach marks a growing movement among those interested in cognition and in cognitive development.

To more fully appreciate these contrasting views of cognition, we will examine three cases that illustrate the debate between these different ways of understanding human thinking and its role in our behavior. The first case addresses the study of political beliefs and cognitive information processing. The second case focuses on moral reasoning. The final case looks at our everyday cognitive activities.

. . . .

Politics and Cognition:
Integrative Complexity and Political Ideology

The first case is based on the publication in 1950 of a classic study, *The Authoritarian Personality* (Adorno et al., 1950). To understand the terms of the debate between conventional and sociohistorical positions on cognition, we will first briefly examine the original study and the perspective it adopted.

After World War II, many people wanted to understand why the institutionalized brutality and genocide of Nazi Germany took place.

Who could participate in such crimes against humanity? Could the Nazi atrocities happen again today and in our own country? It was supposed that one answer to these troubling questions might be found in a particular personality type attracted to the sadistic lure of fascism.

Partly driven by this quest, a team of investigators at the University of California in Berkeley combined their skills as clinical psychologists who had worked mostly with disturbed patient populations and social psychologists who studied the attitudes of normal populations, to produce a monumental study of what they called *the authoritarian personality*. The immediate horrors of the Nazi era were past, but the possibility that authoritarian personalities were among us brought home the worry that the Holocaust could be repeated.

The search for a certain configuration of personality traits led Adorno and his colleagues to posit the existence of a character type, the authoritarian, who might be uniquely susceptible to the appeals of fascism. The investigators used a diversity of methods to determine whether or not such a character existed. They developed sets of paper-and-pencil tests inquiring about persons' political, economic, and social attitudes, and conducted in-depth clinical interviews with individuals selected on the basis of attitudes they revealed on the questionnaires. One of their major findings was that the authoritarian has certain cognitive deficiencies.

In particular, the authoritarian personality was found to be extremely intolerant of ambiguity and so quick to provide structure and organization to otherwise ambiguous situations. If presented with a situation not clearly defined as either black or white, for example, the authoritarian would quickly categorize it as black or white, not being comfortable with shades of gray (for example, see Block & Block, 1952; Kelman & Barclay, 1963). Another cognitive deficiency of the authoritarian is the tendency to project intolerable personal impulses onto others and so see other people as possessing the very qualities most feared in themselves. For example, being highly anxious about their own sexual and aggressive impulses and refusing to accept them as their own, authoritarians project these threatening impulses onto others and so see others as being obscene, dangerous, and needing to be carefully controlled.

When it came to defining their political attitudes, Adorno and his colleagues found a tendency for authoritarians to be on the right, or conservative, end of the political spectrum. This description linking authoritarianism with political conservatism annoyed many critics of the concept of the authoritarian personality (for example, see Hoffer, 1951; Rokeach, 1960; Shils, 1954). These critics believed that the investigator's own liberalism had biased their work, leading them to posit only a politically conservative, but not a politically liberal, kind of authoritarianism. Given the anti-communist fervor in America in the early 1950s—the Cold War, the Korean War, and McCarthyism—the implication that the primary danger the world faced stemmed from a group of far-right political extremists seemed to contradict the perceived far greater danger of the extreme left. Was it not also possible to find an authoritarian way of thinking on the far left as well as on the far right?

Rokeach suggested that there may be a dogmatic or closed-minded *way of thinking* that characterized both politically left and right extremes; presumably, those in the political center would be less dogmatic and more open-minded in the way they thought. Rokeach developed a test to measure this closed-minded dogmatism and reported support for his views. In other words, the cognitive style that had been identified as authoritarian—the intolerance of ambiguity that leads people to organize information into simplistic, black–white categories—appeared to describe extremists of both ends of the political spectrum. Rokeach's studies provided scientific confirmation of Hoffer's "true believer": the kind of political extremist whose mind disposed them to be attracted to the irrational appeals of mass movements of all kinds.

Structure Versus Content

The suggestion that, regardless of the *content* of the person's beliefs—whether far right or far left—all extremists' cognitive systems operate in much the same closed-minded manner, introduces us to an important distinction in cognitive social psychology: that between the *structure* of a person's mind and the *content* allowed by that structure.

Underlying this distinction is the conventionalists' assumption we previously encountered of the human mind to be like a central processing system located within the individual that transforms the information received from the world as a function of its particular properties. In the case of the authoritarian or dogmatic personality, this central processing system is characterized by a highly simplistic structure that allows information to be organized into only one or two categories—black or white, good or evil, for me or against me, and so on.

There are several intriguing implications that follow from the distinction between the structure and content of a person's beliefs. In the first place, by studying the structural characteristics of the central processing system, we should be able to learn a great deal about how people transform the rich information of their world into their own particular ways of experiencing the world. This knowledge of the structure of the system, in turn, should help us to better understand why people behave as they do.

If the central processing system of the authoritarian individual is more simply structured than the nonauthoritarian, we can see why the former is so quick to join movements that offer simplistic interpretations of complex social problems. For example, since both fascists on the far right and communists on the far left are presumed to have the same kind of simple cognitive structure, they tend to see the world in the same polarized terms.

In the second place, once we can distinguish between the structure of the mind and its specific content—for example, political beliefs—it would seem reasonable to argue that although the content may vary extensively among people—some line up politically on the left, others on the right, and still others in the center—there may be a limited set of structures that describe all human minds. If we could discover the properties of these universal structures, then we could build a firm cognitive science on universal laws of cognitive processing. Recall that it is this hope of discovering such universal laws of mental functioning that motivates those who have adopted the conventional model of cognitive social psychology.

Integrative Complexity: The Tetlock Program

Now that we have examined the background and some of the issues involved in the original debate, we are prepared to see where things have moved more recently. Once again, as with the original study of authoritarianism, we will return to Berkeley, but now to the important work of Phillip Tetlock and his associates (1981a, 1981b, 1983, 1984, 1986, 1988; Tetlock & Boettger, 1989). As we examine Tetlock's work, we will notice a significant transformation in his own understanding of the relationship between cognition and political beliefs. In short, Tetlock began by probing the structural properties of persons' cognitive systems and relating these to their political beliefs and behaviors. His data, however, led him eventually to conclude that the internal structure was less important than the external circumstances in which the political beliefs gained expression. In other words, Tetlock moved from advocating a conventionalist position on cognition to adopting a sociohistorical one.

Tetlock based his initial efforts on the pioneering research of Harvey, Hunt, and Schroder's (1961; also see Schroder, Driver, & Streufert, 1967) theory of cognitive complexity, referred to by Tetlock as a theory of *integrative complexity*. The original work on cognitive complexity sought to describe two main structural features of each person's cognitive system: (1) the degree to which the system is differentiated and (2) the degree to which the system is integrated.

The first concept, *differentiation,* refers to the extent to which a cognitive system allows many different ways to process information. If we think of differentiation as a continuum, then highly differentiated systems allow an individual to have many different ways of categorizing information; individuals with less-differentiated systems have few ways. Differentiation thereby comes very close to describing one of the cognitive qualities noted earlier in work on both the authoritarian personality and on dogmatism. Both authoritarians and dogmatic, closed-minded thinkers would have a minimally differentiated cognitive system because they tend to make few distinctions among the rich array of information potentially available to them. They experience the world in terms of minimal categories such as black vs. white, for-me vs. against-me, and so on.

Someone whose cognitive system is highly differentiated has a diversity of ways to categorize information, and can thus more easily process contradictory information without having to resolve the contradiction on one side or the other. For example, consider two proverbs: "birds of a feather flock together" versus "opposites attract." These are contradictory assertions. Presumably, someone with a cognitive system low in differentiation can accept one or the other, but not both, while someone with a highly differentiated system should be able to accept both beliefs. It is obvious that because most people and most issues are complex, a person whose cognitive system is highly differentiated should be better able than the person with a less-differentiated system to assimilate this kind of complexity.

The second feature posited by Harvey and his colleagues to describe a person's cognitive system involves its degree of *integration.* This refers to the ways in which the differentiated elements of the system are interconnected. Again, we can picture a dimension going from low to high integration. On the low-integration end are people for whom ideas are more or less isolated from one another; on the high-integration end are people whose cognitive systems are richly interconnected networks of ideas. A person with a less-integrated cognitive system sees each individual tree, but fails to notice the relationship that joins them together into a forest. A person with a highly integrated cognitive system sees both the trees and the forest.

If the two key structural dimensions of an individual's cognitive system—differentiation and integration—are combined, we arrive at what Tetlock refers to as that individual's degree of *integrative complexity.* Low integrative complexity describes a cognitive system of low differentiation and low integration. High integrative complexity describes a system combining both high differentiation and high integration. Other points between these extremes vary in their degree of differentiation and integration.

We now have a theory about the structure of an individual's central processing system. But how can we measure an individual's degree of integrative complexity? The original measurement approach used a Sentence Completion Test: individuals were presented with incomplete sentences and asked to write out a completion. For example, if presented with "Rules . . . ," the task would be to write a sentence beginning with the word "rules."

An individual's completions can be scored for their degree of integrative complexity using a 7-point rating system, where 1 is a minimally integrative answer and 7 is a highly integrative answer. Using the example of "Rules . . . ," someone would be scored towards the low end if his or her response suggested an unawareness of different views of the concept of rules and their role in society: "Rules are made to keep society from deteriorating into complete anarchy and chaos" (Tetlock, 1988, p. 104). If the answer indicated a more complex view of rules, he or she would be scored towards the upper end: "Rules are one way by which human beings regulate their social relationships. Rules serve different functions in different situations" (p. 104).

Tetlock found that, within a few weeks of training, his associates learned to score responses in a highly reliable way. Note that what is being scored is the structure of the person's cognitive system—how they think about a situation—not the actual content or ideological position they profess. Thus, in theory at least, an individual whose political beliefs were on the far left and an individual whose beliefs were on the far right could receive very similar scores: their cognitive processing of information could be either simple or complex based on how they framed their beliefs rather than in the left–right content of their beliefs.

Once a scoring system of the sort used with the Sentence Completion Test is in place, it is possible to apply it to *any* written or verbal material—speeches, written statements, answers to interview questions, and so on. This means that one could undertake the systematic examination of a wide variety of beliefs and public expressions in terms of their degree of integrative complexity. Indeed, this is exactly what Tetlock and his associates have done in an extensive and fascinating exploration of the integrative complexity of political leaders. Before we review some of his findings, however, let us return to the theoretical issue that first led us to this case.

In its original conception, integrative complexity was intended to describe a structural characteristic of the individual's mind: the way that individuals process information as a function of the complexity of their cognitive system. Therefore, as originally understood, integrative complexity is located inside the individual as a structural property of the person's mind. After his extensive examination of the integrative complexity of political leaders from the United States, Great Britain, and the Soviet Union, however, Tetlock reached the following conclusion:

> . . . the appropriate question is not "What kind of machine is the human information processor?" but rather "What kinds of machines do people become when confronted with particular tasks in particular environments?" *(Tetlock & Boettger, 1989, p. 388)*

As we examine this conclusion and the data on which it was based, we will see how it is difficult to continue arguing that integrative complexity is a structural property of the individual's cognitive system; perhaps we need to consider it to be a property of the social situation that political leaders confront. In other words, situations may call forth different forms of cognitive functioning, and most people are capable of using whatever form the situation requires. If this conclusion is reasonable, then perhaps it is to situations rather than minds that we should turn to understand more about human information processing. This, of course, is the sociohistorical formulation of cognitive social psychology. What data led Tetlock to his conclusion?

Tetlock reports that high integrative complexity among political leaders is less likely under conditions of national or international crisis—when quick decisions under threat are required—than in quieter times. He also finds that United States presidential candidates tend to make integratively simple speeches while running for office and become more integratively complex once in office. In today's reliance on television coverage to cover elections, with its demands on candidates to say something brief and pithy, simplicity is preferred over complexity. Tetlock also finds that competitive situations call forth integratively simple ways of interacting, while cooperative situations call forth greater complexity.

These findings cast some doubt on the conventional view that cognitive processing goes on inside the individual. If the particular situations in which people find themselves differ in their demands for high integrative complexity, we may learn more by studying those situations than the mind.

Conclusions

What can we conclude from this first case about the relationship between cognition and political ideology? Let us review the several possibilities:

1. The Adorno study of authoritarianism suggested a clear link between cognition and political beliefs, arguing that politically conservative thought was cognitively simple.

2. Adorno's critics (for example, Rokeach) argued that while there was a definite link between cognition and belief, this connection revealed that extremists of both the political right and left shared the same tendencies towards simplistic information processing.

3. Both 1 and 2 suggest that cognitive structure is related to the kinds of political beliefs that people hold. In other words, both conclusions support a conventional view of cognition.

4. Tetlock's program of research raises some serious questions about the validity of either 1 or 2. He finds a variety of social and even historical factors that play a role in whether people think in simplistic or complex ways. Although there may be people who tend toward simplistic thinking, for the most part the pressures toward either simplistic or complex thinking seem to reside more in the social world than inside the individual. Tetlock's conclusion directs our attention away from how the mind structures political beliefs and toward the ways in which circumstances in which political beliefs are expressed structure the ways in which people think.

This first case, therefore, seems to point to a sociohistorical version of cognitive social psychology by raising serious questions about the "inner" view of cognitive processes.

. . . .

Moral Reasoning:
Formal Operations or an Ethic of Caring?

The second case that illustrates the debate between the conventional and the sociohistorical approaches to cognition examines moral reasoning, and contrasts those who are searching for a universal form of human cognition found in the structure of the mind (conventional) and those for whom the social context is the centerpiece of our un-derstanding (sociohistorical). Consider the moral dilemma of abor-tion. Should a woman be allowed to choose to have an abortion or is it in the state's interest to protect the rights of the unborn and so regulate the conditions under which an abortion can be performed? While rational arguments can be summoned on both sides of this complex issue, is there a universal—and, thus, fundamental—stan-dard of reasoning to which we can appeal to resolve the debate?

The more we probe such controversial issues as abortion, gun control, and capital punishment, the more we realize that intelligent and reasonable people can and do disagree. It would appear, there-fore, that the *content* of such issues cannot be submitted to some uni-versal standard as a basis for objectively deciding a proper from an improper position. Submitting such an issue to the judgment of a court may result in a legal resolution, but the morality of such a decision remains open to continued debate.

According to some investigators, however, our search for a uni-versal standard of moral judgment need not be totally frustrated. What if we ignore content and focus instead on the structure of a person's moral reasoning? Furthermore, what if we can demonstrate that this structure is universal, shared by all people throughout history? If such a universal structure of the human mind were found, then we could at least suggest that arguments in support of a given position in a debate reflected morally inferior or superior ways of thinking. This approach should sound familiar. It involves the distinction between structure and content that we encountered in the first case on cogni-tion and its role in politics. In that case we saw that some social psychologists argued that people could differ in the content of their political beliefs and yet maintain the same structure of thinking and reasoning. Is there a similar possibility in the case of moral reasoning? Perhaps the same or a similar universal structure of thinking applies here as well.

In pondering this complex matter, Lawrence Kohlberg (1969, 1981, 1984) called upon the pioneering efforts of Jean Piaget (1965) as one of the bases for his analysis. Piaget argued that the human mind passes through a sequence of stages as the infant matures into adulthood. These stages inexorably take the infant away from the im-mediate, concrete here-and-now into the world of highly abstract mental operations, which Piaget termed *formal operations*. These formal op-erations conform to the advanced logical and mathematical principles of western scientific thought. When achieved by the mature individ-ual, they not only permit people to process information in a very different way than was previously possible, but also allow them to more closely approximate the truth about reality without the kinds of distortion associated with the earlier stages of thinking.

According to Piaget, a *stage* of mental functioning involves qualitatively different ways of processing information. We can think of the individual's cognitive system as comprised of various *schema*, or ways by which information is processed. The immature child's schema are centered around his or her immediate and concrete context, thereby providing the child with a particular understanding of the world. Schema not only shape the kinds of experiences that are possible but, over time, are themselves transformed by experiences with the world. When experiences occur that challenge the existing ways of knowing, the schema begin to change, eventually creating a qualitatively different stage based on different schema. In effect, schema both transform what we experience and, in turn, are transformed by our experiences.

Piaget referred to the ways by which schema transform our experiences as *assimilation;* he referred to the ways by which experiences transform the schema as *accommodation.* We assimilate experiences to the prevailing schema; and yet, as experiences occur that cannot readily be assimilated, the schema themselves accommodate and eventually result in a new stage of cognitive operations.

Piaget demonstrated the existence of a developmental sequence to cognitive schema, and argued that this course of cognitive development described a universal process. As people mature, the schema by which they relate to reality pass through a sequence of stages, moving towards the highest stage of all—formal operations—characterized by highly abstract, formal, logical, and mathematical ways of relating to the world. At this point, they are about as close to encountering reality "out there" as is possible.

Kohlberg applied these Piagetian ideas to the stages of reasoning about moral dilemmas. He suggested that there were three main stages of reasoning, each having two subtypes. At the earliest, least advanced stage of thinking, termed the *preconventional,* the individual's ability to separate the interests of the self from the situation is minimal. Thus, there is a tendency for the individual to emphasize egocentric concerns in reasoning about a moral dilemma. In this stage of thinking, for example, "stealing is right as long as you can get away with it" or "people with the greatest power should have the right to get whatever they want out of life." Similar to Piaget's notions of an immature stage of cognitive development, Kohlberg viewed reasoning centered around these egocentric concerns as immature or primitive.

With development, the individual begins to encounter the needs and wishes of other people, as well as the duties and demands of society. The immature, egocentric schema for organizing information are challenged by these new forms of experience. In time, a transformation from the preconventional to the *conventional* form of reasoning occurs: egocentric schema begin to accommodate to the realities of social living.

At the conventional level, the individual can better differentiate self from other and begins to adopt a much less egocentric stance vis-à-vis the world. People recognize and try to accommodate themselves to others' needs and wishes. As people progress in the conventional forms of reasoning, they begin to consider the necessary rules and conventions of their society. These become important tools for human survival and the focus for reasoning. Considering the demands of others and carrying out societal obligations, rather than living entirely for one's own self, comes to define what is morally right and proper to do.

For Kohlberg, a further transition in human reasoning occurs when persons begin to think in terms of schema much broader and more abstract than those involved in conventional reasoning. At this *postconventional* stage of reasoning, the person employs highly abstract formulations of human rights and obligations, recognizing principles that apply to all humanity, not just to specific people in one's own orbit or society.

Kohlberg and his colleagues report that (a) people move through these three main stages (b) in a specific order—preconventional, conventional, postconventional—and (c) this describes a fundamental and universal feature of the human mind as it develops. Cognitive development allows a person to keep an increasingly greater distance from any specific context, thereby decontextualizing thinking to adopt the broadest and most abstract reasoning about any moral issue.

Let us now see how Kohlberg's theory would address a complex moral issue like abortion. While it does not specifically judge which position on the abortion issue is morally correct, his theory does indicate whether the way people reason about the position they take is primitive or advanced. Remember that the universal standard does not refer to which content is superior or inferior—pro- or anti-abortion—but only tells us whether the structure of the reasoning employed is developmentally primitive or advanced. At the highest stage, reasoning turns to general principles not rooted in self-interest or specific societal obligations, but rather in all of humankind. A person who reasons that abortion "would be good for me, and therefore the right thing to do," would be considered to be thinking about abortion at a primitive level.

Note that the framework that Piaget and Kohlberg present tells us that decontextualized thinking is more advanced than any more contextualized form. That is, the highest stages of thinking are the most abstract and general, and hence the most removed from the specific context of the individual or society. Clearly, therefore, this analysis opposes the central thesis of the sociohistorical view of cognition, for which the social context is central. The position developed by Piaget and used by Kohlberg emphasizes the advanced quality of decontextualized thinking. This contradicts the position developed by Vygotsky and Luria, among others, that thinking does not reside within the individual, but within society. Is Kohlberg's theory convincing?

A "Different Voice" of Reasoning

An associate of Kohlberg's on the moral reasoning project expressed concern about the decontextualized quality of the model. Carol Gilligan (1982) was especially concerned about the possibility that decontextualization placed many women at a morally inferior stage as compared with many men. For example, in reasoning about the issue of abortion and taking into consideration its effects on the unborn fetus, on the father, on one's friends, and on one's self, the woman would be considered to be thinking at a more primitive level than someone (male or female) who based his or her view of abortion on some highly abstract principle. A personal and interpersonal focus was too context-bound to suit the Kohlberg–Piaget understanding of moral development, in which abstraction and distancing from the concrete immediacy of the situation was said to reflect the most advanced form of human reasoning.

Gilligan's own research addressed these issues directly by examining a group of women who were personally confronting the abortion decision. How did they reason as they made up their minds? By conducting extensive interviews with these women, Gilligan found what she termed "a different voice" of reasoning. This voice was different in that it offered a form of reasoning equal to, not inferior to, that identified by Kohlberg. The different voice emphasized an ethic of caring rather than an ethic of individual rights. Just what does this distinction involve?

If a person's reasoning remains within the context of relationships and responsibilities towards other people; if that person's primary interest involves how best to care for others and not to harm anyone, the voice in which they speak follows an ethics of caring. This voice cannot seek a principle that lies outside the immediacy of a situation and those people involved in it. In Gilligan's view, every move towards abstraction is a denial of the caring and responsibility for other people. Reasoning in this different voice, however, does not produce an easy or necessarily satisfying resolution to a moral dilemma. In the case of abortion, for example, there is no decision that can be made in which someone is not harmed—the mother, the fetus, the father, friends, relatives, and so on.

In contrast, Kohlberg's voice of individual rights seeks a solution to a moral dilemma in terms of a generalized, abstract principle that can be justified precisely because it is not concerned with any specific context or people but with doing what is generally and universally right. Although this kind of reasoning might lead to a painful decision in some situations, the course to follow becomes increasingly apparent the further one becomes removed from the concrete details of circumstances.

In assessing a person's stage of moral reasoning, Kohlberg developed a series of hypothetical dilemmas which he presented to his subjects and asked them to indicate what should be done and why. One typical dilemma involved Heinz, whose wife was dying from a disease for which the cure was too costly for Heinz to afford. The druggist had the medication that Heinz needed but refused to sell it to Heinz for anything other than the high price which Heinz could not pay. Heinz decided to break into the store and steal the medicine. People were asked to decide whether or not Heinz should have done this, and to offer a rationale for whichever choice they think is proper: to steal or not to steal.

By scoring their responses to this and other similar scenarios, Kohlberg was able to assess a person's level of reasoning. Those who said that Heinz should not steal because he would get caught or that he should steal if he could get away with it, were scored at a much lower level (preconventional) than those who reasoned in terms of societal rules about stealing (conventional); in turn, they were both rated lower than those who reasoned in terms of an abstract principle—for example, valuing human life over property (postconventional).

Gilligan's female subjects were also asked to respond to this and other similar hypothetical dilemmas. According to Gilligan, her female subjects did not view Heinz, his wife, or the druggist as cardboard figures to be manipulated as mental abstractions toward some principle, but as real people. Indeed, Gilligan found her subjects imaginatively filling in details of their lives. The more details they supplied, the more real these characters became; the more real they became, the less possible it was to find any principle that could justify stealing or not stealing.

In other words, unlike the voice that Kohlberg found to reflect the highest levels of reasoning because it could distance itself from the immediate situation, the different voice that Gilligan uncovered could find no abstract principle that in some way did not violate the ethic of caring: someone was always getting hurt whatever choice was made. If Heinz stole in order to save his wife, then she might survive, but if he were caught, he would be put in prison and then where would they be as a couple? In much the same way, every other possibility was agonizingly examined from the perspective of the relationships between the people: no solution without pain to someone could be found.

It should be noted that some analysts have been critical of Gilligan's formulations, calling upon two different arguments. First, it appears that others' work has not consistently supported Gilligan's contentions that males and females use a different voice in reasoning about moral dilemmas (for example, see Colby & Damon, 1983). Second, to maintain, as Gilligan appears to have done, that reasoning varies by the gender of the reasoner seems to undermine a genuine sociohistorical analysis by failing to address the broader social context that may actually account for different forms of reasoning (for example, see Mednick, 1989).

Mednick argues, as have several other researchers (for example, see Deaux, 1984; Eagly, 1983), that social position rather than gender may be the actual source of differences in reasoning. The point is not that men and women differ, the differences being somehow intrinsic to one's biology, but rather that a person (male or female) whose social position has been centered in the home and family may come to reason in a manner different from someone (male or female) whose social position operates in the public world of work, where following abstract and impersonal principles tend to be requirements for effective functioning.

Conclusions

What does the Kohlberg–Gilligan debate imply for our two contrasting views of cognition? Gilligan's case that there is at least one other voice of reasoning casts doubt on the universalistic claims of the Piaget–Kohlberg thesis. It would not be unreasonable to suggest that the Piaget–Kohlberg view reflects only one culture's (or perhaps only the male part of one culture's) proposal about human reasoning. In other words, rather than describing something fundamental about the reality of human thinking, the benefits of formalization and abstraction recommended by this approach may simply reflect a bias in favor of a conventionally scientific view of thinking.

As Gilligan suggests, the male voice and the female voice of reasoning seem to differ. The dominance of males in the science of social psychology has perhaps given prominence to their theories at the expense of females. In her view, this suggests that there is an ideological slant even to these discussions about thinking. If thinking abstractly is not the way all minds necessarily must work when functioning at their best, but rather describes the way some minds work to accomplish certain social purposes, then perhaps the Kohlberg–Gilligan debate illustrates the sociohistorical view that different ways of understanding reflect different proposals about reality, *not* good or bad descriptions of its fundamental nature.

While it does seem likely that Gilligan has overly emphasized the role of gender while deemphasizing social position in her analysis, to focus on social position rather than on gender simply adds further weight to the sociohistorical analysis. Indeed, as Mednick suggests, a scheme that restricts itself to innate male–female differences carries the seeds for advancing societal gender discrimination disguised as social scientific discoveries in a way that the focus on social position does not allow.

We cannot, in effect, come away from the Kohlberg–Gilligan debate assuming that men are not concerned with interpersonal relations while women are. First, if the preceding differences are found, these are less likely to be reflections of intrinsic differences between men and women than they are of the differential social positions that men and women have thus far occupied in society. Second, insofar as we can find different forms of reasoning that vary as a function of the social positions of the reasoner, we have raised serious doubts about the conventionalist framework that animated the Piaget–Kohlberg approach.

. . . .

Everyday Cognition

The final case we will examine that illustrates the debate between the conventional and sociohistorical views of cognition focuses on common, everyday forms of thinking. Much of our understanding of human cognitive activity has been derived from examining people in highly contrived laboratory situations who are usually presented with formal problem-solving tasks (for example, see Galotti, 1989). In gaining the kinds of control over extraneous factors that the laboratory provides, investigators may have "inadvertently" adopted a conventional model of cognition to the detriment of the sociohistorical alternative. The laboratory approach assumes that the cognitive processes discovered in this artificial situation can be generalized to processes outside the laboratory because they are fundamental: the way the mind works; the way that people think, reason, and process information; and so on. As we have seen, this conventional perspective reflects but one of the two points of view we have considered. If the sociohistorical perspective were adopted, cognition would be understood as processes organized not by structures in the individual's mind, but by social environments. Therefore, because the laboratory is only one kind of social situation with its own particular demands and requirements, it leads to a restricted form of thinking. Far from being universal and fundamental, laboratory cognition would differ from everyday cognition because different settings organize and regulate different patterns of thinking, reasoning, and information processing.

According to the sociohistorical framework, then, cognitive activity is constituted in the social world, and so by restricting ourselves to studying cognition in the laboratory we do not learn about more basic processes (as conventionalists believe) but only about how people operate under conditions that emphasize only one type of human cognitive activity. If our interest is in human cognition, the sociohistorist argues, we must get out of the laboratory to see how thinking is structured within commonly encountered social settings. Galotti (1989) outlines some of the important ways in which formal reasoning of the sort commonly studied in the laboratory differs from everyday cognitive activity:

1. In the laboratory, people are usually provided with full information about the opening premises or assumptions of a reasoning problem they will be asked to solve. In everyday activities, we do not usually have premises so neatly outlined for us. Indeed, it is one of our everyday tasks to generate these opening assumptions and proceed from there.

2. In the laboratory there is usually one correct answer to a reasoning problem, and the experimenter examines either how a subject arrives at that solution or, if the answer was incorrect, what kinds of errors he or she made. In the everyday world, however, there are usually many different answers to any one problem, all of which are "correct." Solutions tend to vary as a function of values and interests they serve, not their correctness in some formal, mathematical sense.

3. In the laboratory there is usually a standard used to judge when a reasoning task is completed—a correct answer to a problem, for example. In our everyday world, however, we

are usually never quite sure when our task is over; we make do with our decision and move on to something else.

4. The kinds of reasoning problems used in the laboratory are usually very narrowly defined by the investigator's particular interests and rarely have much personal relevance or consequence to us. In the everyday world, we must deal with a wide and complex variety of problems that often have serious personal relevance and important implications for our lives.

Mehan (1984) observed how different decision-making processes in social contexts were from those studied in the laboratory. His research focused on decisions whether or not to place children in special education programs in a large school system. These are institutional rather than individual decisions, he points out, because the outcome—where the child is placed—emerges only after numerous individuals and committees have considered the specific case and made their evaluations. As he notes, the process usually begins in the classroom, where the ways in which the teacher decides whether or not to refer a child can be examined. The subsequent decision processes, however, involve a wide range of other persons and committees: assessment by examination; evaluation of the assessment; recommendation for counseling; recommendation for further assessment; Education and Placement Committee evaluation of the case; and so on.

Insofar as our models of rational decision making are based on the study of how individuals in the laboratory reach decisions about contrived experimental tasks, and insofar as our theories are based on assumptions about rational cognitive processes in the head of the individual who faces several clear alternatives, we tend to miss the process that occurs when institutions make decisions about a person's fate. As Mehan indicates, most rational models place the decision makers at a choice point with several available alternatives. People act rationally if their choices conform to a model of rationality—maximizing personal gain, achieving stated purposes, and so on.

Within institutional contexts of decision making however, these elements do not exist. "The decision making is distributed across participants in that information about the case is not under the control of any one committee member. . . . Decision making is distributed through time in that bits and pieces of the final decision are made at various stages in the referral process" (p. 64). Because of this more complex process, the alternatives are not known in advance, but emerge through time. Thus, there is no way to stand at a choice point in advance. All one can do is reconstruct several choice points *after* the fact.

If we examine organizational decision making, we see how everyday cognition departs dramatically from the laboratory model that assumes rational cognitive activity occurs inside the head of the individual. Mehan tells us that cognitive activity is socially distributed, organized, and regulated; it is more a property of the organization than of any one individual. How rationality emerges or even what it means, therefore, is not the result of any one person's thought processes, but rather is a function of how the many parts of the whole institution operate. A group of highly sophisticated thinkers, each of whom does marvelously well on laboratory tasks of rational cognitive ability, when placed into the kind of institutional setting that Mehan has examined might perform no better or worse than people whose laboratory performance is far less superior. In short, cognitive processes vary with the kinds of social settings that prompt them.

Other Examples

There are many other examples that illustrate how differently people think in different settings. Research has examined people's arithmetic reasoning in a grocery store (Lave, Murtaugh, & de la Rocha, 1984), a dairy (Scribner, 1984), in educational and employment settings (Wertsch, Minick, & Arns, 1984), and so on (also see Greeno, 1989; Kessen, 1979). In each case the findings generated in the laboratory not only fail to apply to everyday settings, but are also based on a flawed model of human cognition.

For example, Lave, Murtaugh, and de la Rocha's (1984) research examined how supermarket shoppers actually made the various pricing decisions that led them to purchase one product over another. The investigators compared this cognitive behavior with the same individuals' performance on formal, laboratory cognitive tasks. Their data suggest that the supermarket imposes a practical cognitive structuring of the shopper independent of the formal cognitive activity required to solve the simple arithmetic problems used in the laboratory. Experienced shoppers know how to use this situated cognition very effectively even if they do poorly on the formal measures of their ability.

Wertsch, Minick, and Arns (1984) compared how mothers and teachers worked with the same children on a learning task. They found that teachers ignored the efficiency of the children's performance, whereas mothers emphasized efficiency. Similar research has found that where learning a skill is part of a culture's economic framework, errors are not allowed and high efficiency is sought—the mother's view of training children. In the context of the classroom, errors are permitted and efficiency is much less required—the teacher's view of teaching children. In short, the kind of cognitive activity that emerges varies as a function of the goals of the individual "teacher" and the cultural context in which the activity occurs.

Perhaps the most succinct summary of these approaches to everyday cognition is found in Greeno's (1989) conclusion: because "most cognitive activity occurs in direct interaction with a situation, rather than being mediated by cognitive representations" (p. 139), advanced, critical thinking may be "more a social phenomenon than it is characteristic of individuals" (p. 139). This is a clearly sociohistorical view of human cognition. It suggests that we would benefit more from focusing on the kinds of social environments that encourage advanced, critical thinking than on the individual who, according to the conventionalists, is the seat of all thinking.

By locating cognitive activity in the social environment that organizes and regulates it rather than in the individual, efforts to induce a particular kind of thinking—for example, critical thinking—must turn to the environment that structures thinking rather than to the individual who is doing the thinking. The laboratory environment, then, is a very narrow and even peculiar location to study cognitive activity that may teach us very little about everyday thinking.

Conclusions

In this chapter we have compared two different approaches to understanding human cognitive activity. Each approach reflects the two perspectives in social psychology. The conventional approach seeks fundamental, universal cognitive structures and processes that describe how individuals think, reason, remember, process information, and so on. The sociohistorical approach emphasizes how cognitive activity is a feature of the social world rather than a description of the individual's mind. By stressing the importance of social contexts in structuring, organizing, and regulating the ways we think, reason, and understand, the sociohistorical approach gives social psychology a special place in the study of human cognition.

Since about 1980, there appears to be a clearly emerging trend away from the study of cognition as an individual process and towards the kind of social cognitive model advocated by Vygotsky and Luria. Replacing universal processes, structures, or stages with a context-linked or socially situated view seems increasingly to characterize the dominant models of theory and research. It must be noted, however, that changes of firmly established scientific models do not occur rapidly or easily, especially the kind of dramatic changes required by a social model of cognitive activity.

In the social model, "Thinking is situated in physical and social contexts. Cognition, including thinking, knowing and learning, can be considered as a relation involving an agent in a situation, rather than as an activity in an individual's mind" (Greeno, 1989, p. 135). This not only demands study of the social situation in order to understand human cognitive activity but, in moving away from the individual as thinker, challenges several hundred years of commonsense understanding in the western world.

The sociohistorical view that situations structure, organize, and regulate knowledge to more of an extent than individuals structure, organize, and regulate situations inverts the traditional conventional view of cognitive science; individuals are no longer the locus of the structuring, organizing, and regulating principles. If situations are the structuring source and persons in interaction with those situations consequently think, reason, and understand in particular ways, those concerned with a recent decline in human reasoning need to address our present social and cultural circumstances. This is an interesting and challenging task that social psychology, with its unique interest in examining the interaction of individuals and society, must face today.

4

....

Attribution
and Explanation

WHAT WOULD OUR everyday lives be like if we behaved as scientists do? Because some of the major objects in our world are other people, we would presumably have a definite practical interest in knowing how to predict and control their behavior. Without such knowledge our interpersonal world would be confusing and chaotic, pushing most of us into the security of solitude.

Scientists typically order the universe according to the underlying causes of these phenomena that interest them. If we were to behave comparably, we could achieve order in our own interpersonal universe if we knew the underlying causes of people's behavior. One place that most people reared in the western tradition look for these underlying causes is in the personality. Concluding that John yelled at us *because* John is aggressive, for example, would help prepare us to deal with John if and when on future occasions we run into him.

But how do we know that John's behavior is caused by his aggressive personality rather than by something else? For example, perhaps we ran into John immediately after an argument with his wife; his anger is most likely a direct consequence of that event rather than of something deeply embedded in his personality. Knowing about the argument leads to different predictions about John's future behavior than simply attributing the anger to his personality. It is therefore important to be able to make accurate analyses of the underlying causes of people's behavior to best know how to deal with them.

Although we may not commonly think this kind of cognitive activity has anything to do with scientific study, several social psychologists have argued that our everyday behavior more or less follows the traditional scientific method (for example, see Heider, 1958; Jones & Davis, 1965; Kelley, 1973). We make observations of John's behavior; we develop hunches about the probable causes; we test them out and reach conclusions. The conclusions become the basis for our own behavior towards John. We are likely to be sympathetic and understanding if we attribute John's aggressiveness to the fact that he just had an argument with his wife; we are likely to be cautious if we attribute his aggressiveness to a difficult personality. Let us look at a somewhat different example that also illustrates how we approach our interpersonal world scientifically.

Suppose you have studied for an upcoming examination. You take the exam and leave feeling uncertain about how well you did. Next week when the exams are returned, you learn that you did poorly. What went wrong? Even as we use observations to test our hunches and explain others' behavior, we are said to use a similar process to explain our own behavior: (a) "I didn't study enough"; (b) "the exam was far too difficult for the level of this course and so no one could be expected to do well"; (c) "I simply lack the capacity to handle this subject matter"; (d) "staying up late with friends the night before backfired on me." Undoubtedly, there are other possibilities, but these are a fair sampling. Which hunch is "correct"?

Your performance on future exams as well as feelings about how you did on this one will depend on which explanation you accept. If you did poorly because you did not study enough, your task in preparing for the next exam is clear; but if the material is beyond your capacity to grasp, then perhaps you should accept your performance as the best that could be expected of you under the conditions.

Both of these examples illustrate what in social psychology has come to be called *attribution theory*, which is really more of an approach than a comprehensive theory. Attribution theory is concerned with how people explain both personal and interpersonal events in their world, and how the consequences of the conclusions they draw will affect their future behavior. While the genesis of the attributional approach in social psychology may be in some doubt, its most important early advocate was clearly Fritz Heider (1958). Heider called attention to the importance of attribution and explanation, saw the process in our everyday life to be like the scientific method itself, and pointed out some of the key concepts still being used today.

. . . .

An Organizing Framework

The table on page 56 is a helpful way to organize the approach to attributional analysis in social psychology. This chapter will examine inputs and antecedent conditions, and causal attributions; Chapter 5 will consider outcomes and applications.

We will first look at some of the conditions that affect the attributions we make. We will begin with a model proposed by Kelley (1973) that helps us see the kinds of information we use when making causal inferences about another person's or even our own behavior, attributing the behavior either to the person or the situation. We will then compare the attributions actors make about their own behavior to those they make about other people's behavior. This discussion will introduce us to the so-called "fundamental attribution error" (Ross, 1977), the tendency to overly attribute to person-centered rather than to situational causes.

We will then take an even broader view of attribution theory, exploring the very terms of attributional mediation to determine whether attributions to the person or the situation may be culturally determined. In doing so, we will look at the question: What meaning does the person–situation distinction have when no clear line can be drawn, (as it can be in most western cultures) between what is within the person and what is within the situation?

Finally, we will consider the concept of intergroup relations. We will see how our own and others' group memberships influence the kinds of attributions we make. For example, there is a tendency for us to see our in-group's behavior in a more favorable light than the same behavior performed by an out-group member.

We will move from inputs and antecedent conditions to the two major classes of cognitive mediation that almost every attribution theory assumes, differentiating between locating the causes of behavior within the person or within the situation. As we have already seen, attributing causes of behavior to the person leads to very different consequences than attributing causes to the situation. If you did poorly on the exam because you are stupid, for example, you will act and feel differently than if you did poorly because the exam was too difficult.

Outputs and applications of attribution theory will be taken up in Chapter 5. Briefly, we will first explore issues involving the kinds of attribution people make about their performances in achievement situations and the consequences of these attributions. We will then

A Model for Attribution

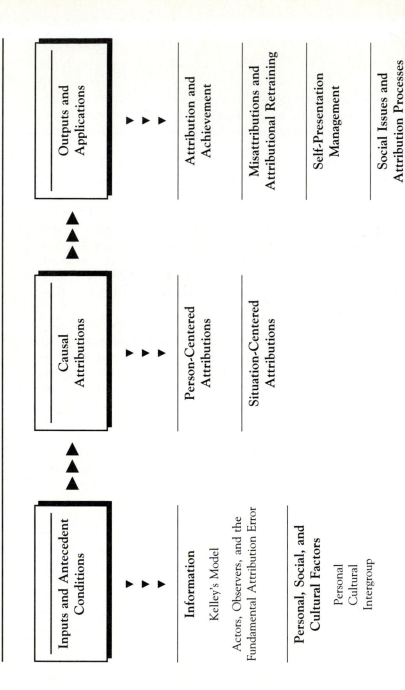

see how we can use some of the insights of an attributional analysis to help people deal more effectively with several emotional and behavioral difficulties. The following discussion suggests that many of the attributions we make serve important face-saving purposes in addition to providing us with an accurate assessment of the underlying causes of behavior. Finally, we will examine some of the social applications of attributional analyses to several topical issues, including rape, poverty, racism, and so on.

Inputs and Antecedent Conditions

Our initial concern is to examine what Heider and other major attribution theorists, but in particular Kelley (1973), have had to say about the kinds of information we use to explain personal or interpersonal behavior. Heider maintains that when people conduct their own scientific analysis of the social world, seeking to uncover the underlying structure that permits them to carry on effectively, they tend to infer two main types of underlying causes: those that refer to something about persons and those that refer to something about the environment.

Heider suggests that people are rarely comfortable with merely registering the raw items they observe, but rather try to discover the invariances that place them in a more stable and predictable world. In doing so, people turn either to something about persons—their underlying motives, needs, personality, and so on—or to something about the environment.

Kelley's Model

Building on the underlying framework established by Heider, Kelley sought to understand the kinds of information that would induce people to give their observations person-centered or situation-centered explanations. Kelley expanded Heider's original view of there being only two sources for stable invariances—person and situation—into a three-factor model involving the person, the stimulus entity, and circumstances. The first source is Heider's person-centered causal analysis, while the remaining two sources reflect Kelley's more complex view of environmentally based analyses.

To better understand Kelley's model, consider the following example (from Orvis, Cunningham, & Kelley, 1975). Suppose we observe John complimenting Mary for a job she has just completed. To what do we attribute John's behavior?

- ❑ Is John complimenting Mary because that is the kind of person that John is? This would involve making an attribution to something about John's *personality*.

- ❑ Is he complimenting her because her work is actually good? This would involve making an attribution to something about the *stimulus entity*, in this case, to Mary's work.

- ❑ Or is John complimenting Mary because of something unique about this one occasion? This would involve making an attribution to something about these specific *circumstances*.

Kelley identified three kinds of information relevant to the attributional decision we eventually make:

1. *Consensus information.* This tells us how usual it is for people to compliment Mary's work. If Mary's work is always being complimented by others, then consensus would be high. However, if Mary's work rarely receives compliments, then consensus would be low.

2. *Distinctiveness information.* This tells us something about John's behavior. If John freely gives out compliments to almost everyone, then the distinctiveness of his current compliment is low. However, if John rarely compliments anyone, then the distinctiveness of the present situation is high.

3. *Consistency information.* This tells us something about the particular occurrence we have observed compared with previous ones. If John has been known to frequently compliment Mary's work, then consistency is high. However, if John has rarely ever complimented Mary for her work, consistency is low.

Research indicates that the following configurations of the preceding categories of information produce specific kinds of attribution (for example, see McArthur, 1972; Orvis, Cunningham, & Kelley, 1975).

PERSON ATTRIBUTION: LOW-LOW-HIGH   (LLH)   PATTERN
Attribution is made to the personal—that is, to something about John—when consensus and distinctiveness are low, but consistency is high.

In other words, we infer that John's complimenting of Mary's work is more informative about John than about Mary's work if we learn that (a) few others besides John compliment her work (low consensus); (b) John is not very discriminating in giving away compliments (low distinctiveness), and (c) John has complimented Mary for her work in the past (high consistency).

ENTITY ATTRIBUTION: HIGH-HIGH-HIGH (HHH) PATTERN
Attribution is made to the stimulus entity—that is, to something about Mary's work—when all three sources of information are high. In other words, we infer that John's complimenting Mary's work is informative about the quality of her work if we learn that (a) John is not alone in finding her work to be exemplary (high consensus); (b) John's compliments are not usually given out freely to everyone (high distinctiveness); and (c) on previous occasions in which he has had a chance to evaluate Mary's work John has almost always found it to be commendable (high consistency).

CIRCUMSTANCE ATTRIBUTION: LOW-HIGH-LOW (LHL) PATTERN Attribution is made to the circumstances—that is, to something special about this particular situation—when consensus and consistency are low, but distinctiveness is high. In other words, we infer that John's compliments were given to Mary on this particular occasion for some special reason if we learn that (a) John, but few others, compliment Mary's work (low consensus); (b) John, however, is usually quite discriminating in complimenting people (high distinctiveness); and (c) John has not been known to compliment Mary for her work in the past (low consistency).

There are some important assumptions built into Kelley's model. First, the information patterns that lead to the different kinds of attributions—for example, the LLH, HHH, and LHL patterns—are presumed to be schemata built into a person's cognitive system. A person is presumed to compare information about events with these three schemata before making causal attributions.

Second, although experiments on Kelley's view of attribution typically present people with an informational pattern—for example, HHH—and ask for their causal explanations in terms of person, stimulus entity, or circumstances, it seems likely that in most situations in our everyday lives we seek out the information we need. Several investigations have evaluated this possibility (for example, see Hastie, 1984; Hilton, Smith, & Alicke, 1988; Holtzworth-Munroe & Jacobson, 1985; Major, 1980; Weiner, 1985; Wong & Weiner, 1981).

For example, Major (1980) created an experiment in which subjects were presented with a behavior they were to explain and could request various kinds of information prior to offering their explanation. They were told, for example, that John, who has been in prison for five years and is currently being considered for parole, recently got into a fight with another prisoner, Reggie. What caused John to get into this fight? Subjects could get additional information about John's behavior toward other prisoners (distinctiveness information), about other prisoners' behaviors toward Reggie (consensus information), or about John's past behavior toward Reggie (consistency information).

Somewhat surprisingly, Major found a general paucity of informational use on the part of most of her subjects: people sought only between 25% and 33% of the total amount of information they could have obtained before presenting their causal explanation. She also found that when information was sought, there was a definite preference for consistency information over the other two types. In this case, consistency information informed the subjects primarily about John's past behavior toward Reggie; and they apparently found such information helpful in explaining his current actions.

Several other efforts have been made to examine the conditions under which people seek information, using a somewhat different approach than Major's. For example, Wong and Weiner conclude that people spontaneously seek causal information primarily when something unexpected or unpleasant occurs. In other words, if events correspond to what we expect, we have little reason to seek additional information in order to understand the event; it is only when something unexpected or unpleasant occurs that we seek additional information to help us explain an event.

Hastie's (1984) examination of "When we ask why" tends to confirm Wong and Weiner's findings while adding several other circumstances under which we are likely to seek additional attributional information:

1. When we are explicitly requested to come up with an analysis of a person's actions, then we are likely to conduct an informational search. In some occupations, such as personnel interviewer, clinical psychologist, or judge, making attributions is part of the very job itself.

2. When we find ourselves dependent on another person for getting things we want—for example, a student's dependency on a teacher's good will, a child's dependency on a parent, a worker's dependency on a boss—we tend to seek information more than when our fate is less dependent on another person. In effect, there are certain conditions under which we

need to "psych out" the other person in order to protect our own interests.

3. When we have failed on some task—for example, an academic assignment—we are likely to engage in an attributional search to better understand why (we will return to this topic later in Chapter 5).

4. To this listing of Hastie's we might add the findings from a study of married couples reported by Holtzworth-Munroe and Jacobson (1985). Their data suggest that (a) early in the relationship there is more "attributional activity" than later in the relationship when stable expectations about one another have been formed; and (b) when marital conflict appears, the couple are more likely to seek information at that time to explain the troubled situation than when the conflict has passed.

Actors, Observers, and the Fundamental Attribution Error

In the studies we have just examined, the subject is an observer asked to make causal attributions about another person. Do people make the same kinds of attributions about their own behavior as they do when observing someone else?

Research on this question reveals two different tendencies: (1) supporting the original theory proposed by Jones and Nisbett (1971), there appears to be a slight, but reliable, tendency for people to attribute their own behavior to something about the situation and others' behavior to something about their personalities; and (2) observers tend to prefer person-centered attributions over situation-centered attributions. This latter finding has been termed the *fundamental attribution error* (Ross, 1977). We will examine each of these tendencies and review possible explanations for them.

ATTRIBUTION: SITUATIONAL EXPLANATION FOR BEHAVIOR OF SELF VERSUS PERSONAL EXPLANATION FOR BEHAVIOR OF OTHERS There are several ways to compare how we tend to attribute our own behavior with others' behavior. Goldberg's (1981) approach is typical. In one of his studies, he asked 1,400 subjects to use a near-exhaustive list of 2,800 trait terms commonly found in the English language to describe themselves and three other people they knew quite well. In addition to using the trait terms (which offer a person-centered attribution), subjects could also indicate that "it depends on the situation." Checking this option rather than a trait term would indicate a preference for a situational rather than a personal attribution. Goldberg's data indicate a rather clear preference for subjects to check the situational option when describing themselves, while using more trait terms when describing others. Despite some criticisms of this approach Goldberg's extensive work and the careful review of other relevant research reported by Watson (1982) continue to show this to be a slight, but reliable attributional tendency. But why do people respond this way at all?

WHY THE DIFFERENCE? Jones and Nisbett (1971) originally suggested several rather plausible reasons why people might make more situational attributions in explaining their own behavior while emphasizing person-centered explanations of others' behavior:

1. People have greater access to information about themselves than they do about others, and so are more aware of how their own behavior tends to shift in different situations. We might then reasonably expect people to use more situational attributions to explain the behavior of their good friends as compared with strangers because we are generally more familiar with how our friends' behavior varies by situation than how strangers' behavior changes.

    Some of Goldberg's (1981) data support this expectation. He finds that "on the average subjects used the situational response about 40% of the time when describing themselves, about 32% of the time when describing any of three other individuals whom they knew personally (their best friend, their father, or an admired acquaintance), and only 25% of the time when describing the television commentator Walter Cronkite. Seemingly, subjects have seen themselves in many situations, others in less, and Cronkite in only one" (p. 519). On the other hand, after carefully reviewing a large array of data examining the plausibility of this information-access explanation, Watson (1982) concludes that its importance "has yet to be established" (p. 690).

2. Because the self and others have different visual orientations, it is possible that this accounts for the self–other attributional differences that have been found. For example, we can more readily see other's actions than our own; when we look at someone else, they are the center of our focus. On the other hand, when we act, we focus more on the situation

around us and how best to manage ourselves within it. However, Watson suggests that here too the available evidence does not clearly support what is an otherwise reasonable explanation.

3. A third explanation for the self–other attributional effect is that we use information differently when it is about ourselves than when it is about others. Watson proposes that this third factor can be divided into two separate elements: (1) the salience of the self versus the environment; and (2) our degree of concern about controlling our interactions with others.

First, Watson suggests that situational, rather than personal, attributions can be increased by making the environment the focus of our attention, while personal attributions can be increased by conditions that increase the salience of the self. If our attention is drawn to ourselves—for example, by leading us to believe that we are being filmed (Arkin & Duval, 1975)—more personal than situational ratings of the self are likely. On the other hand, if the environment becomes more salient, we tend to attribute it as the locus of causality. This research suggests how salience can modify the self–other effect, but still leaves us somewhat ignorant as to why the environment appears more salient when people rate themselves than when people rate others.

Second, Watson proposes that to interact effectively with others, we need to find something internal and stable about them; this personal knowledge helps smooth our interactions with them. On the other hand, when we are behaving, we are primarily concerned with adjusting our behavior to the shifting situations we encounter, and so we are more likely to pay attention to the situations than to ourselves. Watson's review suggests some indirect support for this interpretation of the self–other effect, and concludes that both salience and control currently seem to be the most fruitful candidates for explaining the effect (pp. 98–99).

THE FUNDAMENTAL ATTRIBUTION ERROR   As we have seen, we tend to attribute other people's behavior to their personalities, ignoring or discounting situational factors that might equally account for it. Ross called this tendency to make personal, rather than situational, attributions the fundamental attribution error. This error typically occurs in research studies when subjects witness someone playing a role and are then asked to explain that person's behavior. If the subjects focus on the fact that the person is role-playing, they will attribute the behavior they observe to the situation—that is, to the role the person was asked to portray rather than to something about the person. However, if the subjects discount the role-playing, they will make a personal attribution, believing that something about the person rather than the situation explains the behavior. We commit this "error" every time we see a film and identify the actor with the character he or she is portraying.

In one of the classic studies of this error, Ross, Amabile, and Steinmetz (1977) asked their experimental subjects to observe a simulated quiz show in which they saw one person assigned the role of questionner and another person the role of contestant. Unknown to the subjects, both persons were accomplices of the experimenter. The questionner was instructed to make up questions, which the contestant was to answer. It was very clear that the roles had been assigned by chance. Subjects were to make ratings of each person's general knowledge. Results demonstrated that subjects rated the questionner's ability significantly greater than that of the contestant. In other words, subjects disregarded the fact that the people they were observing had been randomly assigned to roles. By attributing personal qualities to each person—high ability to the questionner and low ability to the contestant—the subjects committed the fundamental attribution error.

This effect has been frequently replicated (for example, see Block & Funder, 1986), leading Ross and his associates to proclaim that we seem all too ready to jump "to conclusions about others and underestimate the potential impact of relevant environmental forces and constraints" (p. 492). Some of the reasons we have previously encountered for explaining self–other attributional differences have been posited to account for this error as well. We will later enlarge our perspective and consider several cultural and historical explanations.

Personal Factors

We will now consider several issues, some raised by sociohistoricists, that, at least in some cases, question the conventional positions that attributional dynamics are both universal and located within the individual. As we will see, the sociohistorical framework offers us a somewhat different angle from which to view the complicating and enlightening factors—personal, cultural, and intergroup—involved in an attributional analysis.

INTERPERSONAL SENSITIVITY Several personal or individual-difference factors influence the kinds of causal analyses people make.

There is research, for example, that suggests some people are more sensitive to interpersonal information than others (for example, see Snyder, 1976). Those who are more sensitive tend to make more situational attributions for their own behavior than for the behavior of others, while insensitives—people for whom interpersonal information is less important—emphasize more personal attributions when focusing on their own behavior.

COGNITIVE-DEVELOPMENTAL FACTORS   One type of personal factor involves the impact of cognitive development on the person's ability to do the complex information-processing manipulations that attributional operations require. Allen and her colleagues (1987) suggest that only those capable of thinking in terms of Piaget's stage of formal operations can manage the complexity of weighing consensus, distinctiveness, and consistency information.

Allen and her colleagues assessed individuals' cognitive capacities and presented them with a typical attributional task. Data indicate that, indeed, only those capable of formal operations could manipulate the information in the manner predicted by the logic of attributional theory.

Both Karinol and Ross (1976) and Kassin, Lowe, and Gibbons (1980) focused on the role of cognitive developmental factors in attribution. Each investigator addressed the *discounting principle* that comes into operation when several plausible causes for an event are present. How does the individual choose among these competing possibilities? For example, what if Jane is promised a reward if she agrees to undertake an activity that is in itself very interesting and rewarding? If she agrees to take on this task, is it because of the reward (external cause) or because the task is interesting to her (internal cause)? Kelley's theory suggests that when an external reason is present people tend to discount the internal reason, to a large extent because the external reason is easier to verify.

The question that Karinol and Ross, and Kassin, Lowe, and Gibbons examined is whether or not discounting requires a certain level of cognitive ability. Previous research suggested that discounting does not appear until children are somewhere between grades 2 and 4. Karinol and Ross presented children in kindergarten, first- and second-grade children, and a group of college students with a situation in which both a plausible internal cause and external cause were present as explanations for a target person's behavior. Their data confirm that the discounting principle increases with age.

They also found that discounting is especially pronounced when the external cause is a command, rather than a reward, to the target person to behave in a particular way. In their view, a command is

much clearer than a reward in the information it provides to the subjects. For example, a reward for doing something may be seen as a
"bonus," whereas a command more clearly seeks to manipulate the
person into carrying out the activity, thereby facilitating those cognitively capable of attributing the target person's behavior to the command and not to something about the person.

Employing a different experimental situation, Kassin, Lowe, and
Gibbons did not find the same developmental differences that Karinol
and Ross reported. In fact, their study suggested that even kindergart-
ners were able to use the discounting principle. Why the different
findings? Kassin, Lowe, and Gibbons suggest that when a verbal task
is presented to subjects of different ages, younger children are at a
greater disadvantage than older children, and thus show a general
inability to adopt the discounting principle. On the other hand, when
a purely nonverbal, perceptual task is used, as in their own research,
this age disadvantage disappears along with the apparent difficulty in
discounting.

Given that we now have several plausible explanations of the
role of cognitive-developmental factors in attribution before us, which
among them is the most adequate? Because Kassin, Lowe, and Gibbons' work seems to integrate all previous findings, and suggests the
conditions under which discounting will or will not follow a developmental pattern, theirs would be the most complete explanation.

ATTITUDES AND VALUES   Another type of personal factor that seems
to be important in attributional analysis involves a person's attitudes
and values. These should be especially relevant when the attributions
do not involve the kinds of abstract, hypothetical circumstances encountered in laboratory research, but situations where people are asked
to explain important social events like poverty and unemployment.
Feather's (1985) research is especially relevant in this context.

Feather evaluated his subjects' degree of conservatism as well as
their adherence to the "Protestant Ethic"—the belief that the individual is personally responsible for success or failure. He related these
factors to the subjects' explanations of youth unemployment. His data
suggest that conservative subjects tended to attribute unemployment
to such personal factors as lack of motivation and personal problems,
while less conservative subjects emphasized governmental failure. (We
will return to this finding again in Chapter 5.)

Feather also finds a relationship between his subjects' adherence
to the Protestant Ethic and the kinds of attributions they make. The
value implies that whenever we find people who have "failed" in life—
for example, who are chronically unemployed—their failure has some-

thing to do with them personally rather than the particular circumstances they are in. Feather's data confirms this expectation: subjects scoring higher on adherence to the Protestant Ethic tended to judge bad outcomes like unemployment as a consequence of something internal to the individual rather than of his or her external circumstances.

Feather's data from this and several other studies suggest that attributions are not merely neutral outcomes of careful and thoughtful information processing, as Heider, Kelley, and many others have proposed. Rather, the kinds of attributional analyses we make tell a story about our own political values and ideologies.

This important conclusion takes us one step from a conventional to a sociohistorical perspective. Attributions are not simply processes that take place inside the head of the individual thinker; they refer to prevailing social processes and values. In examining attributions, then, we should focus on the kind of society in which they occur and the role they play in that society.

Cultural Factors

Our discussion in Part I should have prepared us to question the universality of the kinds of attributional processes we have been considering. Cultures in which the individual is less clearly differentiated from other people or from the environment—most nonwestern cultures, for example—might not subscribe to the theories Kelley and others suggest. In this respect, Joan Miller's (1984) research is particularly instructive.

Miller gathered her data from samples in Mysore, India and Chicago. All subjects were asked to give an example of two behaviors they considered to be deviant and two they considered to be helpful or kindly. They were also asked to explain why people engaged in each type of behavior. She scored all responses into the by-now familiar attributional categories—situation-centered versus person-centered. Because her samples not only differed by culture, but also by age, she was able to examine both cultural and developmental differences. The latter were important because Miller contends that children learn their culture's dominant theories only over time.

In comparing adults from Mysore and Chicago, Miller found a greater tendency among the Chicagoans to offer person-centered explanations. For example, of all the reasons offered to explain behavior, an average of 40% of those mentioned by the subjects in the American sample made reference to personal traits and dispositions, compared with only 20% of those in the Indian sample.

A specific example from her research will help clarify this difference. When asked to describe and explain a deviant act with which they were familiar, an American subject told about a neighbor who cheated on her income taxes by overreporting charitable donations. When asked to explain this deviant behavior, the subject responded by noting, "That's just the type of person she is. She's very competitive" (p. 967). In comparison, an Indian subject reported as a deviant act his being cheated by someone who had agreed to complete some construction on his house and who ran off with the money without ever doing the promised work. When asked to explain this behavior, the Indian subject commented that, "The man is unemployed. He is not in a position to give that money" (p. 968). In other words, it appears that Americans' explanations for behavior are more likely to be person-centered, while Indians' explanations tend to be situation-centered. Miller also reports finding no striking age-related differences in comparing American and Indian 8- and 11-year-olds. The absence of such differences suggests further the important role socialization plays in our theories of attribution.

Miller's intriguing data lend credence to a sociohistorical perspective. If attributional analyses reveal how the human mind works, then there is little reason to expect cultural differences. Miller's research suggests, however, that attributional analyses do, in fact, vary by culture. If Miller is right, the causal schemata that attribution theory has identified—for example, Kelley's informational patterns—are less a depiction of some universal mind at work than a particular cultural framework. In the conventional view, when we see that only John compliments Mary's work, and that John is noted for complimenting nearly everyone, we conclude that the compliment tells us less about Mary's work than about John's character. But have we thereby captured an essential feature of the way that the human mind processes information and reaches a conclusion? Or, as Miller's sociohistorical approach suggests, is this kind of attribution better seen as a feature of our own current society which, in making the attribution to John's character, we help to re-create? Likewise, is the fundamental attribution error, in which we overattribute to persons and underestimate the importance of situations, a naturally occurring function of the human mind or of our current society?

Jellison and Green's (1981) research turns the tables on the attribution theorists by observing that the very explanation of most attributional effects, such as the fundamental attribution error, can itself be either person-based or situation-based. As noted earlier, the tendency among most theories we have examined is to adopt a person-based interpretation and so attribute this fundamental error to something about the way people's minds work. Miller's cross-cultural findings illustrate a situationally based explanation, as does Jellison and Green's emphasis on social norms.

According to their normative explanation, when individuals propose a person-based attribution, they are following a learned social norm which, at least in our culture, favors internal over external attributions. When our attributions conform to our cultural norms, we are more likely both to be understood and to receive the social approval of our peers.

In one of the several studies they report, for example, Green and Jellison asked their subjects to respond to a standardized questionnaire in such a way as to gain social approval. Findings indicated that the subjects selected responses focusing on something within the person that causes behavior. In other words, they knew that the kinds of responses necessary to gain approval were person-based, internally oriented responses. Although by no means definitive, Jellison and Green's findings add further support to the sociohistorical view of attributional analyses as descriptions of how a culture, rather than an individual mind, operates in explaining events.

Intergroup Factors

We have so far examined the attributions that a person makes in explaining the behavior of another person without regard for either's *group membership*. The following personal account illustrates what we mean when we speak of a person's group membership.

When I was just beginning my graduate studies at the University of Michigan, a friend and I decided to see if we could find an apartment or even a large room to share. We wandered all over Ann Arbor checking out various leads and finally came upon what we both considered an excellent possibility—a large, affordable room in a good neighborhood near the campus. In showing us the room, the very friendly landlady commented how pleased she was with the two of us, saying almost parenthetically that she would surely never rent any of her rooms to anyone who was Jewish or Catholic. My friend and I paused a moment and glanced knowingly at one another: he was Catholic and I was Jewish. We said nothing, but left quietly. In that brief moment, we each became aware of our membership in groups, an awareness that neither of us had most other times in our lives. After all, this was my friend, an individual, the guy I played tennis with. We rarely, if ever, approached one another as Catholic and Jew. Until that day.

This story shows how, as we begin to relate to people as representatives of particular groups rather than as individuals, we may begin to see them differently. One of the consequences of group membership is the possibility of an in-group–out-group bias effect (for example, see Billig, 1976; Tajfel, 1978, 1982; Taylor & Moghaddam, 1987): once different group memberships are identified, people may begin to evaluate one another in terms of in-groups and out-groups. Some of Tajfel's research has demonstrated how even an apparently minor factor, such as aesthetic preferences created in the laboratory, can serve as a basis for dividing the world into in-groups and out-groups.

What difference does this group membership effect have on the kinds of attributional analyses people make? The effect is substantial, and results in in-group favoritism and out-group denigration: behavior is positively evaluated when performed by the in-group but negatively evaluated when performed by the out-group. For example, people tend to hold in-group members—those seen as similar to themselves—less responsible for a bad event than out-group members—those seen as dissimilar to themselves (for example, see Shaver, 1970; Veitch & Piccione, 1978). Some of the most striking research, however, does not manipulate the in-group–out-group factor in the laboratory, as in the preceding studies, but builds on real group differences.

In a dramatic demonstration of the out-group biasing effect, Duncan (1976) presented a sample of white male college students with a videotaped interaction of an argument between two people, a protagonist and a victim. At the end of the argument, the protagonist shoved the victim. Some of the subjects saw a videotape in which a white protagonist shoved a black victim; others saw a black protagonist shove a white victim. The subjects' task was to evaluate the act of shoving and to explain why it occurred.

When the white subjects saw a white protagonist shove a black victim, 17% described the act as "violent," while 42% thought it merely "playful." When the white subjects saw a black protagonist shove a white victim, 75% described it as a violent act and only 6% thought it to be playful behavior. In other words, the "same" behavior is evaluated more positively when performed by a member of the in-group. In addition, Duncan found white observers of white protagonists to attribute the shove to some feature of the situation rather than to the person, which they did when the protagonist was black.

Taylor and Jaggi's (1974) research confirms this same out-group biasing effect. All of their subjects were Hindu clerks asked to evaluate the behavior of either a fellow Hindu (in-group) or Muslim (out-group) protagonist. Brief stories were presented to the subjects in which the protagonist was placed in four different situations and behaved in either a positive or negative manner. For example, the protagonist was a generous shopkeeper or one who cheated his customers; he was a teacher who praised or scolded his students; he either provided help to an injured person or ignored the injured person; he provided shelter to someone caught in a rainstorm or denied them shelter.

Subjects were instructed to offer explanations for the protagonist's behavior. These explanations were examined to see if any in-group favoritism or out-group denigration occurred. The results of the study were impressive. When an in-group member's behavior was positive, an internal explanation was offered—"fellow Hindus are like that"; when the in-group member's behavior was negative, an external explanation was offered—"something in the situation prevented him from acting properly in this case." When an out-group member acted positively, the explanation was significantly less internal and emphasized the unique situation: to admit generosity as a trait of out-group members would grant them too much credit, so something about the situation must explain their momentarily beneficent action. But when the out-group member's behavior was negative, internal explanations increased: the characteristics of out-group members disposed them to act negatively.

As we can clearly see, when people make attributions to members of their own groups, they tend to place things in the best light possible, dismissing negative acts as momentary effects of the situation while claiming positive acts to reflect permanent qualities they possess as a group. On the other hand, the same actions performed by members of the out-group tend to be much less generous: their positive acts are passed off as momentary features of the situation, while their negative behaviors are treated as though they were expected.

It is interesting to consider the relationship between these effects and the perpetuation of group stereotypes. Given these findings, it appears to be difficult for out-group members to shake off in-group members' stereotypes of them. Whenever they do something positive, it is attributed not to their personality but to some temporary feature of their situation; on the other hand, when they do something negative that fits the stereotype of their group, then the act is seen to be just what was expected of "people like that."

Hewstone and Ward (1985) sought to replicate the Taylor and Jaggi study in all but one of its details: they used a different sample of subjects in two separate studies. In the first study, their subjects were Malay and Chinese University students in Malaysia. Subjects were presented with the same task that Taylor and Jaggi had used and asked to explain the protagonist's behavior in terms of something internal—"Chinese are very generous" or "Malays are very hospitable"—or something external—"the Chinese shopkeeper didn't cheat his customers so there must have been something wrong with the scales he was using" or "the Malays provided shelter during the rainstorm because everyone else in the village was doing so."

Confirming Taylor and Jaggi's original results, Hewstone and Ward report a definite *ethnocentrism effect*—that is, a tendency to show favoritism in attributions about the in-group as compared with the out-group. Using the percent of person-centered attributions as the key measure, Hewstone and Ward found that Malays were more likely to attribute positive actions of other Malays (66%) to person-centered reasons than their negative actions (18%). Malays were not as generous in their evaluations of Chinese protagonists, however; they were more likely to attribute negative actions of Chinese (46%) to person-centered reasons than the positive actions of Chinese (27%). Many Chinese subjects, however, seemed to favor the Malay protagonists at the expense of their own group. For example, Chinese subjects were more likely to attribute the positive behavior of Malay protagonists (57%) to person-centered reasons than negative actions of Malays (24%). In turn, they tended more to attribute their own groups' negative actions (54%) to person-centered reasons as then positive actions by members of their own group (39%).

In seeking to explain this puzzling finding, Hewstone and Ward turned to broad social factors in Malaysia. They noted, for example, that at the time of their research Malaysia was a nation in upheaval: the Malays were deeply nationalistic, and the minority of Chinese showed a kind of anxious accommodation to this situation. The nationalistic spirit among the Malays is consistent with the Hewstone and Ward results indicating an ethnocentric preference for their own people. In turn, the Chinese subjects' reluctance to openly express pro-Chinese feelings by favoring their own group may have been their way of protecting their own interests. To test this interpretation, Hewstone and Ward conducted their second study.

For this second study, they selected Singapore because of its reputed multicultural harmony, a nation with many ethnic groups living together in apparent harmony and with few intergroup stereotypes. Once again, they presented subjects, now Malays and Chinese from the National University in Singapore, the same stories used in the first study.

In this case Hewstone and Ward found few, if any, attributional biases based on in-group favoritism, although there remained a tendency for some in-group favoritism among the Malay subjects. However, the Malays did not denigrate the Chinese out-group, nor did the Chinese show the same self-effacing strategy used in Malaysia.

Hewstone and Ward's data suggest the importance of social, cultural, and political factors in shaping the kinds of attributions people make. In contrast to the "naive scientist" model that has guided a considerable amount of social psychological understanding, this study describes subjects whose sensitivity to group membership and to political realities shape their way of understanding their own and other's behavior. Even the ethnocentric or out-group biasing effect that seemed to describe the way the mind works now seems to be a function of cultural and political realities. We will return again to this theme in Chapter 5 when we examine the strategic use of attributional analysis in self-protective face-saving.

Conclusions

Several philosophers and social scientists distinguish between the *cause* of something and the *reasons* offered to explain it (for example, see Peters, 1958). In the case of most human behavior, when we say that we are seeking the cause of an action, we really mean that we are seeking the reasons for that action.

Using Peters' own example, if we want to know why Steven is crossing the road, explaining how the sensory and physiological apparatus make his walking movements possible will not satisfactorily explain his behavior, even though it provides the basis for a causal answer. What we want to know are the reasons for his action—for example, he crossed the road because he saw a flower shop and wanted to buy some flowers to take home to his wife. Although the term "causal attribution" has been applied in conjunction with the theories and research we have examined in this chapter, reasons, not causes, have been our focus. Reasons in this instance refer to something internal—the person's motivation, ability, personality, and so on—or to something external—the particular circumstances involved—that explain behavior. Peters also notes that we are likely to seek explanations only when something out of the ordinary occurs. For example, if rather than walking across the road Steven hopped on one foot, then we might be sufficiently intrigued to probe further into why he behaved in such a peculiar manner. At this point, according to Peters, we might seek causal explanations rather than reasons, looking for something special about Steven.

It is interesting to note that reasons require knowledge of the culture in which the activity occurs. In effect, reasons refer to a culture's way of accounting for or explaining human behavior. Crossing the street to purchase flowers to take home makes sense to most of us. If we said, however, that Steven crossed the street because he was overweight, this would not likely be an acceptable answer. Unacceptability is not a function of either its being true of false (he may or may not be overweight); rather, it lies outside our cultural framework of acceptable reasons for people's actions (also see Gerth & Mills, 1953; Mills, 1963).

If reasons have explanatory power for us because they are acceptable accounting devices within our culture, this suggests that they are cultural properties we learn in order to explain both our own and others' behavior. In spite of this culture-specific quality of attributions, those social psychologists doing work on attribution who follow the lead of its originators (for example, Heider and Kelley), not only have presented their cases in terms of causes rather than reasons, but have also located the principles of attribution inside the mind of the individual.

Although the conventional case that Kelley and others make has been framed in terms of the person's search for the underlying causes of behavior, from the sociohistorical viewpoint we should substitute reason whenever we see the term "cause." In our own society, we find it helpful to explain people's behavior by claiming that it is caused by something we call their personality: John is aggressive because he has an aggressive personality. In another culture we might just as well explain John's aggressiveness as due to his being under the spell of an evil spirit. While this kind of reason would not be convincing in our culture, our explanatory theory would be equally unconvincing in a culture for which the concept of personality did not offer an acceptable reason for a person's behavior.

It would seem then, that rather than referring to causes, attributional analyses might better be seen as referring to reasons that are acceptable accounts within a particular culture. It would also seem, therefore, that rather than assuming the processes said to characterize attributional analyses reflect some internal cognitive principles of the individual's mind at work, they are better seen as properties of a given social system. Both the cross-cultural examples we have introduced in this chapter and the self-presentational examples we will encounter in Chapter 5 are more compatible with this sociohistorical way of understanding attributions than with the conventional view that still dominates current research.

5

....

Attribution: Outcomes and Applications

IN THIS CHAPTER we will continue our examination of attribution theory, focusing on the various ways that attributional concepts have been put to practical use.

We will first look at attribution in achievement situations—situations where people succeed or fail. Much of the work in this area has been conducted in academic settings, and is primarily concerned with how we explain our academic failures and the consequences that follow from the kind of explanation we use.

We will next consider some of the therapeutic uses of attribution theory, based on the view that attributional retraining—in which people are helped to reattribute the sources of their difficulties—may help them improve their everyday functioning.

The next discussion introduces us to an understanding of the attributional model compatible with the sociohistorical perspective. The argument is made that attributions serve strategic face-saving functions and that people learn how to manipulate attributions in order to manage the impressions that others form of them.

Finally, we will see how attributional analyses lead to interpretations of the causes of some common social problems, and the implications of those interpretations for the kinds of action proposed to resolve them.

Attribution and Achievement

Two interrelated approaches have been used to examine how attributional processes deal with achievement experiences in academic settings. The first approach owes much of its impetus to the work of Weiner and his associates (1971, 1979); the second approach emerged out of research on learned helplessness (for example, Peterson & Seligman, 1984; Seligman, 1981).

In Weiner's view, people's attributions of their success or failure can be internal or external. There are at least four internal possibilities: the outcome was due to *ability, unstable effort, stable effort,* or *personality.* Two external attributions are also possible: the outcome was caused by *other people* or *luck.* According to Weiner, the kind of attributional analysis we make determines our emotional reaction and influences future activity.

For example, if you fail an examination and attribute your failure to some enduring negative trait—"I lack ability" or "I never seem to be able to study sufficiently hard to do well"—you are less likely to work harder in the future than someone who attributes his or her failure to a temporary or uncharacteristic letdown. In the latter case, the future can be changed since the cause is presumed to be modifiable—"I didn't put in as much effort as I could have, but next time I know what to do." Research by Weiner and others suggests general support for the motivating consequences of less enduring, internal attributions, and also suggests what might be done to increase a person's future efforts in response to a failure experience.

For example, Wilson and Linville (1985) report the results of three separate studies based on Weiner's model in which they tried to improve the academic performance of first-year college students. They reasoned that students who had not done well during their first semester and who had attributed their poor performance to some deep-rooted flaw in themselves might give up trying, thereby perpetuating a failing pattern. In order to reverse this possibility, they created an intervention strategy in which they provided the students with information suggesting that the causes of early college failure are unstable and thus modifiable. For example, they presented statistics showing that grades typically increase after the first year; in addition, the first-year students saw interviews with seniors who reported failure while in their first year, but success in later years.

Wilson and Linville's results suggest both significant short- and long-term effects from this kind of attributional intervention. For example, shortly after the intervention, subjects took a set of sample items from the Graduate Record Examination. Males who had been given the intervention strategy did significantly better than males in the control conditions (students in similar situations who had not received the intervention designed to change their attributions). To measure the long-term impact of their intervention, Wilson and Linville looked at year-end grade point averages, finding that those in the intervention condition had a higher GPA than those in the control conditions. As the authors conclude: "Communicating to college freshman that the causes of low grades are temporary has . . . beneficial effects, on both short-term and long-term performance measures" (p. 291).

Wilson and Linville's work focuses on performance, but what about those emotions felt as a function of the kind of attribution people make for their failures? Weiner, Russell, and Lerman's (1979) research is instructive. They asked subjects to write about a personal experience in which they had either been successful or had failed. Weiner and his colleagues then evaluated the emotional experiences their subjects reported. They found two different sets of emotions: one set appeared for success and failure regardless of the kind of attributional analysis the subject made; the other set was linked to the attributions that were made.

Not surprisingly, success led people to feel happy and good, regardless of what kinds of attributions they made, while failure produced feelings of upset and displeasure. What is of particular interest, however, are those emotions linked to the kinds of attributions people make. Weiner and his associates report that when people attribute success to something internal, such as ability or stable effort, their feelings are pride, competence, and contentment; when they attribute failure to something internal, the resulting feelings are incompetence, resignation, and guilt.

It is clear that how we explain our academic failures has a significant impact both on what we are likely to do and how we feel. We can offer explanations that focus either on something about us (internal) or something about the situation—"I just had bad luck this time" or "other people interfered with my ability to study this time around." Depending on the attribution we make, we will experience different kinds of emotions and will plan different future actions.

Feelings of resignation and hopelessness that come from attributing our failure to something internal and stable, as we have seen, might prevent us from trying harder; and so we give up and sink further into failure. By helping us change those attributions from internal and fixed to another source (for example, unstable effort), both our behavior and emotions can be transformed.

Learned Helplessness as an Explanatory Style

Approaching these same issues of failure from a slightly different point of view, another group of investigators built their case around the concept of *learned helplessness*. The original idea was based on research indicating that if dogs were unable to escape from a painful situation, they soon gave up trying and became "helpless." We can imagine two different situations: in one, our actions permit us to escape; in the other, regardless of what we do, we cannot escape. In the first situation, relief is contingent upon our actions; the second situation involves a noncontingent relationship between our behavior and relief. In its original formulation, learned helplessness involved a passive yielding to the inevitable—that is, noncontingent—suffering.

Moving away from this original view, the *reformulated* theory of learned helplessness called upon an attributional analysis (Abramson, Seligman, & Teasdale, 1978). According to this view, learned helplessness is not so much a function of expectations of noncontingency between behavior and relief as it is a matter of the kinds of attributions people make when explaining a distressing situation. Three types of causal attribution were suggested as important:

1. *Internal versus external.* If an internal explanation is offered, people hold themselves personally responsible for the difficulty they face. Where the explanation is external, people blame something or someone else for their discomfort.

2. *Stable versus unstable.* Attributing our current fate to a stable cause implies that the cause is not likely ever to go away; we are forever trapped in the disagreeable situation. On the other hand, attributing the current difficulty to something unstable implies that things will change.

3. *Global versus specific.* Where people attribute the causes of their current problems to something global, they believe that the problem pervades every facet of their lives. Where the attribution is more specific, people believe that only a limited part of their life is affected by the current difficulty they are facing.

In general, the sense of helplessness that leads people to give up trying goes along with a tendency to define the current difficulty by the ISG trio: internal–stable–global. This makes intuitive sense. If I have done something poorly and attribute my poor performance to something about me (internal) that is a relatively enduring negative trait (stable), and see this failure to be true of most things in life that I do (global), then I might just very well give up even trying.

A question that intrigues adherents of this reformulated learned-helplessness model asks if people have their own particular explanatory styles. Are some people characteristically pessimistic (the ISG pattern), while others characteristically optimistic (an EUS pattern of external-unstable-specific attributions)?

Several investigations that have pursued this idea of attributional or explanatory style have found support for some of its theoretical formulations (for example, see Burns & Seligman, 1989; Peterson & Barrett, 1987; Peterson, Seligman, & Vaillant, 1988; Riskin et al., 1987). For example, Peterson and Barrett hypothesized that students who attribute their academic difficulties to internal, stable, and global causes (the pessimistic ISG pattern) are more likely to have ongoing difficulties with academic success than students who attribute their current difficulties to external, unstable, and specific causes (the optimistic EUS style).

To test this hypothesis, Peterson and Barrett used an academic version of the Attributional Styles Questionnaire (ASQ). Students were to imagine themselves in each of 12 negative academic situations: for example, you cannot get all the reading done that your instructor assigns; you do not have high enough grades to switch to your desired major; you get a D in a course required for your major; you cannot understand the points the lecturer makes. Subjects were asked to indicate what they believed to be the one major cause for each event, and then to rate that cause in terms of its degree of internality/externality, stability/unstability, and specificity/globality.

Peterson and Barrett compared students with different explanatory styles on several outcome measures. Students with a pessimistic explanatory style (the ISG pattern) tended to do less well in their end-of-term college grades as compared with students whose explanatory style was more optimistic (the EUS pattern). This relationship held even when differences in students' ability levels were controlled. In addition, students with the pessimistic style tended to be much more passive, not trying to improve themselves in school, as compared with those who had a more optimistic style.

Confirming the meaningfulness of the concept of explanatory style as an enduring trait that characterizes individuals, both Peterson,

Seligman, and Vaillant (1988) and Burns and Seligman (1989) presented some interesting longitudinal data. It appears that people who earlier in their lives tend to adopt a pessimistic style are at greater lifetime risk for various kinds of psychological and physical disorders—depression, various physical illnesses, and so on. Not everyone, however, confirms this formulation of a pessimistic explanatory style.

Follette and Jacobson (1987), for example, not only failed to find some of the anticipated effects, but in one instance even report that students with a pessimistic style who did poorly on a classroom examination are *more,* not less, energized to try new study habits. Although this was not quite what the theory would predict, it is similar to Mikulincer's (1988) data showing that, with small failures, pessimists are more likely to improve on a subsequent task; only with repeated failures is future performance impaired.

Attributional Retraining and Misattribution

The last section introduced us to the topic of attributional retraining, suggesting the use of misattribution as a way to change people's feelings and behaviors. Recall Wilson and Linville's (1985) research, in which students who were led to reattribute their current academic difficulties from a stable to a temporary cause improved their academic performance. This illustrates the potentially powerful use of attribution theory in effecting behavior.

Two attribution approaches have been used:

1. Wilson and Linville illustrate attributional retraining in which people are helped to reattribute from something internal to something external, or from the pessimistic (ISG) to the more optimistic pattern (EUS). This is done to encourage them to keep trying rather than give up and sink into a state of depressive helplessness.

2. Another approach, best described as involving *misattribution,* attempts to provide individuals with a neutral explanation for their disturbed feelings. For example, if snakephobic people can be led to believe that it is not the snake that is making them feel so anxious but rather something neutral and benign, they should be better able to deal with the snake.

We will now look at a few illustrations of each approach.

Attributional Retraining

The majority of efforts involving attributional retraining have been carried out in the context of the learned-helplessness model. If a sense of helplessness is the result of the characteristic way people explain negative experiences in their lives, then the goal of attributional retraining is to redirect people's ways of analyzing the causes of those experiences so that they no longer feel helpless to minimize or prevent them. Försterling (1986) summarizes several of the most important studies that have used this model. In each case, after evaluating people's characteristic ways of explaining negative events, an effort is made to influence them to reattribute their failures from something fixed and immutable about themselves to something temporary and modifiable and, hence, subject to their future actions.

As Försterling has pointed out, however, what if people actually lack the ability to do well in a particular area? Under these conditions, attributing their failures to something internal and stable about themselves—"I simply lack the ability"—is genuinely true, not simply an error in their judgment. To lead them to believe that the real cause of their failures is something unstable—"I just didn't study hard enough"—or external—"I had bad luck this time"—might only delay inevitable disappointment. As Försterling comments, "It generally appears to be quite functional for individuals to know when they have failed because of limited abilities" (p. 278). This realization might help them move to an area of work that is more suited to their talents. In our rush to help people deal with failure, we might overlook this realistic possibility.

Försterling is clearly calling for a realistic appraisal of the actual causes of a person's difficulty in confronting negative life experiences, in addition to their pessimistic ways of explaining them. At times, attributional retraining will empower those people who *can* do well to do well; there are times, however, when the best advice might be to avoid optimistic projections. We will encounter a similar theme in Chapter 6 when we examine different views about the potential benefits of being "out of touch" with some of the harsh realities about ourselves.

Misattribution

Suppose that we are anxious whenever we are asked to speak in public, and that the anxiety disrupts our ability to do well. What if we could learn that the cause of the anxiety we feel is not our fear of speaking in public, but something neutral and impersonal on which our attention is focused, like a noise in the room? If we misattribute our anxiety to the sound rather than to the thought of speaking in public, we may actually feel less anxious and so perform better. A couple of research studies demonstrate this effect.

Brodt and Zimbardo (1981) took a group of very shy people who said they had great difficulty interacting with members of the opposite sex, and placed them in a setting in which they were required to do just that. The anxiety symptoms they subsequently experienced included increased pulse and heart rates. The investigators then informed their subjects that the actual cause of these symptoms was the presence of a very loud noise rather than the fear of meeting others. Brodt and Zimbardo wanted to know if shy people who learned that the noise and not other people caused their anxiety, would be better able to interact than those who were equally shy but who had never received the misattributional information. Their research, in fact, confirmed that those subjects who believed the cause of their shyness to be the noise and not others actually became less shy as evaluated by how much talking they did with the other person.

In a similar study, Olson (1988) asked his subjects to read a speech in front of a camera, knowing that this is precisely the kind of situation that makes most people anxious. His subjects were informed that while reading the speech they would hear a subliminal noise in their earphones; this served as the neutral misattributional source. What they actually heard was a kind of buzzing sound that presumably meant that the subliminal sound was being piped into their earphones.

Olson created several different experimental conditions. The misattribution experimental group was informed that the subliminal sound had been found to cause unpleasant emotional arousal (for example, increased heart rate and agitation). A second group was informed that the sound would have absolutely no effect on their emotions. A third group was told that the sound would lead them to feel calm and relaxed. A fourth group was given no information about the purported effects of hearing the sound.

Olson predicted that subjects in the misattribution group would show *less* emotionality, and thereby reveal fewer speech problems—stuttering, stammering, making reading errors, and so on—while reading in front of the camera. After all, they could misattribute their anxious feelings (increased heart rate and general agitation) to the unpleasant sound rather than to the speech they were reading. The subjects who were told that the sound would cause pleasant arousal were expected to show signs of anxiety. Because they are already anxious about the speech, they should be even more anxious when the sound fails to reduce their anxiety as they are told it should. "I'm anxious about the speech; meanwhile, the sound that is supposed to make me relaxed, isn't doing so. Therefore, I must be *really* anxious!"

Olson's data support these predictions. Those who had been informed that the subliminal sound was the source of their anxiety had fewer speech difficulties than either the group who had been told that the sound would have no effect or the group that expected the sound to make them feel good. By being able to misattribute the source of their emotional arousal from the situation causing it (giving a speech in front of a camera) to a neutral event (the sound), people's levels of emotionality were reduced, leading them to make fewer errors than the other groups in the study.

Other investigations have used either a sound, as in the preceding two studies, or an inert chemical substance (a placebo) to help subjects misattribute their level of emotional arousal. In general, the research demonstrates a similar effect: subjects with a variety of phobias and difficulties were able to manage the situation better once they could misattribute the cause of their emotional arousal to something benign rather than the actual object they feared (see Reisenzein, 1983, for a good summary).

This does not mean that every investigator has invariably been successful. There is some evidence that the misattribution effect is more likely to be discovered when the dependent variables involve actual behaviors—talking to a stranger, reading a speech, and so on— as in the preceding studies, than when self-reports of changed feelings are used. Furthermore, as several investigators have suggested (for example, Ross & Olson, 1981), when the symptoms that misattribution hopes to change are deeply embedded in the individual's pathology, as are some kinds of phobias, it is difficult to offer a persuasive story convincing people that their fears are really caused by something benign. In spite of these limitations, the use of attribution theory to help people reattribute or misattribute the causes of their difficulties has produced sufficient success to suggest its potential usefulness in many cognitively designed therapies.

· · · · · · · · · · · · · · ·

Self-Presentation and Impression Management

Several years ago, Erving Goffman (1959) proposed what he referred to as a dramaturgic analysis of human behavior. The term "dramaturgic" is intended to convey a theatrical metaphor, calling forth the image of people as role players portraying certain characters before an audience. It was Goffman's contention that a great deal of social behavior could be understood as efforts on the part of each one of us to present ourselves in such a way as to create and maintain a desired social identity. We try to manage the impressions we convey to others (our audience) so that they will infer that we are a particular kind of person. We would stage a different performance if we wanted to be seen as sensitive and caring than if we wished to portray a much tougher and more assertive character.

But why all this concern with self-presentation and image management? According to Goffman, the answer involves control. We want to control our relationships with others by permitting information to appear that fits the character we are creating and by concealing information that would "blow our cover." A person who wishes to be seen as gentle and humane, for example, will try to perform in ways that fit that image rather than reveal their hidden, abusive side.

All of us have learned how to manage our self-presentations by learning about the kinds of information that produce certain impressions in our culture. In other words, we each know the "other side" of attribution theory. With few exceptions, until now we have been considering how observers draw inferences about the underlying causes of the behavior of another person—that is, why the actor did what she or he did. The "other side" therefore shifts focus to the ways in which the actor uses this shared cultural knowledge about attributions in order to present and manage a particular impression.

In other words, if you and I are both knowledgeable about the kinds of information used to make attributional inferences, then each of us can use that knowledge to create the kind of impression we want others to have of us.

Although by no means completely consistent with this formulation, the ideas presented by Schank and Abelson (1977), and more recently developed by Read (1987), have much in common with this way of thinking. For example, Schank and Abelson talk in terms of social scripts that people follow in most situations. Read concludes that rather than view people as naive scientists, as most attributional models insist, it is far better to see people as "story understanders and storytellers" (p. 300).

In noting this quality of human understanding, Read shifts our focus from the mere manipulation of events inside the individual's head to the more complex processes required to tell a story. To tell an intelligible story, the storyteller must use the culture's system of knowledge; otherwise, the reader or listener will have no idea what is going on. Likewise, as Goffman's ideas about impression management suggest, our knowledge of these cultural narratives, scripts, or stories permits us to manipulate them so that others see us as we so choose.

To illustrate an impression-management view of attribution, we will now return to Kelley's theory (see Chapter 4, pp. 57–59) to see how people use cultural knowledge to generate excuses for their own behavior.

Excuses

One interesting way to examine an image-management perspective on attribution is to study excuses. Giving others excuses for our real or perceived social misbehavior is something we all do, some of us perhaps more than others. In attributional terms, an excuse tries to displace the cause of our misdeeds from something central to our sense of who we are to something far removed: ideally, to something not even identifiable with us (Snyder & Higgins, 1988).

For example, suppose I do rather poorly on a task for which I supposedly should do well. In this case, my poor performance reflects on my sense of who I am. In order to avoid this kind of attribution, I might very well try to find an excuse that shifts responsibility for my poor performance away from me. I might try to find a situational explanation or possibly seek to downplay the relevance of my poor performance to my identity.

Consider the example of a professor trying to get tenure at a major university. This requires successful publication and, to a certain extent, good teaching. If the professor submitted an article to be published and it came back rejected, he or she might try to find an excuse to "save face": "The reviewers were too stupid to understand what I was trying to say." If the professor's friends accepted that explanation then, of course, the failure would lie somewhere else. There might be times, however, when he or she would agree with the reviewers' judgments (the paper really wasn't very good); on those occasions, the professor might excuse his or her failure by downplaying the importance of publication and highlighting a history of teaching excellence. A poor teaching review, of course, would reverse this process of rationalization.

Obviously, in order to generate plausible excuses, people have to know what works and does not work in their particular culture. To excuse a poor performance on grounds that no one else in our social milieu would find plausible—"I was possessed by devils"—would run counter to the face-saving reason for offering excuses in the first place. Because most of us are quite familiar with our own culture, we construct excuses our audience will find convincing. It is likely that what works for our audience works for us as well: if they accept our excuse, we are likely to believe it and so, in a sense, deceive ourselves as well.

The same processes that Kelley suggested operate when observers try to account for other people's behavior can also be used by other people to excuse their own behavior. People develop an excuse based on their understanding of how consensus, distinctiveness, and consistency information lead the observing audience to attribute their poor performance to the situation, rather than to something about themselves.

If excuses deflect failure away from us and toward the situation, then we would try to portray our poor examination performance, for example, in terms of either high consensus, high distinctiveness, and high consistency or the other pattern that Kelley identifies as leading away from a person-centered attribution—low consensus and consistency but high distinctiveness. Both cases involve situational rather than personal attributions.

We might claim that everyone did poorly on this particular examination because nobody understands what the professor is saying. This claim for high consensus might lead our audience and, perhaps, even us to blame the professor rather than ourselves and so preserve the image of us as bright and competent students. Or we might claim that because we generally do well on exams taken in other courses, there must be something very unique about this exam; perhaps the professor simply does not know how to write clear questions. This claim for distinctiveness also helps deflect the blame from us to the situation or the professor. We might similarly try to claim either high or low consistency, either one of which in combination with the other sources of information also removes the onus from us and puts it on the professor or on the situation. Obviously, if our performance on this exam is not representative of our usual performance on other exams in the same class (consistency is low), then the exam must be at fault, not us.

Mehlman and Snyder (1985) conducted an experiment that examined these possibilities for excuse-making. Their subjects were provided with feedback about their performance on a multiple-choice test which they were told was a measure of intelligence known to predict academic performance. Some subjects received feedback noting that they had 40% correct (the failure group), while others were told they received a score of 90% correct (the success group). Needless to say, this information was created for purposes of the study and did not indicate the subjects' real performance or the real meaning of a score on the test.

After receiving this information about themselves, half of the subjects were placed in what was called a *bogus pipeline* condition; the other half did not receive this kind of manipulation. The bogus pipeline is so named because it is designed to lead people to believe that their true feelings about things can be determined by the experimenter. It is a device, in other words, to make all aspects of the subjects' behavior appear to be open to public scrutiny. In the Mehlman and Snyder study, subjects were told that in order to evaluate the accuracy of their written responses, the experimenter would connect them to a physiological recording device that would provide a measure of their true feelings.

Finally, half of the subjects were given an excuse questionnaire that permitted them to explain their test performance in terms of Kelley's three informational categories: consensus (they estimated how well they had done compared to others who had taken the same test); distinctiveness (they were asked to judge how well they would do on a different test of their intelligence that, like the one they had completed, was also a good predictor of academic performance); and consistency (they predicted how well they would do on the same test if they were to retake it again soon).

The results showed that subjects made excuses for their poor performance by calling upon both consistency and distinctiveness information, but *not* consensus. Specifically, subjects who performed poorly tried to excuse their performance by claiming that they would do much better in the future on the same test (low consistency) and that they would score much higher on a different kind of intelligence test (high distinctiveness). Both of these sources of information help displace the blame from the person to the situation.

Interestingly enough, subjects did not try to base their excuses on consensus information; that is, they did not claim that others had also scored poorly. The investigators reasoned that this otherwise plausible explanation might not have been operative in their situation because the experimenters could readily check the accuracy of this excuse. In effect, because we know something about our audience and the kinds of information to which they have access, we avoid building excuses on information that will make us look worse than not excusing our behavior at all.

The bogus pipeline manipulation also reveals an interesting effect. Although poorly performing subjects who offered excuses tended to feel better than those who did not, subjects who believed that their true feelings were known by the "audience" felt more emotionally negative. Mehlman and Snyder suggest that the latter group had the double onus of making excuses *and* being caught at it by an audience who knew their true feelings.

More recently, Basgall and Snyder (1988) found the same tendency for excuse-making subjects to lower consistency and raise distinctiveness but not turn to a consensus-raising tactic.

Self-Serving Attributions and Impression Management

Once we adopt an impression-management view of our social behavior, it is clear that many kinds of attributional processes are self-serving. As we have seen, excuses are a form of self-serving attribution designed to remove responsibility from ourselves and locate it as far away in the situation as possible. Social psychologists studying attributional phenomena have noted several other self-serving attributions. We will consider two in this section: (1) the tendency to attribute our good acts to something internal and our bad acts to something external; and (2) self-handicapping strategies. Keep in mind that several of the attributional biases we will consider later in this chapter and in Chapter 6 can also be seen as self-serving impression-management techniques.

The tendency for people to attribute their good acts to internal causes and bad acts to external sources parallels for the individual the intergroup bias effects we first encountered in Chapter 4 (see pp. 69–73) for the evaluation of ingroup members—the tendency to see the same behavior favorably when carried out by an ingroup member and critically when carried out by an outgroup member. In this case, although the focus is the self, the same basic process occurs: we try to present ourselves in the best possible light, claiming personal credit when things go well and externalizing excuses when things go badly.

Bernstein, Stephan, and Davis (1979), for example, examined the kinds of attributions students made about their performance on examinations. Before each exam, students were instructed to report the grade they expected to make; after the exam, they were asked to explain the reasons for their performance. The data indicated the operation of a self-serving bias: "Ability and effort, the internal factors, were emphasized as the causes of good outcomes, whereas task difficulty and luck, the external factors, were perceived to be the cause of poor performance" (p. 1819).

In a review of the experimental literature on this form of self-serving attributional bias, Bradley (1978) notes that the majority of studies place people in a situation under the direct scrutiny of the experimenter-audience. This provides a perfect setting for them to try to make a good impression by taking credit for positive outcomes while denying responsibility for negative outcomes. As Bradley also notes, however, there are times in all our lives when the best impression we can make to others, especially when we would be even more embarrassed if caught in a deceptive performance, is to confess our personal responsibilities for negative outcomes.

Bradley reports a study conducted by Beckman and by Ross and his colleagues that offers us some insights into this process. A sample of teachers and students was asked to make attributions about the reasons for the student's academic successes or failures. Results indicated that more attributions implicating the teachers were made when the student failed than when the student succeeded. In other words, rather than blaming the students when they failed and accepting credit when their students did well, teachers accepted responsibility for their students' lack of success. As Bradley notes, it is likely that teachers' claiming all the credit for their students' success or denying any blame for their failure would not sit well with their audience: they would lose more face by presenting themselves in terms of the usual self-serving bias than by accepting personal responsibility.

Self-Handicapping

When people are placed in a setting in which they are going to be evaluated, they may attempt to anticipate how others will see them by providing an excuse-making, self-handicapping storyline, as though to say, "Given my tragic personal history, what more could you expect of me"? This is exactly what happened in a study by De Gree and Snyder (1985). Their subjects reported trauma-filled personal histories as a strategic impression-management device to qualify their performance and lower others' expectations.

Initial work on the self-handicapping strategy was reported by Berglas and Jones (1978). They offered their subjects a choice of "drugs" before carrying out an experimental task. One drug purportedly would enhance their performance, while another would interfere with it. Those who had previously done well on similar tasks, but for reasons outside their control, chose the performance-*interfering* drug, as though to protect themselves in anticipation of failing at this new activity: "Blame the drug, not me"!

Kolditz and Arkin (1982) replicated the main elements of the Berglas and Jones study, but varied the public quality of both the act of choosing one of the drugs and performance on the experimental task; the audience in this case was the experimenter, who could either observe (in the public conditions) or not observe (in the private conditions of the study) the subjects' behavior. Results indicated that subjects were more likely to choose the performance-interfering drug under the public-audience conditions, but not under conditions they thought were private. This is just what an impression-management view would expect: it is when we are in the light of public scrutiny, not in the privacy of our own consciences, that we are most under pressure to make the best impression possible by influencing the attributions others make of us.

Before concluding our analysis of the attribution model, let us briefly re-examine the case we have made on behalf of the impression-management view. The basic idea of this view is that we each make use of attributional information to present a positive image of ourselves to others. We are successful in so applying attribution theory because we are all generally familiar with the norms and expectations of our culture; we know what information is needed in order to create an acceptable account of our behavior. A different culture, or even our own culture at a different time in history, would be likely to have different ways of explaining our behavior.

Our own culture, of course, is particularly heterogeneous, made up of numerous ethnic groups and subcultures that each have their own way of attributing behavior. Insofar as most research on attribution has relied on young college students as subjects, the cultural factors are too "controlled," depriving us of the full story. That story awaits more systematic examination of how different cultures and subcultures explain behavior and use those explanations on behalf of strategic impression management. It is likely, of course, that even the concern with impression management is itself a feature of some cultures more than others.

Social Issues and Attributional Processes

In 1973, Caplan and Nelson reported the results of a study of the attributions that professional psychologists made about one particular social issue, the difficult life experiences of African-Americans. They examined every article referring to African-Americans in *Psychological Abstracts* for a six-month period, scoring the major explanatory perspective employed in each article. They found that approximately 82% of the articles interpreted the difficulties that this ethnic minority experienced as due to some kind of person-centered cause: "the picture that emerges is one of psychologists investing dis-proportionate amounts of time, funds and energy in studies that lend themselves, directly or by implication, to interpreting the difficulties of black Americans in terms of personal shortcomings" (p. 204). It would seem that something like the fundamental attributional error is very evident here, affecting professional psychologists as well as the lay public.

Caplan and Nelson were not content to let their findings speak for themselves. They suggest several possible implications of a person-centered analysis of a social issue. For example, attributing the prob-lems of a minority to personal shortcomings implies that those with fewer problems have succeeded because of their own character, drive, motivation, ability, and so on. In other words, if failure is caused by something internal, then surely so too is success. Those who have "made it" in society should feel rightfully proud of their ability to control their own destiny. Of course, this kind of analysis ignores the possibility that both success and failure are related either to the ab-sence (for success) or presence (for failure) of societal racism, sexism, ageism, and so on.

Caplan and Nelson also comment on the ways in which a per-son-centered causal analysis helps focus our treatment programs on the person rather than on the society. If we attribute the difficulties of African-Americans to personal defects rather than their circum-stances, it follows that our treatment programs should be designed to transform persons, not improve the conditions of society. As Caplan and Nelson note, this approach also legitimates recruiting special-ists—psychologists, social workers, and so on—to treat people rather than transform society. Caplan and Nelson's analysis helps us see how the prevailing view of the causes of social problems fits into the over-all fabric of the culture and is not simply a feature of the individual's internal information-processing system. Several other analyses support this way of thinking about social attributions.

Brickman and his associates (1982) argue that it is important to distinguish between the analysis made about the *causes* of a social problem and the analysis of its *solution*. As we have seen, Caplan and Nelson suggest a relation between these two aspects: if persons are held responsible for causing their own difficulties, then they are re-sponsible for solving them. According to Brickman and his col-leagues, however, this reflects only one of four possible relationships between (a) the responsibility for causing a problem and (b) the re-sponsibility for solving the problem.

They refer first to the *moral model,* in which persons are held responsible both for causing their difficulty and for solving it. This is similar to Caplan and Nelson's suggestion. If people's own laziness and lack of motivation got them into trouble, for example, then we should exhort them to shape up and help themselves. Our role as helpers in the moral model is to remind "people of how responsible they are for their own fate and how important it is that they help themselves" (p. 371).

The *compensation model* maintains that, although people may not be responsible for the problems they have, they are definitely responsible for solving them. This view recognizes that circumstances may have caused the difficulties people experience, but nevertheless insists that they must find their own solutions. It is compatible with Caplan and Nelson's view of the role of the professional helper to help downtrodden people pick themselves up again.

In the *medical model,* people are responsible neither for the difficulties they face nor for the solutions. The victim of multiple sclerosis, for example, is not held personally responsible for the disease or for its treatment: medical personnel supervise the treatment, while the cause remains beyond human control. The case of clearly behavior-related diseases like AIDS presents us with a somewhat different picture, which we will examine shortly.

The final model that Brickman and his associates identify is termed the *enlightenment model.* In this view, people bear personal responsibility for their problems, but the solutions fall outside their own hands. Because of their past behavior (sexual promiscuity, drug use, eating behavior, and so on), people are held to be causally implicated; the helpers' role is to work to restore the control that the person is unable to accomplish on his or her own.

Weiner, Perry, and Magnusson (1988) examined elements of the work of Caplan and Nelson, and Brickman and his colleagues, in a laboratory study. Their subjects were presented with a list of ten items the authors termed *stigmas:* AIDS, Alzheimer's disease, blindness, cancer, child abuse, drug addiction, heart disease, obesity, paraplegia, and Vietnam War syndrome. Subjects were instructed to rate each in terms of (a) the kinds of causal attributions made about it (for example, responsibility, controllability, stability); and (b) the kinds of helping strategies that would be effective (for example, job training, educational training, psychotherapy, medical treatment).

It is obvious that the results of an extensive study with such an array of items would be quite complex. Yet, a definite pattern was discerned revealing linkages between "the sources of the stigmas, perceived controllability, affective reactions, and judgments regarding help" (p. 741). Weiner and his associates' data generally support the contention of Brickman and his colleagues that it is important to distinguish the causes of a problem from the responsibility for its treatment. In the case of AIDS, for example, victims are held responsible for causing it, but not for its treatment (like the enlightenment model).

Weiner and his associates also compared physical with so-called mental-behavioral problems. Their subjects generally regarded the victim as less responsible for causing the former than the latter. In addition, subjects felt more pity for those with physical problems and more anger for those with mental-behavioral problems, and so expressed a greater desire to provide more help to those with the former than those with the latter. Indeed, the data suggest that when the cause of the problem is seen to be a consequence of the individual's voluntary actions, there is less sympathy for providing help to the victim.

Weiner and his colleagues also found a tendency for intervention strategies to vary with the kind of analysis made of the cause of the problem. Professional training is recommended to help people cope better with disabling conditions like blindness, for which they are usually not responsible and which are unlikely to improve. On the other hand, intervention is suggested for reversible medical conditions like cancer and heart disease. Psychotherapy, of course, is recommended for those people with conditions to some extent their own doing, and who must bear some of the responsibility for treatment.

A close examination of the social problem-solving analyses of both Weiner's and Brickman's groups appears to confirm Caplan and Nelson's critique of professional psychology's blindness to social causation. Caplan and Nelson found the same tendency for social psychologists to attribute the causes of a particular group's plights to the group's character (a person-centered attribution) rather than to the society (a situation-centered attribution).

The following example illustrates this point. Suppose it could be demonstrated that most types of cancer are caused by industrial wastes and pollutants; to advocate the medical treatment of cancer victims ignores the very social institutions that cause the problem in the first place. Even when a sophisticated analysis of a social predicament is offered, therefore, it often narrowly conforms to our culture's view that tampering with the system itself is less favorable than treating the individual victims.

Rape

In late 1989, news accounts reported the findings of a rape trial in Fort Lauderdale, Florida. A jury comprised of three men and three women exonerated the alleged rapist because they believed that the female victim had "asked for it." Although she had apparently been abducted from a restaurant parking lot and raped at knife point, her provocative manner of dress (she wore a lace miniskirt and no undergarments) convinced the jurors that she, not the rapist, was to blame. The example clearly illustrates what Ryan (1971) refers to as a cultural tendency to "blame the victim." Ryan's main concern was with sufferers of crimes and accidents who tend to be doubly victimized—first during the event itself, and then by society's tendency to hold them responsible for what happened. As the Florida case illustrates, rape provides us with more than ample evidence of this process of double victimization and the pattern of blaming the victim.

Janoff-Bulman (1979) obtained information from people in several rape crisis centers throughout the United States. She mailed questionnaires to a total of 120 such centers and obtained a 53% return rate. The questionnaires which focused on the issue of the rape victim's self-blame, were to be answered by the rape crisis counsellors at each center. Janoff-Bulman distinguished between two kinds of self-blame: *behavioral* and *characterological.* In the case of behavioral self-blame, the victim acknowledges doing something foolish, such as walking alone late at night, letting a stranger in the house, hitchhiking, not locking the car, and so on. These kinds of behavior are voluntary, and hence avoidable in the future. On the other hand, characterological self-blame finds the fault to lie in the person's own character—"I'm a weak person, a nonassertive person, an immature person who cannot take care of myself" and so on. Characterological self-blame is clearly more difficult to modify than behavioral self-blame.

The rape crisis counsellors were told to evaluate the percentage of the people they counselled who blamed themselves in each of these two categories. First, Janoff-Bulman reports that self-blame is a frequent response of the rape victim: an average of 74% of the women held themselves at least partly to blame for what happened. Second, behavioral self-blame exceeds characterological self-blame. In her study, 69% demonstrated the former while only 19% the latter. As Janoff-Bulman comments, it is rather disturbing to see the widespread acceptance on the part of the victims of their own responsibility for what happened to them.

Howard's (1984) research reminds us that these tendencies to blame the victim, especially the female victim, are cultural beliefs rather than something about the way the human mind works. Howard examined the ways that people attribute responsibility to victims of various types of crime including rape. Her data suggest a tendency both to hold female victims more responsible for what happened to them than male victims, and also to attribute behavioral self-blame to male victims and characterological self-blame to female victims.

These findings reveal the impact of social and cultural factors that doubly victimize certain victims. Research reported by Brekke and Borgida (1988) confirm Howard's findings, but also reveal important differences between men's and women's ideas about victim responsibility for rape: "women attributed significantly less responsibility to the victim [and] considered it significantly less likely that she consented to have sex" (p. 375) as compared with the evaluations that men made.

Howard's study also included a measure of her subjects "gender attitudes." This permitted her to compare those with traditional sex-role stereotypes about women and men with those not holding such stereotypes. Howard reports that the traditionalists were more likely than the nontraditionalists to find fault with the female victim and with her character; indeed, nontraditionalists treated male and female victims in a similar manner.

Several other studies have added to this victim-blaming picture. Wyer, Bodenhausen, and Gorman (1985) report that men hold the rape victim more responsible when the male and female are friends than when they are strangers, whereas females do not find women similarly responsible. These data are relevant to the issue of "date-rape," in which the male assumes a right that the woman does not. These findings also confirm the Brekke and Borgida data indicating male-female differences in their views about rape responsibility.

Field's (1978) survey of the attitudes about rape held by rapists, crisis counsellors, police, and average citizens reveals some parallel findings. For example, as compared with women, men tend to see women as generally more responsible for the rape. Paralleling Howard's research, Field also reports that people holding nontraditional views about women's roles tend to view rape more as a crime of power than sex.

So what can we conclude? First, it is still common, particularly among those with traditional attitudes about the proper role and behavior of men and women, to blame the rape victim, especially if the victim is female. Second, many women clearly accept the victim-blaming perspective, at times even more strikingly than men. As Howard concludes, "These attributional patterns are consistent with societal stereotypes about women and men" (p. 503). This echoes the point we have repeatedly made: attributions are better understood as features of society than of the internal operations of the individual's cognitive system.

Accidents

Although the research findings have not always been consistent, when people are asked to explain the responsibility for an accident there is again a general tendency to blame the victim. After his extensive review of the research literature, Berger (1981) reports a weak tendency to attribute more responsibility to an accident victim as the *severity* of the accident increases. There is, however, a tendency to downplay the responsibility of the accident victim when the subject and the victim are similar to one another.

A useful way to understand these results within a cultural framework is to consider the *just world theory* proposed by Lerner and Miller (1978). According to this theory, the world is said to be just if people get what they deserve. In a study by Lerner (1965), student subjects concluded that a fellow student who won a cash prize in a lottery must have worked harder than those who had not won. In other words, since we believe that we live in a just world where everyone gets what they deserve, even beneficiaries of seemingly random events are assumed to have contributed in some way to their good fortune. It is as though justice in our culture is served so long as winners and losers deserve what they get.

To maintain a sense of justice, people will presumably hold the victim responsible for an accident. Since people who get into trouble deserve what happens to them, there must be something wrong with them. The greater the severity of the accident, the greater the challenge to the belief in a just world; consequently, the greater the effort to restore justice by finding fault with the victim.

When the severity of a disaster, whether natural or man-made, is great, the belief in a just world becomes harder to accept. Survivors of floods and earthquakes often feel guilty that they survived while others more deserving were killed. In this case, justice is not restored by believing that the victims got what they deserved; rather, the survivor is momentarily unable to make sense of the tragedy. The difficulty in restoring a sense of justice may also be met by turning to a religious belief—"it was God's will." For example, a study of Holocaust survivors (Leon et al., 1981) found that many attributed their survival to luck and to God's help rather than derogate those who perished under such extreme conditions.

In terms of the just world perspective, however, luck is hardly equivalent to justice. Perhaps when the victim's world is turned upside down and there is no way to restore faith in justice, luck by default becomes the dominant reason for what happened. Luck is a somewhat frightening explanation. Unlike the belief in a just world, which offers us a sense of some personal control over our fate, there is nothing we can do to influence luck. Of course, with a truly horrible event like the Holocaust, perhaps luck is an accurate description: there was no justice.

Unemployment

Another important issue that has been examined in terms of an attributional analysis involves the way people face unemployment. Because of the centrality of work in most of our lives, losing our job not only comes as a severe blow, but also demands some kind of explanation. As we have noted, Feather has been especially involved in studying the different kinds of attributions that are made to explain unemployment.

For example, Feather and Davenport (1981) report that unemployed youth in Australia feeling the most depressed about their circumstances were more likely to blame society's economic conditions than themselves. When economic conditions are blamed, many people have doubts about controlling their own fate and so feel, quite accurately, helpless and depressed.

In another study, Feather (1985) examined attributions made by those explaining other people's unemployment. University students were asked to rate a variety of possible causes for the unemployment of youth, including factors that were predominantly external (for example, ineffective government, economic conditions) and factors that were predominantly internal (for example, deficiencies in competence, lack of skill). While the overall findings suggest a tendency to favor external over internal explanations, competence and skill were also seen to be relevant.

Both studies found a similarity between how the victims and the observers of unemployment judged its causes: both focused on external rather than victim-blaming attributions. On the other hand, as we noted in an earlier study by Feather, politically conservative observers as well as those subscribing to Protestant Ethic values tended to underattribute to external factors and emphasize the internal factors in explaining unemployment.

A longitudinal study reported by Schaufeli (1988) combines some of the features of the preceding research. He first collected the attributions of a group of subjects about unemployment; he then compared these attributions with those made six months later by the same people, some of whom were employed and others unemployed. His findings indicated that there was virtually no change in the earlier attributions, despite the different life experiences of the subjects after six months. In considering imagined unemployment at that earlier time, both said that successful employment would primarily be a function of internal factors, while failure to get a job would be due to external factors. When they were assessed six months later, those who were employed attributed their success to internal factors; those who remained unemployed attributed the causes of their unemployment to more external factors. In other words, in either imagining or personally experiencing unemployment, people make the same kinds of self-serving attributions: employment is seen to be a result of something about the person, unemployment a result of something about society.

. . . .

Conclusions

We will now review the main differences between a conventional and sociohistorical understanding of attributional phenomena, combining points raised in both Chapters 4 and 5. Three differences are important to emphasize: (1) The "location" of attributional accounts of behavior; (2) individualistic versus collective approaches to attributional retraining; and (3) the place of attributional analyses in a society's arrangements of social privilege and power.

The "Location" of Attributional Accounts of Behavior

Consistent with the still dominant conventional view of cognitive processes, the majority of social psychologists who have contributed to an attributional analysis of human behavior locate attributional processes inside the mind of the individual rather than in social situations. The many signs of this tendency can be most directly documented through the explanations offered for actor–observer differences in attribution.

Recall that three kinds of explanation were offered for the tendency of people to attribute their own behavior to the situation and others' behavior to their personalities: differential access to information about self versus other; different visual orientations; and differential processing of information about self versus other. All three are "internal" rather than "cultural" explanations for the differences found between actors' and observers' attributions.

That is, in each case the empirical finding of an actor–observer difference is attributed to how the individual's cognitive system operates on information to arrive at a particular attributional conclusion. In no instance does the analysis call upon some feature of the cultural framework that may organize and structure different analyses of one's own and others' behavior.

Lutz's (1988) work with the Ifaluk, however, illustrates a different cultural understanding than our own. For example, she notes how the Ifaluk often attribute the causes of their own behavior to other people, holding others responsible for their own inner states. In a similar manner, Lutz also notes that the Ifaluk rarely refer to themselves by trait terms (person-centered) but usually describe both self and other in terms of the immediate situation. These findings suggest that people's attributions are culturally organized and structured rather than being properties of the individual mind.

This is not to say that the three main explanations of attribution offered by social psychology are incorrect. It is simply to suggest that social psychologists tend to adhere to a conventional approach to attribution by seeking events inside the mind of the individual rather than within the culture or social system. This tendency to search for our explanatory principles within the individual reflects our current western ethnopsychological bias, not a fundamental, universal truth about the nature of attributions.

Individualistic Versus Collective Approaches to Change

We have noted instances throughout Chapters 4 and 5 in which attributional analyses are used to change individual's dysfunctional behavior: helping students who tend to do poorly on academic tasks and who blame themselves to find a less immobilizing attributional analysis of their failures; helping people with social anxiety reduce their anxiety by misattributing their feelings to a neutral source; and so on. In these cases, efforts are concentrated on the individual who is in need of some kind of transformation.

Focusing on the individual who has the problem and providing some kind of therapeutic intervention is, of course, a very familiar approach in our current culture. If the individual can be empowered to think differently, then the individual can improve her or his lot in life. However, as McClure (1985), among others (for example, Caplan & Nelson, 1973; Furby, 1979), have commented, this individualistic approach not only misses the point, but also may exacerbate the dysfunctionality of the individual's behavior.

What if the individuals under study are members of particular groups in society—women, ethnic minorities, laborers, and so on—for whom failure-like experiences are a sign of their oppression rather than symptoms of personal pathology? To help these individuals try harder to overcome failure by convincing them that their problems are rooted in internal conditions they can individually control may backfire dramatically if the conditions are external and beyond any one person's ability to change. Prejudice and discrimination that are built into the very fabric of a social system and its institutions, for example, change by virtue of collective action. Michael Lerner's (1985) attempts in this regard are exemplary.

He reasoned that labor union members experiencing extreme stress on their jobs and who tended to commit the fundamental attributional error of blaming themselves for their difficulties would be empowered to seek change if they could learn to blame the social system rather than themselves. However, Lerner did not want to produce the discouragement that appears when one individual tries alone to fight the system; and so he developed group techniques designed to help workers and their families collectively learn about the disabling nature of self-blame. His aim was not to produce individual change but collective change. He knew that placing the responsibility for change on individuals alone would only exacerbate their problems. Helping people see how their fates are linked and that their empowerment is collective, not individualistic, increases their opportunities of creating the kinds of change that are effective in the long run.

By focusing entirely on the individual, however, and making that individual personally responsible for reattributing the sources of his or her difficulties, investigators and attributional therapists have failed to address the far more potent concept of collective empowerment. As McClure (1985) notes, while working exclusively to improve one's self might be effective if that alone is the source of the difficulty, it would be foolish and dysfunctional if the problem is rooted in the social system. If that were the case, collective empowerment oriented towards producing social change is more likely to work. But of course, moving in that direction is a greater threat to the prevailing arrangements of power and privilege than focusing on changing the individual.

Attribution, Power, and Privilege

In terms of the sociohistorical perspective, an attributional account of human behavior is not a neutral description of how the mind operates while processing information, but rather involves social analyses of human behavior that those growing up within a society learn and that play a part in the system of power and privilege within that society. If we can accept personal responsibility alone for our collective fate, then we will surely ignore the role other factors play in our present social dilemmas. By relocating the focus of attributional analyses from the individual mind to society, we can see how they do not simply refer to discoveries about the way the world is (for example, people blame victims), but rather propose versions of the world that may very well benefit one group at the expense of another.

The more that people peer into the machinery of the mind for some basic and universal truth about themselves, the less likely they are to examine the social circumstances that led to that way of thinking in the first place. A culture that holds people completely responsible for their fates clearly differs from a culture whose attributional analyses hold witches or gods to account for humanity's ills. In western society, as Gergen (1989) and others (for example, Harré, 1984) have noted, we emphasize accounts based on the mind and its operations rather than those based on different social theories. In each case, however, the dominant accounting system helps sustain the society in which it has been generated and usually plays a role in sustaining the ongoing pattern of privilege and power within that society.

Gergen comments on the "vast importance in social life of hegemony in world construction" (p. 73), noting that the ways we make sense out of our lives have significant consequences for nearly every facet of our existence. Every attribution is a statement about what a society believes to be true about people; these beliefs benefit some people and may potentially harm others. The current emphasis on individualistic accounting practices helps deflect attention away from the very structures of power and privilege in our own society that can truly challenge the status quo. We will return to this theme throughout the text.

6

Accuracy, Biases, and Errors in Social Cognition

MAGINE LEARNING FROM your doctor that you have cancer, and that there is a risky experimental treatment that may arrest the disease. Your doctor informs you that the treatment offers a 68% chance of survival. Would you be less likely to accept this risky treatment if you were told that it offers a 32% chance of death? Most people are more willing to accept the risk if the survival rate is emphasized (for example, see Kahneman & Tversky, 1984; Passell, 1989a, 1989b). The probabilities of survival are identical (68%) in both presentations of the treatment, so preferences for one over the other must tell us something about the ways people process information.

The case above illustrates several points. For instance, knowledge about the outcomes of such information processing could prove useful to, for example, public health officials who want people to adopt a certain health practice: they would know that how they phrase information is more or less likely to produce the outcomes they desire. For our immediate purposes, however, the example illustrates a situation in which we can evaluate individuals' information-processing ability against a standard—probability statistics—and determine the degree to which they conform to or deviate from that standard.

Now consider another example. Suppose you work in sales and your entire income is based on commissions from customer orders. It is extremely important that you be able to make accurate evaluations of your customers' psychology. You need to know how best to approach them, and also when not to waste your valuable time with someone clearly not likely to make a purchase. But what is the standard against which we can measure your ability to perceive others?

Unlike the earlier case, in which we can judge people's processing against a statistical standard, this case does not have a comparable statistical norm. Three standards against which to evaluate an individual's judgmental accuracy, however, seem reasonable in this second case:

1. We can see how much your judgments about other people's personalities agree with the judgments others make about the same people. We would conclude that you were an accurate judge of character if your judgments agreed with those of other people.

2. We could evaluate your judgments of other people against their own judgments of themselves. We would conclude that you were accurate if the ratings of you and the people you judged agreed.

3. We can evaluate your judgments of other people against their behavior, determining whether or not the predictions you made about what they were likely to do were accurate. If your judgments helped you make good predictions, then we would conclude that you judged accurately.

We all know how difficult this process can be. For example, even if our judgments agree with a dozen others about a particular person, we might all be wrong. All of us base our judgments on prevalent cultural stereotypes, which produce the agreement. In addition, even if our ratings agree with other people's self-ratings, we might still be in error: they may not be aware of some of their characteristics; they may be trying to conceal aspects of themselves in order to make a desired impression, and so on. Finally, even if we make an accurate prediction about their behavior, it might be the result of information not available to us: for example, they personally may not have chosen to behave as they did but were told to do so. In this instance, we consider ourselves to be good judges of character because we predicted accurately, while their behavior was guided by other requirements of which we were unaware.

The two cases we have just examined—the cancer treatment

and the sales job—illustrate the general approach of social psychologists to understand how people judge situations and, especially, other people. In the first case, there is a normative standard against which to evaluate the accuracy or inaccuracy of a person's judgments; this is usually a statistical norm. Thus, people are compared against a statistical probability model in order to see how well or poorly they do. A related normative standard involves a theoretical model concerning human judgment. Kelley's attribution model, for example, tells us how people would evaluate another's behavior if they behaved like perfect scientists in processing information. To the extent that their evaluations deviate from this model, we would conclude that they are processing information in an unscientific—that is, biased—manner.

Using agreement or prediction as the basis of evaluating the accuracy of a person's ability to judge other people, as illustrated in the second case, forms the other major approach used by social psychologists interested in evaluating the accuracy of people's information-processing systems. As we noted, however, this approach might lead us astray if our goal is to make unequivocal claims about how generally accurate people are in judging others.

. . . .

Two Approaches
to Errors:
Shortcomings or Blessings?

There are at least two different approaches to the judgment situations we have considered. The first considers all deviations, whether from a statistical norm, or from agreement or prediction, to be informative about how the mind processes information. If we adopted this view, we would not be concerned with bias or error per se, but rather with trying to use these deviations to learn more about how the mind operates on the information it receives. So-called errors would not lead to the associations most of us have when the terms "error" or "bias" are used to describe our performance. Rather, as Funder (1987) has commented, we would find errors to be

> . . . an indispensable tool for studying the processes of human judgment. They can provide valuable insights into how the cognitive system transforms, augments, and distorts an initial stimulus "input" on the way to a final judgment "output"   (p. 75).

Although we might suppose that this first approach was used by most social psychologists, the vast majority of investigators have treated error and bias as *failures, shortcomings,* or *deficiencies* in the human cognitive system (for example, see Ross, 1977). Consider some of the biases we encountered in Chapters 4 and 5. The fundamental attribution error describes our tendency to overattribute to the person and underattribute to the situation. It is considered an *error* because its use deviates from how a scientific information-processing model suggests we should ideally use information. That model, however, fails to consider a whole range of other factors that might make it very useful for someone in our culture to focus on people's responsibilities for their own activities rather than situational factors that relieve people from responsibility.

For example, Block and Funder (1986) replicated the experiment we considered earlier (see p. 64) by Ross, Amabile, and Steinmetz (1977) that demonstrated the fundamental attribution error. In their replication, however, Block and Funder evaluated their subjects' social adjustment. They concluded that subjects prone to making the so-called attributional error were in fact more socially adjusted than those not making the error. In other words, this "error" might well indicate a high level of social competence and a healthy emotional adjustment rather than a shortcoming.

Might the same interpretation be made of self-serving or self-handicapping biases (see pp. 88–90)? These are said to be errors because they depart from a scientific model of how judgments should be made given such and such information. Insofar as people guide their actions in a self-serving way, however, taking credit for successes and denying responsibility for failures, they may function better than people lacking such a bias. As we will see later in this chapter, the trend among some investigators is to emphasize the healthful benefits of these so-called errors (for example, see Greenwald, 1980; Taylor, 1989; Taylor & Brown, 1988).

Several reviews of the research on error and accuracy (for example, see Funder, 1987; Markus and Zajonc, 1985) have commented on the trend away from a concern with how accurately we process information about other people to deficiencies in the human cognitive system. Markus and Zajonc, for example, note that the image of people as rational information processors has changed to one of people so error-prone and biased that they can hardly be trusted to make rational judgments. Markus and Zajonc report five times as many studies adopting this less flattering image of people's cognitive abilities. The pendulum of opinion, however, seems to be swinging back to a more positive image. Either people are increasingly seen as "not so bad" in their social judgments (Funder), or the errors that they make are seen to be signs of health (Block & Funder; Greenwald; Taylor; Taylor & Brown). As we study accuracy, biases, and errors in social judgment, we will see all of these positions represented.

Illustrations of Some Social-Judgment Biases

It should now be apparent how complex making judgments about other people in social situations really is. There are many places in the overall process where problems can arise: we may distort the kinds of information to which we attend, our recall of the information we use to reach our conclusions, and the way in which we process or integrate the evidence on which our judgment is based. Markus and Zajonc (1985) identified over a dozen kinds of error and bias that can occur at several points in this overall process. We will now consider several examples of error and bias that social psychologists have examined extensively.

Beliefs and Expectations

Distortions can occur in the kinds of information we process: people may attend only to instances that confirm their preexisting beliefs about another person and so fail to include disconfirming information. If we believe someone to be unkind, for example, we may fail to note those occasions when they acted kindly and so continue to conclude that they are unkind.

A different example is presented by Crocker (1981). Our expectations about the relationship between two events can also influence our judgments—for example, expecting the amount of time put into practice to be related to the outcome of a tennis match. The following four-celled table will help us better understand Crocker's general approach and research findings:

Outcome		Win	Lose
Amount of Practice	Little	1	2
	A lot	3	4

Reviewing the table indicates that information from two cells (2 and 3) would *confirm* the expectation that practice produces winning, while the two remaining cells (1 and 4) would *disconfirm* that expectation. Which kinds of information do people prefer to know?

Crocker reports that 77% of her subjects preferred to learn about the frequencies in the confirmatory cells; far fewer wanted to have the disconfirming information obtained by examining the entries in cells 1 and 4. From a scientific standpoint, however, before we would be willing to accept the claim about the relationship between practice and winning, we would want to know what all four cells were like. Because people seem to prefer confirmatory over nonconfirmatory information, however, they behave like poor scientists, permitting their hopes rather than hard evidence to influence their judgments.

Heuristics

Tversky and Kahneman (1974; also see Kahneman, Slovic, & Tversky, 1982) identified several kinds of biases people are prone to make in their judgments. They were especially concerned with identifying the errors that result from using short-hand, simplistic rules of thumb to guide our judgments. They termed these unreflective short-hand methods of judgment *heuristics*.

As a judgment process, the use of heuristics can be contrasted with the more thoughtful and careful analysis that a properly trained scientist or statistician might make (for example, Sorrentino et al., 1988, make this distinction). In Crocker's four-celled table, for example, a short-hand approach might simply examine cells 2 and 3, while a more thoughtful analysis would take the entire table into consideration. In general, it is assumed that when we are faced with the task of making a judgment based on little information—that is, under conditions of uncertainty—we are likely to use these mental shortcuts. We will now examine two of the several important heuristics identified by Tversky and Kahneman: representativeness and availability.

REPRESENTATIVENESS Steven is someone you have never met before, but others who know him have provided you with some information about him. If you are asked to make a judgment about Steven's occupation, it would obviously be made under conditions of uncertainty. The others tell you that Steven is shy and withdrawn, and respects order and tidiness. Do you think Steven is more likely a farmer or librarian? Tversky and Kahneman found that people generally believed Steven was more likely to be a librarian, primarily because the characteristics describing Steven are representative of the stereotype people have of librarians.

Of course, Steven may or may not actually be a librarian; the point is that as a short-hand tool, the representativeness heuristic can lead us to make erroneous judgments. Because it is based on the degree to which personal characteristics correspond to social stereotypes it fails to consider population base rates. A base rate offers information about the number of people in different categories of a population; for example, there are more farmers than librarians in the population of the United States.

If we base our judgments on this base-rate information, rather than rely on representativeness alone (which is likely to lead us astray), we would predict that the probability of Steven being a farmer is greater than being a librarian simply because there are more farmers than librarians in the general population. Although this prediction might be wrong, we have a far greater chance of being correct because we are guided by base-rate information rather than the simplistic representativeness heuristic. Note that "correct" in this case means conforming to the probability model. If we are in error, therefore, it is because we depart from that model, not because Steven actually is or is not a librarian or farmer.

Let us look at another example that Tversky and Kahneman provide both in order to reinforce the understanding of the representativeness heuristic and also to show its connection with accurate versus erroneous judgments. In another one of their studies, they provided subjects with personality descriptions of several individuals who had been drawn from a group of either lawyers or engineers. Half of the subjects were told that the group from which these descriptions were drawn contained 70 engineers and 30 lawyers; the other half were informed that the sample descriptions were drawn from a group containing 70 lawyers and 30 engineers. The subjects' task was simply to indicate the probability that a given description was of an engineer or a lawyer.

If the subjects truly based their judgments on probability, they would view a given description as more likely to be that of an engineer when it was drawn from the group of 70 engineers and only 30 lawyers; they would similarly view a given description as more likely that of a lawyer when it was drawn from the group of 70 lawyers and 30 engineers. Tversky and Kahneman, however, report negligible difference between the two groups of subjects in their judgments. In other words, the subjects ignored base-rate information about the population and used the representativeness heuristic to conclude that a given description was surely of an engineer because the personality description fit their stereotype of an engineer.

When subjects were provided only with population information (no personality descriptions), they made their choices very clearly in terms of the base-rate probabilities. That is, they said that an unknown individual is more likely to be an engineer when they knew he had been drawn from the group containing 70 engineers, and more likely to be a lawyer when they knew he had been drawn from the group containing 70 lawyers. The moment personality descriptions were provided, however, people used the short-hand representativeness heuristic, ignoring the base-rate probabilities. Their error is the failure to match the statistical standard.

While other studies have confirmed the use of the representativeness heuristic, some have challenged the whole idea, noting that under appropriate conditions, even as Tversky and Kahneman have shown, people can and do use base-rate probabilities. Ajzen (1977), for example, demonstrated that if subjects are provided information that has a causal connection to the behavior they are asked to predict, they are more likely to call upon base-rate information than to rely on the biasing representativeness heuristic. When this information is not causally connected to the behavior to be predicted, however, then they will turn to the representativeness heuristic.

Ginossar and Trope (1987) demonstrated the importance of *context* in determining whether people will or will not use base-rate information. For example, when the context involved making judgments about college entrance examinations, they found that subjects were very good in matching base rates. For example, when told that the sample entrance exam score was drawn from a population containing 70% engineers and 30% lawyers, subjects accurately concluded that a particular score presented to them was an engineer's.

AVAILABILITY   According to Tversky and Kahneman, another rather common heuristic people use in making judgments involves the ease or availability of a specific piece of relevant information. For example, we judge the risks of flying as greater shortly after a few rather striking accidents have occurred because that information is the most readily available to us. In making this judgment, we ignore the statistical facts that suggest the relative safety of flying when compared with, say, driving a car. Thus, availability refers to the relative ease with which we recall some information that enters into our judgment.

Here is another example of the availability heuristic: do more words in English begin with the letter *r* or have the letter *r* in their third position? Our judgment tends to ignore the facts, but rather is based on the ease with which we can think of words beginning with *r*. If the first few words that come to mind begin with *r*, we will probably conclude that *r* is more likely to appear in the first rather than the third position. In fact, the third position is the more frequent location of *r*.

The availability heuristic is especially important in policy issues involving risk and risk management. Because people's perception of danger may be more a function of the ease with which they can recall instances of the risk rather than the actual probability of the risk, they become insensitive to what is really dangerous and overly worried about less probable events. For example, Passell (1989a, 1989b) suggests that comparative statistics show that the United States is much safer today than in the past; yet, most people feel themselves increasingly at risk from polluted water in their taps, pesticides in their food, gang violence in the streets, and sexually transmitted diseases nearly everywhere. Although all of these risks do exist, the ease of availability is more influential in driving our judgments about them than their comparative danger.

Illusory Correlation

Another kind of judgmental bias that has been demonstrated involves what is termed *illusory correlation*. Correlation, of course, involves a relationship between two factors. When we say that a correlation is illusory, we mean that people tend to overestimate the magnitude of the relationship, even positing a relationship when none exists. Markus and Zajonc (1985), for example, note how some psychologists using projective tests in making clinical judgments about their clients assume a higher correlation between response to the projective (for example, seeing someone draw a belt around the waist on a draw-a-person test) and underlying personal problems (for example, being overly concerned about controlling sexual impulses), than is warranted by the research literature (also see Chapman & Chapman, 1967).

The *halo effect* also illustrates an illusory correlation. We tend to see people who have some desired attribute (beauty) to have other desirable attributes as well (intelligence and financial success), regardless of the actual relationship that exists among these variables. The halo effect is an exaggerated correlation that ignores all those instances in which, for example, people not regarded as beautiful are not only very intelligent, but also excel in other aspects of their lives.

False Consensus

Suppose that you are presented with a list of behaviors (for example, "smokes a lot") and attitudes (for example, "favors freedom of choice in abortion decisions"), and are asked to predict how many people in your college either engage in the behaviors or agree with the attitude statement. Suppose that you have also previously indicated your own behaviors and attitudes on these same issues. If you tend, inaccurately, to see others as behaving and believing in much the same way as you do, that is an instance of *false consensus*: seeing greater agreement between our own and others' points of view, abilities, and characteristics than actually exists (for example, see Hoch, 1987; Marks & Miller, 1987).

This tendency is usually seen to be a very self-serving bias. The bias leads us to believe that we live in a world that is more confirmatory of who we are than might really be the case. On the other hand, some have suggested that rather than our considering false consensus to be such a negative bias, there are occasions in which such biasing might work to our advantage. But first let us examine the negative view of the false consensus effect.

In their thoughtful review of some 10 years of laboratory research, primarily involving college students, on the false consensus effect, Marks and Miller (1987) find a rather consistent demonstration of this effect in such target areas as opinions, characteristics, and behavior. In positing some of the reasons why people might be biased towards false consensus, Marks and Miller suggest several leading possibilities, none which is adequate by itself to explain the wide range of findings.

For example, false consensus might result from our reliance on the cognitive heuristic of availability. If we spend most of our lives interacting with people similar to us (a selective exposure effect), then our similarity with others is likely to be the most readily available piece of information. This availability might lead us to see greater similarity in many situations than actually exists.

A less cognitive understanding of the false consensus effect suggests the functional value of exaggerating similarity between ourselves and others to our sense of well-being. We know from our discussion of intergroup attributions in Chapter 4 (see pp. 69–73) that in-group members assume greater similarity with their own group and dissimilarity with the out-group. For example, Wilder (1984) found that when subjects were divided into two groups on the basis of their preferences for paintings, and were later asked about their own and other groups' political attitudes, they saw greater similarity between themselves and the in-group than between themselves and the out-group.

Kinder's (1978) research adds further to an understanding of this effect. Subjects indicated their own and major political candidates' attitudes on the Vietnam war and on urban unrest during the election campaign of 1968. They also indicated their feelings towards each candidate. Results showed that voters saw similarity between their

own positions and the positions of candidates they liked, but contrasted their own views with those of the candidates they disliked.
The former effect involves *assimilation* ("I assume a greater similarity
between my views and the views of the candidate I favor; I assimilate
theirs to mine"); the latter effect involves *contrast* ("I exaggerate the
differences between my views and the views of the candidate I dislike").

Taken together, both Wilder's and Kinder's studies suggest a
tendency for people to reveal assimilation between their own and in-
groups members' viewpoints and contrast between their own and out-
group members' viewpoints. This results in a more homogeneous view
of others than may be factually warranted. Indeed, sometimes we are
abruptly awakened to the discovery that someone from our in-group
disagrees with us on important issues, or that someone from the out-
group is more like us than we had imagined.

PROJECTION   *Attributive projection*—projecting onto others what is
experienced as an undesirable trait in one's self—is often assumed to
be a basis for the false consensus bias (Sherwood, 1981). What might
account for this perceived relationship? First, both are self-serving biases.
Second, both accomplish self-preservation by seeing others as more
like us than they actually may be. In the case of attributive projection, we justify something undesirable about ourselves by noting how
many others also have this fault. This suggests that we see similarities
in others with regard to negative traits as well as positive ones. A
study reported by Bramel (1963) illustrates the attributive projection
effect.

Bramel led his male subjects to believe that they were erotically
aroused by pictures of men in various states of undress. Assuming that
the majority of his subjects felt such arousal not desirable, they might
engage in attributive projection. If they could believe that the other
person working with them in the study was similarly aroused by the
pictures, then their own arousal would be less painful to tolerate. Bramel found a tendency for subjects to rate their own behavior in the
situation and that of their partner as similar, especially when the partner was judged favorably. In other words, attributive projection was
more likely to occur with a liked than a disliked partner, similar to
the false consensus effect in both Wilder's and Kinder's research.

As noted earlier, the false consensus effect is generally regarded
as an undesirable bias: it reassures us by distorting reality. On the
other hand, Hoch (1987) has argued that there are conditions under
which we might make even better predictions about another person if

we were guided *more*, not *less*, by the biasing effect of our own point of view.

Hoch's data suggest that projection onto others of our own characteristics proves to be helpful rather than a source of error, especially when the predictions pertain to others who are very close to us, such as our spouses. His argument is not that projection is the best way to make judgments of others, but that we should use all the information we can derive from our own experiences.

The Self-Fulfilling Prophecy

Most of us are familiar with the self-fulfilling prophecy: the effect our expectations about reality have in generating that reality. For example, if we believe someone is unintelligent (the expectation), we may act in such a way toward that person that he or she feels unintelligent (generate reality).

The self-fulfilling prophecy tells us that our expectancies may not simply distort the way we process information (as with the other biases), but may lead us to *behave* in such ways as to validate these expectancies. In our earlier discussion of biases we likened a bias to poor scientific practice (for example, heuristics). A similar argument could be made for the self-fulfilling prophecy. Good scientists let reality reveal itself; they are not to act in such a way as to create the reality they hope to discover.

Perhaps the most striking piece of research on this phenomenon was demonstrated by Rosenthal and Jacobson (1968). They gave elementry-school students a test purporting to measure the likelihood that they would demonstrate rapid intellectual growth in the coming academic year. Teachers were told the names of those particular students expected to excel; in fact, the so-called bloomers had been randomly selected from each class. Would having this expectation about the students' likely intellectual abilities influence the teacher's behavior and produce a group of real-world bloomers?

Within a brief time after the first term began, the bloomers already showed an increase in their actual I.Q. test scores. By the end of the year, comparisons made between the bloomers and the rest of the class (about whom no expectations had been formed by the teachers) showed that the former had not only made very substantial I.Q. gains, but also received higher grades. Teachers' ratings of the students also differed: nonbloomers were described as less curious, less interested, and less likely to be successful in the future than the bloomers.

Rosenthal's work demonstrates rather clearly the self-fulfilling prophecy: the teachers' expectations produced a reality that confirmed those expectations. Note that the effects produced by the teacher's expectations resulted in actual I.Q. changes.

To better understand how the self-fulfilling prophecy works, Harris and Rosenthal (1985) proposed a model dividing the process into several components, three of which seem especially important: (1) the expectancy, (2) the behavior of the person holding the expectancy, and (3) both the immediate and long-term outcomes. Harris and Rosenthal's review indicates that the majority of research focuses on the relationship between expectancies and the behaviors of those who had them; fewer studies examine the link between the behaviors and the outcomes. To better understand the reasons why a prophecy may be self-fulfilling, however, the link between expectancies and behaviors is precisely what is of interest.

Below are some actual behaviors identified by Harris and Rosenthal that seem to account for the effect:

1. Teachers who expect students to do well create a less negative classroom climate for those students; they behave in a warm, rather than in a cold or distant manner towards them.

2. Teachers tend to keep physically close to these students.

3. Teachers give these students more material to learn and often more difficult material.

4. Teachers have longer interactions with these students.

5. Teachers ask these students more questions and, in general, are more encouraging.

6. Teachers smile at and praise these students more often.

This shows how teachers' actual behaviors towards students they expect to do well can help them advance their learning skills. But what about teachers who hold negative expectancies about some of their students? Harris and Rosenthal admit that we currently know much less about the actual behaviors that mediate negative expectancies, but they suspect that the processes involved might differ in certain ways from those identified as mediating the positive effects that have been more thoroughly studied.

The self-fulfilling prophecy is not restricted to the classroom. Consider people who have a low opinion of themselves and believe that no one would want to be friends with them. They may consequently behave towards potential friends in a manner that alienates them, thereby fulfilling their prophecy. Consider also how the stock market may fluctuate up or down in reaction to an international incident like a terrorist bombing. Expecting the crisis to threaten the stability of the market, many people behave accordingly and sell their own stocks. In this way, they confirm the expectancy that the market will be affected by the incident. In other words, the bombing itself does not cause the market to fall; people's expectancies about its effect on the market leads them to behave in ways to cause the market's precipitous drop.

Not everyone has been as enthusiastic about the reality of the self-fulfilling prophecy as the cited work suggests. Jussim (1989), for example, reports the results of a longitudinal study involving some 27 teachers and over 400 students. His data suggest that the teacher's expectations about students' performances were only modestly related to the students' eventual academic achievement. For the most part, teachers were more accurate than biased in their ability to judge high-achieving students, leading Jussim to conclude that "teacher expectations predict student achievement more because they are accurate than because they lead to self-fulfilling prophecies" (p. 477).

A Different View of Errors, Biases, and Accuracy

Earlier in this chapter we saw that social psychology's views of people's cognitive abilities seem to reflect two major themes: (1) people are reasonable, rational information processors; and (2) they are somewhat defective in their abilities to accurately deal with reality. We also saw that during the last decade the second view has become the dominant one. Two revisionist trends are currently emerging, one new, the other familiar. The new trend sees people as inaccurate in picturing the social world in which they live, but considers inaccuracy to be a virtue rather than a deficiency. The once familiar message sees people to be less error-prone than currently thought.

Inaccuracy Is a Virtue, Not a Deficiency

Writing in 1980, Greenwald suggested that we consider the person to be somewhat like a totalitarian government, designed to manage information so as to keep the dictatorial regime alive and well. For the person, however, this regime is the "ego," the very sense of who we are in the world. Totalitarian regimes involving both people's egos and nation-states distort reality in the hopes of maintaining a stably functioning system. If the distorting shield were to be cast aside, a personal breakdown would be the likely result. Greenwald outlines three cognitive biases that are both common and helpful: (1) egocentricity, (2) benefectance, and (3) cognitive conservatism.

Egocentricity is the tendency to place ourselves more at the center of the universe than is usually warranted, and so view our role as being more important than it really is. In relating a recent conversation, for example, we tend to emphasize our part in it and minimize the parts that others played. In relating some past event, we provide a storyline in which we are one of the main characters. Although most of us have been taught not to think in such terms and even to consider egocentricity a rather despicable trait, Greenwald suggests that it plays an important role in self-preservation.

Benefectance is Greenwald's term for the tendency of people to accept responsibility for positive effects but not for negative effects (see pp. 88–89). Contrary to those who disapprove of this kind of self-serving bias, Greenwald regards this too as one of the individual's healthy mechanisms of survival.

Cognitive conservatism, Greenwald's third member of this totalitarian trio, refers to our tendency to resist change on the basis of new information. By processing the new in terms of the old existing categories of understanding, we shield ourselves from the topsy-turvy events of life.

In combination, these three common biases do indeed distort reality. But rather than regard these distortions as negative qualities to be eliminated, as most social psychologists proclaim, Greenwald sees these biases as serving very useful protecting and self-maintaining functions. In fact, he argues, we may be more seriously damaged without these biases than with them.

Based on rather extensive work with patients confronting a variety of diseases, Taylor (1989; Taylor & Brown, 1988) has adopted a position similar to that of Greenwald. Although she recognizes that most concepts of mental health emphasize the importance of our being in touch with reality, and even evaluate those "out of touch" as mentally ill, Taylor suggests that there is sufficient evidence to revise that point of view: people who adopt certain "illusions" may actually function better than those who insist on facing the world as it really is.

Taylor reports three illusions found to be helpful to a person's mental and physical well-being: (1) the illusion of control; (2) an unrealistic sense of optimism; and (3) maintaining an unrealistically positive view of one's self (Greenwald's egocentricity bias). It is interesting to observe that the first two illusions, involving control and optimism, are very much like the explanatory style identified in Chapter 5 as a helpful way to approach problem situations (see pp. 78–80). In both cases, individuals make attributions that give themselves a sense of control and optimism. These illusions increase people's chances of surviving a serious illness, for example, by helping them cope better than those who sink into passivity and depression because they see few possibilities for intervening on their behalf. We might say, then, that the illusion of control and unrealistic optimism empower people to respond to certain kinds of misfortune better than those who realistically assess their situation and yield themselves to circumstances. Taylor's view of the third illusion essentially parallels Greenwalds' analysis, and so need not be discussed further.

Taylor recognizes that her position on the efficacy of self-enhancing illusions runs counter to current opinion that accurate self-knowledge is necessary for the individual's well-being. She also recognizes, however, that in many instances it is precisely those people who are insistently accurate who give up, while those directed by this trio of illusions continue to strive, thereby improving their own chances of survival.

In reaching this counterintuitive proposal, Taylor and Greenwald join with several social analysts who have commented on the need for people to live by myth and illusion (for example, see Becker, 1973; Campbell, 1968; Rank, 1936). In this view, without illusions we may be too close to the brutal realities of our world; illusions help protect us and provide meaning to what otherwise might be unbearable. Indeed, this may be a key function of faith in our lives: to provide ways we can live in an era that, in hoping to free us from all illusions, has perhaps stripped all meaning from our lives.

Funder's Challenge

David Funder (1987) has mounted a somewhat different kind of challenge to the hegemony of the view that people are deficient information processors. Funder's argument does not turn on the idea that error and illusion are good, as Greenwald and Taylor have suggested, but is based on another, more familiar argument.

As Funder notes, most of the work that demonstrates error in our information processing system occurs in the laboratory using very specific stimulus materials and testing an often narrow theoretical model. In the real world, however, where the contexts in which we act are much more varied, a laboratory error may turn out to be a correct understanding of the situation. In other words, behavior considered inaccurate in the laboratory may prove effective in the everyday world. One example Funder uses to illustrate this point involves the so-called Ponzo, or railroad-ties, illusion:

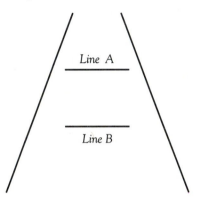

In this common perceptual illusion, line A seems to be longer than line B, even though they are drawn the same length. The illusion seems to be rather firmly established in the laboratory. Does our susceptibility to this illusion, however, indicate that there is something fundamentally deficient about our perceptual apparatus? Funder argues that thinking this way about perceptual, as well as more strictly cognitive, illusions and biases is absurd.

Can we think of circumstances in which seeing line A to be longer than line B makes sense? Funder notes that if we had a three-dimensional picture, in which lines A and B were the edges of a plane moving away from our visual field, we might very well *correctly* claim that the lines were of very different lengths. Which understanding is correct—that defined by the laboratory results or that defined by the hypothetical experience of encountering the so-called illusion in the more complex, three-dimensional world?

Funder observes that investigators of such perceptual "errors" as the Ponzo illusion recognize that in three-dimensional reality correctness differs from the two-dimensional version of the laboratory. Because a judgment made in the lab might differ from judgments made outside the lab, they do not discount their subjects' perceptual abilities. He urges us to adopt a similar attitude when we encounter the kind of so-called cognitive deficiencies we have considered throughout this chapter. Investigators seeking to study laboratory information on cognitive processing may be missing the point: while people seem to be poor scientists, they may in fact be doing very well under the highly restricted conditions of the lab, and would also do quite well under real-world conditions.

Some interesting cross-cultural work on the Ponzo illusion supports Funder's argument. Brislin (1974; Brislin & Keating, 1976) examined an ecological interpretation of the Ponzo illusion. It was hypothesized that people most susceptible to the illusion misapply cues that commonly appear in their natural environment (railroad tracks, highways, paved walkways, and so on), while those whose natural environment contains few such cues (for example, because they live on a somewhat primitive island), are less likely to make the "error" typically associated with the illusion. In support of this hypothesis, Brislin compared Pacific Islanders with U.S. subjects, finding that Islanders were more accurate than Americans who "misapplied an inference, useful in their everyday lives, that objects far away are larger than they appear" (Brislin & Keating, p. 409).

Although the terms "accuracy" and "error" are used to describe the performance of the two cultural groups, we should not treat these terms as we commonly do. The reason why one group was more accurate than the other was not because of some better perceptual apparatus for which the other group was deficient, but because the two groups had experiences in very different kinds of real-world ecologies that would lead one group (the U.S. subjects) to make an inference that was not likely to appear in the other group (the Pacific Islanders).

Funder also suggests that there is substantial evidence even in the laboratory that people are more accurate cognitive processors than is usually assumed. A study by Funder and Colvin (1988), for example, demonstrates that people perceive others quite accurately. Another study conducted in a nonlaboratory field setting by Wright and Dawson (1988) shows that people are very accurate in predicting others' behavior, at least when the behavior is highly salient to them. In this case, boys were especially sensitive to the aggressive behavior of others and so could readily know whom to avoid and with whom to associate. This is hardly a sign of a deficient cognitive system. Research by Funder and Dobroth (1987) and Woodruffe (1985), as well as Jussim's work on the self-fulfilling prophecy (see p. 115), confirms the accuracy of human information processing.

Funder clearly presents several good reasons to suspect the claim frequently made by investigators that people are relatively poor, deficient, inaccurate, or error-prone information processors. Funder has suggested ways in which that negative image is itself inaccurate (because we are more accurate in our perceptions of people than the image would allow) or incomplete (because what is an error in the laboratory might be a correct judgment in the more complex real world). Clearly, most of us get by reasonably well in our relationships with other people. We do not spend our lives in a futile attempt to discover truths about others. There are, of course, occasions in which we may seem more like the cognitive bumbler that current social psychology portrays; but, more often than not, we accurately make some very difficult and complex judgments of other people.

Conclusions

Are people good scientists, with systematic and accurate cognitive processing abilities? Are they poor scientists, burdened with so many biases and errors that achieving an accurate judgment seems a distant dream to be realized, if at all, only by some rigorous retraining? Or are people poor scientists guided by illusions that, rather than impede their abilities to function effectively in the real world, are the very basis of healthful adaptation? In this chapter we have examined evidence for all three images of our cognitive abilities while recognizing, along with Funder, and Markus and Zajonc, that these three positions seem to mark historical shifts in social psychology's framework of understanding even more than the discovery of hidden aspects of human reality.

One conclusion, however, should be fairly evident: because a sociohistorical perspective emphasizes the historical rootedness of our understandings, these contrasting social psychological "images of people" are interesting data to be explained, not dismissed.

Around the turn of the nineteenth century and especially in Europe, where psychology was born, the strains of irrationality seemed to loom large in people's understandings of human behavior. In the area of group behavior, for example, we find Le Bon's (1895/1960) intriguing ideas. According to Le Bon, although people can be rational, when placed in groups irrationality takes over. Most of us are familiar with Freud's (1924–1950, 1954) depiction of people as anything but clear-thinking, rational beings. He portrays people driven by deeply unconscious impulses struggling to break the confining reins of rationality.

As the birthplace of contemporary social psychology, the United States was not very receptive to these images. After all, the masses were regarded as the roots of democracy; they surely could not be treated as irrational hordes intent on tearing down revered institutions. Furthermore, the science of psychology, modeling itself after the natural sciences, could not long endure an irrationalist image of its object of study; nor could it advance as a science if the material it needed to examine was hidden from public view. And so the United States embraced a more rational image of the individual: people capable of accurate and reasoned thinking. The horrors of World War II made it difficult to sustain this image.

If people were rational and capable of thinking accurately, how could the crimes of Hitler and Stalin have taken place? After the Holocaust, reason itself became suspect as our image of humanity sank even lower. The combination of the birth of the computer and the subsequent turn to cognitive science as the basis for psychology, and especially for social psychology, turned around the historical forces once again. Rationality and accuracy of information processing again emerged with a renewed interest.

Perhaps in response to this overly rational image, or broader social trends like the anti-war and civil rights movements of the 1960s and 1970s, the historical tide turned once again. Although computers might be accurate in processing information, and may even serve as the ideal model for the human brain, people seemed to have certain serious cognitive and noncognitive (emotional and self-serving) shortcomings that prevented them from realizing the expectations implied by a computer-based model of information processing. And so we find investigations of the sort we have examined in Chapters 4–6 on people's cognitive deficiencies.

Rather than simply returning to claims of rationality, as the historical pattern would suggest, investigators now admitted that people were imperfect information processors, but that their imperfection was what saved them. This is a fascinating turn. It is almost as though in the latter decades of the twentieth century reality was overtaken by illusion to the degree that either illusion is preferable to reality, or illusion defines reality. In either case it is now fashionable to advocate some degree of self-deception and distortion as effective defensive screens against the complex, brutal reality of the modern world.

Nurtured as we are on television images, perhaps defining illusion as reality makes sense. The speed and glut of information in our civilization compel people to seek refuge in fantasy and appearance. Interestingly enough, the sociohistorical view of science, which proposes a version of reality rather than a definition of its actual nature, can be seen as part of this same cultural and historical trend.

Accuracy and Correction in Science: A Lesson for Social Psychology

As we have seen, many social psychologists studying human information processing have lamented the fact that people do not act as scientists; yet, these critics of our shortcomings have ignored how science rids itself of error. Scientific thinking is self-correcting, but not because any scientist single-handedly manages that feat; self-correction is a feature of the *community* of scientists as a whole. If we built our sciences entirely on the hopes that each scientist was free of bias and entirely rational, we would not see the kinds of scientific advances made today.

Those social psychologists who see the individual as a flawed scientist fail to realize that even if the individual were a good scientist, his or her perceptions and judgments would still be corrected by the community. For example, Foushee (1984) examined the factors that contribute to the poor performance of aircrews. He did not link their difficulties to the accuracy of any one individual's cognitive abilities, but rather to their ability to work effectively together as a group. Accurate information processing was a community-wide, not an individual outcome. Foushee tells us of the importance of the group's processes of working together to achieve accuracy, rather than locating accuracy inside the head of any one individual member as most cognitive social psychologists currently do.

Once again we have encountered the sociohistorical understanding of cognitive processes. In this view, rationality and accuracy of information processing are not outcomes of activities occurring in the heads of individuals but, as in the case of scientific self-correction, are located in the interacting community of individuals who jointly determine what constitutes rationality and accuracy. Rather than concerning ourselves with the deficiencies in the human cognitive system, we should address problems located in the *processes* by which groups work together.

While this reformulation of cognitive social psychology will not be easy to accomplish, given the current commitment to an individualistic and internal view of cognition, a dose of sociohistorical thinking may eventually recast our understanding. Irrationality and inaccuracy would then emerge as problems of the community's ability to work together in a self-correcting manner (as science demonstrates with reasonably good success), not problems of individual information processors with various deficits and shortcomings. If there are shortcomings, they exist in the social world, not in individual minds.

PART THREE
Social Influence

7

· ·

Issues in Social Influence

ONFORMITY IS USUALLY the first thing that comes to mind when we think of social influence. Most of us believe that conformity—that is, a target acting in accordance with the specified standard of some agent—is a product of social influence. Acceptance of an agent's influence constitutes conformity; rejection, nonconformity or deviation. In this chapter we will explore some of the complexities that have marked the social psychologist's study of this fascinating and important topic. We will focus on six different aspects of social influence: (1) majority and minority models of social influence; (2) types of conformity and nonconformity; (3) kinds of tasks studied; (4) informational versus normative influence; (5) target populations and gender effects; and (6) some proposed psychological mediators of social influence.

. . . .

Majority and Minority Models of Social Influence

Before 1969, most social psychologists defined social influence as synonymous with conformity; that is, they saw the outcomes of social influence to be either conformity or deviation. This perspective has come to be referred to as the *majority-influence model,* in which a majority (usually a group of peers) trys to induce the conformity of some minority (usually one individual). In this model, the target (the object of the agent's influence) faces two possible options: conform to the majority view or deviate.

In a paper introduced to American audiences in 1969, Serge Moscovici and his associates suggested an original alternative. Why is it, they wondered, that the only question the target faced was whether or not to conform to the majority? Is it not equally plausible that the target might try to influence or convert the majority, producing what Moscovici referred to as *innovation* rather than conformity? Innovation refers to the change that the minority (now as the agent) induces in the majority (now as the target). Thus emerged the second model for understanding social influence, commonly termed the *minority-influence model.*

We will examine in detail the majority-influence model in Chapter 8 and the minority-influence model in Chapter 9. For now, however, simply be aware of the fact that social influence is no longer identified with conformity but, rather, is considered a very general process that can result in either conformity or innovation. Conformity describes the outcome of social influence as understood from the majority perspective in trying to gain control over the target's behavior. Innovation describes the outcome of social influence as understood from the minority perspective in trying to effect a change in the majority's behavior. Social influence as conformity, then, is concerned with how social control is established and maintained by majorities over minorities. Social influence as innovation, on the other hand, is concerned with how social change results when majorities are successfully challenged by minority points of view.

While a significant body of research has emerged since 1969 on the minority-influence model, and while several efforts have been made to integrate both models into a single theory of social influence (as we will see in Chapter 9), the majority perspective has dominated the field of social psychology. This will become more evident as we explore other issues in social influence.

. . . .

Types of Conformity and Nonconformity

As we have seen, in the majority-influence model there are two possible ways the target can respond to the agent's attempted influence: conform or deviate (nonconform). But isn't the range of possible responses to attempts at social influence more complex? Consider the following personal example.

While preparing my doctoral dissertation on conformity and deviation, I had the opportunity to try out a few of my ideas one evening at a friend's house. His little daughter, Lisa, wanted my attention while we were sitting in the living room waiting for dinner. One idea I was interested in studying was whether I could get people to oppose my efforts to make them see things my way. Since she was already eager to be the center of my attention, Lisa impressed me as a perfect first "subject" for this benign demonstration. I held my hand up, palm facing her, and said, "Lisa, I have the power to get you to follow my hand wherever it moves." She giggled, knowing that she had hooked me into a game. And, of course, I was pleased to see such a highly motivated "subject."

At times, when I moved my hand forward, Lisa dutifully followed it and leaned her little body in my direction acting as though I really had the power to affect her behavior. At other times, however, she would literally bend over backwards in order not to follow the movement of my hand.

Two interesting features of social influence emerge from this example: *congruence* and *anticonformity*. It was clear to me that when Lisa leaned forward in response to my hand moving forward, she was not really following my directions; she was simply doing what she wanted to do in the first place, which also happened to be what I wanted her to do. In other words, her behavior is better seen as an instance of congruence than conformity: sometimes targets react in the same way that the agent wants them to, not because they were responsive to the agent's influence but because that is how they would have behaved anyway.

On the other hand, Lisa's efforts to resist my influence, by literally bending over backwards to avoid following the forward movement of my hand, reflects a process termed *anticonformity*. In this case, her response to my attempts at influence was a very special type of nonconformity. She could have resisted by simply ignoring me or standing still. But she resisted by doing just the opposite of what I told her to do; in other words, anticonformity.

Is it considered conformity to *publicly* adopt the agent's position but *privately* remain unaffected? Would we not want true conformity to be reflected in both public *and* private change? This distinction between public and private conformity has proved to be one of the most important keys to understanding social influence, regardless of whether the governing model is the majority or the minority perspective. As we will see, a great deal of research on conformity, especially within the majority framework, reports public conformity without private acceptance.

Many investigators concerned with social influence have tried to develop descriptive schemes that would incorporate these and related distinctions. Several schemes have been proposed (for example, Jahoda, 1959; Nail, 1986) to account for a variety of responses to social influence. As we review the essentials of one typical scheme (Nail, 1986), we will note that there are several different possibilities for both conformity and nonconformity, all seen through the perspective of the majority-influence model.

To avoid needless complications, let us assume that we are dealing with a situation in which there is a disagreement between the initial positions of some agent and target. There are, then, several possible responses:

1. *Conversion.* This describes a situation in which the target *both* publicly and privately accepts the position advocated by the agent. This is the kind of response most of us intuitively consider to be true conformity. The target thoroughly accepts the agent's influence; it then becomes internalized, altering what the target says in public and what he or she believes in private.

2. *Compliance.* This describes a situation in which the target changes publicly, but privately maintains his or her original position. For the most part, this is a kind of expedient conformity. The target does not really accept the agent's position, but publicly declares acceptance to avoid confrontation, to go along with the group, to avoid looking foolish or ignorant, and so on.

3. *Anticompliance.* This describes a situation in which the target changes privately, while publicly remaining unaffected. While

this might initially seem puzzling, consider a politician who must not appear to have publicly yielded to influence even while privately accepting it. As Nail, among others, has noted, anticompliance can serve very important public face-saving purposes for those privately convinced by the influence agent. As we will see in the discussion of the minority-influence model in Chapter 9, anticompliance is common among majorities who have been influenced by minorities but are either unaware of this influence or will not acknowledge it. From the perspective of the agent, anticompliance is a kind of conformity, although a type that may remain hidden from the agent's view.

4. *Independence.* This describes a situation in which the target both publicly and privately retains his or her original position. This response corresponds to our commonsense impression of truly autonomous individuals who listen to those seeking to influence them but who remain true to their own convictions.

5. *Negative conformity.* This describes a situation in which the target changes his or her own initial position, publicly and perhaps even privately, to one even further removed from the influencing agent's original position. Negative or anti-conformity can occur when the target and agent initially share similar positions, but on learning of the agent's position the target adopts a position contrary to that held by the influencing agent to distinguish himself or herself even more from the agent. A similar response can occur even if the positions of target and agent were originally not that close, but the target nevertheless feels that they are too close and so widens the gap even further.

In originally outlining some of the complexities of social influence, we have already considered the concept of *congruence.* This describes a situation in which the target and agent initially agree and continue to agree after the agent's attempted influence. As we noted, it is important to separate the effects of congruence from those of conformity since it is inappropriate to consider congruence as a response to some current acts of influence agents.

While several other responses to social influence from within the majority perspective have been identified, those listed above sufficiently reveal the range of possibilities for both conformity (as conversion, compliance, or even anti-compliance) and nonconformity (as independence or negative conformity).

Kinds of Tasks
Studied

A wide variety of tasks have been studied by those interested in learning more about social influence. Surprisingly, objective perceptual judgments, often about relatively unambiguous stimuli, have formed the centerpiece of many of these studies—the length of lines, the color of slides, and so on. For example, the classic studies on social influence by Asch (1956, 1958), using the majority-influence model, and Moscovici, Lage, and Naffrechoux (1969), using the minority-influence model, focused on perceptual judgment tasks. (We will examine these studies in detail in Chapters 8 and 9.) Other studies on social influence have concentrated on group discussion and decision making, attitudes, opinions and values, personal preferences, and so on. What difference does the kind of task studied make?

Both Moscovici and his associates (1969) and Ross, Bierbrauer, and Hoffman (1976) argued that a disagreement involving physical stimuli—for example, length or color—poses a more acute crisis for the individuals involved than, for example, one over a matter of opinion. We expect people not to share our opinions, but are somewhat surprised if they do not see the physical world in the same way we do. In the typical majority-influence experiment, a minority of subjects experience physical reality differently than the majority, causing them to doubt their own perceptual abilities. For example, they see the length of lines differently than the majority in the room see them. In a typical minority-influence experiment, the majority confronts a minority who report a different version of physical reality than they are experiencing, thereby posing a potential challenge to their own perceptual abilities. For example, the majority sees color differently than does a minority, presumably also reporting accurately.

In contrast, differences in opinions or preferences have a kind of built-in explanation that permits people to disagree without the kind of anxiety associated with differences in perceptual judgments. Someone whose opinions differ from our own does not challenge our beliefs about reality in the same way as someone who perceives seemingly objective stimuli differently than we do. Unless we can account for the disparity, the latter produces substantial self-doubt. In this case, the kind of task studied is very important, since using physical stimuli in situations of either conformity or innovation clearly provides a greater risk of inner conflict than other tasks.

Later in the chapter we will see another argument raised about the importance of the task chosen for studying conformity. Eagly (1978, 1983) suggests that a definite gender bias in the kinds of tasks chosen for much of the research on conformity favors male life experiences. In general, people relatively inexperienced in a given area are more likely to be influenced by others' opinions. If women conform more than men, for example, this result may only reflect the use of tasks with which women have less experience than men, rather than anything profound about male–female differences. We will return to this topic later in the chapter.

Informational Versus Normative Influence

Another important distinction typically found in social-influence literature was initially proposed by Deutsch and Gerard (1955), the distinction between normative and informational influence. *Normative influence* involves pressure to conform to the norms of a group of which one is a member, hopes to become a member, or even imagines what it would be like to be a member. In contrast, *informational influence* deals with the effect that knowledge, evidence, or information about reality have in changing one's understanding.

An example of this distinction comes from one of my classes on group dynamics. Students usually enter the class without any prior acquaintance with others, and suddenly find themselves a member of a group whose only task is to learn how groups function. Since they have not seen one another before, they have no traditional standard of behavior. Without specific norms developed by the group to define proper member behavior, people follow the norms of their own social experience.

Yet, even without group-developed norms, people are still influenced by the information others present them. For instance, those having difficulty getting into classes in a given term follow the advice of those who have been more successful in beating the system. In this case, we see informational influence at work: the information about open classes is used by others, making those in possession of this information influence-agents.

Over time, however, the group does develop its own norms about proper member behavior. Two typical norms tell us, for example, that silent members are not appreciated, and that emotional expression rather than intellectual debate is appropriate. These become potent norms that significantly shape the behavior of group members, leading those who comply with these norms to be more highly valued than those who deviate from them.

One of the reasons for maintaining the distinction between normative and informational influence is the probable difference in the kind of conformity associated with each type. For example, normative influence is likely to produce compliance (public but not private change) but not conversion (both public and private change); on the other hand, informational influence is likely to produce conversion (for example, see Nail, 1986).

Returning to our example, those in the group seeking acceptance often learn to follow its norms, talking more often and showing more emotion. In many instances, this behavior appears only in the presence of the group, suggesting the public or compliant nature of normative influence. On the other hand, learning about a class that one might be able to get into often can and does lead to immediate conversion: the target follows the agent's directions and has thus changed his or her behavior.

· · · · · · · · · · · · · · ·

Target Populations and Gender Effects

We will now consider two features of the target population that are relevant to understanding social influence. We will first briefly comment on the relevance of group membership for the processes involved in social influence. We will then examine the consequences of people's gender on their susceptibility to social influence.

Because most work on social influence has focused on laboratory experimentation rather than the everyday world, most target populations have been individuals rather than groups or individuals located in their usual group settings. It seems reasonable to maintain that the processes of influence operating on an individual isolated from his or her group affiliations are not the same as those operating on individuals in groups. Studies of brainwashing, for example, have indicated how the agents seeking to brainwash target individuals first isolate them from their groups in order to break them down more effectively (for example, see Lifton, 1961; Schein, 1958).

In a different context, Kurt Lewin (1947a, 1947b, 1958), a major figure in social psychology, demonstrated that it is far easier to change individuals who are alone than when they are in groups. He outlined a three-stage process in which the very first stage, which he termed *unfreezing*, required separating the individual from his or her current group support. The second stage, *movement*, involved changing the individual's opinion or behavior. The final stage, *refreezing*, required placing the changed behavior into a new group context in order to sustain it. Let us look at an example of this process in practice.

Suppose the behavior to be changed involves an individual's overeating habits. The agent wants to help the individual lose weight by eating less. The first thing the agent does is try to understand the target's current eating behavior. The tendency to overeat is not seen as some isolated, individual act, but as a behavior pattern embedded in a social or group context: the family overeats; the individual is encouraged to overeat by the people he or she associates with, and so on.

Unfreezing involves taking the individual out of those social contexts that support their overeating and placing them in a different social group—for example, Overeater's Anonymous or some other organization designed to help individuals change undesirable behavior patterns. Movement, the second stage, involves helping the individual learn better eating habits; and finally, refreezing, the third stage, involves trying to place the changed eating behavior in a supportive social context. This last stage might not be easy if the person's family continues to encourage the old ways, but by continued connection with the OA group, the individual might be helped to sustain a more healthful pattern of eating.

The above example suggests that by studying social influence in highly individualistic settings, in which neither agents nor targets are individual members of real groups, we may miss some of the important features of social influence. Furthermore, as the vast majority of social-influence research—both the majority- and minority-influence models—has focused on relatively isolated individuals rather than individuals as group members, the resulting knowledge may not be directly applicable to real-life social situations, in which group membership is a salient feature in much of our behavior.

Gender Effects

The second feature of the target population relevant to social influence is gender. Our commonsense cultural stereotypes tell us that women tend to be more persuadable than men. But is this true? Alice Eagly (1978, 1983) clearly *rejects* this commonly held belief. She reports that only in situations involving group pressure is there some tendency for women to be more susceptible to influence than men. In what she terms *persuasion studies*, for example, in which a person simply states his or her position and presents arguments for or against it, there is little effect of gender: 82% of the studies revealed *no* male–female differences in persuadability.

In contrast, studies of direct or implied group pressure reveal a slight tendency for females to be more conforming than males: 62% report no sex differences, 34% report females to be more conforming than males, and 3% report males to be more conforming than females.

Eagly was not content to debunk the cultural myth of high female persuadability; she also examined other experimental and cultural aspects that might account for some of the differences that were found (for example, in the group pressure contexts). In one case, Eagly compared studies reported before and after 1970, finding that 37% of the former but only 10% of the latter reported women to be more influenceable than men. She reasoned that historical changes involving the emergence of the women's movement, for example, might have provided a significant impetus to women's independence.

Another illuminating effort on her part led Eagly to examine a variant of the Deutsch and Gerard informational versus normative influence effects. She reasoned that where informational influence is at issue, any person, male or female, should be more easily influenced by information in areas about which they have little or no knowledge. And, indeed, this expectation has been generally confirmed (see Eagly, 1978, p. 96). Eagly also reviewed the social-influence research literature to determine if the tasks used were primarily oriented around areas of information about which males were more likely to have knowledge (and thus be less liable to influence) than females. She in fact discovered a bias towards using tasks favoring the male experience, a fact which might account for the tendency of women to yield more than men in such situations.

The tendency of women to concede to group pressure more than men, Eagly suggested, is part of women's efforts to preserve group harmony and promote good feelings among all members of the group. Calling upon the previous distinctions, it appears that compliance rather than conversion is the most likely response of female subjects under these group conditions. In other words, they change what they say publicly in order to avoid discord within the group.

Eagly's (1983) final conclusion about gender differences in persuadability is that if we ever find women to be more subject to influence than men, we should look for the reason in real-world gender standings in our society rather than in biology. Men occupy more positions of power and influence than women, who in turn are subjected to a lower social status. Thus, the differences we might find among men and women confronting a social-influence situation may very well reflect their differential locations in the structure of society. As those locations change, we should likewise expect to find changes in our understanding of the relation between sex and persuadability.

Some Proposed Psychological Mediators of Social Influence

Various analyses have been made of likely cognitive, motivational or, self-presentational processes that mediate between the agent's attempted influence and the target's eventual response. In this section we will examine: (a) compliance, identification, and internalization; (b) reactance; and (c) impression management. Chapter 8 presents a fourth possibility, an attributional account of influence effects.

Compliance, Identification, and Internalization

Some years ago, Kelman (1958) proposed three processes mediating social influence that he termed compliance, identification, and internalization.

Compliance occurs when the target, whose behavior is under careful surveillance, wants either to avoid punishment for not following orders or to receive the rewards promised by the agent for accepting the influence. As we saw earlier, compliance describes a public but not a private response. In order to avoid being punished or to get the reward, the individual will comply, but only insofar as his or her performance is publicly observed; privately, the individual will continue to maintain his or her original perspective. Compliance is thus an expedient response that should be very familiar to most of us. Children comply with their parents' wishes, for example, to get a toy or avoid a spanking.

Compliance works, however, only when continued surveillance is possible. When surveillance ceases—that is, when the target's performance can no longer be scrutinized by the influence agent—there is little or no reason to conform. Therefore, if the only mechanism assuring conformity is compliance, it is obvious that constant and extensive surveillance would be required to maintain control of, say, a large population. This is evident from recent revelations of the widespread use of secret police and government informants in some Eastern European nations under dictatorial rule until their overthrow in the late 1980s. As Kelman notes, however, there are other processes of influence that operate in somewhat different ways.

With *identification,* the target accepts influence from the agent in order to preserve the strong bond of attraction that the target feels towards the agent—"I do what you wish because I identify with you, want to be like you, and in turn to have you like and respect me." Unlike the mediation of compliance, with identification the change in viewpoint can be both public and private and can therefore endure. With identification, indirect rather than direct surveillance is usually involved. For example, people imaginatively review their behavior with parental figures not present or with a religious figure presumed to be always knowledgeable about their thoughts and actions—"Jesus, God, or my Spiritual Master is always present and serves as a continuing guide for all that I do."

Internalization, the third process Kelman discusses, involves accepting influence from the agent because of its credibility and because it fits the target's existing beliefs and values. Unlike compliance, with internalization the agent need not be continually present to observe the behavior of the target; unlike identification, there need not be any bond of attachment linking the target to the agent. With internalization, the informational value provided by the agent is sufficient to win the target's allegiance. As noted in our earlier comparison of normative and informational influence, with internalization the change in the target's behavior is likely to be both public and private and thus more like conversion than any of the other possibilities we have outlined.

Reactance

Several years ago, Brehm (1966; See also Brehm & Brehm, 1981) formulated a theory of *reactance,* referring to the negative motivational state presumed to occur whenever a person's freedom is threatened. On experiencing reactance, the individual is motivated to restore lost freedoms or prevent the loss of other freedoms. Clearly, most social-influence situations are ripe for inducing reactance, as they lead individuals to experience a potential loss of their own freedom of self-determination when placed under pressure to follow the directives of others.

One way to reduce reactance in a social-influence situation is anticonformity—demonstrating one's own willfullness by doing just the opposite of what the agent desires. In view of reactance theory, then, one of the psychological bases of nonconformity involves individuals' efforts to restore their own domain of self-determination when under pressure from others to conform.

Impression Management

A controversy has recently arisen between proponents of reactance theory and those advocating an impression-management interpretation of reactance effects. A brief look at this controversy will give us an opportunity to examine still another psychological mediator of social-influence effects. Impression management, as we saw earlier in connection with attribution theory (see pp. 83–90), is the idea that people are primarily motivated to create and sustain a positive impression of themselves in the eyes of their audience. In the impression-management view, then, reactance is less a desire on the part of the individual to restore personal freedom than a tactic to assert his or her autonomy in defiance of the influence agent (for example, see Hellman & Toffler, 1976). According to Baer and his associates (1980), "people are more concerned with managing the impression of autonomy than they are with actually maintaining autonomy" (p. 416).

In the impression-management view, the desire to demonstrate autonomy as an impression-management technique should appear on the public, but not the private level. In examining this possibility, Baer and his colleagues created an experimental procedure in which subjects could express their autonomy and respond to a persuasive communication either publicly or privately. Data tended to support the impression-management interpretation; that is, subjects whose freedoms were publicly threatened and who had an opportunity to publicly present themselves as autonomous were less likely to reveal private change in response to the agent's attempted influence than were subjects not provided these opportunities of public presentation. Needless to say, proponents of reactance theory, like Wright and Brehm (1982), have contested the conclusions of Baer and his associates, offering their own theory to account for the data.

We previously considered another kind of impression-management interpretation of social-influence effects in our introduction of anticompliance: the target publicly defies the agent while privately agreeing with the agent's position. In some of the research on minority influence we will consider in chapter 9, for example, a majority might publicly show disdain for the position advocated by the minority and yet privately agree. Their public disdain is a tactic, in this case designed to show their continued allegiance to the establishment.

8

Conformity and The Majority-Influence Model

RECALL FROM CHAPTER 7 that the dominant model for study-ing social influence was, until about 1969, of the majority seeking to influence a minority, usually a minority of one. It envisioned two main classes of response to this majority in-fluence—conformity or deviation. In this chapter we will examine in detail four major cases that illustrate key aspects of the majority model:

1. The Asch paradigm, where a minority of one confronts a majority. This case demonstrates the effects of group pressure on people's judgments of physical reality.

2. The Sherif paradigm, where everyone confronts a highly am-biguous situation. This case demonstrates how people de-velop shared frameworks that structure their perceptual judgments.

3. The Schachter paradigm, where a majority rejects the non-conforming deviate. This case demonstrates both how social influence operates in a group-discussion situation and how groups try to persuade those with deviating points of view to

adopt the majority's position or be rejected from group membership.

4. The Milgram paradigm, where people buckle under to the demands made upon them by legitimate authority. This case demonstrates the role of the agent's legitimacy in creating obedience to orders that may run counter to the target's personal desires not to harm another person.

Asch's Classic Study of Conformity to Majority Influence

Picture yourself in the following situation. You have agreed to participate in an experiment and arrive at the appointed hour. You enter a room, in which you see a group of others like yourself already seated, and are directed towards a chair at one end of the room. The experimenter describes your task; it sounds rather simple and straightforward. You will be presented with a standard line and three comparison lines—A, B, and C—and will be asked to state which of the three is the same length as the standard. You will be required to announce your answer out loud when it is your turn.

On the first trial, you are all presented with the set of lines. You look closely and see how easy the task really is. Obviously, line B is the same length as the standard. You wait your turn to announce your answer. While waiting, you are pleased to note that each of the others who speak ahead of you has announced that line B is also their choice. When your turn arrives you simply, but forcefully, state, "line B."

The second trial moves forward in much the same way as the first. By now, you are settling back rather comfortably in your chair, confident in your ability to do well in this little experiment on perceptual judgments. The third trial arrives, but something perplexing has suddenly happened. You clearly know that line C is the correct answer, but as you wait your turn and listen to the others announce their choice, they all say, "line A." What is going on here? It approaches your turn. What will you do? You think that line C is the correct answer, but everyone else in the room thinks it is line A. Do you tell everyone what your eyes tell you at the risk of facing their ridicule, the embarrassment of standing out as a perceptual ignoramus? Or do you go along with the group, announcing line A so to avoid trouble, but secretly knowing that line C is correct and that something strange is going on?

The above scenario basically describes what Asch's subjects confronted. Unknown to the real subjects, however, Asch hired a group of accomplices trained to provide incorrect answers on certain selected trials. In Trial 1, the standard line was 10 inches long, while the comparisons were 8¾, 10, and 8 inches, respectively. The group's announcement that line B was the same length as the standard clearly corresponded with the subject's own perceptions.

In Trial 3, however, the standard line was 3 inches long and the comparison lines 3¾, 4¼, and 3 inches, respectively. Line C, of course, was the correct answer, but the group of accomplices answered, "line A." Under these conditions, Asch reported that about 33% of the naive subjects' "errors" were in the direction of the majority view—that is, towards the selection of line A rather than line C. This contrasted sharply with the virtual absence of any errors in a separate control condition in which no erroneous group judgments were offered.

You might argue that trial 3 calls for a more difficult judgment than trial 1, which would account for the more numerous errors. Even though this argument does not explain why the control group did not make any errors, let us take a closer look at Asch's study to put that argument to rest. On some of the critical trials—that is, when the majority answer was incorrect—differences between the lines to be judged were rather substantial. On trial 7, for example, the standard was 8 inches, while the incorrect comparisons were 6¼ and 6¾, respectively. Indeed, Asch tried even more extreme discrepancies in the range of 3–6 inches; he comments that "even glaring discrepancies . . . did not produce independence in all" (1958, p. 182), even though the percentage of conformity responses was reduced.

Asch systematically varied some of the conditions of his research to study their effects on conformity. In one instance, he varied the *size* of the majority that the naive subject confronted. He found that conformity vanished when the subject confronted only one other person, but was in full force once the majority consisted of three people. Interestingly, increasing the size of the majority beyond three had no discernable effect.

Asch also varied the degree to which the naive subject confronted the majority alone or with another ally who reported accurately. Of course, this ally was also an accomplice, instructed to report accurately. Data indicated that by having even one other ally, the subject was empowered to defy the majority: "Indeed, we have been able to show that a unanimous majority of 3 is . . . far more effective than a majority of 8 containing 1 dissenter" (p. 180).

In another variation, Asch convened a group of 17 people, 16 of whom were naive subjects and only one a paid accomplice trained to give the incorrect answer on several critical trials. Asch reports that, "Under these conditions the members of the naive majority reacted to the lone dissenter with amusement. Contagious laughter spread through the group at the droll minority of 1" (p. 182). In other words, when the majority confronted a deviate, they ridiculed him. Imagine, then, the painful awareness the naive subject must have experienced in that deviating position, anticipating the ridicule of the larger group if he or she dared to speak the truth.

Asch carefully interviewed his subjects to determine whether or not they actually "saw" the lines differently. In other words, was this a case of true conversion or merely compliance? As you might well have surmised, evidence suggests support for compliance rather than conversion; very few subjects actually said that on learning of the majority's views about the lengths, their own perception was actually changed. Asch does report, however, that even among those subjects who remained independent, not yielding to majority pressure, some evidenced a loss of self-confidence, while others experienced considerable tension and doubt. In other words, the effect of being a minority of one confronting a majority of at least three others who see the world differently can be very disturbing to the individual.

Many other investigators have used the Asch-type social-influence model as the basis for their own research. While Asch's original research program could only study one subject at a time, Crutchfield (1955) developed an apparatus capable of studying several subjects. His apparatus was actually a partitioned table with places for five people. The experimenter could manipulate the information each person received, as well as their response "position" in the group. For example, each subject was led to believe that he or she was the last person to respond after learning of the other's responses, which were in fact programmed by the experimenter to provide false information on selected trials. Using a wide variety of tasks and subjects, Crutchfield confirmed most of Asch's original findings.

Perhaps the two most interesting uses of the Asch-type social-influence situation, however, were reported by Ross, Bierbrauer, and Hoffman (1976) and Frager (1970). Ross and his associates employed an attributional interpretation of the Asch situation, arguing that it caused the subjects a profound crisis in understanding. Facing a majority whose perceptions differed from their own, the subject must have wondered: (a) How can I explain their behavior? and (b) What understanding will they have of my behavior if I fail to agree with their perceptions?

Ross, Bierbrauer, and Hoffman suggested that in most everyday settings, people resolve these questions by assuming that they occupy different positions from others. For example, we disagree because our priorities are different, or because others stand to gain more from seeing things their way than we do. In the original Asch situation, however, there was no easy way for the subjects to arrive at these conclusions. Subjects were confronted with an inability to explain what was happening, and so faced a rather severe "attributional crisis."

What would happen if, in a situation very much like that used by Asch, subjects were provided with explanations for their perceptual differences from the majority? Ross and his colleagues created just such a situation by establishing different payoffs or priorities for the participants. They argued that when an explanation for the differences between the naive subject and the majority was readily available, subjects would experience less pressure to conform to the majority view, and thus would be more accurate in their judgments. Their data demonstrate higher conformity (26%) under conditions that directly parallel the original Asch study, and significantly less conformity as explanations for the differences in perceptions were readily available. For example, they found a conformity rate of 18% when people could infer that different priorities governed behavior in the situation; they found a conformity rate of 10% when people could infer that the perceptual judgments were caused by different payoffs.

Frager's study offers a fascinating variation on Asch's work, reporting *anticonformity* as a response to majority influence. Frager replicated the essentials of the original Asch study in Japan with Japanese subjects. He reports finding "slightly over one-third of the subjects exhibited anticonformity" (p. 207) by giving answers further separating them from the majority point of view *on the neutral trials*—that is, when the majority presented a correct judgment. For example, on one trial, the standard was 2 inches, with comparison lines of 2, 1, and 1½ inches, respectively. When the majority answered line A (the correct choice), the anticonforming naive subjects (a total of 46 people) answered line C.

Comparing these results with the control-group figures adds to the picture of anticonformity: overall, the control group exhibited 95% accuracy, but on the particular item illustrated above, the control group was 100% accurate in judging line A to be the correct choice. Furthermore, Frager had the opportunity to re-examine 12 of the anticonforming subjects a full year later, finding an average accuracy of 96% at that time from the very same people who had anticonformed earlier. Thus, anticonformity to the majority influence in the Asch-type situation does not appear to be a function of some perceptual deficit in the subjects.

Frager reports that anticonformity was significantly related to the subjects' alienation, especially in the case of male anticonformists. Frager speculates that because anticonformity appeared so early in the study—even before subjects were aware that the majority was going to make inaccurate judgments—their negativistic response seemed to be a deliberate violation of normative expectations. That such a response appeared to correlate with cultural and social alienation suggests the possibility of a kind of Japanese countercultural movement similar to that which took shape in the United States during the 1960s and led to the wholesale rejection of major institutions and practices in our society. What better way for an alienated youth in Japan (in the late 1960s), a culture noted for its high level of conformity, to show rejection of that culture than by anticonforming!

. . . .

The Sherif Approach to Studying Social Influence

Another approach to studying social influence that falls within the majority-influence perspective involves the pioneering research reported by Sherif (1935), using what is called *the autokinetic effect*. The effect refers to the apparent motion of a pinpoint of light exposed in an otherwise darkened room. Although the source itself does not move, the light appears to move; various judgments about how far it moved during a specified interval of time can thus be made.

Sherif demonstrated that when a group of people in this situation are asked to announce their estimates of the distance the light moved out loud, their judgments eventually converge. Suppose, for example, that Sarah initially says the light moves 5 inches, Betty that it moves 8 inches, and John that it moves 2 inches. Over a period of several trials, their judgments converge so that they implicitly agree that the light seems to move about 3–4 inches.

Sherif reports that once this convergence has been established, its potency persists. Subjects who have first been in the group situation where the judgmental norm is established, and are then placed alone in the same situation, persist in maintaining the established group norm. On the other hand, subjects who begin this experience alone, establishing their own personal norm, show convergence once placed in a group. However, as Sherif comments, convergence in the latter case is not as substantial as among those who first begin in the group situation. Thus, establishing one's own norm can serve as an insulation against total convergence in the future to the position of the group.

Social influence, in this case, does not involve any direct or intentional effort on the part of a majority to change the behavior of a minority; rather, the sheer ambiguity of the situation leads people to seek social information that will help them anchor what would otherwise be a chaotic experience. Once that anchor is found, others brought into the situation quickly learn to adopt its persuasive hold. Unlike the Asch trials, which produced compliance rather than conversion, Sherif's experiment involves an actual change in the subjects' perception of the light movement, resulting in conversion rather than compliance.

Sherif also presents interview data showing that "the majority of subjects reported not only that their minds were made up . . . before the others spoke, but that they were not influenced by the others in the group" (1958, p. 228). Since we know that they were actually influenced to converge with the others, it appears that the change represents a perceptual shift, even if they publicly disclaim being influenced at all. This could be seen as a form of anticompliance—private change without public change.

Another fascinating use of the Sherif model of social influence was reported by Jacobs and Campbell (1961). They created an influence setting in which subjects reported the light's movement in groups of 30 trials called "generations." In the first generation, Jacobs and Campbell used three accomplices and one naive subject. The accomplices were instructed to report a movement of some 16 inches, thereby establishing a generational norm that influenced the naive subject by the end of that generation's life (by the 30th trial). In the second generation, one of the accomplices was replaced with a new naive subject. Thus, generation 2 consisted of two naive subjects (one from generation 1 and a new one) and two accomplices. They too went through 30 trials, the accomplices continuing to claim 16 inches movement with the support of the original naive subject who had previously accepted this norm. Convergence was again found on the part of the new naive subject, so that by the end of generation 2 everyone agreed to the same perceptual norm.

In generation 3 the same procedure was employed: one accomplice was replaced, leaving only one behind. Generation 3 thus consisted of the one remaining accomplice, a generation 1 and a generation 2 naive subject, and one new subject. Again, convergence on the common norm was found. By the time of generation 4 there were no accomplices, only "naive subjects": one from generation 1, one from generation 2, one from generation 3, and the new subject.

If this same procedure is continued, each generation replacing the oldest member with a newcomer, by about generation 7 none of the original subjects is left. Yet, there is still convergence on the original norm. With this procedure, Jaccobs and Campbell have demonstrated experimentally what most of us learn socially: the lessons of past generations shape our current understandings and behaviors.

. . . .

The Schachter Approach to Studying Majority Influence

Whereas both Asch and Sherif employed perceptual judgments as the basis for their research on social influence and conformity, Schachter's (1951) research employed group discussions and decision-making tasks. Schachter convened groups of 8 to 10 people in "clubs" that were to meet and discuss various topics: a case-study club, a movie club, an editorial club, and a radio club. Unknown to the naive subjects, each group contained three paid accomplices instructed to take on a particular role within the ensuing discussion.

The case-study club, for example, was presented with the case of a juvenile delinquent, Johnny Rocco; they were to spend some time together discussing it and eventually make a recommendation about Johnny's disposition. In making their recommendation, they were to use a 7-point rating scale (the love–punishment scale): position 1 argued for a "loving" treatment for Johnny, while 7 urged "punishment." Schachter knew that his subjects would be likely to select a position on the lower, or "loving," end of the scale, and so he could instruct his accomplices to take on various positions and see how the group handled them.

He defined three distinct roles for the accomplices: (1) the *deviate* was instructed to argue for position 7 throughout the entire discussion, regardless of what happened; (2) the *slider* was to begin with position 7, but halfway through the discussion to "slide in" toward the majority position of the group; and (3) the *mode* was instructed to hold the group's normative position throughout the discussion.

Schachter observed the patterns of communication within the groups and, at the end, how they dealt with the deviating member. He found that there was a great deal of communication with the deviate and the slider to persuade them to change their ways of thinking about Johnny, but very little communication with the already right-thinking mode. Once it became clear that the deviate was not about to change, however, communication dramatically decreased; once the slider adopted the group's own position, the need to communicate with him was also reduced.

At the conclusion of the discussion, Schachter indicated that the groups were simply too large for their next discussion and that he wished to be guided by their desires in deciding whom not to include. As expected, the recalcitrant deviate was rejected from future discussions. We will consider this rejection of the deviate again in Chapter 9, when we examine the minority influence model; there we see that, rather than influencing the majority, the deviant minority might at any time simply be ignored or rejected as in the Schachter study.

Schachter provides two additional features of interest for us to consider. He was able to vary both the cohesiveness of the groups and the relevance of the discussion task for the groups' original purposes in being convened. *Cohesiveness* refers to the degree to which a group of people have high morale and feel good about being together as a group. Schachter created two degrees of cohesiveness—high and low. *Relevance* was varied simply by having those groups who had been convened to discuss radio, for example, first deal with the Johnny Rocco case (low relevance); groups convened to deal with case studies would consider the Rocco case to be of high relevance to their purposes.

Schachter's findings indicate that the pressures on the deviate are greatest and the chances of rejection highest when both cohesiveness and relevance are high. In other words, when the majority has a strong sense of togetherness and is involved in discussing and deciding about something of particular relevance to their group, they are much less tolerant of people holding minority opinions than when cohesiveness and relevance are low.

Of course, in the Schachter study the deviate is a paid accomplice, shielded from the pressures at least to a certain extent by the role he has been paid to portray. But the Schachter data indicate the intense pressures that deviates in real life must face as they are hammered everyday by the influence-oriented communication of the majority and, if they are not converted, face social ostracism.

The Milgram Study of Obedience

Even if they are not familiar with his name, many people are generally familiar with the study Milgram conducted in 1965. A disturbing television movie about this study captured the imagination of the American public because the research suggested that people will agree to harm another person for no other apparent reason than the request of a scientific investigator. The findings brought forth images of obedient German citizens committing horrible crimes against other human beings under the Nazi regime. Although there are some important differences between the Milgram approach to the study of obedience and the approaches of Asch, Sherif, and Schachter, we will first examine some of the details of his study before examining these differences and the issues they raise.

The basic design of Milgram's research was to have two subjects, one of whom was an accomplice of the experimenter, placed into a situation in which one (the naive subject) was supposed to be the teacher who uses punishment to motivate the learning performance of the student (the accomplice). The student was presented with a learning task; every time the student made an error on this task, the teacher was to administer punishment. In this instance, the punishment consisted of increasingly high voltages of electric shock. The student was attached to an apparatus that delivered the shocks. The device consisted of a series of levers, each one providing increasingly strong levels of voltage. For example, the lowest, marked "Slight Shock," began with 15 volts and moved to 450 volts, marked only "XXX" on the apparatus. Each error made by the student warranted increasing the voltage by one step. The teacher's task was to listen to the student's learning performance and, every time an error was made, motivate improved performance by increasing the shock by one step, up to 450 volts if necessary.

Unknown to the teachers, of course, the student was an accomplice and never received any actual shock; furthermore, the accomplice was instructed not only to make errors (on cue), but also to make loud protestations (again on cue) when receiving the "shock." Initially, the protest was simply a grunt or verbal protest of pain when receiving the shocks; as the experiment progressed, however, the student complained more seriously about the pain, especially about the possible effect of the shocks on his or her heart. Finally, somewhere around the 300-volt level, the student was no longer heard. On inquiring what to do about their nonresponse, the teachers were told to count silence as an error and continue increasing the shock levels!

Milgram's findings were disturbing, even to Milgram. In his own language, "With numbing regularity good people were seen to knuckle under the demands of authority and perform actions that were callous and severe" (1965a, p. 74). He reports approximately 62% of the subjects studied obeyed the experimenter's requests and went all the way to the final 450-volt shock level. Furthermore, these were not abnormal, disturbed, or particularly vicious people; under the conditions created in his laboratory, most people would have, as he says, "knuckled under."

Milgram tried several variations to see if he could reduce this very high number of obedient subjects. For example, would varying the immediacy of the student victim make a difference? He found that as the student was more physically remote from the teacher, obedience increased. As the teacher and student were brought closer together until the teacher actually had to hold the student's hand on the apparatus in order to deliver the shock, obedience decreased. Yet, even here, 30% were obedient all the way to 450 volts.

Milgram reasoned that perhaps the closeness of the authority would make a difference in the levels of obedience he had originally found. For example, would an experimenter who could directly view the subject's behavior produce more obedience than an experimenter increasingly removed from a position of direct supervision? Milgram reports a sharp drop in the levels of obedience as the experimenter became increasingly removed from having direct surveillance over the subject's behavior. An experimenter in face-to-face proximity produced nearly three times as much obedience as one who was distant. In fact, with the experimenter removed from the scene, several subjects "cheated"; that is, without experimenter surveillance, they administered shocks that were at a lower level than they were required to provide, and never told the experimenter of this deviation from approved procedure. This seems to illustrate the strong degree of compliance that existed in the original study and the degree to which subjects privately did not agree with what they were told to do. Yet, as we can see clearly in this context, despite their private reservations, they still performed just as expected by the experimenter when under surveillance. Some solace for the student-learner that the subjects harming him did not really want to do so, but were simply following orders!

Seeking still other ways to reduce the 62% level of obedience, Milgram introduced a group-pressure condition. For example, the naive subject was to co-teach with two others, both of whom were accomplices. At designated points in the study, one by one the co-teachers dropped out. And at each point, the experimenter appealed to the remaining teachers to continue with the research. Obedience under these conditions decreased to only about 10%.

Recall that in the Asch situation, the presence of only one ally helped empower the naive subject to defy the authority of majority-group pressure; in the Milgram study, although the context was different, allies who defied the experimenter's authority once again helped empower subjects to do likewise. Milgram viewed these allies as models for defiant behavior, whereas Asch considered allies as simply confirming the subjects' own versions of reality. It is possible, of course, that allies serve a variety of functions, including those proposed by both Asch and Milgram.

In a variation of the group-pressure situation, co-teachers complied with the experimenter, producing a 72% obedience rate, not much greater than the 62% obtained without additional help from allies. In other words, the potency of the experimenter's authority was sufficient in itself to influence the subject, and did not require any additional help from compliant accomplices.

In another variation of this design, Milgram moved his research from Yale University to downtown Bridgeport, Connecticut. He reasoned that the authority associated with a prestigious institution like Yale would be lessened in Bridgeport, resulting in a lower degree of obedience. Results indicated a general confirmation of this expectation, with rates dropping in Bridgeport to about 48%, rather than the 62% found in Yale.

Milgram's approach to the study of social influence differs in certain respects from the majority-influence models of Asch, Sherif, and Schachter. Milgram's research does not provide us with a majority seeking to gain the conformity over a minority of one. Yet, Milgram's research clearly falls within the conformity framework as it rather convincingly demonstrates the potency of legitimate authority in gaining conformity. Although the authority in the Milgram case is only one other person, the scientific investigator, rather than a group of peers, the subject nevertheless confronts a dilemma of choice—to conform or deviate—that may be even more severe than in the previous cases.

Although the scientific investigator is only one human being, he or she represents an entire social institution. The scientist in Milgram's study did not bully or threaten his subjects, but simply requested that they carry out their obligations to be a good scientific subject. When a subject faltered and became unsure of whether or not to continue, the scientist simply reminded him that he must continue. It was unnecessary for the scientist to say any more.

It is clear that this potent influence was not a function of the character of the individual scientist—his intelligence, attractiveness, skill, ability to persuade, and so on—but rather his representing an entire institution of science. That institution is what was present in the room; *science* was the majority that Milgram's minority of one faced. Although the majority in this case was not physically present, like a group of one's peers, the abstract force of scientific expertise and legitimacy became even more potent. It is one thing to look foolish in the eyes of one's peers by claiming to see something differently than they do; it is entirely different to defy the scientific establishment for some ambiguous reason.

In short, although Milgram's work does not appear within the usual majority-influence paradigm, there are parallels as well as differences with the basic model. In Milgram's study an abstract authority is legitimized by representing a potent kind of institutionalized majority interest—science itself. When complying can mean doing harm to another, the costs of compliance are substantial; under Milgram's conditions, publicly complying while feeling privately virtuous takes on a different meaning. To defy the authority of legitimate and respected social institutions—science, education, government—may place the deviant individual at risk, well beyond anything typically considered in the social influence–conformity model. Milgram's work gives us some perspective on the stakes involved for a minority in confronting the majority.

9

Innovation and the Minority-Influence Model

I N CHAPTER 7 WE saw that, until recently, the study of social influence focused on how the majority produces conformity in a minority. Since 1969, however, the focus on social influence has shifted perceptibly from a majority- to a minority-influence model. In this view, social influence is more than the majority's efforts to produce conformity on the part of a minority; it is also a minority's effort to convert the majority to its own way of thinking. In terms of minority influence, innovation and social change, not conformity, is the potential outcome.

This change in understanding began with the 1969 publication in an American journal of the work of a group of French social psychologists led by Serge Moscovici (Moscovici, Lage, & Naffrechoux, 1969). Moscovici and his colleagues initially wanted to know how a minority, generally lacking the kinds of power majorities possess, might nevertheless influence the majority's point of view. That is, how does a minority challenge the majority rather than always yield to the demands of the majority?

Consider how majorities and minorities differ in their respective degrees of potential influence. Moscovici and his colleagues contrasted two sources of power available to any influence agent: *dependency* and *behavioral style*. For the most part, the source of influence available to the majority are those resources they control on which a minority depends. For example, the majority can use its standing to humiliate or even expel a minority (see Mugny, 1984). Recall that in one variation of Asch's study on conformity, a deviating minority of one faced a majority of 16 people, all of whom ridiculed his failure to report the line lengths as they did. Recall also the deviate in Schachter's study who was finally rejected from the group by the majority for not adopting their views.

In contrast, it is difficult to think of a minority having comparable resources that would make the majority dependent on them. Thus, Moscovici and his associates turned to an alternative source of minority influence, what they termed *behavioral style*. One of the major sources of minority power is its ability to create uncertainty and conflict among the majority. A minority that firmly backs its position always poses a serious problem for the majority. It creates a sense of uncertainty among the majority about their own position, and conflict over how to restore the harmony upset by the minority's presence.

Behavioral style refers to the way a minority presents itself. Mugny (1984; see also Maass & Clark, 1984) has distinguished between behavioral style and *negotiating style*. Behavioral style refers to the degree of *consistency* with which a minority presents its position, while negotiating style involves the degree of *flexibility* or *rigidity* it adopts in negotiating a compromise with the majority.

According to Mugny, "It is essentially through its consistency that a minority acquires its capacity to generate a social conflict which becomes unmanageable for the system as long as the consistent minority refuses to negotiate or to compromise . . . the minority causes the system to lose its equilibrium and stresses its fallability" (p. 504). The central idea in the minority-influence model is that a consistent minority will have an influential impact on a majority, setting the terms for an innovative rather than conforming resolution. Unlike conformity, which suggests a movement of a minority to the position advocated by the majority, innovation suggests a movement on the part of *both* minority and majority. The outcome of this influence process is therefore referred to as innovative because it reflects a compromise.

Although they faced many real-life opportunities to examine how minorities evoke innovation rather than yield to majority influence, Moscovici and his associates chose the experimental laboratory to test most of their ideas. There is nothing more convincing to the majority of social psychologists than empirical laboratory research clearly demonstrating an effect predicted by theory. Indeed, it is likely that by virtue of their extensive program of experimental studies Moscovici and his primarily European associates were able to turn the field around in the United States, so much so that by 1985 Moscovici himself authored the chapter on social influence in the third edition of the prestigious *Handbook of Social Psychology* (Lindzey & Aronson, 1985).

In their pioneering research effort, Moscovici, Lage, and Naffrechoux (1969) brought groups of six subjects together, four of whom were naive and two of whom were carefully trained accomplices of the experimenters. Their initial decision to have two minority-group members rather than one was based on speculation that the majority could more easily dismiss the consistent deviation of one person as due to some defect in the individual. This attribution is more difficult to make, however, when the majority consists of at least two people. Later research confirmed the wisdom of this move, as minorities of one were found to be less effective than minorities containing at least two people (see Maass & Clark, 1984, for a summary).

All six subjects were seated in front of a screen on which slides were to be projected. They were informed that this was a study of color perception; their task was to judge the color and intensity of each slide and to announce their judgment. Colors were to be named in simple terms—for example, blue or green—while intensities were to be named according to a scale from 0, representing the dimmest intensity to 5, the brightest.

In order to both eliminate subjects who had difficulties with color perception and reduce the likelihood that the naive subjects would attribute any "deviations" on the part of the minority to their poor visual ability, all subjects were given a color test. The test was scored and all subjects informed "that everyone in the group had normal vision" (p. 369).

Several design variations were employed in the study, but mostly the four naive subjects confronted a unanimous minority of two persons (unknown to them to be confederates of the experimenters) who consistently saw "green" when it was obvious that the slides were "blue." Would a unanimous and consistent minority influence the majority's own perceptions?

A minority-influence effect would appear if, under the conditions of confronting a consistent minority saying "green," the naive majority shifted their own judgments towards "green." Results supported this expectation. Comparisons between control groups (groups without minority influence attempted) and these experimental groups revealed a significant tendency of the latter to show increased use of "green" in response to the "blue" slides.

Moscovici and his associates next asked themselves whether the minority-influence effect was merely a verbal response—that is, what the subjects publicly reported—or went somewhat deeper. In order to test this possibility, they created another kind of experimental variation of the same basic design. In this case, subjects were examined for their actual blue and green thresholds. Somewhat surprisingly, the investigators found an even *greater* tendency to *perceive* green than to report green verbally. In their words, "We can conclude that the consistent minority has an even greater influence on the perceptive code of the subjects than on their verbal response to the slides" (p. 373).

This finding appears to be an instance of anticompliance—private, but not public, change toward the position of the influence agent. From the minority's perspective, however, the change is akin to conversion: disregarding what the majority says publicly, a minority has converted at least some of the majority to its point of view. It is as though subjects in the majority were publicly reluctant to violate their allegiance to the group, but in private, possibly even unknown to themselves, their perceptual thresholds had been influenced by the minority responding "green" to actually "blue" slides. Moscovici boldly suggested that perhaps majority influence produces compliance while minority influence produces conversion.

Notice what is meant by conversion in this case. When we think of conversion in the majority model, we usually think of the influence agent's producing both a public and private change; in Moscovici's usage, however, conversion occurs when the majority yields privately rather than publicly to the position advocated by a minority. This may be a kind of face-saving device on the part of the majority or, as Moscovici also suggests, may represent the more typical case: "Great innovators have succeeded in imposing their ideas, their discoveries, without necessarily receiving direct recognition for their influence" (p. 379).

The implication of this interpretation is that the minority's challenge causes the majority to reconsider its own positions when they take the minority's arguments seriously. The result of this self-questioning might be a change towards the position advocated by the minority without any real recognition that such a change has occurred or even that it reflects a concession to the opposing point of view.

Their thoughtful review of some 15 years of research using the minority-influence model has led Maass and Clark (1984) to conclude that Moscovici's initially bold statement based on the 1969 study has generally been substantiated in other studies involving a variety of different tasks and situations. In other words, the majority evokes public compliance without significant private acceptance from a minority, while a minority evokes private acceptance without public recognition from the majority.

Why might private, but not public, change occur? Is something more than face-saving involved? Maass and Clark suggest that private change seems to accompany a high degree of cognitive activity (for example, generating arguments and rebuttals). They suggest some reasons why a minority might motivate such a high level of cognitive activity.

For example, because a minority so actively resists the majority pressure to conform, the minority point of view might warrant more serious consideration: anyone who is that dedicated must have something to offer. Another possibility involves the consequences of accepting the minority position. As Maass and Clark note, "a person may think twice before accepting a minority opinion" (p. 446), given the implications of taking their side. While these explanations are speculative and lack systematic examination, they do offer a way to understand how minorities might motivate increased cognitive activity that could produce significant private change, even without corresponding public recognition.

Consistency and Minority Influence

Many other efforts have been made to find out more about what consistency is and how it operates in the minority-influence paradigm. Nemeth and Wachtler (1974), for example, found that where an individual *chooses* to sit in a group discussion, plus the consistency of his or her point of view, can have a significant effect on the majority. When the experimenter's accomplice (who was the minority in a group discussion situation), chose to sit at the head of the table, his influence on the majority increased. Choosing to sit at the head of the table led subjects to rate the confederate as more confident in his attitude than when he was assigned to occupy the same position.

Nemeth and Wachtler also report that the confederate who adopted the minority position was usually seen "as more consistent, independent, active, central, strong-willed, more of a leader and more confident . . . than were the naive subjects. Subjects also said that he made them think more . . . and made them reassess their own positions more . . . than did the other subjects" (p. 537) in their group. Nemeth and her colleague concluded that a minority who freely chooses his seat and argues consistently has a greater ability to influence the majority to seriously consider or adopt his point of view.

In another study examining the meaning and impact of consistency, Nemeth, Swedlund, and Kanki (1974) suggest that literal consistency seems to be less important than the *perception* that the minority's position is held consistently and that it offers a viable alternative to the majority's own point of view. This study replicated much of the original research by Moscovici and his associates (1969), employing color slides but with some modifications. In one experimental group, the accomplices patterned their naming of the color to correspond systematically with the intensity of the slide; for example, the brightest slide was always said to be green while the dimmest slide was said to be green-blue. In another experimental group, the brightest slide was said to be green; sometimes, however, the dimmest was said to be green. Data indicated that the minority was not effective when they were simply consistent in naming green, but only when this consistency correlated with some visible feature of the slides (for example, their brightness). It seems that following a pattern of this sort increased the viability of the minority alternative in the eyes of the majority.

Is Consistency Always Necessary?

Although his ideas did not develop within the European tradition, Hollander's (1958, 1964) work builds on a notion that is opposed to consistency. Hollander introduced the concept of *idiosyncrasy credit:* people who initially conform to a group build up credits upon which they can later draw so that when they deviate from the group they can do so with relative impunity. He suggested that this approach offers a technique leaders can use to influence a group: first gain acceptance by conforming, then move the group towards their point of view.

This approach seems to contrast with Moscovici's emphasis on minority consistency in behavioral style. In order to build up Hollander's credits, the individual must behave inconsistently, first conforming and then deviating. Bray, Johnson, and Chilstrom (1982) tested to see whether Moscovici's consistency or Hollander's programmed inconsistency was more effective in changing the majority's viewpoints. In terms of which theory was more accurate, the research findings were somewhat equivocal; they were not at all equivocal, however, with regard to minority influence. The data rather clearly demonstrated that under both Hollander's conditions of inconsistency (conform first and then deviate) and Moscovici's conditions of consistency (deviate all the time), there was a significant impact of the minority on the majority when compared with a control group in which no influence was attempted.

. . . .

Other Factors in the Minority-Influence Model

During the last several years, research on the minority-influence paradigm has focused on aspects other than consistency: (a) attraction; (b) rigidity; (c) zeitgeist effects; and (d) double minorities.

Attraction

One issue raised by the minority perspective involves a time-honored piece of advice: "You can catch more flies with honey than vinegar," meaning that people are more likely to be influential if they are liked. A more familiar expression of this axiom is, "One first wins friends—then influences people" (Nemeth & Wachtler, 1974, p. 539). According to the minority paradigm, however, the majority has no love for a minority; indeed, it may actively dislike them. According to Nemeth and Wachtler:

> **Our confederate was never liked. He was considered unreasonable, unfair . . . unliked, unwanted. . . . While not liked . . . He had stability and he had strength. We suggest that it is this stability and confidence that rendered him effective, not whether he was liked or disliked** (p. 540).

It would seem, then, that we need to develop a new set of homilies, perhaps something about catching flies with vinegar rather than honey.

Remember that the "task" of a minority is to create conflict, thereby forcing the majority to contend with them in one way or another. While this obstinacy is unlikely to endear a minority to the majority, minorities still seem to have considerable influence over the majority. Needless to say, there are situations, as Schachter's study demonstrated (see pp. 145–46), in which the majority not only dislikes a minority but may ostracize or expel it.

Rigidity

If it is true that a minority that holds firmly to its position will not be liked but will be influential, what are the limits to the majority's tolerance of a minority? As we noted earlier, Mugny (1984; see also Maass & Clark, 1984) argues that while consistency describes the behavioral style of a minority, its degree of rigidity determines its negotiating potential. It is his view, supported by several empirical investigations, that a rigid style leads to attributions of dogmatism, thereby reducing the potency of a minority to influence the majority. On the other hand, a flexible style of negotiation is more likely to get the results desired by a minority.

Picture this situation from the majority's perspective. When a minority is intractable, refusing to cooperate or soften its position, the majority is inclined to use its power to get rid of the troublesome deviants rather than carry on pointless negotiations. Something like this may very well have occurred in Schachter's study. The deviate (an accomplice of the experimenter's) was instructed to adopt the most extreme position and *never* waiver from it. After trying to influence the deviate, the majority finally gave up and, when given the chance, expelled him from their group. If Mugny is correct, and the deviate had shown some signs of willingness to reach a compromise with the majority, he probably would have been retained by the group and possibly even achieved a substantial degree of influence.

Mugny's research indicates that excessive rigidity communicates an unwillingness to make any concessions whatsoever, thereby eliminating any hope of ever reaching some kind of compromise. Rigid consistency is seen to be a sign of dogmatism; the minority loses the impact they would otherwise have had. In contrast, a more flexible consistency leaves open the possibility of a settlement with the majority and may even stimulate a more serious examination of the minority's position.

Furthermore, as Mugny notes, excessive rigidity on the part of a minority invites the majority to search for some inherent defect as a rationale to discount what might otherwise be an influential position. If it is possible to define the minority as "crazy" or "out of touch," there is little reason to listen to them, and every reason to try to exercise firm social control to silence them.

Zeitgeist Effects

The German word *zeitgeist* refers to the "spirit of the times," the general cultural or intellectual climate of a given period in history. For example, in the current zeitgeist of the United States, the civil rights of many once disenfranchised groups—blacks, women, and so on—are actively supported. Thus, to oppose a woman's right to equal education, for example, would be to oppose the cultural spirit or zeitgeist of our time. Several investigations (for example, Paicheler, 1976, 1977; see also Maass & Clark, 1984, and Mugny, 1984 for an overview) have demonstrated that a minority is more likely to influence the majority if it upholds a position consistent with the zeitgeist (for example, favoring a woman's right to an equal education).

Another experiment by Moscovici and Lage (1978) created two different normative contexts within groups, one emphasizing objectivity, the other creativity. They found that conditions of creativity facilitated serious consideration of the minority point of view by the majority; when objectivity was stressed, however, the majority tended to disregard the minority and remain relatively immune to their influence.

Double Minorities

Several investigations within the minority-influence model compare the effects of single and double minorities on the majority. A *single minority* is made up of those people who adopt an opinion or perceptual judgment different from that of the majority but are otherwise similar to them. A *double minority* refers to a minority distinguished from the majority by at least two factors—for example, the minority's race *and* opinion (see Maass & Clark, 1984).

Many studies (see Maass & Clark for a summary) have found that double minorities were *less* influential than single minorities, in part because the majority considered the minority's position as primarily self-serving. For example, a gay minority arguing for gay rights in a group of otherwise nongay subjects was less influential than a nongay minority arguing for gay rights. It was easier for the nongay majority to dismiss the gay minority as self-serving than it was for them to dismiss the nongay minority advocating gay rights.

The Continuing Debate Over Minority Influence

Because passionate debate is part of the nature of science, it should not be surprising to find continuing controversy over the many theories dealing with minority-influence effects. We will examine three different theoretical approaches to these effects: (1) attributional accounts; (2) Latané's social-impact model; and (3) Tanford and Penrod's social-influence model.

Attributional Accounts

Perhaps the most straightforward account of minority-influence effects has called upon a version of the attribution model we first considered in Part Two (see Chapters 4 and 5). In this view, a consistent minority forces the majority to make certain attributions that mediate their influence. As we saw in the Nemeth and Wachtler (1974) study, for example, when the minority accomplice chose to sit at the head of the table in a group discussion, other subjects attributed greater confidence to him, and so listened more attentively to his opinions, than when he was assigned to that same position.

It is likewise assumed that consistency is effective because it generates attributions of confidence and competence. By virtue of his or her social status, a minority must walk a tightrope between being seen as confident (which could gain the sympathy of the majority) or being seen as dogmatic and eccentric (which will surely lose the sympathy of the majority). These different attributions thus have major consequences for the minority's effectiveness. An effective minority strives to elicit helpful personal attributions, like confidence and competence, to raise its credibility. If the majority considers the minority point of view a function of the situation—for example, different perceptual judgments are based on the majority and minority's respective seating positions—the minority's effectiveness is correspondingly reduced. The same is true if the majority sees the minority position as dogmatic or eccentric.

Latané's Theory of Social Impact

Latané, as well as Tanford and Penrod, sought to integrate both the majority- and minority-influence models by developing a formal, quantitative theory of social influence. Latané's theory is one of social *impact,* while Tanford and Penrod refer to theirs as one of social *influence.*

According to Latané (1981; Latané and Wolf, 1981), a social impact refers to any effect other people have on a target individual. Latané first introduces a Principle of Social Forces. He argues that social impact is a multiplicative function of three factors: (1) S, the strength of the agent (the agent's status, power, and so on); (2) I, the agent's immediacy (the proximity of the agent to the target, whether the agent is close or distant in time and space); and (3) N, the number of agents involved (how many people are trying to influence the target).

Latané also introduced a second principle, the Psychosocial Law. Basing his reasoning on the old economic adage that the first dollar is worth more than the hundredth, he suggested that "the first other person in a social force field should have greater impact than the hundredth" (p. 344). How well do these two principles account for both majority and minority influence?

Latané considers his model reasonably workable. According to his critics, like Tanford and Penrod and Maass and Clark, it is interesting but unable to account for many effects found in both paradigms. For example, Tanford and Penrod observe, as even Latané acknowledges, that in the Asch majority-influence situation, the presence of one or two agents had little impact but three produced the maximum impact. This would not seem to work well in terms of Latané's second principle, in which the first agent should be the most influential.

As Maass and Clark point out, Latané's model also has difficulty in minority-influence situations. Indeed, if the model were adopted literally, only majorities should be influential. By definition, the majority has a greater number of influence agents (the N-factor); when this number is entered into the equation, it should produce a greater social impact for the majority. Yet, as we have seen, research consistently reveals a real minority-influence effect, difficult to account for in terms of Latané's integrative theory of social impact.

Tanford and Penrod's SIM Model

To provide an integrative theory of social influence free of the kind of problems associated with Latané's approach, Tanford and Penrod (1984) proposed their SIM, or Social Influence Model. It is more formal than Latané's, and is based on certain features presumed to exist in any majority- or minority-influence situation—group size; number of influence sources; probabilities that a majority member will choose the minority position without any influence attempted by the minority; individual differences in members' susceptibility to persuasion; and so on.

Tanford and Penrod initially tested their model by computer simulation, and later applied it to reexamine many of the classic majority- and minority-influence studies. They report impressive success with their model, and are led to conclude that "both empirical and computer simulation results support the hypothesis that majority and minority influence are part of a single process" (p. 221). They admit, however, that their model does not take into consideration any of the so-called psychological mediators that might be involved. For example, they conclude that minority influence is greatest in small groups with a minority of two, and smallest in large groups with a small minority. The mysterious psychological mechanisms by which this effect operates, however, are not addressed by their theory.

The ability of the SIM model to account for a substantial number of research findings on majority and minority influence is impressive. On the other hand, Tanford and Penrod's approach, as well as that of Latané, lead to conclusions opposed to Moscovici's own views. Both of these approaches sought to develop a formal model that would integrate the majority- and minority-influence perspectives in one scheme; indeed, for Latané it would include all kinds of "social impact." After reviewing their model's ability to account for much of the research literature, Tanford and Penrod concluded that "majority and minority influence are part of a single process" (p. 221). Not so, claims Moscovici, citing the differences he finds in the outcomes of each model: compliance in the case of majority influence, conversion in the case of minority influence.

From Moscovici's perspective, formal, quantitative analyses that fail to consider the *qualitative* differences between these two modalities of influence are inevitably incomplete. As we have seen, he is especially intrigued by the possibility that the nature of the change produced under majority influence is public but not private, whereas the nature of the change produced under minority influence is private, but not public. In his view, this difference must involve qualitatively different intervening psychological and social processes; it demands two distinct bodies of theory, not one. And so the debate continues. Perhaps, like the debates between the conventional and the socio-historical frameworks, this one will also not be resolved by mere empirical findings.

· · · · · · · · · · · · · · · ·

Conclusions

In this chapter we have examined recent alternative approaches to social influence proposed by Moscovici and others on the influence of minorities on majorities. Moscovici's concern is with innovation and social change rather than conformity and social control, the focus of majority-influence models that until recently dominated social psychological inquiry.

Because minorities do not have the same kinds of resources as majorities, the search for the mechanisms of minority influence turned towards behavioral and negotiating styles. We saw that consistency and flexibility on the part of a minority presenting its point of view emerged as central to most analyses.

We concluded the chapter by reviewing efforts to integrate the minority and majority paradigms in terms of a formal, quantitative theory, and considered Moscovici's continuing doubt about the feasibility of such an integration given his view that two different processes are involved; that is, that majority influence produces only public change while minority influence is private and more enduring.

Just how good is the minority model? We saw earlier that social psychologists primarily rely on laboratory methods to establish credibility. Now that the model seems reasonably well established, however, it is time, even as supporters of the model have suggested (for example, Maass & Clark, 1984), to see how it functions in real-life situations. The difficulty with typical laboratory research is that the groups involved are rarely real groups with a past tradition, ongoing structure, or any future anticipation of continuing to work together. How will minority influence operate under these more realistic conditions?

Although we have been using the words *minority* and *majority*, we have been ignoring real differences in power and status that go along with membership in those respective groups. As numerous historical examples suggest, especially among totalitarian regimes, the majority has the power to oppress or even exterminate minorities. We cheered on the students occupying Beijing's Tiananmen Square and then, with horror, witnessed the brutal crackdown of the demonstration by troops and tanks. Quick trials and executions for many of the dissidents soon followed.

The struggles of minorities for equality in the United States also reveal a harsh and often violent history; consistency alone did not win over the majority. On the other hand, in late 1989 the world witnessed several major populist uprisings in Europe that challenged entrenched governmental institutions. The changes initiated were not accomplished on the basis either of a consistency in argumentation or a simple flexibility in negotiating style. Massive protests in the streets combined with a changed global political situation started the process of democratization.

An awareness of the harsh realities of life does not mean that we should now reject the minority-influence model; rather, we need to see the broader social contexts within which minorities are able to wield influence and the conditions under which they are ruthlessly put down or even benignly pacified. We will examine this issue in more detail in Chapter 11.

10

Attitudes, Persuasion, and Change

ARDLY A DAY goes by without the media reporting the results of some recent survey of public opinion on a controversial issue—a political race, a product, a health practice, and so on. Although most of us are so accustomed to these polls that we rarely give them a second thought, a close examination of how we measure public attitudes would lead to some rather intriguing realizations.

We would see that when interviewing someone, the pollster is trying to reveal something that can only be inferred from the person's behavior, but not be directly apprehended. That is, we do not "see" attitudes and opinions; we can only learn about them by listening to what people tell us. We would also realize that to be asked for our opinion on some issue is not a puzzling request. In fact, we find it natural to discuss our attitudes with others; it is part of our common sense understanding of people and how they function.

Of course, we happen to live in a culture in which the assessment of attitudes in public-opinion polling or focused group discussions is routine. In fact, literally billions of dollars are spent annually simply to influence our attitudes and the behaviors they presumably produce—voting, purchasing, and so on. McGuire (1985) has estimated, for example, that about $50 billion is expended each year in the United States on advertising alone. The goal of these ads is to induce attitudes in us about products that persist with us until we enter the store and make our purchases. Cacioppo, Petty, and Morris (1983) refer to a *Newsweek* article by columnist George Will, who notes that on an average day each of us is bombarded with approximately 1,500 persuasive messages from national advertisers alone, designed to influence our attitudes about various products. To these, he could have added public service announcements to get us to improve our health and well-being and a variety of political announcements designed to win our loyalties to one or another cause or candidate. In other words, attitudes are big business!

The concept of attitude—its measurement, understanding its internal structure and processes, and examining its relation to our overt behavior—has always been central to social psychology. Although the focus has shifted over the years, McGuire has observed that each year about 5% of the *total* literature published in psychology—5% amounts to about 1,000 new studies annually—deals with some aspect of human attitudes. This is an impressive body of new material which, accumulated over time, represents an extraordinary investment of professional time, energy, ingenuity, and expense.

Our current commonsense understanding of attitude and its dominant place in our culture, however, is a relatively recent phenomenon. It is especially interesting, as Billig (1987) notes, that the meaning of attitude has shifted since the middle of the seventeenth century from a technical reference in painting and sculpture referring to the posture of the body to the "posture" of the mind. Use of the terms "stance" and "position" reflect this semantic transformation, as in "What is her stance on abortion?" or "What position does he take on Gorbachev's reforms?" In Chapter 11, we will explore this change in detail.

For now, however, it is only important to recall the two scientific perspectives we introduced in Part One. The conventional approach views attitudes in the following way: (a) attitudes are something located within each of our minds; (b) they have specific properties that can be discovered and described; (c) although not seen directly, they are inferred from what we can see, namely people's behavioral expressions; and (d) attitudes are related to our behavior. In contrast, in the sociohistorical view attitudes are historically rooted cultural inventions. They do not have a reality in the mind independent of the society that proposes them for its own particular purposes. As we would expect, most of the research social psychologists have conducted on attitudes derives from a conventionalist point of view; only recently and even then with some hesitation, have sociohistorical analyses begun to emerge (for example, Billig, 1987; Gergen, 1982, 1987).

Because the vast majority of work has been guided by the conventional model, we will provisionally adopt that approach in this discussion, as we have done previously, to familiarize ourselves with the current understanding of attitudes and their relationship to those social-influence processes we have been considering in Part Three. Of course, we will also continue to balance our analysis with sociohistorically advised commentary.

In this chapter we will explore three major topics: (1) the definition, properties, and functions of attitudes; (2) the relationship between attitudes and behavior; and (3) persuasion and attitude change.

The Definition, Properties, and Functions of Attitudes

While many different definitions of attitude have been proposed—some estimates put the number at 500 (McGuire, 1985)—there seems to be general agreement on two points. First, an attitude is a mediational concept; second, an attitude must involve "responses that locate 'objects of thought' on 'dimensions of judgment' " (McGuire, 1985, p. 239).

To call an attitude "mediational" is simply to suggest that it represents something inside the head of the individual that mediates between outside stimuli and the consequent responses that the individual makes. Attitudes, then, are only one of several mediational concepts found in social psychology, joining the cognitive mediators we considered in Part Two.

To define an attitude as an evaluative judgment about an object of thought is to say that when we talk about people's attitudes, we mean that they have a positive or negative evaluation of some object, issue, or person. So when we read the results of an opinion poll telling us that over 70% of those surveyed believe a woman has a right to terminate a pregnancy without governmental restrictions, we assume that we are dealing with people's positive evaluations of the abortion issue.

This definition of attitude is founded on a central western cultural belief that all human experience is divided into three components: (1) knowing, or the cognitive component; (2) feeling, or the affective/evaluative component; and (3) doing, or the conative/behavioral component (for example, see McGuire, 1985; Rosenberg & Hovland, 1960). The cognitive component represents knowledge of the issue—for example, abortion—about which a judgment is to be made. The affective component represents the positive or negative evaluation made of the issue; for example, we noted that over 70% of those surveyed reflected a positive evaluation of the pro-choice position. Finally, the conative component represents what is assumed to be the action or behavioral intention (for example, see Ajzen, 1988; Ajzen & Fishbein, 1980) that follows from the affective evaluation; for example, we would anticipate that those 70% favoring the pro-choice position would not vote for candidates who clearly wanted to restrict a woman's right to free choice.

It should be pointed out that this tripartite division of human experience does not characterize the frameworks that all cultures employ in their understanding. Lutz (1988), for example, suggests how even the seemingly "natural" division between cognition and affect does not appear to be so neatly separated in other cultures. What for us signifies an emotion may be understood by another culture—for example, the Ifaluk islanders—as a combined emotion/cognition or thought/feeling; the slash between each pair of terms suggests an intertwining rather than a neat separation. It is for this reason that the tripartite analysis of human experience—knowing, feeling, and doing—is a western view rather than a universally shared understanding.

Attitude Structure

The tripartite framework implies that an attitude has some kind of internal structure. This possibility leads to two questions: (1) are these three components independent or are they highly intercorrelated? and (2) will a change in one component produce a change in the others? Although research has failed to resolve these issues, high correlations among the three components have been reported, raising doubts about their independence. However, some investigators have questioned these correlations; it is possible, for example, that the high correlations among the three components result from an overemphasis on the evaluative component (for example, see McGuire, 1985).

Breckler (1984) reports a study which directly examined the independence of the three components proposed in the tripartite model. The study design permitted Breckler to meet some objections to previous research: he used both verbal and nonverbal measures of affect and behavior, plus the physical presence of the attitude object. For example, he obtained the affective reaction of his subjects to a caged snake, checking their moods on a questionnaire (verbal) and measuring their heart rates (nonverbal). Likewise, he had his subjects respond to such statements as "Whenever I see a snake I scream" (verbal) and also determined how close they agreed to get to the live snake (nonverbal).

Breckler's data indicated strong support for the model (that is, that the three components were independent) when both verbal and nonverbal measures were used and the attitude object was present as in the above illustration. In a second study, however, where only verbal measures were obtained and subjects were asked only to imagine the snake (it was not present), higher correlations among the three components—and thus less clear support for their independence—was found. Yet, because he had found conditions under which the three components functioned independently, Breckler concluded that we should continue to separate these three components of attitude and treat them as independent.

THE BILLIG VIEW   A different understanding of an attitude's internal structure appears in Billig's (1987) approach. He suggests that attitudes have the same structure as a debate. In other words, according to Billig an attitude is composed not merely of cognitive, affective, and conative elements, but also of the kinds of criticisms and justifications found in a public debate. He argues that these qualities are an integral part of the composition of attitudes.

To demonstrate his claim, Billig called upon some of McGuire's (1964) work on innoculating people to be resistant to persuasion. In medicine people are innoculated with attenuated doses of an illness-causing virus in order to increase their resistance to the disease. Extending this principle to the study of attitudes, McGuire reasoned that if you present people with cultural truisms about which they have probably given little thought (brushing your teeth twice a day, visiting a doctor once a year, and so on) and present some of them with a small dosage of an opposite point of view ("the attenuated virus"), you may be able to strengthen their resistance to a full-blown influence campaign. Data from several investigations indicated that providing subjects with refutational arguments helped innoculate them better than supportive arguments, presumably because the former are better in building up people's defenses.

Billig sees this work as testimony to the debate structure of people's attitudes. It demonstrates how beliefs never before tested in public debate have not yet developed the argumentative component Billig sees as a constituent part of most of our attitudes. McGuire's innoculative approach encourages people to develop this internal structure of their attitudes by justifying their views and critiquing the opposing views of others.

THE EXPECTANCY × VALUE MODEL   Another popular formulation of attitude structure is the so-called *expectancy × value model*. In this model, each attitude is said to be comprised of two central elements: (1) the expectancy or probability that the attitude object has certain characteristics, multiplied by (2) the perceived value of the characteristic. Ajzen and Fishbein's approach represents one version of this model. Ajzen (1988) provides the following useful illustration.

Let us suppose Mr. Ketchum believes that being on a low-salt diet will lead to both beneficial outcomes (lower blood pressure) and some less beneficial outcomes (restrictions on the kinds of food he can eat). Mr. Ketchum's overall attitude toward the prospective behavior (going on a low-salt diet) is said to be determined by his evaluation of each of these outcomes (the value component) and the probability that each will be obtained by adopting the behavior in question (the expectancy component). By multiplying the probability by the value term for each possibility and summing the products, we arrive at a quantitative estimate of Mr. Ketchum's attitude toward going on a low-salt diet. Ajzen summarizes several investigations demonstrating the usefulness of this expectancy × value formulation.

STRUCTURAL RELATIONSHIPS   Having examined the idea of an attitudinal internal structure, we can now turn to our second question: does a change in one component effect the other components? This question was examined in some of Rosenberg's early work (for example, Rosenberg, 1960; Rosenberg & Hovland, 1960). He reports evidence that altering the affective component (through hypnosis) modifies the cognitive component so as to preserve internal consistency. In other words, if someone's attitude is composed of a cognitive belief about some object consistent with the feelings about that object, and the affect is changed through hypnosis, then the beliefs will also change to be consistent with the new affect. For example, if I like chocolate cake and believe it is healthy, I am likely to question its health benefits if a hypnotist tells me I dislike chocolate cake.

Although it is based on a very different formulation, McGuire's (1960) work on the *Socratic effect* offers yet another illustration of how attitude structures operate to preserve consistency—in this case, a logical consistency among the attitude's constituent parts. McGuire presented his subjects with a series of three-part syllogisms, separating the parts and inserting them in a set of other statements as part of a longer questionnaire. When his subjects learned of the inconsistencies with which they had evaluated each of the separate parts of the syllogism, they later shifted their overall attitudes towards greater logical consistency.

Attitude Functions

Some of the earliest work on attitudes used what has been called the *functionalist* approach (for example, see Katz, 1960; Katz & Stotland, 1959; Smith, Bruner & White, 1956). While interest in this approach has waned during the last two decades, many investigators are rediscovering its relevance to understanding how persuasion might produce or fail to produce attitude change (for example, De Bono, 1987).

Attitudes serve four main functions for the individual: (1) object appraisal; (2) social adjustment; (3) value expression; and (4) ego defense.

The *object-appraisal,* or knowledge, function that attitudes serve involves their role in providing us with a simplified, organized "road map" of the objects, issues, and people in our world. An attitude is a ready-made framework for interpreting and understanding events. Hymes (1986), for example, argues that our political attitudes help us categorize people in much the same way as we categorize them on the basis of their race or gender.

Hymes suggests that this organizing function of our attitudes structures not only our perceptions, but our memory as well. He found, for example, that people who favored a woman's right to an abortion were better able to recall both favorable and unfavorable information about abortion as compared with those whose attitudes were neutral. Data showed that impartial subjects had difficulty with recall because their neutrality on the abortion issue did not provide them with the kinds of issue-schema that would help them organize the information presented in the experiment.

The *social-adjustive* function of attitudes involves their role in helping us fit into the various groups to which we either actually belong or wish to belong. For example, an individual who is generally not very prejudiced might adopt more prejudiced attitudes to become a member of an exclusive country club. In this case, his or her attitudes serve socially adjustive functions.

The *value-expressive* function of attitudes refers to their role in helping people communicate their values to others. For example, an individual might voice very strongly liberal attitudes to express her belief in liberal causes.

Before examining the ego-defensive function of attitudes let us review a recent effort to examine social adjustment and value expression in a persuasion context (De Bono, 1987). One problem De Bono noted with the original functional approach was its difficulty in identifying the functions a given attitude served for an individual. He argued that measuring individual differences in *self-monitoring* might be helpful in identifying people for whom a given function predominated.

Snyder (1979) first proposed the concept of self-monitoring to describe differences between individuals' concerns with fitting their behavior to the requirements of a given situation. High self-monitoring individuals are very concerned about the appropriateness of their actions to a given situation; they are attuned to how well their performances fit the social circumstances they happen to be in. In contrast, low self-monitors are less oriented to the situation than to inner cues directing what they should and should not do. Snyder's ideas about self-monitoring are reminiscent of Riesman's (1950) description of other-directed individuals who are always attuned to what others expect of them, and inner-directed individuals whose primary concern is with following the dictates of their internal guidance system.

De Bono suggested that high self-monitors are more likely to be concerned with the social adjustive function of attitudes, low self-monitors with the value-expressive functions. This interpretation has face validity. If other-directed, high self-monitors are concerned about adjusting their behavior to the situation, then they would surely want their attitudes to conform to situational expectations—the social-adjustive function. On the other hand, if inwardly directed, low self-monitors are concerned with being true to some inner evaluation, they are more likely to want their attitudes to reflect these inner values—the value-expressive function.

De Bono made an initial assessment of a pool of subjects' self-monitoring and value scores. His eventual sample consisted only of those who were either above or below the median in self-monitoring, and who rated the values of "being responsible" and "loving" as high, and the values of "being courageous" and "imaginative" as low. His subjects were then presented with a persuasive message emphasizing either value-expressive or social-adjustive concerns by a fictitious psychologist, Dr. Gregory Stevenson, purportedly a well-known leader in the field of mental health. For example, he argued that his research demonstrated some of the underlying values of people who had different attitudes towards the care of the mentally ill, claiming that those who favored institutionalization tended to value responsibility and love while those who favored deinstitutionalization emphasized values such as courage and imagination. Subjects who received Dr. Stevenson's socially adjustive message learned that 70% of a sample of people like themselves favored institutionalization, 23% favored deinstitutionalization, and 7% had no opinion. After listening to one of these two talks (both of which were presented on tape), the subjects completed various questionnaires, including measures of their attitudes.

The hypothesis was that those for whom attitudes serve a primarily value-expressive function should be more influenced by Dr. Stevenson's value-expressive persuasive message, whereas those for whom attitudes serve a social-adjustment function should be more affected by his social-adjustive message. Results generally confirmed these expectations. Specifically, high self-monitoring subjects developed more favorable attitudes towards institutionalization of the mentally ill after hearing the social-adjustive message. In contrast, low self-monitoring individuals expressed more favorable attitudes towards institutionalization after hearing the value-expressive message. As more sophisticated ways to measure the primary functions of given attitudes are developed, as in De Bono's research, the functionalist perspective may once again occupy a central place in the study of attitudes.

The final attitude function proposed within the functionalist perspective involves *ego defensiveness*. In some respects, this is the most fascinating function because it suggests that some of the attitudes we hold protect us from otherwise threatening realizations about ourselves. Some prejudiced attitudes, like those revealed in work on the authoritarian personality (see pp 33–36), are of this sort. Rather than directly encountering their own unwanted impulses, bigoted individuals project these impulses onto others and regard them as bad and dangerous people. As long as their attitudes toward these out-groups remain negative, individuals are protected from encountering the badness within themselves.

As De Bono's work suggests, knowledge of an attitude's primary function can be essential in designing a program of attitude change. It is obvious, for example, that if individuals' attitudes serve ego-defensive functions, providing them with information about reality might induce them to withdraw even further. For example, suppose that bigots' hate of homosexuals is based on a fear of their own sexuality. Helping them learn that homosexuals are reasonable, upstanding, and decent citizens is likely to make them cling even more tenaciously than ever before to their narrow-minded attitudes.

On the other hand, not all of our attitudes are held in the service of ego-defensive functions. Thus, rational appeals may work very well on those for whom an attitude serves object-appraisal functions, social appropriateness on those for whom the social-adjustive function is primary, and something like De Bono's value-oriented approach on people for whom the value-expressive function is most important [also see Rokeach's (1973) value-confrontation approach for another possibility].

Attitudes and Behavior

In this section, in which we examine the relationship between attitudes and behavior, the story of attitudes should reach its climax. The payoff, after all, lies in being able to predict people's behavior from a knowledge of their attitudes. The story begins on an optimistic note, quickly becomes discouraging and apparently hopeless, and ultimately concludes with confidence and hope restored.

Investigators once anticipated finding a direct, clear-cut relationship between attitudes and behavior. It was hoped that a person's behavior in the presence of some object could be predicted based on his or her attitudes toward that particular object. In short, there should be a consistency between what people say (their attitudes) and what they do.

Let us briefly examine the logic of expecting such a relationship. Ajzen (1988) offers several reasons why we might expect an attitude-behavior consistency, two of which are that (1) consistency describes a property of the way the human mind operates and (2) it serves to increase our effectiveness in the world.

According to the first view, the human mind is constructed, either through genetic programming or some kind of early social learning, to prefer consistency over inconsistency. An inconsistency between what we think and what we do, therefore, would be distressing to a mind built to favor consistency. According to this point of view, an inconsistency between an attitude and a relevant behavior would be disturbing because it violates our preference for consistency in our mental operations. We will examine this view in more detail later when we discuss cognitive dissonance (see pp. 183–84).

A second reason for expecting a consistency between attitudes and behavior is that society would be fairly chaotic if people said one thing and did another (Sampson, 1963; Tedeschi, Schlenker, & Bonoma, 1971). Our effectiveness in the world requires consistent principles of operation. We could not predict how people are likely to behave toward us if they expressed attitudes only randomly related to their behavior: for example, the person who claims to be our best friend rejects us; the person who says she favors a particular political

candidate, votes for that candidate's opponent. Consistency is important to our everyday lives even if it is not invariably found in practice.

Given, then, a reasonable expectation for consistency between
attitudes and behavior, what has research revealed? In 1934, when
there was a prevalence of anti-Chinese sentiment in the United States,
La Piere conducted his classic investigation. He traveled around the
United States with a Chinese couple, calling on some 250 hotels and
restaurants. They were refused service on only one occasion. However, six months later, when La Piere sent a letter to each place they
had visited inquiring about whether or not they would accept Chinese
as guests, over 90% of the places that responded said they would not.
This was a clear example of inconsistency; only one establishment
actually refused to provide service even though 90% indicated they
would refuse service in the same hypothetical circumstances.

Minard (1952) found that coal miners who worked with blacks
would not associate with blacks above ground in the community.
Harthshorne and May (1928–1930) found that people who would tell
a lie outside of class would not necessarily be dishonest in the classroom by cheating on an examination. After reviewing the extensive
literature examining the relationship between attitudes and behavior,
Wicker (1969) concluded that, "Taken as a whole, these studies suggest that it is considerably more likely that attitudes will be unrelated
or only slightly related to overt behaviors than that attitudes will be
closely related to actions" (p. 65).

Ajzen's Perspective

Though discouraged, many social psychologists did not abandon
the assumption that attitudes are relevant features of human life somehow related to behavior. They sought improved methods to assess
both attitudes and behavior, and a somewhat modified understanding
of the expected relationship between them.

If we consider the methods by which attitudes are assessed, we
can see some of the flaws in the original work and ways to remedy
them. Suppose that we have only one measure of people's attitudes
and only one measure of their behavior. We know from measurement
theory that any single measure is unreliable and that multiple measurements increase reliability.

For example, many people are concerned about their levels of
blood cholesterol. Assessments obtained at any one time give us an
indication of the level, but multiple measurements over a period of

time provide a much better picture of our blood chemistry. Indeed, were we to contemplate any major medical intervention, we would be well advised not to do so merely on the basis of a single measurement. Similarly, multiple assessments of both attitudes and behaviors will provide us with a more accurate picture of the relationship between them.

Ajzen observes that, strictly speaking, when we say that we are measuring attitudes and relating them to behavior, what we really mean is that we are looking at two different measures of the same underlying factor: one is a verbal measure of attitude on a questionnaire, the other a verbal or nonverbal measure of behavior. For example, we interview people to determine their voting preferences. This is a verbal, self-report measure of their attitudes toward particular candidates and issues. We then relate this measure to their vote, which is usually obtained in another interview with them immediately after they have voted. What we are actually doing, therefore, is relating one verbal measure obtained at one time and in one context to another verbal measure obtained at another time and in another context. We refer to the former as their attitude and the latter as their behavior when, in fact, each is a manifestation of their behavior. Presumably, each is also a function of some underlying "attitude" that we cannot see but only infer from consistencies in their "behavior" at these two points in time.

Given this demystification of the attitude-behavior relationship, it makes sense to use many different ways to determine what we consider to be people's attitudes. As Epstein's (1979) research demonstrates, predictions developed on the basis of a *sample* of assessments, not simply one instance, are more stable and reliable predictors of behavior.

Suppose you are interested in learning whether students are likely to procrastinate in turning in their assignments. There are many ways in which this behavior could be manifested. If you ask students if they have ever handed in an assignment late, for example, you may find it impossible to predict their likelihood of turning in another assignment late based on this one measurement. On the other hand, if you understand procrastination to be a characteristic attitude that some people have, you could make many different kinds of observations and aggregate the data before either concluding anything about the underlying attitude or trying to predict their future behavior.

You would not want to say that a given individual was a procrastinator until you determined whether he or she demonstrated a variety of traits presumably related to this attitude; being late once is not sufficient to earn the label of procrastinator. A *pattern* of behaviors over a period of time, on the other hand, might lead you to conclude that "Yes, indeed, Jim is a procrastinator."

If you now wanted to use your understanding of Jim's attitude to predict his future behavior, you might also want to sample his behavior in a variety of contexts. Any one situation is likely to have unique circumstances and thus may or may not be a proper test of the attitude-behavior relationship. Observing Jim in many different situations, however, would give you a better chance to find a true relationship.

It is also true, however, that it is probably more difficult to predict a highly specific behavior than a general behavioral tendency. For instance, we would have more difficulty predicting whether or not Janet is likely to have a drink at the party she will be attending with Bill on Saturday night from a knowledge of Janet's attitudes about drinking than predicting whether or not Janet generally has a drink in social gatherings.

The former prediction is so highly specific that we would have to know a great deal about the party to feel that our knowledge of Janet's general attitudes about drinking were even relevant. Suppose there is no alcohol at the party or that very few others are drinking? What if Janet's date drinks a lot or a little that evening? On the other hand, the latter prediction—based on knowing Janet's behavior in social gatherings—might turn out better because we would have considered a variety of social settings in which Janet may or may not drink. In that case, we should be able to predict with reasonable accuracy about the chances that she would have a drink while out socially.

Ajzen's analysis suggests that those wishing to make a simple prediction of people's behavior from a knowledge of their attitudes are acting naively. Indeed, it is simplistic to expect a direct attitude-behavior relationship; it is more reasonable to expect a complex connection requiring many measurements of both components.

Moderator Variables and Complicating Factors

Another way to deal with the apparent inconsistencies between attitudes and behavior is to examine complicating factors. We saw these illustrated in the earlier example involving Janet: intervening between her attitude about drinking and her behavior on Saturday night were a host of situational factors that might either restrict her from acting in a manner consistent with her attitude (Bill does not drink and disapproves of anyone who drinks), or might encourage her to act in an attitude-consistent manner (the party is loaded with drinks and heavy drinkers).

The term *moderator variables* is often used to describe these complications. A moderator is something that intervenes between the statement of an attitude and the behavior that presumably should follow from it. Moderator variables modify the relationship so that on some occasions or for some persons the expected relationship appears, while under other circumstances or for other people the expected relationship does not occur.

Obviously, there can be numerous moderating variables, including almost everything we know or can imagine about individual personalities, needs, cognitive processes, and so on, as well as various situational factors as in the example involving Janet. Indeed, as Ajzen (1988) notes, one of the problems with the moderator-variable approach is that almost everything imaginable has been considered. This generates a great deal of research, but not necessarily any real advances in our understanding of the attitude-behavior relationship.

To avoid reproducing the nearly endless array of moderator variables, we will examine in detail a few currently interesting leads, primarily from the field of cognitive social psychology.

Accessibility

Fazio and several of his colleagues (Fazio, Powell, & Herr, 1983; Fazio & Williams, 1986) have argued that the attitude-behavior relationship is influenced by the accessibility of individuals' attitudes from their memory. An attitude is said to represent an association the individual makes between a given object (for example, a presidential candidate) and an evaluation of that object (for example, positive or negative feelings toward the candidate). Such associations vary in their strength. Accessibility from memory is said to be a function of the strength of this association: strong object-evaluation associations are more accessible from memory than weak object-evaluation associations. By repeatedly calling people's attention to the object and to their evaluation of it, for example, we should increase the strength of the association and thus increase accessibility from memory.

High accessibility would mean that whenever the object is present, the associative link is more readily recalled than when accessibility is low. Under high-accessibility conditions, therefore, there should be a greater impact of the attitude on people's behavior. In other words, with high accessibility, we should expect to find a stronger attitude-behavior relationship than with low accessibility. In conditions of high accessibility, the presence of the object evokes those evaluative associations less likely to be recalled in conditions of low accessibility.

In order to examine these possibilities, Fazio and Williams studied attitudes, perceptions, and behaviors during the 1984 presidential race between Reagan and Mondale. In the first phase, people's attitudes on a wide variety of public issues were measured, including school prayer, gun control, nuclear power plants, as well as the candidates themselves. In the second phase, they contacted subjects by mail after the second televised debate, inquiring about their perceptions of the debate performances of the two candidates. The third and final phase of the study focused on actual voting behavior. Subjects were contacted shortly after the election and asked to indicate which candidate they voted for.

One issue Fazio and Williams were able to examine is the relationship between people's attitudinal preferences and their *perceptions*. In this case, it was possible to see if people who favored one candidate over the other saw their candidate's debate performance to be superior to his opponent's. Results clearly demonstrated support for this relationship. In effect, people's attitudes toward Reagan or Mondale colored their judgment of each candidate's performance in the debate. This finding confirms a well-known effect linking attitudes with perceptions (for example, see Ottati, Fishbein, & Middlestadt, 1988, for both confirmation and a complication). Fazio and Williams also found that people's attitudes towards the presidential candidates colored their perceptions of debate performances of the vice-presidential candidates as well.

The key analysis examined the question of accessibility that motivated the study in the first place. Subjects were classified into high- or low-accessibility groups. In previous research, accessibility was measured by response time—that is, the time it took an individual to answer questions about the attitude object. Presumably, the shorter the response time, the more accessible the attitude. The methodology employed by Fazio and Williams in their study permitted them to assess the speed with which their subjects responded to questions about the two candidates. Although certain complications forced them to modify the procedure, accessibility was assessed by the speed with which the object (Reagan or Mondale) elicited evaluations (favorable or unfavorable feelings).

Having divided subjects into high and low accessibility on the basis of these response times, the question was whether the predicted relationship between attitudes and behavior would hold *more strongly* for high-accessible subjects than for low-accessible subjects. They tested this expectation in several ways. For example, Fazio and Williams compared the correlations between the subjects' attitudes toward the candidates and their perceptions of the candidates' debate performances separately for high and low accessibles. Data revealed a consistent pattern of stronger correlations for the high- than for the low-accessible subjects.

The next test of the accessibility hypothesis more directly examined the attitude-behavior relationship. The procedure was similar to that in the debate-perception test but, in this case, the correlations between the subjects' attitudes and their voting behavior were examined separately for the high- and the low-accessible groups. Once again, a clear and consistent pattern emerged: higher correlations between attitudes and behavior were found for the high- than for the low-accessible subjects. As the authors note, "The high correlation evident among respondents with a highly accessible attitude towards Reagan is all the more astounding when one keeps in mind that the attitude was measured via a single item some 3½ months prior to the election" (pp. 510–11).

Self-Focused Salience

A second moderating variable in the attitude-behavior relationship is *self-focused salience,* the effect of focusing attention on one's own thought processes. For example, if you are asked why you have the attitude you do, will the consequent attention to your thought processes increase or decrease the relationship between your attitude and your subsequent behavior? There are two ways of considering this possible effect, deriving from somewhat different theoretical frameworks.

Wicklund and his associates (Wicklund, 1975, 1982; Duval & Wicklund, 1972) suggest that situations that increase attention to ourselves—public self-consciousness—produce an increased correspondence between the expression of our attitudes and our behavior. For example, Pryor and his associates (1977) had some of their subjects participate in a study in front of a mirror to simulate high public self-consciousness, the assumption being that a mirror makes people more aware of how they are feeling, thinking, and so on. They hypothesized that this increased access to their own thoughts would increase the correspondence between their attitudes and behavior.

The subjects were instructed to complete a questionnaire measuring their sociability in front of a mirror and, several days later, were placed in a social situation in which their sociable behavior could be assessed (for example, the volume of their voices in talking to others). Data indicated a higher correlation between sociable attitudes and behavior for those subjects who completed the questionnaire when the mirror was present than when it was not. Several other studies have supported this finding (for example, see Wicklund, 1982).

On the other hand, research by Wilson and his associates (1984) reports an opposite effect. Some subjects were asked to explain their attitudes toward a group of puzzles, and this attitude assessment was later correlated with measures of their actual behavioral reactions to the puzzles (for example, how much time was spent with each puzzle). In this case, the attitude-behavior correspondence *decreased* for the group asked for the reasons for its attitudes, while it increased for the group that was not asked to explain its attitudes.

Millar and Tesser (1986) argued that perhaps these contradictory findings could be explained by considering the three components of an attitude—cognitive, affective, and conative—that we encountered earlier in the chapter (see pp. 166–67). We saw that while not everyone recognizes this tripartite differentiation, it nevertheless remains a viable way to represent the internal structure of an attitude. Millar and Tesser's work built on this tripartite model, emphasizing the cognitive and affective components.

Millar and Tesser reasoned that attitude-behavior correspondence is likely to be high if the part of the attitude on which the person focuses matches the kind of behavior the attitude motivates. Referring to the puzzles used by Wilson and his colleagues, Millar and Tesser suggest that people can be asked to focus on either the cognitive component of their attitude toward these puzzles (for example, "the puzzle is challenging, imaginative, clear"), or on the affective component (for example, "the puzzle makes me feel happy"). Likewise, people who want to test their analytic ability have a cognitive motivation for doing the puzzles; on the other hand, those who only want to please themselves have a more affective motivation for doing the puzzles.

Millar and Tesser suggest that the contradiction between the results of Wicklund's and Wilson's research may be due to each study calling on a somewhat different component of either the attitude or the behavior. Their own hypothesis is that we should expect high attitude-behavior correspondence when the attitude component on which the person focuses matches the behavioral component. In other words, if people are asked to think about the cognitive reasons for doing puzzles, and are then placed in a situation in which doing puzzles is said to be a test of their analytic or problem-solving abilities, we should find a greater correspondence between what they report as their attitude about puzzles and their behavior in the puzzle task than if there is no match between attitude and behavior components. They make a parallel hypothesis for the affective component.

Millar and Tesser created an experimental situation in which it was possible to compare matched and mismatched combinations on a set of puzzle tasks. Their findings generally supported their predictions. For example, subjects were asked to think about the affective component of their attitudes (for example, "how do you feel when performing each of the puzzles?"), and were then placed in a situation in which their behavior was affectively driven (for example, the puzzle-solving task was unrelated to a later activity they were to carry out) so that they did the puzzles only because they were interesting or did not do them because they were boring. This group was compared to another whose behavior was more cognitively driven (for example, the puzzle-solving task was to be followed by another task for which the skills learned on the puzzle task were relevant). The former group—the one whose attitudinal and behavioral components were both affectively focused—showed higher attitude-behavior correlation than the latter group—the one whose attitudes were affectively focused, but whose behavior was cognitively driven. Likewise, those subjects asked to think about the cognitive component of their attitude showed higher attitude-behavior correspondence when the behavior was cognitively driven than when it was affectively driven.

In summary, what reasonable conclusion can we draw about the attitude-behavior relationship? It seems fair to say that careful methods designed to obtain a sample of both attitudes and behaviors, in combination with a sensitivity to a variety of moderating and complicating factors, can increase the correspondence between attitude and behavior. On the other hand, as Billig (1987) has commented, focusing our energies on closing this gap may blind us to the reasons for the gap in the first place.

For example, are there any cultures in which an attitude-behavior inconsistency might be an important feature of life? Slugoski and Ginsberg (1989) report that in Japan, attitude-behavior consistency is *not* as valued a sign of integrity as it is in most western cultures, but rather is seen as a sign of immaturity and inconsiderateness. People are encouraged not to behave in accordance with their attitudes to avoid appearing insensitive and impolite. On the other hand, most western cultures seem to favor attitude-behavior consistency. Perhaps we should try to understand the social functions this preference serves.

In a culture in which billions are spent on advertising to influence consumer consumption habits, and by government agencies and corporations to help improve people's lives and anticipate crises, having good attitude-behavior correspondences is vital. After all, why would an advertiser want to spend so much money to get consumers to change their attitudes about products if their shopping decisions were made spontaneously? Likewise, what good would it do a government agency to learn about its citizens' views if there were no relationship between the expression of those views and citizens' behavior? Every good politician wants to know the public's opinion, and would balk at a young social psychologist's admission that "Yes, I can measure attitudes, but no, they have little if any connection to how your constituents are likely to vote this fall"!

Perhaps our cultural concern with attitude-behavior consistency, therefore, has less to do with personal integrity than with social control. While social psychology seems intent on finding ways to develop a more predictable connection between attitudes and behavior, it might be equally useful to explore the presence or absence of such a relationship as a cultural feature.

Persuasion and Change

The persuasion model of attitude change is based on some ideas about human communication in which a (a) *source* communicates a (b) *message* via some (c) *medium* or *channel* to a (d) *receiver* to influence (e) *targeted attitudes* or *behaviors*. The model is typically examined in terms of the separate effects of each of these elements. However, it is usually understood that the elements do not operate independently; indeed, as we will see, they often interact in rather intriguing ways. Rather than examining the work conducted on all five factors, we will instead focus only on the source, message, receiver, and some of their interactions.

Source Factors

We will first examine those characteristics of sources that increase or decrease their effectiveness in producing attitude and behavior change in receivers. Three main categories of source variables have been identified: credibility, attractiveness, and power.

Credibility

The credibility of sources refers both to their expertise as well as their trustworthiness. Obviously, an expert source is more likely to be influential than one who is not an expert. Numerous studies have demonstrated the importance of expertise in effective persuasion. As McGuire (1985) points out, however, expertise alone is often insufficient, especially when trustworthiness is missing. Trustworthiness appears primarily when people believe that the source has nothing special to gain. When sources are disinterested, they appear to be more trustworthy than when they are personally interested in the outcome. The perennial favorite—the used-car salesman—is a prime example of a source usually considered to be much too concerned with the outcome (selling a car) to be trusted.

Some research indicates that sources who forewarn receivers of their intention to influence them are actually considered more trustworthy and thus more persuasive. On the other hand, forewarning can also provide the receiver an opportunity to plan a defense against the persuasive message.

Attractiveness

Source attractiveness is a familiar device used by sources to increase their persuasive impact. Communications literature generally reports that sources who are liked are more persuasive than those who are disliked. Furthermore, the greater the perceived similarity between source and receiver, the greater the receiver's attraction to the source and, presumably, the greater the receiver's susceptibility to the source's attempts at influence.

Recall the findings from Chapter 11, however, in which we examined the minority-influence paradigm (see p. 157). We learned that even when minority sources are disliked and clearly different from the majority receivers, they are influential as long as they are consistent and flexible in their appeals. Thus, even liking works in complex ways. We will now explore other similarly paradoxical findings involving attractiveness and persuasion.

COGNITIVE DISSONANCE   The theory of cognitive dissonance was originally proposed by Festinger (1957), who suggested that an internal state of cognitive tension, called cognitive dissonance, appears whenever a person holds two contradictory thoughts—for example, "It is raining outside" and "I am standing outside but not getting wet." Presumably, the mind abhors dissonance and so strives to get rid of it and restore the happy state of cognitive consonance. Paradoxically, the theory predicts that we are *less* likely to be persuaded by a source we like than a source we dislike when asked to do something distasteful to us.

The "logic" of this prediction is based on the concept of *insufficient justification*. When we have a sufficient external justification for doing something unpleasant, we experience *less* dissonance than if we do it with insufficient external justification. A usually honest person, for example, who agrees to lie for a great sum of money (sufficient external justification) experiences less dissonance than if he or she lies without receiving a significant monetary inducement (insufficient external justification). In this latter case, we have to get rid of the dissonance; one way of doing so is by coming to believe that perhaps we really didn't tell a lie after all; we now believe as true what we originally thought was a lie.

Extensive research demonstrates the effects of insufficient justification. It reveals, for example, that people who receive one dollar for reporting to a subject in the waiting room that the boring experiment they have just completed is "really interesting" reevaluate their attitude and regard the experiment as "more interesting" than those paid twenty dollars for telling the same lie (see Festinger & Carlsmith, 1959). Twenty dollars provided sufficient external justification, causing subjects little dissonance and, therefore, little need to change their attitude about the task. On the other hand, one dollar was little external justification for having lied, causing subjects a great deal of dissonance that could only be relieved by rationalizing that the task was more interesting than it really was.

Applied to source likability, dissonance theory predicts that more cognitive dissonance is experienced doing something unpleasant for a disliked source than for a liked source. It is like lying for one dollar: complying with someone we dislike is insufficient external justification for doing something distasteful. To restore cognitive consonance, we may rationalize that what we did was actually not so bad. On the other hand, complying with someone we like is akin to telling a lie for twenty dollars: helping our friends is sufficient external justification for doing something unpleasant. Because little dissonance is created, there is little need to change our evaluation of what we have done (see Zimbardo et al., 1965). In conclusion, according to dissonance theory there may be a greater persuasive impact (under very specific conditions) deriving from a source who is disliked than one who is liked!

IDENTIFICATION WITH THE AGGRESSOR Another kind of paradoxical connection between the likability of sources and their effectiveness as influence agents, involves an effect first proposed by Bettelheim (1958) termed "identification with the aggressor." Bettelheim noted how some prisoners in Nazi concentration camps so identified with their guards that they emulated them in as many ways as possible. Insofar as people identify with an aggressor—presumably someone they, at least initially, do not like—they will come to comply with that person's requests (see McGuire, 1985).

Power

The third major factor sources use to produce attitude and behavior change in receivers is power. In addition to attractiveness and credibility, French and Raven (1959) identified the ability to provide rewards or punishment and legitimacy as other bases of source power.

Obviously, sources who have the power to determine the receiver's rewards and punishments should be more influential than those lacking this ability. As we noted earlier in our discussion of Kelman's ideas about social influence (see pp. 135–36), however, sources wielding this kind of power must constantly monitor receivers' behavior to reward or punish them for their performance. In addition, sources using punishment are likely to get immediate compliance but no lasting change, while those providing rewards may, over time, induce more permanent change in the receivers' attitudes or behavior.

We first encountered legitimacy as a basis of power in our earlier discussion of the Milgram study of obedience to an experimenter's requests to apply painful electric shocks to another person (see pp. 147–50). The study illustrates how the institutional contexts in which we live create legitimacy for certain people to issue commands and others to follow them by virtue of their respective positions in the hierarchy. When a legitimate source—our boss, for example—makes a request of us, he or she is more likely to gain our acceptance than an illegitimate source—a temporary employee working in the mailroom, for example—would making the same request.

Source Dissociation: The Sleeper Effect

One familiar effect related to the source of a message is known as the *sleeper effect:* the tendency of a message not immediately persuasive to become persuasive later in time (see Hovland, Lumsdaine, & Sheffield, 1949). This effect runs counter to the usual view of influence as dissipating over time; here is a case in which influence actually *increases* over time. One rationale offered for the sleeper effect is that people come to *dissociate* the source of the message from its content, and are influenced by the content alone.

This dissociation is especially important when the source is initially disliked or seen as somehow illegitimate. Over time, we forget that the message came from someone whom we normally do not listen to, only remembering the persuasive message itself. This failure to remember the source whose influence we have come to accept is reminiscent of Moscovici's interpretation of the potent influence of those minorities we resist publicly but accept privately.

According to the dissociation interpretation of the sleeper effect, the disliked source of a position we have rejected because of that source over time becomes lost to our memory; if the message remains, however, we might later be influenced by its content so long as the source of the message is not reinstated, reminding us of why we rejected it in the first place.

Until the series of investigations reported by Gruder and his colleagues (1978), evidence for this effect was irregular and often inconsistent. They managed to demonstrate that the sleeper effect occurred reliably, but only (a) when the message was initially very impactful but was discounted because of the source; and (b) when over time, there was a dissociation between the discounting source and the message, allowing the message's impact to take over. Recently, Pratkanis and his associates (1988) generally confirmed the reliability of the sleeper effect under very specific conditions, although they are less convinced than others that the source dissociation interpretation is the correct explanation for the effect.

. . . .

Message Factors

Message factors in a social-influence situation involve how the influential message is phrased and presented. For example, suppose you have a position you want others to adopt. Is it better to present only arguments supporting your position or arguments both supporting and opposing your position? Some experimental research suggests that if the audience is already aware of both sides, it is better to spend time reviewing and refuting the counterarguments rather than simply ignoring them (see McGuire, 1985). Yet during the 1988 presidential campaign, some political commentators were quick to fault Dukakis for his tendency to do just that, letting Bush control the campaign and eventually win the election. Other research suggests that a more intelligent audience is more likely to want to hear both arguments and counterarguments on an issue.

A second message factor involves the question of whether positive or negative appeals are more persuasive. Some early work suggested that more negative arguments—for example, those that might arouse people's fears—did not work well because fear arousal interfered with their ability to hear and understand the message. On the other hand, some reviews of the research literature suggest the effectiveness of limited fear-based appeals.

More recently, Meyerowitz and Chaiken (1987) examined whether messages framed in terms of their negative consequences would be more or less influential than those framed in terms of their positive consequences. The messages in their study involved breast self-examination by women. A positively framed message, for example, indicated the potential health benefits of spending only five minutes each month doing a breast self-examination; a negatively framed message indicated the potential dangers of failing to spend five minutes each month doing a breast self-examination.

Data indicated the following results: (a) the negatively framed message was more influential in shaping the subjects' *opinions* about conducting breast self-examination than the positively framed message; (b) when subjects were asked about their *intentions* to do a breast self-examination, once again the negatively framed message was more effective than the positively framed message, but in this case only after a four-month follow-up questionnaire with these same subjects; and (c) when actual self-examination *behavior* was studied, it was found that during the four-month period since the persuasive messages had been administered, subjects who had received the negatively framed message were more likely than those who had received the positively framed message to have actually carried out their intentions and done breast self-examinations.

Receiver Factors

Receiver factors involve how the properties of the person receiving the message affect its impact. In Chapter 7, for example, we examined how the receivers' *sex* affected their influenceability. As we saw in Part One, young college students appear to be more open to influence than older adults: this suggests the potential importance of *age* as a receiver factor in persuasive communications (see also Krosnick & Alwin, 1989). Of all receiver factors, however, *self-esteem* has been the most important in research.

Early research argued that people with high self-esteem are generally less open to influence than persons with low self-esteem. McGuire's (1985) thoughtful review of the literature, however, suggests that a variety of factors affect the relationship between self-esteem and persuadability: we find a positive relationship under some conditions and a negative relationship under others. As with the gender effects we considered earlier, the matter is neither simple nor yet clearly resolved.

Interactions Among the Factors

Several investigators have recently been concerned with the interaction effects among receiver, source, and message factors. Petty and Cacioppo (1981; see also Chaiken, 1980) led the way by examining the role of *issue involvement* on persuasion. They identified two cognitive routes to persuasion: (1) a route involving central processing and (2) a route involving heuristic or peripheral processing.

In central processing, individuals "actively attempt to comprehend and evaluate the message's arguments as well as to assess their validity in relation to the message's conclusion." (Chaiken, 1980, p. 752). Petty and Cacioppo (also see Petty, Cacioppo, & Goldman, 1981) note that the central route leads the individual to consider the message's arguments, to counter them with her or his own arguments, and to try to integrate these elements into a coherent reaction to the message. In contrast, with heuristic or peripheral processing people tend to do little processing of the arguments, but rather rely on peripheral cues like the credibility, prestige, or power of the source.

Having identified two different routes to persuasion, their next step was to consider (a) what determines which route is followed and (b) what consequences for persuasive impact follow from adopting the central, as opposed to the peripheral, route. Petty and Cacioppo suggested that one answer to the first question involves the personal relevance to the individual of the topic of the message: personally relevant messages will follow the central route while personally nonrelevant messages will follow the peripheral or heuristic route.

If central processing is involved because the issue is of high relevance to the individual, then we would expect strong arguments to be more persuasive than weak ones. On the other hand, if the issue is of low relevance, so that peripheral rather than central processing is involved, we would expect the quality of the message to be secondary to other factors, such as the credibility or attractiveness of the source. Several studies have substantiated this expectation.

For example, Sorrentino and his associates (1988) found that strong arguments had a significantly greater impact on receivers than source expertise under conditions of high relevance. In another kind of study Axom, Yates, and Chaiken (1987) found that subjects were more influenced by an audience's overheard response to a persuasive message than by the quality of the arguments contained in the message under conditions of low involvement; under high involvement, subjects were more affected by the quality of the message.

Leippe and Elkin (1987) argued that the concept of involvement, or personal relevance, has a somewhat ambiguous meaning that would benefit from conceptual clarification. They suggested that the idea of involvement as used by Petty and Cacioppo, and by Chaiken, differs from the idea of ego-involvement or issue commitment traditionally used in the literature on attitude change. Issue commitment refers to the degree to which people are committed to a particular issue; in this case, research has shown little or no influence effects when ego-involvement is high.

In contrast, involvement or relevance refers to the degree to which people not committed to an issue are receptive to more input. Involvement can take two possible forms. First, people may find the issue raised by the persuasive message to be personally relevant to their future concerns; this is called *issue-involvement.* For example, the message is relevant to a college student if it deals with his or her career goals after getting out of college. *Response-involvement* occurs when people find the actual attitude position advocated in the message relevant; for example, they know that they will soon be asked to discuss the issue in some public forum and so need to pay close attention to the position they are hearing.

Leippe and Elkin report previous data suggesting that while both issue- and response-involvement seem to follow the central, rather than the peripheral, route of information processing, they differ in terms of their persuasion effects. Specifically, issue involvement produces greater persuasion effects than response involvement.

To further examine these possibilities, Leippe and Elkin designed a study in which subjects were presented with variations in (a) the quality of a message (high versus low); (b) the degree (high versus low), and (c) kind of involvement (issue-only, response-only, or a combination of the two). They studied the various persuasive impacts of these several variables, as well as their impact on the consistency between attitudes and behavior.

Data indicated that subjects for whom the issue-only involvement was made relevant were most strongly influenced by the quality of the message: they agreed more often and had more favorable thoughts about strong, rather than weak, messages. Furthermore, confirming an earlier finding of Sivacek and Crano (1982), Leippe and Elkin also found that issue-involved subjects were more likely to engage in attitude-consistent behavior. In contrast, subjects for whom relevance was of the response-only type were not affected by the quality of the message.

The complexity of findings we have examined suggest the growing sophistication with which social psychologists have addressed issues involving the persuasive attitude-change model. We can no longer simply deal with source, message, and receiver as independent factors; we now have a theoretical framework and some useful data to suggest how certain qualities of sources (for example, their credibility) may be ignored or become important as a function of certain properties of their message for a given audience—for example, whether the arguments are strong or weak and whether the message is personally relevant or not to the audience.

It is interesting to observe that people routinely bombarded with persuasive messages do not possibly have the time to adequately review alternatives. Thus, peripheral rather than central processing may prevail, leading more and more people to attend primarily to the superficial features of the situation rather than to the persuasive strength of the arguments.

Furthermore, if by admitting the personal relevance of what we hear we are "compelled" to engage in central processing, the glut may increasingly lead people to distance themselves from finding much in the daily news that is personally relevant. That is, by distancing ourselves from issues and seeing most things as unimportant, or at least not personally relevant to our own interests, we can avoid thoughtful consideration and engage in the kind of mindlessness to events some psychologists have examined more extensively (for example, Langer, Blank, & Chanowitz, 1978).

• • • • • • • • • • • • • • • • • •

Conclusions

There is perhaps no subject in social psychology as intriguing and complex as the study of attitudes. As we saw at the beginning of the chapter, even the task of defining an attitude is difficult. There is general agreement that an attitude refers to some internal characteristic of people that must be inferred from their verbal and nonverbal behavior. When we refer to an attitude, we mean some affective judgment about an object. We reviewed the evidence for and against a tripartite structure of an attitude—involving cognitive, affective, conative components—concluding that this kind of division is nonetheless valuable, and considered the functions attitudes might serve for

the individual, noting in particular object appraisal, social adjustment, value expression, and ego defense. Next, we looked at the relationship between attitudes and behavior. We noted that while little
correspondence was initially found, as the field became more meth-
odologically and conceptually sophisticated a definite, if tenuous, link
began to emerge. Finally, we examined social influence and attitude
change, focusing especially on source, message, and receiver factors
and their interactions as facilitating or thwarting attitude and behavior change in response to persuasive appeals.

11

Society and Social Influence

I N THIS CHAPTER we will examine two dominant issues in the study of social influence. The first issue, raised by Moscovici, is why conformity rather than innovation has been the focus of most investigations. The second issue is why social psychology has failed to deal with the issues of power and ideology when discussing social influence. Our examination of these two important issues should not lead us to dispose of the understandings we reached in earlier chapters. Rather, it should provide us with a better sense of why those understandings are incomplete and what alternatives still remain to be examined. Our purpose is not so much to cast out the old as it is to put it in a broader context to better see where to look for our new approaches to understanding social influence.

Harmony or Conflict? Two Models of Society

To find out why social psychologists studying social influence were more concerned with conformity rather than innovation, Moscovici examined the dominant model of society in the United States, where most of the work on conformity has been conducted. Although Moscovici's terminology and mine is somewhat different, in general he found that most people, including social psychologists, regard society as made up of harmonious individuals sharing certain basic interests. The alternative view is to see society as made up of conflicting groups, each with their own interests. We can call these models, respectively, the harmony and conflict views of society.

According to the *harmony view*, people basically agree about the fundamental values and structure of their society. If there is social discord, there is no attempt to change to the underlying framework, but rather those individuals or groups responsible for causing the trouble. Social influence describes the various ways to control individuals who for some reason have challenged the otherwise harmonious social system. The object of this influence is to restore order by transforming deviates into good citizens who will conform to social laws and customs.

To be sure, we still value independent and autonomous behavior and disdain those who conform to mob rule. This may seem paradoxical, but consider that autonomy does not describe behavior challenging the underlying social system; rather, it refers to actions governed by the parameters of the system. For this reason, Fromm (1955) suggested that in our consumer society we value people who can make up their own minds about which products to purchase, but not those who question the very idea that the increasing consumption of goods is desirable.

In other words, autonomy means deciding what products to purchase without being unduly swayed by the irrational appeal of group pressure or devious advertising. It involves reviewing the issues and arguments and finally making up one's own mind. In no way, however, does autonomy involve refusing to participate in consumerism. Indeed, those who do appear to be odd or even deviant.

In contrast, the *conflict view* offers a more pluralistic vision of society. Modern, complex societies are composed of various competing interest groups which differ in their views about the best way to organize society or distribute its wealth. Groups in powerful, dominant positions defend the status quo as the most natural and beneficial to society. On the other hand, disadvantaged groups aim to transform the social order to improve their relative status and realize their own particular interests.

In the conflict view, society is characterized by disagreement and conflict. This need not involve violence, but rather a healthy competition among organized interests for a fair share of limited resources and a clear and distinct voice in determining what goes on. Under these conditions, social influence negotiates agreements that are *mutually* satisfactory; it does not evoke conformity on the part of one party to a dispute. Moscovici called these outcomes innovation, because any negotiated agreement requires each side to compromise and accept a new position. In contrast, conformity usually involves a minority yielding to the majority's point of view.

The Hawthorne Project

Early research on employee productivity at the General Electric Company's Hawthorne plant provides a useful demonstration of these two models of society in operation. The series of studies reported by Mayo (1933) and Roethlisberger and Dickson (1939) focused on those conditions in the workers' physical environment that affected their productivity. It was assumed that if those physical conditions were improved, productivity would increase.

One of the first efforts was directed toward the lighting of the room where the work was carried out. To study the effects of illumination on productivity, the investigators selected a small group of workers for their experiment. These workers were placed in a setting in which the lighting could be systematically varied while they carried on their normal work routines. Somewhat surprisingly, results showed that productivity increased regardless of the variations in the lighting, suggesting that illumination was *not* related to their productivity. What, then, accounted for their increased productivity?

At the time, it was not popular to consider social and interpersonal factors as possible contributors to worker productivity. The investigators, however, reasoned that if physical factors were not the major cause of increased productivity, then social factors—in particular, the increased attention shown to those workers selected to participate in the study—must be. After all, a group of somewhat anonymous workers was now the center of considerable attention; even their opinions were sought. Perhaps it was management's attention to these workers, not the physical environment, that led to their greater productivity.

This finding became known as the *Hawthorne effect*: regardless of physical conditions, workers given a great deal of interpersonal attention and caring concern from management will work harder. This "discovery" led to a major transformation in theories of good management and to the human-relations approach to managerial training. No longer would managers be encouraged to be impersonal and entirely task-oriented; good managers show concern for workers and are sensitive to their needs and problems.

Generations of managers have been nurtured on this interpretation of the Hawthorne effect, but writers like Bramel and Friend (1981) take exception to it. In terms of the two contrasting models of society, the original Hawthorne work was carried out under the auspices of the harmony view, whereas Bramel and Friend base their analysis on the conflict view.

If we see management and labor as having basically harmonious interests about what each wants, it makes sense that worker compliance to managerial directives might best be attained if management works in an interpersonally sensitive and caring way. This is somewhat like arguing that a manager who is liked will be more influential than one who is disliked, and that the best way to be liked is to show a genuine interest in the workers.

In contrast, Bramel and Friend's position argues that labor and management have several conflicting points of interest. For example, top-level management is interested in high profits. Since wages cut into profits, it is in their interest to keep a lid on wages. On the other hand, for many kinds of industrial jobs, about the only benefit workers can obtain is higher wages. Their interest in increasing their wages thus conflicts with management's interest in keeping wages at a level it considers reasonable. Any resolution to this conflict will require that each side compromise, revealing a process more like Moscovici's innovation than the kinds of conformity usually studied in the laboratory.

This analysis demonstrates that conflict describes the labor-management relationship better than harmony; we can also see that appeals to harmony may actually disguise this underlying conflict of interest. Who benefits from perpetuating a harmony view? Following Bramel and Friend, we might find our answer in the world of management: As beneficiaries of the system's current structure, managers subscribe to the harmony view to justify their high salaries and the workers' low wages, while the employees, who feel exploited by a system insufficiently sensitive to their needs, use the conflict view to agitate for a higher percentage of company profits and better benefits. Bramel and Friend suggest that, in fact, the Hawthorne effect has very little to do with managerial sensitivity to worker needs, and everything to do with the managerial exercise of its power and authority.

Not everyone who has reexamined the original Hawthorne findings concurs with Bramel and Friend's conclusion. Of course, there is little reason to expect agreement given the contrary views of the nature of the management-worker social system. From their perspective, however, Bramel and Friend examined the actual use of managerial power that appeared in the reports of the original study. They concluded that it was management's power to fire workers, not their caring concern for the workers' well-being, that gained worker compliance.

Obviously, if management and workers have conflicting interests, especially in how net profits are distributed, for example, workers will not comply simply because management is benevolent. Under these conditions, tough negotiations between the two conflicting groups will be required. If management is unwilling to negotiate with the workers, they will have to use their power to fire workers to gain their compliance. Bramel and Friend report numerous instances in the original Hawthorne study in which precisely this occurred, made all the more potent by the simple fact that the study was conducted during a time of poor employment opportunities for workers and thus even greater pressure on them to comply.

Melting Pot or Mosaic?

When the Hawthorne studies were conducted, the United States was somewhat less sensitive to group differences and the conflict perspective than is currently the case. At that time, people still lived under the happy myth of America as a "melting pot," a land where poor immigrants from all over the world came for economic opportunities and social progress. As everyone shared in the American experience, differences would fade and one people with shared beliefs and values would emerge.

While some continue to believe this myth, recent events have made it increasingly difficult to sustain. One key consequence of the social upheaval in the 1960s was the realization that the United States was not a great melting pot where everyone shared the same goals, aspirations, and outlook on life. A mosaic comprised of different shapes and colors was a more appropriate metaphor.

The popular challenge to the Vietnam War revealed a group of people openly opposed to their government's policy-making decisions. The countercultural youth movements questioned the very work ethic that served as a moral foundation for the social and economic order. The various civil-rights movements that sought equality for blacks and Hispanics led to a variety of other minority-rights groups for women, gays and lesbians, the handicapped, the aged, and so on. The ecology movement challenged the desirability of unfettered economic growth. All of these movements revealed diverse and often conflicting perspectives on the nature of life and society. The United States was not one nation, but many.

While the country experienced domestic unrest, the global scene also experienced several dramatic changes. American hegemony was challenged by the emergence of Germany and Japan as economic superpowers, as well as the unification of Europe. There is nothing like the loss of influence and authority over others to teach people the need to revise their understanding of the nature of the world they live in. The message for the United States was that many voices, not one, would have a say in how the world entered the twenty-first century.

Under these conditions, it would have been virtually impossible for a discipline like social psychology to continue to follow only a harmonic view of social life. Even Moscovici's advocacy of minority influence needs to be seen against the backdrop of recent global changes. Because these changes give more credence to a conflict view of social life, the outcome of social-influence processes must inevitably be social change, not simply conformity on the part of minority groups.

. . . .

Social Control, Domination, and the Formation of Realities

Suppose that you and I are playing a game by a set of rules that gives me an advantage over you, and that neither of us is aware that our game is "rigged" to give me this advantage. As far as we know, we are simply playing the only way we have been taught. "A preposterous situation!" you say. "Highly improbable!" Now suppose that you are black and I am white, or that you are female and I am male. Is it possible that we are involved in a "game" that operates by historical rules giving me certain advantages over you? Is it possible that as we go about living our lives, we affirm those rules and so perpetuate your relative disadvantage?

The historical process that creates, and continues to sustain, this kind of situation exercises an extraordinary degree of influence over many people. If I could create a set of rules that gave me and my kind an advantage over everyone else I would be extremely powerful in determining various outcomes, both good and bad. But what if I personally did not create the rules? What is wrong with simply playing the game and reaping the benefits that come to me and people like me? If we no longer played by the same rules, I might quickly lose my relative advantage. That advantage would require you to play the game by certain rules, and to never examine those rules. Even if I did not create the system, by participating in it I would help perpetuate a system of social domination.

For the most part, social psychology has not been concerned with the background or context of rules within which social influence operates. Most social psychologists operate within an already constituted reality, ignoring how that reality—which is the outcome of social history—is itself a significant locus of influence. In this section of the chapter we will examine this alternative focus: how social rules themselves come into being, whose interests they serve, and how this represents a potent basis for power and domination. The intent is not to be critical of the field's oversights but, more importantly, to open up new vistas of theory and research in an area clearly needing more systematic examination.

To begin, briefly recall the major distinction we noted in Part I between a conventional and a sociohistorical perspective. While the conventional view emphasizes the ways our theories *refer* to the nature of reality, the sociohistorical view emphasizes the ways those theories *form* reality. In terms of the sociohistorical perspective, theories about the nature of reality are not so much descriptions of the way the world is than proposals that form our ideas about the way the world is. The sociohistorical approach, then, is actually a story about social influence and how one group has come to dominate another.

What is missing from our consideration of the sociohistorical perspective is the idea that a given theory about the nature of reality—the "rules of the game"—did not arise spontaneously in some neutral climate; each is the victor in an historical battle of ideas. If we were to take only the prevailing theory as our measure of truth and reality, we would freeze in place *its* understandings and *its* rules as though they were the only proper ways to play the game. In doing so, of course, we would fail to recognize how those rules came into being and the special advantages built in to benefit certain players.

Clearly, this kind of social influence is quite unlike either the majority- or minority-influence approaches we considered in Chapters 8 and 9. In both of these models, social influence refers to something taking place between an agent and a target. In the majority model, a dominant agent tries to influence a less dominant target; in the minority paradigm, agent and target try to influence one another.

When we consider social influence to involve the outcomes of historical processes deeply embedded in the system and that permit one group to dominate another, we can better see how both agent and target operate within a preexisting framework binding them both to its terms. If we look at agent and target as two chess players, for example, we can see that while each is trying to make winning moves, both are still bound by the rules of the game. The agent cannot use an extra queen to checkmate the target, nor can the target use two kings to force a draw.

Although we may agree that the rules of chess do not give an unfair advantage to one player over another, beyond differences in their ability to play, we may well be less sanguine in our interpretation of the rules of everyday social games. We may legitimately inquire about the contentious, perhaps even repressive social and historical processes that created those rules and a group of people who benefit from them. While social psychologists have largely avoided this aspect of social influence, it clearly lies squarely within the purview of the sociohistorical perspective and its concern with the formative quality of our understandings.

Agenda Control

As we have seen, power and influence can be measured by the ability to determine and enforce the rules of the game; that is, to form the nature of social reality people confront. Several analysts have adopted this approach (for example, Dahl, 1989; Foucault, 1979, 1980; see also Dreyfus & Rabinow, 1982; Stam, 1987).

Citing the work of Lacey, for example, Stam distinguishes between power that stems from control over outcomes and power that derives from control over agendas. *Agenda control* is either limiting what is on the agenda or excluding certain items from discussion. Dahl presents the concept of agenda control as one of the primary criteria for a democratic political system. For example, a system is not truly democratic if one group sets the agenda and then lets others vote only on items preselected for their consideration by the dominant group.

The Hawthorne study provides one illustration of agenda control. The original investigators placed only physical features of the work environment on their agenda for understanding worker productivity. As we saw, their research suggested that another kind of agenda item—managerial style—needed to be added. By adding this item to the social psychological agenda, they set the terms of inquiry for years to come. The failure by the original researchers to include labor–management conflict as an agenda item was also a form of agenda control. In this case, since a conflict view was never discussed, it never entered public debate. As Moscovici pointed out, by defining social influence as conformity, social psychologists set the agenda for proper research on this topic for years. He and his associates have now placed a new item—minority influence—on the social-influence agenda. It has already gained legitimacy in work on social influence. And I am trying to set another item on the agenda, namely, the underlying processes by which terms are set on the agenda itself!

Anyone interested in understanding the dynamics of social influence cannot ignore the role of agenda-setting or rule-setting. To do so is to help perpetuate systems of control and domination. Suppose you are in a debate. Every time you raise a good point for your side, someone interferes, declaring what you have said to be irrelevant and out of order. The agenda is thus set in such a way that you are powerless to make a persuasive case. But who has the right to restrict your freedom to argue?

A case from Great Britain illustrates the problem of how agenda control can be used as a form of social influence. Kemp (1985) presents an analysis of a series of public hearings on nuclear waste management. He notes that such hearings had become almost routine in various areas of national decision making in Britain, involving, for example, the location of new motorways, the possibility of developing a third airport to serve London and, in the present case, nuclear energy policies. It is commonly assumed that public hearings make whatever eventual decision is reached more legitimate because the public is given an opportunity to enter into a dialogue with the government and thus participate in the decision-making process.

The public hearings Kemp studied took place over a 100-day period beginning in 1977, and involved a state-owned company seeking approval to build a nuclear waste reprocessing plant. Several organized groups attended the sessions to protest its construction. These groups spent two months preparing their cases to present during the hearings. Nevertheless, by mid-May, 1978, final parliamentary approval for the project was obtained after what appeared to be a full public inquiry.

Kemp concluded that "the communication process that occurred at the . . . public inquiry was in fact systematically distorted . . . the decision to allow the construction . . . did not reflect a genuine consensus on the issue and was not reached solely due to the force of the better argument" (p. 190). His analysis of some of the reasons for the protestors' failure reveals the exercise of genuine power in society, including the power to set the terms by which public debate itself can occur.

Kemp makes several observations. For example, the objectors lacked the same kind of financial resources the government possessed, and thus could not possibly gather the body of facts and figures needed to develop a persuasive case. Furthermore, because the government could restrict access to officially "secret" information, the protesters were unable to marshal important evidence. In effect, certain areas were deemed off limits to them, thus undermining their position. Indeed, as Kemp notes, "government policy was exempt from discussion" (p. 195). In effect, the agenda set by the government did not include probing the government's agenda-making itself!

This case clearly demonstrates how the power to set the very terms of a debate, based on both superior resources and control over access to information can reduce an open public hearing to a fixed game with largely predetermined outcomes. While agenda control still awaits further examination, Kemp clearly demonstrates that anyone genuinely interested in social influence must go beyond the traditional majority- and minority-influence paradigms.

PART FOUR

The Self in
Social Psychology

12

The Self:
An Overview

OUR LANGUAGE IS full of "self" terms: self-help; self-improve-ment; self-discipline; self-denial; self-actualization; self-es-teem; self-knowledge; self-made; self-conscious; self-reliant; self-defense; self-seeking; self-control. Our culture seems to be preoccupied with the self. We groom it, nurture it, protect it, conceal it, expose it, develop it; if we are lucky, we share it; some let it go to waste; others never have the opportunity to care for it. Given this near obsession with the self, you may be surprised to learn that our conception of it is a relatively recent historical and cultural phe-nomenon, not something rooted in human nature.

As we explore how social psychology views the self we will en-counter three traditions reflecting different, but usually complemen-tary emphases: (1) the self as a historical and cultural construction; (2) the self as a knowledge structure that organizes our experiences; and (3) the self as an ongoing product of immediate interpersonal relationships. In this chapter we will examine the first two traditions. In Chapter 13, we consider the third point of view.

. . . .

The Self in History and Culture

Several analysts date the emergence of our current conception of the self around the late sixteenth and early seventeenth centuries (for example, Baumeister, 1987; Slugoski & Ginsburg, 1989; Wilden, 1980). According to Wilden's account, the noun "self" first appeared in 1595 in the Oxford English Dictionary. This should not be taken to mean that people suddenly acquired an identity around that time; it only suggests that earlier views of the self were different. When we think of the self today, we usually think of something both personal and private. We mark off clearly recognized boundaries that separate us from others and the rest of the world, and complain when those boundaries are intruded upon.

As Ariès and Duby (1988) point out, however, life in the Middle Ages conveyed a very different understanding of privacy and self. They note, for example, that privacy meant separation from the public sphere and the usually dangerous life outside the home or community, not personal separation from everyone and everything else. The typical home had one large, multipurpose room; only later could the wealthy afford houses containing several rooms, thus introducing the possibility of personal privacy. But even then the bedroom, what we regard as the most private of places, was hardly private by today's standards.

While it is true that the bed was the most private part of the medieval household, beds were very large to accommodate more than the marital couple—children, other family members, and even servants. The "master's bedroom" served not only as a kind of family sleeping place, but was also used "for conversation, work, and even prayer" (p. 187) and for hiding the household valuables. Nearly every facet of both life and death were private only in the familial sense of the term. Every event included the large, often extended family; rarely, if ever, did the individual have privacy as we think of it. Under such conditions, of course, it is difficult to develop a concept of an independent self.

In addition, as Tuan (1982) observes, individual chairs replaced benches as seating for everyone except the highest of the nobility only well after the medieval period. In other words, until relatively recently in western history, we even sat collectively. Tuan (1982) argues that these kinds of household furnishings are important in either muting or encouraging "a growing sense of self and for an increasing appreciation of privacy and comfort" (p. 77). In his view, the growing segmentation and privitization of nearly every aspect of life marked the movement from the medieval to the modern period, and with this change there emerged a growing sense of self and self-conciousness.

Culture and the Self

If our own western past offers testimony to the historical relativity of our current notions of the self, what does the cross-cultural evidence suggest? Does every culture have a concept of the self? Or is our culture rather unique in this regard? Current studies show that while all cultures appear to have a concept of self, they vary extensively in their understanding of this concept. Heelas and Lock (1981) conducted an extensive analysis of different cultures' concepts of the self, noting that while all of them distinguished between a self and not-self, they varied widely in where they drew the boundary line. Our own concept of the self usually includes only the private interior of the person, excluding nearly everything and everyone else. Having a healthy personality, for example, is usually identified with having a well-bounded sense of self, a prerequisite to the later formation of positive interpersonal relations (for example, see Erikson, 1959; Mahler, Pine, & Bergman, 1975).

We need to keep in mind, however, that these are historical and cultural constructions, not veritable truths about all humankind. Indeed, Geertz (1973, 1984), a cultural anthropologist who did most of his research in Java, Bali, and Morocco, suggests that the western idea of the person "as a bounded, unique . . . center of awareness, emotion, judgment and action organized into a distinctive whole and set contrastively against both other such wholes and against its social and natural background, is, however incorrigible it may seem to us, a rather peculiar idea within the context of the world's cultures" (1984, p. 126). Geertz's cross-cultural studies have thus led him to conclude that the western concept of self, especially as it is recognized in the United States, is not only relatively recent, but also somewhat unusual in a broader cultural context.

For example, Geertz cites the different concepts of self he encountered in Java. The Javanese consider a person's inner feelings and outer behavior to be separate, each operating according to its own principles. Thus, those who do not act on their feelings are behaving properly. This concept radically departs from our own view, which assumes a consistency between people's inner feelings and outer behavior, and regards a disparity to be either unhealthy or a sign of insincerity.

The Javanese insist that in both inner feelings and outer expressions, people must be *alus*, not *kasar*. To be *alus* is to be pure, refined, polished, ethereal, smooth; to be *kasar* is to be impolite, uncivilized, vulgar, coarse, and rough. One should never display any untoward behaviors or imbalanced inward feelings; this would be impolite and uncivilized. Geertz presents an example of a young man who, after his wife died, appeared in public with a smile on his face, making "formal apologies for his wife's absence" (1984, p. 128). To a Javanese, he was not concealing his real feelings and putting on an insincere, false front but being *alus*. To do otherwise would have been *kasar*. If we were therapists, we might see his behavior as an unhealthy manifestation of repressed grief. In trying to push him in a way contrary to his cultural notions of a right and proper self, however, we would be upsetting not only him but the entire fabric of his culture.

Geertz informs us that the Balinese reveal yet a different version of the self, dramatizing and stylizing all facets of their lives. This helps to mute all personal signs of individuality or uniqueness, and focuses rather on the "never-changing pageant that is Balinese life" (p. 128). Whereas the performer is central to our understanding, for the Balinese it is the performance. Performers come and go, but the drama continues forever, connecting past, present, and future generations. The goal is to sustain a proper performance, not to reveal something special about the self engaged in the performance. Geertz insists that the performances in which the Balinese mute the performer's individuality are neither make-believe nor pretense designed to disguise real feelings and a real self. This is our way of thinking, not theirs.

Turning to another culture, Rosaldo (1984) examined the Ilongot of the Philippines. The Ilongot do not recognize an autonomous self operating in opposition to the life they express outwardly. "For Ilongots, in short, there is no necessary gap between 'the presentation' and 'the self' " (p. 146). This is quite different from our own view of a real self hidden from others through the many guises and masks we affect when presenting "ourselves" to others.

Lutz's work with the Ifaluk, to which we referred earlier (see pp. 19, 167), illustrates a collectivistic conception of the self. She cites an event that occurred during her first few weeks on the atoll. When she asked a group of Ifaluk women if they wanted to join her on a trip to get water, their faces expressed a shock of disbelief. As she discovered, the use of first-person singular pronouns—"*I* am going to get some water"—connotes excessive egocentrism among a people for whom the plural form—"*We'll* go get some water now, O.K.?" (p. 44)—is considered more appropriate. The use of "we" does not center activities around the speaker nor presume the separation between speaker and listener that the use of "I" communicates.

Lutz also notes that "On observing something unusual, a person would be more likely to say, 'We (speaker and listener) don't know what's going on here' than 'I don't know what's going on here' " (p. 44). In effect, "the relevant viewpoint is taken to be that of the group rather than the individual" (p. 44). Therefore, when Lutz indicated that she was going to get some water, she had communicated too much self-centeredness, failing to take cognizance of the presence and needs of others. In simple terms, while we identify *the self* and *I,* the Ifaluk identify *the self* and *we.*

Critics might argue that of course the Ifaluk think about themselves in collectivistic ways; they are a very tiny cultural group (some 430 people), living their lives on a very small atoll (about one-half square mile) isolated from others (about 500 miles from Yap and Truk in Micronesia). They *have to* think more collectively in order to survive under those conditions. Does it not also make sense that our own concept of self is neither more natural nor universal than theirs, that it too is dictated by the times and places we inhabit and the demands made upon us?

Given Japan's international success after World War II, many people have become increasingly interested in the distinctions between American and Japanese notions of the self. Japan is a modern, highly industrialized, and prosperous world power, not one of those quaint primitive tribes anthropologists seem fond of studying. Yet we still find striking differences between our own understandings of the self and those of the Japanese.

The Japanese define self in a much more inclusive, harmonious way than we do (for example, see Cousins, 1989; Kojima, 1984; Rotenberg, 1977). For example, Kojima suggests that "the concept of a self completely independent from the environment is very foreign" (p. 973) to the Japanese; therefore, they "do not think of themselves as exerting control over an environment that is utterly divorced from the self, nor over a self that stands apart from the environment" (p. 973).

Cousins captures the difference between American and Japanese notions of the self in the conclusion to his research: "When a Japanese college student describes herself as being shy at school, her referent is not an isolated ego but a self-in-human-nexus vivified in characteristic ways in the school setting; when her American counterpart says that at school she is 'sometimes shy with my teachers,' she is objectifying herself as an independent actor for whom school is background" (p. 130). This bears out Geertz's description of the western notion of the self as bounded and oppositional.

Rotenberg comments on the Japanese concept of *amae*, which can be roughly translated as a kind of desired dependency: "*Amae* exists between husband and wife, between student and teachers, between foreman and subordinate, and between doctor and patient" (p. 8). Therefore, while our culture values a fully self-contained, autonomous self, the Japanese believe in a kind of willful submersion of the self to their society.

The historical and cross-cultural accounts we have reviewed thus far invite us to adopt a sociohistorical view of the self. They lead to one clear conclusion: our current concept of the self and the importance we place on it cannot be universalized to apply to all nonwestern cultures. The self is not something fixed and immutable, with properties transcending geographical, cultural, and temporal contexts. It cannot be separated from the society and historical circumstances that define it. The self does not have an existence apart from the society and history that constructed and now describes it.

It might be useful to recall the research on caretaker–child interactions in western and nonwestern cultures reported by Ochs and Schieffelin (1984), which we first encountered in Chapter 3 (see pp. 31–33). In brief, it demonstrated how different patterns of interaction and conversation help constitute two different kinds of selves. Western caretakers talk with their children, inculcating in them a sense of the self as a distinct entity with its own particular needs, interests, and requirements to which others must learn to adapt. In nonwestern cultures, however, a different pattern of communication between caretakers and their children generates a notion of the self oriented toward others, one that must learn how to meet the requirements and demands of the family and society.

But what then *is* the self? From a sociohistorical point of view, the self is a cultural *theory* or set of beliefs about the person. According to Harré (1985), "to be a self is not to be a certain kind of being but to be in possession of a certain kind of theory" (p. 262). As we mature, we learn our culture's theories about the world, other people, and even ourselves. Different cultures have different theories. Our culture envisions the person to have a very richly furnished mental interior; many other cultures envision a much less richly furnished interior to the person's self. Our culture expects consistency between inner feelings and outer actions; other cultures regard the inner and outer worlds of the self as independent. Our culture insists on a firm boundary between self and not-self; other cultures either see a more inclusive boundary or mute the self and not-self distinctions.

Borrowing Macpherson's (1962) concept of *possessive individualism,* Shotter (1985, 1989) presents a rather intriguing idea about our own cultural beliefs about the self. Macpherson suggests that the doctrine of possessive individualism characterizes most modern western societies. According to this doctrine, each person is believed to be "an owner of himself" (Macpherson, 1962, p. 3). We believe that each individual has a natural ownership of his or her own person and own capabilities.

In other words, we believe that in addition to being able to possess (own) external possessions (for example, cars, computers, land), we are also the proprietors of everything that makes up ourselves: our assets, our abilities, our minds, and so on. For example, have you ever heard someone urge a friend "to own" his or her feelings? This illustrates this sense of self-ownership. Of course, as owners we can dispose of our capacities as we wish; no one else is responsible for their coming into being and no one else is responsible for what we do with them. We owe nothing to society for what we personally own.

We can better appreciate possessive individualism by contrasting it with the Native American concept of ownership. In this view, people are caretakers, not owners. Because they do not own the land, for example, it is not theirs to give or to sell, but only to nurture. Likewise, the self is not a private, personal possession to be dealt with as one personally wishes, but part of something greater than the individual given to his or her care.

Shotter maintains that possessive individualism helps to structure a particular idea of the self as a separate entity with its own center. Therefore, prevailing concepts of the self in western cultures are a product of their particular belief systems; there is nothing natural or inevitable about them. Alternative ideas about the self are possible and, some would argue, desirable.

The Self as a Knowledge Structure

Most contemporary social psychologists studying the self have tended to adopt the conventional rather than the sociohistorical perspective. Consequently, (a) empirical findings on the self are considered "discoveries" about a naturally occurring object rather than a cultural construction; and (b) both historical and cultural factors involved in constructing different notions of the self are ignored or minimized. On the other hand, the current cognitive emphasis in social psychology has led a growing body of investigators to regard the self as a knowledge structure that organizes our experiences, a view potentially compatible with the sociohistorical understanding of the self as a culturally constructed belief system.

What does it mean to call the self a knowledge structure? Having reviewed social psychology's most commonly accepted definitions of the self and finding most of them deficient in one way or another, Epstein (1973) recommends that we understand the self as a *theory*; that is, an organized arrangement of beliefs about the self and the world that help people function better. An example Epstein (1985) cites is of a person's theory about authority. The theory contains descriptions of what authority figures are like ("In my experience with them, they are dangerous"); what must be done when around them ("I have found it best to placate them"), and so on. Similarly, a self-theory will contain many other beliefs the individual has built up from his or her personal experiences.

Retaining the main thrust of Epstein's argument, other investigators have leaned more heavily on the cognitive concept of *schema*, or knowledge structure, rather than the term "theory" in defining the self (for example, Greenwald & Pratkanis, 1984; Markus, 1977; Markus, Smith, & Moreland, 1985; Pratkanis & Greenwald, 1985). A schema describes a central knowledge structure involved in processing information—in this case, information about self-experiences. Markus, Smith, and Moreland, for example, see the self to be "a set of self-schemas that organize past experiences and are used to recognize and interpret relevant stimuli in the social environment" (p. 1495).

In spite of some similarities in terminology between the conventional and sociohistorical frameworks, we thus have two contrasting points of view about the self. Although the differences will become clearer as we examine specific examples, it will be useful to briefly highlight the most important differences between the two perspectives as a summary of where we have been and a preview of where we are going.

1. The conventionalists' emphasis continues to be on the self as a property of the individual's cognitive system; for the sociohistoricists, the self is a property of the culture. Thus, the conventional view emphasizes how self-schemas are built up by individuals as a function of their unique individual experiences. In contrast, the sociohistorical emphasis is upon the

dominant cultural beliefs that the individual later internalizes: "What we talk of *as* our experience of reality is constituted for us very largely by the *already established* ways in which we *must* talk in our attempts to *account* for ourselves . . . to the others around us" (Shotter, 1989, p. 141).

2. Whereas the conventionalists approach their findings about the self as discoveries about a real phenomenon presumably having meaning independent of any particular social or historical context, the sociohistoricists insist that the culture proposes both a self and its properties, and that neither would exist without a cultural theory.

3. Although the conventionalists' view of the self as a structure of knowledge learned on the basis of personal experiences appears compatible with the sociohistorical position, conventionalists remain trapped by the idea that the knowledge structure or schema is located inside the individual; this sharply contrasts with the sociohistorical view that the knowledge structure is rooted in particular historical and cultural circumstances.

Understanding the Self in Social Psychology

We will now examine three central issues social psychologists have addressed in their search to understand the nature of the self: (1) Is there one self or are there many selves? (2) Is the self stable and consistent, or malleable and inconsistent? (3) How is the self related to a person's behavior? Since most research has been conducted using the conventional model, we will primarily use that perspective.

One Self or Many Selves?

It is likely that each of us has had contradictory experiences involving his or her self. On the one hand, we like to consider ourselves unitary; that is, we believe in one true self that describes who or what we really are, even if we sometimes have difficulty finding it. This experience of oneness is usually facilitated by a sense of continuity to our experiences. When we go to bed at night, we seem to be the same person who wakes up in the morning; even over a long period of time we feel like the same person. There is thus a continuity in our experiences, even though they are separated by different times and circumstances, that conveys to us a feeling of oneness.

On the other hand, sometimes we speak as though we were made up of many selves, sometimes in conflict and sometimes in harmony. Although Freud did not refer to the self as such, his tripartite division of our psychic apparatus into an ego, id, and superego portrays many selves in constant conflict: an impulsive id that, like a child, strives to satisfy its desires immediately; a watchful superego that, like a stern parent, punishes the child with feelings of guilt; and an ego trying to balance the id and superego with the current demands of reality.

William James (1910), a major figure in the history of psychology, also proposed a variety of selves dwelling within each of us, ranging from a bodily self to a social self to a more spiritual self. Several prominent sociologists and social philosophers have proposed similar views of the individual as made up of many selves. Cooley (1902) proposed a model of the self as a mirror or looking glass that reflects each person we meet. This gives us as many selves as there are people whose reflections we adopt. Mead (1934) offered a view of the self as a property of social interaction similar to Cooley's formulation. We will examine Mead's ideas in more detail in Chapter 13.

Building on these ideas, Alexander (Alexander & Knight, 1971; Alexander & Weil, 1969) proposed a "situated identity" perspective on the self. In this view, each of our actions in a social setting has implications for the kind of person we are and "obliges others to regard [us] as being that kind of person" (Alexander & Knight, p. 66). Because situations call for different situated identities, we are likely to have a wide variety of selves as a function of the many situations we are in. We will also have more to say about this idea in Chapter 13.

The idea of having many selves seems to coincide with many of our everyday experiences. We complain, for example, that "I just wasn't myself today" or "I don't know what got into me." Some normal, healthy people talk of dialogues they have with themselves, especially when trying to make a tough decision: "My rational and reasonable self told me to study, but my fun-loving self said, 'What the hell, go out and have some fun tonight!' " Many of us are also aware of the more pathological manifestations of having many selves. Classic cases, like that of Sally Beauchamp (Prince, 1920), and more popularized accounts, like *The Three Faces of Eve*, demonstrate so-called multiple personality disorders. Currently, there is an interest in how the self splits under conditions of childhood incest or abuse. In these circumstances, the abused self is separated from the remaining self, which grows into adulthood tormented by the efforts of the split-off abused self to destroy it.

Current thinking in social psychology seems to favor a multiplicity, rather than a unity, of selves (for example, see Gergen, 1967; Markus & Kunda, 1986; Markus & Nurius, 1986; Pratkanis & Greenwald, 1985). For example, Markus and Kunda have noted that "the self is not a unitary structure or even a generalized average of images and cognitions. Instead, the self-concept encompasses . . . a wide variety of self-conceptions—the good selves, the bad selves, the hoped-for selves, the feared selves, the not-me selves, the ideal selves, the possible selves, the ought selves" (p. 858). The authors reason that at any given moment, we function according to a *working self-concept:* the most currently available view of ourselves.

Markus and Nurius suggest that of this wide variety of selves the *possible self*—the person we might become—is often neglected. This self is said to serve as both an incentive to future activity and a standard against which we can measure progress. Markus suggests that by adopting this multidimensional view of the self she and her associates propose, we will improve our ability to understand and predict a person's feelings and behavior.

Some Unresolved Questions

If we accept the idea of multiple selves as healthy rather than pathological, two intriguing questions come to mind. First, where is our *real* self? Many of us believe that somewhere under our many masks is a real "we" and that our task is to discover that real self and let it guide our everyday lives. This belief is very much rooted in our culture, and so is perhaps better examined from a sociohistorical point of view.

The question is not whether we have one real self among our several selves. Social psychologists will never be able to answer this kind of question, nor will they resolve the argument whether it is healthier to have many selves or only one. We live in a culture in which various beliefs exist concerning the nature of the self. These cultural beliefs propose certain shapes for reality; multiplicity or singularity are not properties of something that can be empirically identified.

The real question, then, is not whether people have one or many selves, but what role the belief people have in one self or many selves plays in our culture. Why has there been a shift from viewing multiple selves as a pathology to a sign of good mental health? What cultural functions are served by believing in a real self, and that we are at our best only when we allow our true self to guide us? For example, it could be argued that as our society becomes increasingly complex, it functions more efficiently if we believe that, rather than playing different roles, we are revealing our many different selves. We don't worry about a "real" self denied expression in our lives because we see ourselves in everything we do. On the other hand, it could prove just as comforting to deny responsibility for our role-playing and preserve some sense of personal integrity through a belief in a real self independent of our different roles.

Relationships Between Our Selves

A second question raised by the possibility of multiple selves is, What are the relations among them? One of the most extensively examined aspects of this issue is the discrepancy between people's *ideal self* and their *current self*. This discrepancy is often taken to be a measure of people's level of self-esteem. That is, people whose ideal and current selves have low correspondence have less self-esteem than those with a high correspondence between ideal and current selves.

Finding this approach too simplistic, several investigators have introduced several refinements. For example, Ogilvie (1987) has suggested that rather than the ideal–current self discrepancy, we should examine differences between people's current self and what Ogilvie calls their *undesired self*, what the person does *not* wish to become. He suggests that the current–undesired self discrepancy reveals self-esteem from another, more negative approach: the farther our current self is from our undesired self, the happier and more satisfied we are.

Ogilvie studied this possibility by giving a group of college students a series of questions to answer. They first listed the various identities they currently had. Next, they indicated those qualities they liked and disliked in themselves and others. They then listed those qualities that corresponded to each of their several identities. Finally, they completed a measure of their life satisfaction. From the data, Ogilvie determined to what degree the subjects' ideal–current self and current–undesired self discrepancies respectively contributed to their life satisfaction.

Results confirmed the importance of both kinds of discrepancy for the experience of life satisfaction. However, the data more clearly supported the notion that "the implicit standard individuals use to assess their well-being is how close (or how distant) they are from subjectively being like their most negative images of themselves"

(p. 383). Ogilvie points out that this finding runs counter to our cultural intuitions that we are driven more by positive goals—achieving our ideal selves—than by negative ones—avoiding becoming our undesired selves. Even if the "push" factor is stronger than the "pull" factor, however, it is probably safe to say that both impulses affect people's self-esteem and sense of satisfaction.

Extensive research on discrepancies among our several selves has also been reported by Higgins (1987). In one investigation, for example, Van Hook and Higgins (1988) suggest that many people find themselves caught between the pull of two positively valued selves. In other words, discrepancies do not always involve a conflict between where we are now and where we would like to be (current–ideal self discrepancy) or between where we are now and where we do not want to be (current–undesired self discrepancy), but may also involve discrepancies among two valued selves. For example, we may value both assertiveness and sensitivity to others.

Van Hook and Higgins thus suggest that there may sometimes be conflicts among discrepant *guides* for our behavior. Their research examined the particular psychological vulnerabilities of people experiencing these kinds of conflicts. Their findings indicate that people confronting a discrepancy between two valued selves, each of which presents a different guide for behavior, tend to feel more confused and uncertain than those not experiencing such a conflict. Given so many guiding selves, discrepancies even between valued selves can prove distressing, especially in conjunction with current–ideal self or current–undesired self discrepancies.

In another investigation, Strauman and Higgins (1987) studied how people react emotionally when their own self discrepancies are revealed to them. They focused on discrepancies (a) between subjects' ratings of their current self and their ideal self and (b) between their rating of their current self and their *ought self*, who they felt obligated to become. An actual–ideal self discrepancy would occur, for example, if I evaluate myself as a cold, distant, and analytic person who wishes to be more warm, understanding, and compassionate. An actual–ought self-discrepancy would occur if I evaluate myself as a cold, distant, and analytic person whose position as a kindergarten teacher obliges me to take on much more nurturant functions.

Strauman and Higgens' data showed that when either type of discrepancy is activated, negative emotional consequences follow, but that the actual reaction depends on which discrepancy is involved. Current–ideal self discrepancies, for example, produce a saddened and dejected state; current–ought self discrepancies produce a state of activation and increased arousal.

Stability or Malleability?

Is the self stable and consistent or more malleable and inconsistent, shifting with different situational demands? If we assume that there is one dominant or true self, then we would likely regard the self as stable and fixed; if we insist on the notion of multiple selves, we would likely come down on the side of malleability and situational specificity.

Compelling personal experiences as well as research data support both perspectives. For example, we know that people go to extreme lengths to maintain a particularly desired image of themselves, resisting information that threatens to undermine the version they most value. This is the position we saw in Greenwald's notion of the totalitarian ego (see Chapter 6, pp. 116–17). In this conception, people operate like a dictatorship, modifying and distorting information to protect their desired self-images. Swann and his associates (1987; Swann & Ely, 1984; Swann & Hill, 1982) likewise demonstrate how people act in such a way as to verify both positive and negative images of themselves and resist any efforts to change them. (We will explore this theme in more detail in Chapter 13.)

On the other hand, there are indications of great variability in our selves as a function of our particular circumstances. Both Cooley (1902) and Mead (1934) proposed social origins of the self suggesting its inevitable situational specificity. The situated-identity concept and research of Alexander and his colleagues (1969, 1971) has confirmed these ideas. It appears that malleability would be more likely than stability for a self conceived as thoroughly embedded in social interaction. In this view, stability is an achievement that (as we will see in Chapter 13) takes careful work to accomplish.

Markus and Kunda (1986) examined the stability–malleability issue more directly. They experimentally created a situation in which subjects found themselves to be either unique in their group (made up of the experimenters' accomplices) or very similar to it. For example, subjects would experience themselves to be unique in their group if their judgments were frequently discrepant on a task they were presented; subjects would see themselves as similar to the group if they gave roughly the same responses on the task.

On completing the experimental manipulation inducing either uniqueness or similarity, all subjects completed several questionnaires, including measures of the self. One measure assessed their reaction time to a series of slides containing self-relevant words dealing with uniqueness of traits (for example, "original" or "independent") or similarity of traits (for example, "average" or "normal"). The subjects' task was to press a "me" button or a "not me" button for each word, indicating whether it did or did not describe them. A second measure asked for the subjects' associations to words, one set of which pertained to similarity (for example, "ordinary"), the other to uniqueness (for example, "unusual").

The study design created a situation in which the way people habitually thought of themselves ("I am similar to others" or "I am unique") would be either confirmed or disconfirmed by the experimental treatment into which they were placed. For example, those who believed themselves to be like others and who were put into a situation where they saw themselves as unique would have received some disconfirming evidence about themselves. Markus and Kunda assumed that people would try to restore consistency to their selves: those whose similarity was disconfirmed would try to restore consistency by emphasizing how similar they were to others; those whose uniqueness was disconfirmed would try to restore consistency by emphasizing how dissimilar they were to others.

Data supported *both* the stability and the malleability perspectives, as Markus and Kunda suggested they might. On the one hand, being subjected to the experimental situation did not fundamentally alter their subjects' self-conceptions; they retained a certain consistency or stability to their sense of themselves. The core selves with which they entered were similar to the core selves with which they left even though they had received information discrepant with their sense of self. On the other hand, response time and word-association data did suggest the influence of the experimental manipulation on the subjects' working selves; that is, the current, temporary view subjects held of themselves. For example, those individuals made to feel that they were unique and who were apparently disturbed by this view of themselves offered more negative associations to uniqueness-related words and more positive associations to similarity-related words. Likewise, they revealed more rapid response times to words emphasizing their similarity to others and slower times to words indicating their difference from others. In short, Markus and Kunda found that their subjects recruited self-images that would counter the information provided them by the experimental manipulation of uniqueness or similarity. They argue that such findings at least reveal people's temporary malleability because they demonstrate how momentary environmental influences (such as the experimental manipulations) can influence the self-conceptions people have.

It is reasonable to conclude that we are characterized by both a general stability and consistency over time and across situations, and by a temporary malleability as a function of the kinds of situations we are in and the information they provide us. We are obviously sensitive to the events that surround us, and so take these into consideration when forming judgments about ourselves; but just as obviously, we are not transformed into a totally different person after each encounter.

Self and Behavior

Once we treat the self as a structure that organizes knowledge about our experiences in the world, we put it in a category with cognitive structures or schemas—attitudes, for example. The issues involved in relating self to behavior are just as complex as those we considered in Chapter 10 relating attitudes to behavior. Several reviews of research studies linking self and behavior have shown important connections (for example, Hales, 1985; Pratkanis & Greenwald, 1985; Markus & Nurius, 1986). For example, people tend to pay more attention to and have better recall of self-schema information that is relevant than self-schema information that is irrelevant. Likewise, there appears to be a relationship between self-schema and a wide variety of phenomena, including our perception of others, attributional biases, impression formation, stereotyping, and so on. (We will discuss this relationship in detail in Chapter 14.)

Conclusions

This chapter has presented an overview of the self in the context of social psychology, considering it from both the conventional and sociohistorical perspectives. We began by examining the definition and meaning of the self, noting that for most social psychologists today the self is a knowledge structure or schema that organizes our self-relevant experiences and guides our behavior. We examined several issues involving whether the self was multifaceted or singular as well as whether it was stable or malleable.

From the perspective of the sociohistorical framework, the self is an historical and cultural invention. Our descriptions of the self are therefore proposals about what the self is like rather than discoveries about its real nature. This does not make the self any less real, but leads us to determine what social functions are served by proposing that the self has particular characteristics.

If the sociohistoricists are right and the self is part of the cultural fabric, it seems likely that cultural changes will produce new conceptions of the self that will guide the understandings of future generations. For example, I have recently suggested that western civilization is undergoing a transformation as profound as the change from traditional to modern society—a segmented world of independent nations and clearly defined boundaries to a globalized world of interdependent nations and blurred boundaries (Sampson, 1989).

We noted earlier in the chapter that the socioeconomic transformation of western civilization in the late sixteenth and early seventeenth centuries brought with it a more modern conception of the self. Similarly, the transformation from modern to postmodern, global civilization will revolutionize our beliefs about the nature of the self. If today the focus is on a single, sharply bounded self, the pressures of globalization are leading social psychologists to think in terms of a more fluid, loosely bounded self.

We are already witnessing dramatic changes in the world. Economies, no longer confined within national boundaries, link the fate of individuals in distant lands. Satellites, communicating the common hopes and fears of people around the globe, likewise connect nations with an invisible thread. Pollution and the threat of nuclear war affect everyone. Political and religious policies in almost every nation have potentially serious global consequences. Dated theories of the self reflecting a segmented world view must yield to theories more suited to a global world view. Future social psychologists will undoubtedly "discover" very different qualities of the self than is demonstrated by current work.

13

The Dynamics of Self-Negotiating

U P TO THIS point we have examined the idea of the self as (a) a historical and cultural theory about persons and as (b) a knowledge structure for organizing experiences. As we have seen, despite their differences these views tend to be more complementary than contradictory. The same can be said about the view we will examine in this chapter, the idea of a self as the ongoing product of immediate interpersonal relationships.

This view differs from the first approach by examining specific interpersonal relationships that give rise to, sustain, and transform the person's self rather than the broader forces of history and culture. It differs from the second tradition's emphasis on the properties of the self as a knowledge structure by concentrating on the processes by which such knowledge structures emerge in social interaction. This interpersonal focus has been influenced more by the writings of Mead (1934) and Goffman (1959) than by the cognitive-science literature upon which the second tradition is based. In this chapter we will use it to explore the ways we manage, or negotiate, our self-images.

The idea of self-negotiating in interpersonal settings to a large extent is derived from Mead's *symbolic interactionist* perspective and Goffman's *dramaturgic* analysis.

The Meadian View of Interpersonal Dynamics

Mead suggested that the interpersonal process in which the self emerges involves three stages: (1) A person makes a gesture, either verbal or nonverbal that (2) indicates a resulting behavior to which (3) another person responds. For example, Peter says, "Please pass the butter" (1). The words indicate a resulting behavior, in this case Peter receiving the butter from its location at the other end of the table (2). Sandy's response of passing the butter to Peter completes the third phase of this interpersonal process (3).

The process is interpersonal in that while it is initiated by one person (Peter), it is completed by another (Sandy). In Mead's view the meaning of Peter's gesture is not communicated in the words he utters (1), or even in the behavior he anticipates resulting from having uttered those words (2); the full meaning emerges only as Sandy makes her response (3). If rather than passing the butter, for example, Sandy passed the salt, the meaning of Peter's gesture would be different.

Now suppose that Peter raises his hand above his head and makes a fist. He anticipates that this gesture will be taken by Sandy as playful; that is, for Peter the action indicated by the gesture is not threatening. However, Sandy's response is to drop back defensively. She experiences the gesture as anything but playful. The meaning remains incomplete and unclear until Sandy responds. At that point, the process is completed and the meaning emerges. Meaning thus emerges in social interaction, as one person's gestures are completed by another person's responses, rendering the gestures meaningful.

According to Mead, because both Peter and Sandy can mentally represent this entire process to themselves, they are able to communicate together. Although he was in error in the raised-arm example, in general Peter is able to place himself in Sandy's position and anticipate what her likely responses will be to the various gestures he makes. It is because we can look at ourselves from other people's point of view that we can anticipate what our gestures are likely to mean to them. Taking the role of the other person is therefore a central idea in Mead's scheme. Thinking itself is said to involve this same kind of internal conversation of gestures, one person taking the role of the other person and imaginatively carrying on a conversation. There is always an audience in our thinking, a presence we imagine to complete the gestures we initiated.

The self emerges from this same process. The gestures we make are representations of who we claim to be. We are able to gauge which gestures will accomplish the desired responses from others because we can complete the entire three-phase process imaginatively, anticipating their reactions to our gestures. For example, if Peter is interested in appearing to be a sensitive intellectual, he knows that carrying a well-worn copy of Nietzsche will communicate his intellectual qualities to others familiar with this material. Peter thus imaginatively puts himself in his audience's place, looking upon his gesture (carrying the book) as evoking the meaning "intellectual."

In the Meadian view, we develop our self-concept through this same process. We initially take the role of the significant others in our immediate world—parents, playmates, and so on. They are the primary sources of our self-attitudes, and so we acquire a sense of who we are by seeing ourselves in their terms. Over time we learn to enlarge our framework for viewing ourselves and, in Mead's terms, learn to take the role of the *generalized other*—our culture. We learn how our culture generally interprets certain gestures, building up our self-concept by seeing ourselves through its eyes.

It is for this reason, of course, that when we venture into a very different culture, we may be unsure of how we appear and thus who we really are. Since our identities are not self-contained but the products of social interaction, we are unsure of ourselves in a foreign culture because we are unable to gauge others' reactions. We may, for example, think that our copy of Nietszche evokes a response of "intellectual" from our audience, only to learn that because both the author and even the very concept of a book is alien to our audience, it is irrelevant to the responses they make to us.

Social psychologists adopting the Meadian framework have generally pursued two somewhat different, though conceptually related, lines of investigation:

1. The first approach, self-presentational or impression management, explores the implications of a dramaturgic formulation of human behavior—the idea that people elicit others' responses to their behavior in order to project certain self-images. This, of course, is what Peter tries to do by carrying around *The Genealogy of Morals* or *Beyond Good and Evil.*

2. The second approach examines how the interpersonal process itself gives rise to the self. In particular, it focuses on

the degree to which our self-appraisals are matched by others' actual appraisals of ourselves.

Before we examine either of these two approaches, however, we must first deal with one conspicuous feature of the Meadian view—the *vulnerability* of the self to others. Given that who we are is derived largely from social interaction, we are always potentially vulnerable to others' responses.

Vulnerability

If your presence is required to confirm my sense of self, then without you I remain unsure of who I am. Sartre (1954) beautifully captured this sense of vulnerability in his play, *No Exit.* Sartre's vision of hell has three characters trapped together for an eternity. We will examine the relationship between two of them—Estelle and Inez.

Estelle is an especially vain woman who will go nowhere without her mirror; the source of her comfort and self-validation. Yet here, where she will spend an eternity, there are no mirrors. How can she be sure if she even exists? Inez agrees to be Estelle's mirror. Inez beckons Estelle to approach closely and look into her eyes, where she can see herself reflected as a tiny object in Inez's pupils.

As Estelle takes pleasure in seeing herself through Inez's eyes, Inez announces that she sees a tiny blemish, a pimple fouling Estelle's otherwise perfect face. Horrified, Estelle is unsure of what to do. There is actually no blemish; Inez is only teasing. The joke barely conceals the dilemma that Estelle faces. With Inez as her only mirror—the only source that can validate who she is and what she is like—Estelle is trapped into believing whatever Inez tells her. Inez's report of a blemish becomes a real blemish. No wonder, then, that for Sartre "hell is other people" whose reflections of us establish who we are.

The relationship between Estelle and Inez illustrates three points about the self as understood in the symbolic interactionist tradition:

1. We can see how Estelle is dependent on Inez to verify her existence, and thus how the self becomes a property of social interaction. This point is driven home when Estelle protests Inez's teasing behavior. At that point, Inez threatens to shut her eyes and cease being Estelle's mirror, thereby causing Estelle to nearly panic. Without Inez to look, would Estelle have a self?

2. We can see how the interpersonal nature of our selves makes us vulnerable. Inez's proposal of a blemish frightens Estelle

because she has no means of verifying her identity other than through Inez's eyes.

3. Estelle is not an entirely passive victim of Inez's whims. It later develops that Inez has a romantic interest in Estelle; this gives Estelle a negotiating position from which to manage the situation. Estelle can play off Inez's feelings to get her to validate Estelle's beauty. In other words, even though Estelle's sense of her self is dependent on Inez, Estelle is able to actively manage her performances to create the self she desires, not passively accept whatever self Inez is willing to provide her.

If the self was a complete and intact entity, immune to the comments of others, Estelle's vulnerability in *No Exit* would make little sense. In the Meadian context, however, the self is given meaning only through social interaction. Since other people define who we are, like Sartre's characters we become their existential "prisoners."

As Mead points out, however, we are not passive prisoners of others. He suggests that people actively manage their identities to minimize their degree of vulnerability. While the self is constituted on others' responses to our gestures, in time we learn to put ourselves in their positions and anticipate how they would react: "What would someone be like who acts in this manner?" This imaginative process permits us to make those gestures that will evoke the kind of responses from others that reinforce the self-image we want to project.

Of course, a certain vulnerability is always present. We may "read" our audience incorrectly, anticipating a favorable response to our gestures and instead being judged as unsophisticated or vulgar. How many times have you told a joke you were certain would evoke laughter from your audience, only to be answered with silent reproof or disapproval. In these instances, our efforts to manage our self-images backfire, leaving us feeling even more vulnerable than before.

We are also vulnerable when we "read" our audience correctly but they reject the image we are trying to project through our gestures. They see through our phony performance, judging us as insincere or disingenuous for representing ourselves as something we clearly are not. The suitor who arrives with bountiful gifts and gushy compliments for his date may be rejected because his behavior is seen to be a maneuver designed only for a quick seduction.

Self-Presentation and Impression Management

Goffman (1959), whom we first encountered in Chapter 6 (see pp. 83–85), pioneered naturalistic studies of the ingenious processes people use to present themselves to others and manage their self-impressions. According to Goffman, there are virtually no limits to human stagecraft in trying to manage both onstage performances and offstage events that sustain or undermine desired self-images. We choose our costumes carefully; select our props wisely; we place ourselves in situations that show us off as we would like to be seen; we provide our best profiles for the camera; we associate with those who confirm our self-images; we manage both verbal and nonverbal presentations to create favorable impressions of our character.

Both sociologists and social psychologists have found this perspective intriguing. Although their research tends to differ in predictable ways—sociologists tend to examine real-life settings, while social psychologists tend to work in the laboratory—both their findings reveal some of the ways that the self, at least in today's society, can be defined in terms of self-negotiation processes.

Routine and Precarious Situations

You might think that people spend all of their time engaging in self-presentations either to achieve a desired identity or confirm the identity they think they already have. Fortunately, however, so much of our daily lives are routine that we are often oblivious to the various processes of self-negotiation at work. For example, we sit in the classroom and watch our professor pace back and forth lecturing and writing on the chalkboard. This is a very familiar routine, so familiar that we usually pay little attention to the subtle ways that the situation structures the selves of both students and the professor.

Context plays a significant role in the emergence of the self. There are few places in our lives other than a classroom in which we would simply sit passively and let someone else talk on and on and on. The very structure of the classroom also contains a message about who is who in this drama. The professor is standing; the students are seated. The professor is alone at the front of the room; the students are clustered together in the back. The professor speaks; the students do not, except under special conditions under the control of the professor. In these and other ways, routine situations like this conceal the processes that create and help sustain the participants' selves.

Although routines are usually just that—bland, unthinking, repetitive—they, too, can leave people vulnerable. I remember teaching a social psychology class at Berkeley to some 500 students one day in the late 1960s when suddenly the lights went out and a display of music and flashing, colored lights filled the room. Some of the students had decided to disrupt the routine and create their own classroom: *they* were going to teach *me*. While I sat, astonished at their inventiveness, several students approached and asked me to do something. They wanted me to reclaim my professorial self and take control back from those who had usurped it. One student even came forward crying over this terrible event, claiming it not only deprived her of my wisdom (she clearly deserved an A) but also challenged the identities that had been so carefully protected by the normal classroom routine.

Garfinkel (1967) gave his students practice exercises outside the classroom designed to disrupt routine situations in order to study how the identities of those involved in the routines would be affected. While most of these disruptions raise serious ethical questions, they generally demonstrated the precarious possibilities of even routine situations. In one case, for example, he instructed his students to "be a guest in their own home." For most of us, there is probably no environment more governed by routine than the home: everyone knows who they are and what is expected of them, and so they act out their roles without much thought. Being a guest in your own home, however, disrupts those routines and forces everyone in the setting to reassess what is done to sustain the identities achieved there.

Since guests do not walk into a house without first knocking, Garfinkel's students given this assignment first had to knock. But what did this mean to those inside their home? "Probably forgot the keys." Guests also do not walk in and simply take a seat, help themselves to food in the kitchen, or look through the mail piled on the table. When the students waited for a seat or the offer of food, they were met with disbelief, puzzlement, and often anger. By disrupting normal routines and thereby making the situation precarious, they exposed some of the rules by which routine situations operate and maintain participants' identities.

The same processes of self-presentation we examined earlier thus occur in routine situations. We only become aware of them, however, when those routines are somehow disrupted. At those moments, we can see how our everyday gestures evoke responses that confirm our (routine) identity. My behavior and that of my students evoked responses confirming our respective identities until the routine was disrupted. By intentionally acting as guests in our own home, we call attention to how home routines confirm us as members of the family.

Rather than artificially create problematic situations by disrupting normal routines, some investigators have examined naturally occurring problematic situations. Emerson (1975), for example, studied how male physicians and their female patients sustain their respective identities as "doctor" and "patient" during a gynecological examination. She observed that the language each used when referring to body parts and the setting of the exam—for example, having another female present—avoided sexual inferences to sustain a professional relationship. More recently, Young (1989) conducted a similar analysis of a routine medical examination that, regardless of the gender of the physician or patient, involves a bodily violation that must be thoughtfully stage-managed by everyone.

Disconfirmation in the Laboratory

Experimental social psychologists seeking more precision in their research have turned to the laboratory to study the effects on the individual of precarious-identity situations. The typical way to create such a situation is to provide individuals with disconfirming information about themselves. That is, people receive information in the laboratory contradicting beliefs they had about themselves before going in.

What will people do when they receive information clearly disconfirming their self-image? We saw one example of this in the study reported by Markus and Kunda in Chapter 12 (see pp. 218–20). For the most part, subjects resisted yielding their self-images to the disconfirming information provided by the experimenters. Swann (1987) reports several investigations, carried out as part of an extensive research program, in which people were given information disconfirming their self-images. There are at least two possibilities available to people under such conditions: They can accept the information and change their self-images, or they can refute the information and try to change the source's views. Swann and his associates investigated both possibilities.

In one study, Swann and Hill (1982) provided subjects with information discrepant with their current sense of themselves. Some of the subjects were given an opportunity to refute this information, while others were denied this opportunity. Data indicated that the opportunity to reject disconfirming feedback from others permitted people to keep their self-images relatively intact; on the other hand, when they were denied this opportunity, they were more affected and so tended to change their reported self-images.

Swann and Hill note that much of the laboratory research in which people receive disconfirming information does not allow them a chance to refute it. It is this kind of research that reports subjects modifying their self-image in response to negative feedback. On the other hand, in natural settings, where rejection and refutation are probable self-protective responses, less self-image modification is usually reported. It seems therefore that, given the opportunity, people actively manage their self-images by rejecting rather than accepting inconsistent information.

Looking at the refutational possibility from another angle, Swann and Ely (1984) suggested that the *certainty* with which individuals maintain a particular image of themselves influences whether they will accept disconfirming information or confront the source. In studying this possibility, Swann and Ely generally found that when targets' self-images are challenged by a source, the more certain the targets are about their self-images, the less likely they are to concede to the source. On the other hand, targets relatively unsure of themselves change their self-images.

Because Swann and Ely consider the situation to be a battle of wills between targets and sources, it is legitimate to ask who is likely to win this battle. Their answer is clear: "it was the targets who triumphed" (p. 1298). In other words, targets usually emerged from the experiment with their self-images intact, whereas sources of disconfirming information about the targets changed their impressions to be more congruent with the targets' own self-images.

Self-Confirmation or Self-Enhancement?

As we have seen, when challenged with disconfirming information we strongly resist changing our self-images. Swann (1987) argues further that people try to get others to validate their self-image even if it is a *negative* one. Self-confirmation is thus more important than self-enhancement: "I'd rather be right than liked."

Hales (1985) and Jones (1973) argue that, on the contrary, self-enhancement is more important to us than self-confirmation. In their view, people try to negotiate—that is, establish and maintain—positive self-images and repair negative self-images: "I'd rather be liked than right." Several other investigators also support this view. For example, Brown, Collins, and Schmidt (1988) report that, given a choice between validation/consistency theories (like Swann's) and enhancement theories, subjects preferred the enhancement strategy. Their data also indicate that self-enhancement is predominant regardless of the subjects' level of self-esteem. In other words, both high and low self-esteem subjects behaved in ways they thought would enhance their self-images. Low-esteem groups, for example, did not try to verify their poor self-images: "those with low self-esteem are not disinterested in enhancing self-worth because of overriding concerns with maintaining self-consistency" (pp. 451–52).

Where, then, do we stand regarding self-negotiation? Do people prefer to be correct, as the verificationists maintain, or well liked, as the enhancement perspective argues? In spite of the compelling conclusions some investigators have reached, Swann continues to maintain the verificationist position. Needless to say, it seems only appropriate for a verificationist to try to refute disconfirming evidence! Swann suggests, for example, that because most people have positive views of themselves, the typical study never gives the verificationist position a fair test. He claims that a fair test would require including people who have "chronically negative self-views of which they are reasonably certain" (p. 1046).

Surely, we all have encountered people who seem to enjoy maintaining negative self-images, at least with some audiences. Two personal examples, both university presidents, come to mind. Both presidents claimed that having the faculty view them negatively helped them negotiate with the state legislature and governor, who thought negatively of the faculty. Under these conditions, maintaining a negative self-image, at least in front of one audience (the faculty), is preferable to wanting to be liked by that audience. "Let mine enemies fear me and dislike me!" Is this the rant of someone seeking verification of a negative self-image or someone for whom a negative self-image is useful in a larger context of political negotiation?

If we work within the Meadian framework, the self-confirmation versus self-enhancement debate might well be moot. As Mead argues, self-images emerge in a social context. Thus, a person's self-image may be negative in some contexts and positive in others. This situation appears clearly in the case of the two university presidents cited earlier. The presidents wanted to be confirmed as negative by the faculty audience—a self-confirmation position—but as positive by the legislature and governor—a self-enhancement view. It seems, then, that the rivalry between self-confirmation and self-enhancement theories is more an incomplete analysis of the social side of the self than a true debate between opposing perspectives.

. . . .

Approaches to Negotiating a Self-Image

Regardless of whether people seek to achieve a positive self-image or simply have their existing self-image confirmed, their task remains the same: to evoke desired feedback from an audience. There are several possible ways to do this: (a) We can try to be selective about the audiences before whom we perform; (b) we can be biased information processors; (c) we can adopt strategies of interaction—self-presentation or altercasting—that achieve the image we desire; or (d) we can nullify our challengers or even ourselves.

Selective Interaction

A common finding in social psychology confirms the popular proverb that "birds of a feather flock together." While we can posit a variety of reasons for the tendency of people to associate with others similar to themselves, one plausible interpretation involves using similarity as a basis for selecting confirmatory interaction partners as our audience. That is, we selectively interact with people similar to us because they are more likely to offer us self-confirmatory feedback than people who are dissimilar. Swann (1987) summarizes several of his own studies demonstrating our tendency to interact selectively with those who are more, rather than less, likely to provide us with self-confirmatory feedback.

Newcomb's (1943) classic study at Bennington College also demonstrates the effects of selective association on both self-maintenance and change. His study revealed how young women from politically conservative backgrounds became more politically liberal during their four years at Bennington. One of the central mechanisms of this change was their substitution of the campus culture for the home culture as the audience for self-validation.

A small subgroup of women did not, however, become liberalized during their four years at Bennington. They rejected the campus culture and were, in turn, rejected by that culture; that is, they were generally rated as less popular than those who had adopted Bennington's liberalism. Their audience remained a combination of both friends and family at home and their like-minded, culturally deviant peers.

Newcomb and his colleagues also report a follow-up study done some 25 years after graduation (Newcomb et al., 1967). The women who changed their politics during their four years at college sought marriage partners whose views were congruent with theirs; that is, both were politically liberal. In sum, the Bennington study shows that, based on the kinds of selective associations they maintain, people both change their self-image and sustain that self-image.

Biased Information Processing

Even if we carefully restrict our performances to audiences likely to provide us with self-confirmatory or positive information, there are inevitably occasions when we will get unwanted negative information about ourselves. Yet, even under such conditions our self-conceptions are generally resistant to change. This resistance is facilitated by our tendency to process information in a selective manner—what we attend to, what we recall, and how we interpret material. Both Swann (1987) and Greenwald (1980), whose work we have already considered, show how we often process information in ways to assure self-maintenance or experience positive feedback.

Obviously, if we are more attentive to self-confirmatory than to disconfirming information, we are likely to end up with an insulated sense of self. If we avoid anyone who challenges our self-images or exclude negative feedback in our information processing, however, how would we ever grow or learn to change? People use the self-negotiation process in ways that help them *mute* change, not entirely exclude it. It seems clear that we tend to associate with people who affirm rather than disconfirm us, and that we process information to avoid disrupting our ongoing sense of self. But muting challenges in no way means that challenges fail to leave their mark. People do learn; they grow, they change, they even seek challenging information about many things, including themselves.

Self-Presentational Strategies

Self-presentational strategies involve the ways we present ourselves to others, guiding them to verify our claims to be a particular kind of person. As we noted earlier, if the self-image we want to project is "I am an intellectual," we can manage our presentations to lead others to validate this claim: our clothing, our conversation, what we read, our credentials influence our audience to accept our claim and proclaim, "Yes, you are truly an intellectual."

Several investigators have found the self-presentational approach helpful in reinterpreting a variety of social psychological processes (for example, see Baumeister, 1982; Hales, 1985; Schlenker, 1980; Schlenker & Leary, 1982). Baumeister, having defined self-presentation as the way people use their "social behavior as a means of communicating information about (or an image of) themselves to others" (p. 3), demonstrates how this perspective can be applied to a diverse range of behaviors. For example, people may give help to others, not because they are driven by altruism, but because they want to be publicly seen as being altruistic.

Schlenker and Leary illustrate the self-presentation framework for understanding social anxiety, the anxiety we experience in social situations when our performances are clearly open to evaluation and we worry that we are not quite up to the challenge. They suggest that certain situations are likely to be especially anxiety-provoking—for example, meeting one's fiancé's parents for the first time—and are thus likely to call upon impression management and self-presentational strategies.

Schlenker and Leary examined three kinds of behavior likely to occur when self-presentational concerns are aroused: nervousness, disaffiliation, and direct image protection. People about to enter a social situation that might threaten their self-image are likely to show various behavioral signs of nervousness—speech disturbances, fidgeting, excessive body movements, and so on. Clearly, someone trying to manage an impression would have difficulty subduing these clear signs of stage fright.

Disaffiliative behaviors are those actions that attempt to minimize people's contact with others—being quiet, failing to initiate conversations, avoiding embarrassing situations, keeping distant from others, and so on. This category indicates some of the ways we can avoid threatening encounters and save face.

In the case of direct image protection, people prepare a carefully scripted performance in advance to protect their image against anticipated threats. If it is too late, they try to repair their damaged image, offering excuses (Scott & Lyman, 1968) or engaging in a variety of *facework* strategies involving either avoidant or corrective actions (Goffman, 1955).

The avoidant actions Goffman outlines parallel the disaffiliative actions described by Schlenker and Leary. We avoid contacts that may threaten our self-image. We use go-betweens for especially delicate encounters—for example, asking our secretary or a friend to make a sensitive call for us. We present ourselves as relatively unconcerned or confident, as though to say, "No big deal! This really doesn't bother me at all." We try to ritualize the situation, inventing rules of order to manage events and prevent adverse circumstances. If we have to say or do something that might be offensive, we preface our actions with, for example, "While I don't want to offend you. . . ."

Corrective processes come into play when the damage has already been done and we are trying to return to a degree of normalcy. We may stand firm and act as though nothing really happened, implying that the audience must undo the response that produced our predicament in the first place. The egg might be on my face, but it's your job to wipe it off! We may shrug off our error as a momentary slip, a joke, something beyond our control in an attempt to convince both our audience and ourselves that our self-image remains intact. We may save face by deprecating ourselves or offering to compensate those hurt or offended by our unfortunate performance. For example, a comedian who offends an audience with an improper joke may apologize to them ("Sorry, that was in poor taste"), distract them with compliments ("Hey, you guys are great!") or lower themselves even further through self-deprecating humor ("I'm as offensive as my jokes").

Altercasting

Like self-presentation, *altercasting* is a strategy we can use to project a desirable image of ourselves. Altercasting involves casting someone else—the "alter"—in a role, the reciprocal of which gives us the desired self-image (Weinstein & Deutschberger, 1963). For example, each day my wife and I shared difficult moments in our respective jobs. When I told her how I dealt with problem students she would often criticize my behavior. Although her criticism was usually appropriate, it was precisely what I did *not* want to hear from her. I therefore learned to preface my "problem sessions" with certain words and looks, casting her in the role of "loving, understanding wife" and assuring myself of positive feedback: "Yes, dear, you did have a terrible day and I am here to make you forget it and feel better." This is clearly a case of altercasting, in which I cast my wife into a role so that I could play the reciprocal role of "person in need of comfort," not "person in need of sensible criticism."

Although the following study was conducted in a very different context, it provides us with an additional example of altercasting. Rather than altercasting by what we *say* to the other person, as in the preceding example, we sometimes altercast by what we *do*. By behaving in certain ways we may push people to respond in a reciprocal manner, in effect casting their identity in response to our actions. In a controlled study of cooperation and competition in a laboratory game, for example, Kelley and Stahelski (1970) noted how competitive subjects drove otherwise cooperative subjects into competing to stay in the game. The competitors thus altercast the others into the identity of competitors.

The effect of this altercasting was to legitimate the competitor's rationale for being competitive. Ignoring their initiation of this cycle, the competitors argued that they had to compete given the others' competitive moves! In this case, altercasting by means of game behavior gave the competitive altercasters the desired self-image of people who must compete to survive in our society. Findings recently reported by McClintock and Liebrand (1988) show that competitors in such games are typically not evaluated positively. This gives us a better sense of how altercasting might help people avoid negative self-images: they are not by nature competitive, but forced to compete.

Altercasting may not only serve to establish a more positive self-image than is warranted (as the previous example demonstrates), but may also be used to establish or sustain an undesirable self-image. For example, the person who whines and complains and always seeks help from others is behaviorally casting others in a dominant role and themselves in a submissive role. They may *report* resenting this image of helplessness, and yet fail to see how their behavior casts those around them in the very kinds of roles that perpetuate the conditions of helplessness. In this instance, altercasting appears to sustain a negative self-image that, at some level, the person seems to desire.

Nullification

Another, more distasteful approach people use in self-negotiation is to *nullify* others or even themselves to avoid unpleasant realities. When we nullify other people we minimize their human reality; we reduce their credibility so that we can simultaneously listen to what they say and dismiss it as coming from someone immature or unsophisticated. Children are routinely nullified, permitting us to hear their often harsh comments ("Aunt Em, you're fat and ugly!") without experiencing threats to our self-image. Women and minorities are also routinely nullified in our society and so not taken seriously.

Ralph Ellison (1952) poignantly describes the "invisibility" a black man experiences as he wanders about in society nullified by the white majority, often having to bump into them merely to verify his existence. Servants likewise are often nullified; the master and mistress of the household talk openly about very intimate matters in their presence because, having nullified them, they presume that they are not really there at all.

If we can nullify other people then we can ignore them or discount negative feedback from them. If we can nullify ourselves in the eyes of others, then our imperfections do not reflect on us. Being a comic or buffoon offers a defense against ever having to be taken seriously enough to be disconfirmed. "Don't take me seriously" and "Don't listen to me" are ways of self-nullification that help protect ourselves.

We also nullify ourselves when we blame extenuating circumstances for our behavior. We are not sure what came over us: Fatigue? Drugs? Stress? In each case we make a self-protective bid not to be treated as a normal person seeking validation; we want to be temporarily treated as a nonperson. Another form of self-nullification, noted earlier, involves presenting one's self in a self-deprecating manner. Although the message is not "Ignore me," it does project a less than competent self-image. What is the effect of this strategy?

Powers and Zuroff (1988) report an experiment in which female accomplices presented a self-criticizing, self-enhancing, or neutral persona to female subjects. Powers and Zuroff expected that one of the consequences of the self-deprecating behavior would be public support but private rejection. While publicly we contradict people's self-criticism to boost their self-esteem, privately we often hold them in contempt for their display of weakness. Data indicated that the self-deprecating approach did provide a greater supportive response and greater reassurances, but also led the subjects to make negative self-evaluations—"I'm not good either." Although the investigators report that their subjects' private responses to the self-deprecating behavior were complex and mixed, an overall pattern did emerge: subjects favored the self-deprecators over the self-enhancers for future interactions even though they viewed them as being less capable and even somewhat maladjusted.

Given our understanding of this reaction, we can use self-deprecation to elicit desired responses from our audience. In this case, a self-deprecating presentation produced support. Although it led people privately to look down on the self-deprecator, it also led them to lower their opinions of themselves: misery makes its own company.

. . . .
Theory and Practice

Earlier in the chapter we noted that social psychologists have taken two different, though conceptually related, approaches to Mead's symbolic interactionist perspective on the dynamics of self-negotiating. The first, as we have seen, involves self-presentational strategies and impression management. The second line of investigation focuses directly on the relationships among the several components of the interpersonal process that leads to the emergence of the self. Several social psychologists have divided this interpersonal process into three components: (1) *actual appraisals*—the actual reactions of others to a person's performances; (2) *reflected appraisals*—a person's perceptions of others' reactions; and (3) *self-appraisals*—a person's responses to the perceived reactions of others (Felson, 1989; Shrauger & Schoeneman, 1979).

Theoretically, there should be a clear-cut relationship among these three components: actual appraisals give rise to reflected appraisals that, in turn, result in self-appraisals. We should expect to find a comparable relationship among the components from a more practical, impression-management standpoint as well (De Paulo et al., 1987), although in a different order: self-appraisals guiding a person's performances achieve a desired impression to the extent that they successfully elicit actual appraisals; that is, reflected appraisals correspond to actual appraisals. What, however, does a systematic examination of the interpersonal process reveal about the actual relationship among these components?

After an extensive review of both naturalistic and experimental studies, Shrauger and Schoeneman found that, "Although there is evidence that individuals' self-perceptions and their views of others' perceptions of them are quite congruent, there is less evidence that self-perceptions are related to or influenced by others' actual perceptions" (p. 565). From a theoretical standpoint, this means that people do not clearly derive their self-conceptions from the *actual* judgments of others, but rather from their perceptions of others' appraisals; that is, from reflected but not actual appraisals. From the practical perspective of impression management, these findings suggest that people believe their performances are more successful than they actually are.

In his extensive series of investigations of the interpersonal process, however, Felson challenges these conclusions. He observes that the one successful relationship identified by Shrauger and Schoeneman involves two self-reports by the same individual: self-appraisals (what I say my self-image is) and reflected appraisals (what I think you say my self-image is). Any such correspondences might very well be spurious, governed by measurement artifacts rather than by any real relationship. Felson also notes that the relationship might also reflect projection or the effects of false consensus. That is, in the absence of actual knowledge about what others think of us, we assume that they see us as we see ourselves.

Felson examined, for example, a one-year longitudinal study of correspondences among the three elements in a group of children in the fourth through the eighth grades. He obtained the children's self-appraisals in four areas: physical attractiveness, popularity, academic ability, and athletic ability. Actual appraisals in these same areas were also obtained from significant others, including parents, teachers, and peers. Reflected appraisals—that is, the children's perceptions of how specific significant others viewed them in these areas—were obtained by a questionnaire; for example, "How smart (good in sports, good looking, popular) does your mother (father) think you are?"

Some of Felson's data confirm Schrauger and Schoeneman's conclusion linking self-appraisals with reflected appraisals. However, Felson suggests that this correspondence is due to projection rather than the children's ability to accurately understand their parent's actual appraisals. That is, because they do not have a very clear picture of how their parents actually perceive them, they assume that their parents must see them in the same way as they see themselves. Felson also found that parents' actual appraisals more closely approximated their children's self-appraisals with regard to academic and sports activities than with popularity or attractiveness.

Recall that actual appraisals are theoretically linked to self-appraisals through the mediation of reflected appraisals. This implies that correspondences between actual and self-appraisals should be stronger when the reflected component is included in the analysis. Felson's data show, however, that relationship is every bit as strong when reflected appraisals are excluded. Correspondences did exist between parents' actual appraisals and their children's reflected and self-appraisals, but they were tenuous.

To account for these results, Felson turned to a distinction, first introduced by De Paulo and associates, between two kinds of significant others involved in the interpersonal process and the emergence of the self. The *specific other* refers to a specific person, such as mother or father, from whom the child develops a conception of himself or herself. The *generalized other* is Mead's term for the larger group or community from which self-appraisals are derived.

De Paulo and associates, using their own data as well as a review of others' work, suggest that people have difficulty accurately determining specific others' actual appraisals of their performances because they do not attend closely to others' actual reactions to them; rather, they assume that others see them as they see themselves. If people do not accurately perceive how specific others see them, it is still possible, however, that they are sensitive to how they are seen in the eyes of the generalized other. In other words, although we may not know exactly how a specific friend evaluates us, we generally know that we are well liked. If this is indeed the case, as Felson and De Paulo both suggest, efforts to determine the correspondence between actual and reflected appraisals of specific others would fail to show any relationship, even though people have developed a generalized sense of how they come across to others.

Some Problems

Why are actual appraisals of specific others less implicated in guiding our performances and self-appraisals than our perceptions of those appraisals? The authors we have considered in the preceding discussion offer several possibilities:

1. In most circumstances, feedback from others may either be minimal or ambiguous, allowing for multiple interpretations. Our audience may not be as informative about our performances as we sometimes imagine they are. In particular, they may withhold an accurate response to our performance if it is negative. We may believe we are being accepted as we have presented ourselves, when in fact we are not.

2. Although people give us feedback, we do not interpret it as evaluative of the self we are portraying, but rather reframe it and give it some other meaning. For example, we may think that our audience is intentionally lying or being evasive to win our favor. By viewing their feedback as a tactic of ingratiation, we do not think it is informative about us, but only about what they want from us.

3. As we noted earlier in the chapter, people may assimilate discrepant information to fit already existing images of themselves and thus never accurately receive information.

4. We may reject others' feedback or try to stage a more convincing performance. We may respond to negative feedback by trying to influence our audience to see things our way. In doing so, we may exaggerate our effectiveness.

5. As we noted earlier in this chapter, we may break off our relationships with people who provide us with unwanted feedback, insulating ourselves from others' true perceptions of us.

There are undoubtedly many other reasons, but the overall message is clear: people see a greater congruence between their self-images and their perception of how others see them than actually exists. This makes our performances seem more like private shows than public displays.

This conclusion leads to an interesting paradox. We presumably stage our performances to foster a particular self-image, but if we insistently deny, avoid, or distort the feedback we receive, for whom are our performances being staged? Most of the work on impression management and self-negotiation, including the theory developed by Mead, makes sense only insofar as people successfully present a given self-image.

It may be that our intuitions about the interpersonal process have yet to be verified. It does not make much sense to argue that we stage our performances for private benefit, caring little to learn about how successful we have been. Nor is it plausible to deny the important role that significant others (for example, parents) play in shaping our self-images. In any case, though they may err on occasion, most people are reasonably aware of how others see them.

14

Gender, Self, and Society

RECENTLY I RECEIVED an advertisement in the mail for a new magazine. Printed boldly on the envelope in colorful, capital letters was the question: "How can you tell if you're a man or a woman without looking?" Curious, I ripped open the envelope and was confronted with a series of medical "facts" such as "men have warmer hands" and "women are less prone to hayfever." While I cannot vouch for the accuracy of these statistical findings from some study or another, I can assure you that I am definitely not subscribing to that magazine! Clearly, however, some marketing wizards believe that a magazine promoting itself in terms of medical differences between men and women will capture the public's imagination and become an instant success. Perhaps it will.

A recent article by Carlson (1988) suggests one group for whom such a magazine might have special appeal: the medical committee of the International Olympic Games, which recently has become greatly concerned with chromosome testing of female athletes. The intent of the testing program is to certify that men are not competing disguised as women. As obvious as it might seem to most of us, the definitive determination of who is male and who is female was not obvious to the medical committee. The assumption underlying the test is that the chromosome pattern of a normal female is XX, while that of the normal male is XY; any person tested positive for an XY pattern would therefore be disqualified from competing in women's events.

Leaving aside the possibility that the test may be unreliable, as Carlson notes it is, the identification of gender by means of a chromosome analysis is also fraught with potential difficulties. Although the exact figures are not known, it is estimated that somewhere between one in 1,000 and one in 4,000 people are born with defective chromosomes. These people might come out of a chromosome test with a count discrepant from their lifelong socialization as a male or female. Is their gender defined by their chromosomes or by society? There are also sufficient ambiguities in some people's visible sexual features to further complicate easy identification.

Although the test results may not be clear, what is clear is that it is vitally important to some influential people today to be able to divide the world into two definite, clearly marked categories—male and female. Are those magazine marketing wizards correct after all?

Sex is one of the most important frameworks for organizing ourselves and our world. It has major implications for who we are, what we do, and what our experiences and opportunities will be. Although there are other categories—race, nationality, religion, economic standing, and so on—all of which have major consequences, sex is arguably the most significant form of social division, especially in a western context.

I am aware of the headline-making confrontations between nations and groups divided along religious lines. I am also well aware of the tragedy of racial and ethnic discrimination and the consequences of organizing the world into rich and poor. Why then elevate sex to such a central place? While it will be difficult to convince those for whom race, religion, and other categories are more noxious rationales for discrimination, exploitation, and oppression, I believe that sex and gender perhaps constitutes the most difficult challenge we have yet to face. This position is admittedly a bit ethnocentric, based as it is on experiences primarily in the western world, specifically the United States and western Europe. Paradoxically, the one category for organizing our world—sex—that once seemed so clear has now become seriously challenged. Without really questioning it, we lived in a world constituted for and by men, founded on principles oriented toward the male life and experience. What seemed "clear" and "natural" was simply a one-sided view of the world. Opening that view to scrutiny will challenge the simple clarity that once seemed so comforting to both men and women.

Among others, Scott (1988) has noted that until recently history was of *mankind*, not *humankind*. Women were either excluded or took their places as supporting characters in the male's story of his life—his dreams, his achievements, his desires, his fears. Literature likewise told stories about men and women primarily from the male point of view. Even science, especially the social and behavioral sciences, seemed tilted more toward the male experience and understanding (Gilligan, 1982). As some have pointed out (for example, Gould & Wartofsky, 1976), most western philosophers were men who wrote primarily about the male world view, not about the issues facing all humanity. Even religion reflected a masculine bias (Christ, 1980; Ruether, 1985). The feminist movement has mounted a challenge to this way of thinking. It has exposed some ugly truths which we are only now beginning to admit and confront. Without undergoing a dramatic transformation, however, it seems unlikely that our culture can assimilate these changes in our thinking.

In their thoughtful analysis of utopian thought in the western world, Manuel and Manuel (1979) suggest that many current visions of the future are simply extrapolations from the present. New technologies are posited to ease our lives, but our social and psychological world remains much the same. Changes surrounding issues of sex and gender make tomorrow difficult to imagine today. Our most fundamental ideas about ourselves; about our relationships to other people, nature, spirituality, the way we think, the priorities of life, will be completely different. Tomorrow will not simply be a technologically advanced today; the changes will be much too substantial for that kind of limited vision to encompass.

There are strong forces opposing these changes. The understandings we eventually come to have will be the result of complex negotiation among competing interests. What will a future textbook on social psychology include? What will be the most important issues? The story told then will be very different than the one told today, in great measure because of a movement trying to rewrite that story even as others try to resist.

. . . .

Gender Self-Schema

The centrality of sex and gender to our lives has been a topic of particular interest to social psychologists. Whether we consider gender self-schema to be individualistic or culturally shared beliefs, gender is a major organizing principle for understanding most facets of our own and others' everyday lives. To make this claim is to insist that we guide our own actions and interpret the actions of others in terms of gender-based beliefs. This is not to claim, however, that such beliefs are a central part of *everyone's* daily awareness. Many people are quite oblivious to how gender-based categorization shapes much of what they know and do. In the study of gender self-schemas, several changes in thinking have occurred in the last few decades, reflecting both continuing controversy and misunderstanding.

Masculinity–Femininity

The traditional approach to understanding the influence of gender on behavior envisioned a one-dimensional dichotomy between masculine and feminine qualities. Not surprisingly, masculine qualities emphasized *instrumental* terms describing activities of task completion and goal achievement—things having to do with the public world of work. Feminine qualities emphasized *expressive* terms centering on caretaking and nurturance—things having to do with the private world of the home.

If people were presented with a list of characteristics and asked to rate how much each one described themselves, men would be expected to score predominantly at the masculine end; women presented with the list would likewise be expected to score at the feminine end. Because there was only a single dimension, there was no way people could indicate that both masculine and feminine terms described them. This was not simply a feature of the way the scale was constructed; it also characterized the prevailing cultural view that a sharp line separated what was male from what was female.

This common understanding is congruent with Money's (1987) criticism of the dualistic cast of western civilization's beliefs about human sexuality. Money notes that several different patterns of human sexuality are possible, including heterosexuality, homosexuality, and bisexuality. Comparing the majority of western with several non-western societies, he observes how, "For us, heterosexuality, like health, is taken as a verity that needs no explanation, other than being attributed to the immutability of the natural order of things" (p. 385). We treat our world as though it consisted of two kinds of sexual beings—male and female—and assume that their sexual union is part of the natural order. Any other pattern is considered "deviant" and requires explanation. Money raises several questions about the traditional western view that masculinity and femininity are two separate ends of a single continuum. He cites the Sambian culture, in which a young male who does not pass through an initial homosexual phase is considered deviant. Money calls upon data from both cultural and animal life suggesting to him that bisexuality is actually the more natural norm and that monosexuality, whether heterosexual or homosexual, requires explanation!

Androgyny

Constantinople's (1973) critical review of the either/other nature of the traditional masculine–feminine dichotomy, plus Bem's (1974) comments on androgyny, significantly altered social psychology's view of gender. Bem suggested people who are androgynous—that is, *both* masculine and feminine—would adjust to many everyday problems much better than those sex-typed as either masculine or feminine. Most of us encounter situations—for example, someone has taken your seat at a ball game—in which expressing the traditionally masculine quality of assertiveness is important; other situations—for example, an old person needs help crossing the street—require expressing the traditional feminine quality of sensitivity. A person presumably both masculine and feminine should be better able to deal with these kinds of situational demands than someone sex-typed as one or the other.

To study these possibilities Bem developed a measuring instrument, the Bem Sex Role Inventory (BSRI), that presented people with a listing of self-descriptive terms. Some of the terms were culturally recognized masculine qualities (for example, "aggressive," "ambitious," "assertive," "competitive"), some were culturally recognized feminine qualities (for example, "affectionate," "compassionate," "gentle," "tender") and some were culturally recognized neutral qualities (for example, "conscientious," "helpful," "solemn"). People were then instructed to indicate the degree to which each term was self-descriptive.

Bem's interest was in separating people's gender orientation from their sex. Scoring permitted her to distinguish those persons who were primarily sex-typed from those who were not sex-typed. For example, masculine sex-typed people scored high on masculine and low on feminine terms; feminine sex-typed people scored high on feminine but low on masculine terms; non-sex typed or androgynous people scored high or low on both masculine and feminine terms. Note that both males and females could be masculine sex-typed, feminine sex-typed or androgynous.

Initial work with the BSRI test confirmed Bem's expectations (Bem, 1975; Bem & Lenney, 1976; Bem, Martyna, & Watson, 1976). Sex-typed individuals did indeed appear to have more difficulty adjusting their behavior to meet changing situational demands than either male or female androgynous individuals. Various attempts to replicate her work, however, were not successful (for example, Edwards & Spence, 1987; Taylor & Hall, 1982).

Theoretical challenges were also mounted against Bem's work (Spence, Helmreich, & Stapp, 1975; Spence & Helmreich, 1978). For example, Spence and her associates argued that androgyny should not include both high- and low-scoring individuals. Only those scoring high in both masculinity and femininity were truly androgynous; the undifferented lows needed to be given different consideration. They demonstrated that while those scoring high on both masculinity and femininity were high in self-esteem, for example, those scoring low on both categories were not. As we will see, Spence's distinction was maintained in subsequent work; Bem's original ideas of including both highs and lows in the category of androgyny were abandoned, even by Bem.

Even the Spence-revised formulation of androgyny, however, met with very thoughtful and powerful criticism. Taylor and Hall (1982) reviewed a substantial body of literature, comparing the original Bemian version of androgyny with that posited by Spence and her associates. Their critical review first led them to reject the traditionalist understanding against which both Bem's and Spence's work had been directed. That is, Taylor and Hall found no evidence that healthy functioning required masculinity for males and femininity for females. However, they also found no support for either Bem's original or Spence's revisionist formulations. There seemed to be no clear relationship between androgyny, no matter how it was defined, and healthy functioning.

One effect did clearly emerge from Taylor and Hall's analysis: "it is primarily masculinity that pays off for individuals of both sexes" (p. 362). In other words, people who subscribe to masculine self-descriptions fare better than those subscribing either to androgyny or femininity. As Taylor and Hall comment, this conclusion "serves as a natural take-off point for critiques of a male-dominated social structure" (p. 362).

It is also consistent with a classic study of gender stereotypes. Broverman and her associates (1972) first asked a group of male and a group of female college students to list all the qualities and behaviors they felt distinguished men from women. These lists were compiled and a questionnaire was developed containing those items on which both groups showed generally high agreement. This questionnaire was then presented to another group of men and women, who were simply asked to indicate which qualities were most characteristic of adult males, adult females, and themselves. They were also asked to indicate which qualities they felt to be the most socially desirable and valued in an adult. Results indicated that both men and women judged male qualities to be the most valued and desirable.

Broverman and her colleagues also report results from a sample of mental health professionals (psychiatrists, psychologists, and social workers) asked to indicate those qualities possessed by a healthy adult. Data showed the subjects equated health with male qualities, but not female qualities. In other words, health and masculinity are perceived as more closely aligned than health and any other gender pattern.

Not everyone, however, has accepted the validity of Broverman's work, citing methodological problems with the way the test items were developed (Widiger & Settle, 1987). On the other hand, using a different methodology, Eagly and Kite (1987) report results generally confirming Broverman's conclusion, finding a definite bias in favor of terms that describe masculine rather than androgynous or feminine qualities.

This kind of male bias has also been found in recent work conducted in Israel. Dimitrovsky, Singer, and Yinon (1989) chose a sample of 200 men and 299 women, all of whom were native-born Israeli soldiers. They administered the BSRI to all subjects, afterwards dividing then into the following eight categories that are the standard within the Bemian framework. (The percentages in parentheses reflect how many of their sample fell into each sex-role category.)

1. Sex-typed males: men who score high on masculinity and low on femininity (41%)

2. Sex-typed females: women who score high on femininity and low on masculinity (35%)

3. Androgynous men: men who score high on both masculinity and femininity (21%)

4. Androgynous women: women who score high on both masculinity and femininity (27%)

5. Cross-sex-typed men: men who score high on femininity and low on masculinity (11%)

6. Cross-sex-typed women: women who score high on masculinity and low on femininity (17%)

7. Undifferentiated men: men who score low on both masculinity and femininity (27%)

8. Undifferentiated women: women who score low on both masculinity and femininity (21%)

Dimitrovsky and her colleagues evaluated how well subjects in each category performed, basing their data on the person's own, peer, and officer ratings of their effectiveness in training and their suitedness for the various roles for which they were being trained. Dimitrovsky's conclusion is that "for both sexes superior adjustment is associated with instrumental masculine qualities" (p. 846). In other words, men who were either sex-typed males or androgynous, and women who were either cross-sex-typed or androgynous performed better overall in adjustment ratings than those in the other categories. These findings again demonstrate a bias in favor of masculine qualities.

Bem's Gender-Schema Theory

While not abandoning her basic distinction between sex-typed and non-sex-typed individuals, Bem made several modifications in her theory. Taking a more cognitive approach, she suggested that people have different cognitive schemas for organizing their understanding of themselves and others (Bem, 1981, 1982). In this view, some people are *gender-schematic:* they tend to organize things in their world in terms of gender categories; others are *gender-nonschematic:* gender is not of primary relevance to either their self-conceptions or their understanding of others. People are considered gender-schematic if they score either as sex-typed males *or* females on the BSRI; they are considered gender-nonschematic if they subscribe to both male *and* female self-descriptions.

Bem's gender-schema theory suggests that we should expect differences between people who divide their world in terms of gender and those who ignore gender categories. Compared with a gender-nonschematic person, someone gender-schematic has highly differentiated and organized ways of processing information in the domain of gender differences. We should therefore anticipate more attention to and recall of gender-relevant material by gender-schematics than by gender-nonschematics.

Frable and Bem (1985) report an intriguing study attempting to determine how people's gender-schematicity influences the way they organize their perceptions of others in terms of gender categories: A group of college undergraduates (96 men and 96 women) were administered the BSRI and subsequently divided into the eight sex-role categories we saw in Dimitrovsky's study. Bem considered the sex-typed groups (1 and 2) to be gender-schematic and the androgynous groups (3 and 4) to be gender-nonschematic.

All subjects listened to a tape-recorded discussion, in which six people talked about various aspects of college life—finding an apartment, eating dormitory food, and so on. All subjects were told that while they were listening, a photograph of the person speaking would be projected onto a screen, and that after the discussion they would be asked to answer a few questions about the conversation to see how much they remembered.

The experimenters selected photographs of six men and six women; three of each were black, the other three white. This permitted them to place half of the subjects in a gender-relevant condition and the other half in a race-relevant condition. Where gender was relevant, the photographs depicted racially homogeneous groups of six people, three male and three female; where race was relevant, the photographs depicted gender homogenous groups of six people, three black and three white. The voice the subjects heard on the tape matched the sex of the person whose photograph they saw.

At the conclusion of the discussion, subjects were presented with a list of 72 verbatim excerpts from the conversation, all out of their original order. They were also given a folder containing the photographs of the speakers. Their task was to match each statement with a photograph, guessing if they were uncertain.

This format permitted Frable and Bem to examine the relationship between subjects' gender-schematicity and their ability to discern a speaker's sex. Their hypothesis was that gender-schematic subjects (for whom gender is supposedly important) should be better able to discern a speaker's sex than nongender-schematics, but both groups should be equally capable of identifying a speaker's race.

Frable and Bem report, as they predicted, no significant differences between subjects categorized on the basis of their gender-schematicity in the race-relevant condition. This result confirms that information processing is domain-specific; that is, it does not generalize across the domains of both gender and race. Subjects' recall, however, was not perfect; errors followed a pattern, but not as a function of their gender-schematicity. For example, all subjects tended to confuse speakers on the basis of their race; they were more likely to mistakenly interchange the statements of two blacks or two whites, but not of a black and a white.

Also as predicted, Frable and Bem report important differences in subjects' recall as a function of their gender-schematicity. Specifically, "both sex-typed and cross-sex-typed individuals were significantly more likely than either the androgynous or undifferentiated individuals to confuse the members of the opposite sex with one another" (p. 465). This confusion in recall appeared only with respect to members of the opposite sex; no differences appeared when the sex of the speaker was ignored.

Frable and Bem argue that these results confirm Bem's gender-schema theory. Considering the various kinds of recall errors that a subject could have made, the data show that gender-schematic subjects (including cross-sex-typed individuals) made errors based on gender. If, for example, they incorrectly matched a statement with the actual speaker, they did correctly identify his or her sex. This suggests that gender is important to such people. What is not clearly understood, however, is why these kinds of recall errors are limited to members of the opposite sex. It seems that gender-schematics are especially sensitive to the opposite sex, treating them as though they were equivalent to one another. That is, while male gender-schematics are more attuned to women than to men, they tend to see women as all alike. Female gender-schematics have the same cognitive predisposition, but with respect to males. Why cross-sex-typed individuals seem to function like sex-typed individuals remains unclear, unless we assume that cross-sex-typing has made them as gender-schematic as sex-typed individuals.

Although she did not design her study specifically to examine cross-sex-typing, Frable's (1989) work is insightful in this context. Frable used the BSRI to divide her sample of undergraduates into four gender types: sex-typed, androgynous, undifferentiated, and cross-sex-typed. All subjects were asked to respond to questions about the rules governing social interactions. For example, they were presented with brief descriptions of an interaction in which one of the people behaved in an inappropriate manner. Below each description was a rule, and they were instructed to respond to a series of questions about the rule, for example: "Is the rule fair?" "Should it be changed?" "Do you like the person who violated the rule?" "Does the rule make the interaction run more smoothly?"

The scenarios were varied to include different types of inappropriate behavior. For example, some involved men behaving in ways more culturally sanctioned for women, like crying when feeling sad. Others focused on morality (using violence to settle a disagreement), social convention (abruptly breaking off a conversation with a friend without offering an explanation), or discrimination (not allowing a lesbian woman to teach in a nursery school).

Frable expected gender-schematicity to relate only to those rules involving gender-relevant incidents. Her data demonstrated a strong tendency for the gender-schematic subjects to favor the preservation of social rules pertaining to sex-appropriate behavior. Compared to the other groups, they considered the rules to be fair, disliked the rule violater more, saw no need to change the rules, and tended to see the rules as facilitating social interaction.

The cross-sex-typed individuals differed from the gender-schematics: they felt that gender rules were especially unjust and discriminatory, and they favored those in the scenarios who violated such rules. These findings should not be surprising, considering the likely experiences of cross-sex-typed individuals—that is, males with more culturally female-oriented self-descriptions and females with more culturally male-oriented self-descriptions. Frable also found that gender-schematic subjects did not differ significantly from the other BSRI types in their views of those scenarios in which gender was not central.

Frable next examined the effects of gender schema on sexual stereotyping. Subjects watched a video of what was purported to be a job interview for a managerial position. The tapes had been carefully scripted to present two excellent (one male and one female) and two average (one male and one female) job candidates. Results from this second study indicated that only the sex-typed subjects evaluated the male applicants to be consistently better than the female applicants. In doing so, the sex-typed individuals effectively devalued the performances of the female applicants, whereas the subjects from the other three categories did not.

Frable concluded from her two studies that in clearly gender-related test situations, gender-schema effects occur as predicted by the theory. Gender-schematic individuals' behavior reveals the importance of gender categories in their understanding of themselves and others. In addition, because gender-schematics favor the preservation of gender-maintaining rules, they likewise encourage discriminatory hiring practices (for example, their stereotyping in the job candidate study). While cross-sex-typed individuals also organize their world in terms of gender categories (as we also saw in Frable and Bem's study), they favor social changes rather than the status quo in matters involving gender.

Markus' Self-Schema Theory

In contrast to Bem's gender-schema theory, Markus (see Crane & Markus, 1982; Markus et al., 1982) proposed a self-schema approach to understanding gender. Markus and her associates view a schema as a central information-processing framework that organizes our self-experiences about most matters, including, but not restricted to, gender. Thus, we have self-schemas about a wide variety of domains—our honesty, masculinity or femininity, sociability, and so on.

While Bem focuses exclusively on gender schema, Markus examines self-schema in general. The key difference between their two theories, however, involves their respective approaches to gender schema. While Bem maintains that gender-schematic individuals are concerned with all kinds of gender-relevant materials, Markus contends that gender-schematic people only have a gender schema for either masculinity or for femininity. This difference is important. Markus and her colleagues report that sex-typed males deal better with masculine information, while sex-typed females handle feminine stimuli better. Presumably, if people are sex-typed simply with respect to gender, as Bem maintains, then they should be sensitized to *both* masculine and feminine gender terms regardless of their sex. If Markus and her collegues are right that male and female schematics differ, Bem's formulation becomes questionable.

Markus and her colleagues (1982) first determined whether subjects who describe themselves as masculine, feminine, or androgynous showed differential recall for gender-related words. They hypothesized that since a self-schema for gender is either masculine or feminine, but not both, schematic males should recall more masculine words than words unrelated to gender. Similarly, schematic females should recall more feminine than non-gender-related words. Androgynous subjects, on the other hand, should not show any gendered pattern of recall, since they presumably are not schematic for their own gender identity as male or female.

Subjects were classified into sex-typed males, sex-typed females or androgynous, again using the BSRI as the measuring instrument. Results clearly demonstrated that masculine schematics recalled more masculine words than feminine words while feminine schematics recalled more feminine than masculine words. Androgynous subjects tended to recall more feminine than masculine words, but this difference was much smaller than that found for sex-typed subjects.

Markus and her colleagues' second study examined the speed and the confidence with which subjects processed gender-relevant information. Subjects' response time to masculine, feminine, or neutral words was evaluated by having them press a button labeled "me" each time a word appeared that they felt was self-descriptive, and a "not-me" button for every term they felt not to be self-descriptive. After this response, the subjects were asked how confident they were with their judgment.

According to self-schema theory, the different self-schemas

people have for gender should affect both how fast they process information and how confidently they respond. Masculine schematics should respond more rapidly to masculine words and feminine schematics more rapidly to feminine words. Results from the study generally confirmed these expectations. As predicted, masculine schematics also felt more confident responding "me" to masculine words, while feminine schematics felt more confident responding "me" to feminine words.

Markus and her colleagues report that both androgynous and undifferentiated subjects reveal an overall tendency to respond with *equal* speed to all words, regardless of their gender-relevance. This, of course, is what one would expect if androgynous and undifferentiated individuals are gender-nonschematic, having no special self-schemas for organizing their thinking about gender.

A more careful analysis of the data, however, revealed that undifferentiated subjects tended to be less confident in their judgments than the androgynous subjects, suggesting a less organized, less differentiated view of masculine and feminine qualities and less usage of gendered descriptions when referring to themselves. Markus reasoned, then, that only undifferentiated people are truly gender-nonschematic. The androgyny group probably have "multiple gender-schemas . . . [and] . . . are importantly concerned with both masculine and feminine aspects of themselves" (p. 50).

. . . .

Gender Stereotypes

We have so far emphasized the treatment of gender as a personal schema by which people organize their experiences of themselves and the world. The social world also organizes people according to gender categories, and accordingly treats them differently. The societal division of people into males and females is not an outcome of these self- or gender-schema; rather, these schema are an outcome of differential treatment in society.

Is the societal division natural or is it designed to serve particular interests and purposes? At one time it was commonly accepted that gender was a natural, biological way to divide the world. Men had certain natural qualities that distinguished them from women and accounted for their social dominance. Women's natural talents made them better suited for those activities primarily centered around the home.

Simple observation apparently validated these separate spheres. Men governed nations, ran businesses, and dominated the fields of arts, sciences, and athletic competition; women reared children, cooked and cleaned, and performed other subordinate, domestic services. Early scientific research even verified the natural male–female division of the world. For example, specific regions of the brain thought to be associated with masculine or feminine characteristics were located and examined to see if these were larger in area or weighed more in the appropriate sex (Shields, 1975a, 1975b).

The search for a biological basis for gender has not died with the passage of time. The confidence with which sex differences are attributable to biology, however, seems to fluctuate with new collections of data and the sociohistorical climate. At the beginning of World War II, for example, when men were drafted to fight, women were drafted to work in the large industrial plants required to maintain the machinery of war. At the end of the war, women had to return home so that the men could take back their jobs. For a variety of socioeconomic reasons, however, today it is considered the norm for women to work rather than stay at home. For example, in 1900, only about 20% of women worked outside the home; by 1988, this figure rose to about 56% and is projected to be over 80% by the year 2000 (Matthews & Rodin, 1989; Scarr, Phillips, & McCartney, 1989).

Do we explain these movements of women into and out of the work force as a function of natural sex differences or social attitudes and economic demands? It is true, of course, that women predominantly enter different kinds of work than men; it is also true that, even within the same general type of work, women are paid less than men (Deaux, 1984). Although 47% of the productive working hours worldwide involve women, women earn only 10% of the world's wages (Greenpeace, 1989). But are these current features of our social life caused by natural differences between men and women? Even today, men and women experience different life opportunities and have unequal power to affect society and their lives within it (Hewlett, 1986). A gendered system is also a powered system. Once we distinguish people by sex, we also predetermine their future power and privilege (Scott, 1988).

Many social psychologists are interested in how social gender categorization contributes to stereotyping. Although stereotypes are a result, not the cause, of being categorized as male or female and having disparate life opportunities, they do help to reinforce differences. Obviously, if actual access to positions of power distinguishes the life experiences of men and women (Eagly, 1983; Eagly & Steffen, 1984), then stereotypes depicting men as more powerful than women accurately reflect this reality. Coming to hold and believe in such stereotypes because they have a "kernel of truth" to them likewise helps to maintain differential arrangements of power. The study of gender stereotypes, then, is by no means trivial in effecting a more egalitarian, nonsexist society. Yet, as Eagly and Steffen conclude, societal change is more likely to produce a change in stereotypes than vice versa.

In one of the most impressive demonstrations of gender stereotypes, Goldberg (1968) asked a group of female subjects to evaluate articles purportedly written either by a John McKay or a Joan McKay. Even though the articles were identical, the subjects tended to evaluate the male author as more competent than the female author. It appeared that Goldberg had demonstrated a pattern of female self-denigration, by no means unusual in the history of relations between groups with different power and status (Memmi, 1967).

Attempts to replicate Goldberg's research, however, have met with only mixed success. Recently, Swim and her colleagues (1989) reviewed 123 studies published between 1974 and 1979 that were close conceptual replications of Goldberg's original study. A careful examination led them to conclude that "the size of the difference in ratings between female and male target persons was extremely small" (p. 419), and for the most part insignificant; those differences which did appear could have arisen by chance.

The authors did, however, confirm that the less information provided about the target, the more likely subjects will rely on stereotypes, favoring the male over the female (Deaux & Lewis, 1984; Locksley et al., 1980). This finding suggests that subjects do not use gender stereotypes in making their judgments about other people when they have access to other kinds of information about them. For example, Deaux and Lewis provided subjects with gender information (target is male or female) and either role or trait information. Role information included a masculine role (for example, head of household, financial provider), a feminine role (for example, source of emotional support, caretaker) and a mixed role (for example, financial provider, source of emotional support). Trait information paralleled the role information and presented the target as having a set of culturally masculine, feminine, or mixed traits. The subjects' task was to estimate the probability the target had either masculine or feminine qualities. Results indicated that, "In general, the effects of specific trait or role behavior information was greater than the information provided by gender label" (p. 998).

In another study, Deaux and Lewis (1984) presented subjects with a target's personality traits, physical characteristics, and occupational information and a list of roles culturally regarded as masculine or feminine. They were then asked to estimate the probability that the target occupied each role. Results again confirmed the potency of nongender information in the judgments subjects made about the target. For example, subjects given masculine physical characteristics—tall, sturdy, strong—describing the target indicated a 79% probability that the target occupied a masculine role and only a 54% probability that the target occupied a feminine role. In the authors' view, "the influence of gender can be outweighed by other information, such as role behaviors, traits, and the like" (p. 1002). In the absence of such additional information, however, gender stereotypes take over.

These findings suggest why a study like Goldberg's might be replicated in some circumstances but not others. As Swim and her colleagues suggest, in the absence of additional information, people rely on gender stereotypes of the sort Goldberg found to make judgments about others, but when other information is available, even implicitly, it may preclude a gender biasing effect. This is not to say that gender stereotypes can be completely eliminated. Deaux notes that once a gender-specific piece of information is provided, subjects perceive the target as also having traits, characteristics, or behavior patterns consistent with that gender identification. In other words, information other than the target's sex continues to communicate cultural gender stereotypes.

When researchers conclude, therefore, that people use information other than gender to make judgments of others, we should not be misled into believing that gender-based stereotypes are absent. Other information is in fact used in a manner congruent with cultural gender stereotypes. Being labeled male or female directly, or indirectly by means of stereotypes about other components of gender (physical traits, occupational role, and so on) conveys the same message.

· · · · · · · · · · · · · · · ·

Patriarchy

Hyde and Linn (1988) report that because there are minimal differences between the verbal abilities of males and females, "other explanations must be found for the larger gender differences in earning power and career advancement" (p. 64). In other words, even though men and women have the same talents and capacities necessary for success in today's world, men continue to far outdistance women. This suggests that the basis for male dominance is not ability per se, but other factors that help perpetuate male power and status. Walker (1989) attributes male use of violence against women as a manifestation of male resistance to social change. She points out that while women's acts of violence against men decreased as community services to help battered women increased, men's violence toward their partners significantly increased during the same time period.

A recent newspaper story, revealing the extent of violence practiced against women outside the United States, examined the continued use of mutilating puberty rites in over 20 African nations (Perlez, 1990). Ostensibly in order to insure female virginity, an operation is performed on young women in which either the hood of the clitoris is slit, or in some cases, the clitoris is excised and the sides of the vulva are stitched together. Although several governments and physicians have protested against these practices, Perlez notes the strong social pressure to perform the operation, citing the father of three young girls who recently had the procedure performed on his daughters: "There is no way girls can command respect here if they are not circumcised and ready for marriage." Does this not suggest the use of male violence against women to sustain male domination?

Some professional journalists have employed a similar interpretation to understand the antiabortion movement. For example, Salter (1989) suggests that "A woman in complete control of her sexuality and reproductive functions is a threat to this carefully constructed system of male dominance." Both Walker and Salter, among others whose ideas we will soon consider, argue that the current social system is not only prejudiced against women but also reacts with violence and oppressive restrictions whenever male dominance is threatened.

Several feminist writers, including both historians (Scott, 1988) and psychologists (Hare-Mustin & Marecek, 1988; Kitzinger, 1987), have referred to this male domination by the term *patriarchy*. They have provided both an analysis of the nature of patriarchical domination and suggestions on how to eliminate it.

Scott suggests that a condition of patriarchy exists once we accept a clear division between men and women as biologically based and completely natural. This division creates a binary world containing two unitary opposites—men versus women. We are invited, even encouraged, to define and evalaute men and women in terms of their oppositeness to each other. Scott, for example, notes how in the nineteenth century men's work was defined only by contrasting it with women's work; the very meaning of worker "was established through a contrast between the presumably natural qualities of men and women" (p. 175). Such a binary division thus privileges one side at the expense of the other.

Scott argues that reversing this situation, as some have proposed, so that females are privileged over males, would leave us in the same predicament. We would continue to have two protagonists defined as opposites according to a natural dividing line and a hierarchical principle privileging one over the other. A genuine solution would be to deny a natural male–female division and its built-in prejudices.

Scott illustrates the hold of the patriarchal worldview in her discussion of an employment discrimination case that pitted the Equal Employment Opportunities Commission (EEOC) against Sears Department Stores. Sears was accused of discriminating against women in hiring for certain kinds of commission sales positions, as evidenced by both an underrepresentation of women in such positions and questionable job-interview procedures. Sears agreed that more men than women were hired for commission sales positions, but denied that this reflected discriminatory hiring practices. Rather, because of the *fundamental* differences between men's and women's interests, women were less interested in certain kinds of work and so *chose* not to seek those particular jobs. In other words, because men and women have different basic natures, they naturally have different career interests. Thus, Sears claimed, natural tendencies, not employer discrimination, resulted in the unequal hiring patterns. The EEOC responded to this appeal by insisting that *no* differences—including so-called "natural" male–female ones—should be used as the basis for hiring practices.

The case between the EEOC and Sears was thus basically one of equality versus difference. The *equality* position argues that, to avoid discrimination in the workplace, any biological differences between men and women must be ignored. The *difference* position argues that natural differences between men and women must be taken into consideration; for example, women in the workplace require extended leave for pregnancy.

Scott points out, and Hare-Mustin and Marecek concur, that equality and difference are generally seen as opposites: equality insists on no differences, while difference insists on uniqueness. Arguing either position, however, leaves one in a no-win situation. To claim equality is to forget a long past in which women were denied opportunities and relegated to the role of second-class citizens. To claim difference, however, is to invite unequal treatment because of natural dissimilarities. As Scott says of this dilemma, "the only alternative . . . is to refuse to oppose equality to difference . . ." (p. 174).

Scott illustrates how the rules of the game (equality versus difference), defined through centuries of patriarchal rule, trap the players in a situation in which the female position invariably loses. In the employment discrimination case, for example, the judge decided in favor of Sears. He reasoned that the company had not intentionally discriminated against women because naturally occurring, real differences between men and women do not allow equal treatment. The EEOC's arguments were dismissed in part because they seemed somewhat inconsistent, sometimes favoring equality over difference, sometimes difference over equality. The latter position, of course, confirmed Sears' argument and the judge's determination, thus aligning the feminists with the employer!

As long as the patriarchal division of the world into men and women, based on an assumption of naturally occurring, biological differences, exists there will be no opportunity for genuine equality. This is precisely the outcome intended by a system of male domination without, however, ever blatantly appearing to be coercive.

Kitzinger's Case Example

Approaching patriarchy from a different angle, Kitzinger (1987) presents a critical analysis of the social scientific treatment of the gay and lesbian life style. Kitzinger notes an historical shift in social psychology's view of homosexuality. Originally, homosexuality was understood as a disease, but with the advent of what Kitzinger calls liberal humanism, the disease shifted from the homosexual to the homophobe. Rather than considering the homosexual to be sick, the person fearful of homosexuality was now seen as having the real problem.

Samelson (1976) has commented on a similar shift in social psychology's study of race relations: from early work documenting the defects of different ethnic and racial groups to the current liberal humanist study of the defects of those prejudiced against them. Kitzinger argues, however, that liberal humanism itself is part of the problem of patriarchical domination. She maintains that as long as we focus our professional attention on examining either the illness of homosexuality or the illness of those who fear homosexuality, we gloss over the political picture of power and domination that lies at "the root of all forms of oppression" (p. 64).

The liberal humanist values that emphasize individualism and personal privacy for one's sexuality "make it very difficult seriously to entertain the idea that such values might . . . serve the interests of the patriarchy . . ." (p. 192). While the tolerance of the liberal view is more appealing to most of us than the intolerance of early understandings, by turning every social issue into a matter of individual private choice, the liberal-humanist interpretation fails to address underlying issues of power, conflict, and domination. For example, to regard lesbianism as a matter of individual sexual preference is to fail to see it as a challenge to patriarchical control over sexuality. In other words, homosexuality is not simply private individuals expressing a personal preference, but political groups defying the patriarchical directive about how men and women should properly behave.

. . . .

Conclusions

As we have seen, social psychologists have taken several approaches to the study of gender. While people were originally seen as having either masculine or feminine selves, in the current view people organize information about themselves into various gendered categories. We saw that some emphasized the either/or quality of gendered selves, while others saw a self composed of both masculine and feminine characteristics. We reviewed some of the evidence suggesting that these gendered self-schema are important to various other aspects of a person's life.

We moved from the topic of gendered self-schema to a brief consideration of gender stereotypes, noting how stereotypes both reflect and reinforce real differences between men's and women's life opportunities. We considered the argument that in the absence of other information, gendered stereotypes are used to judge other people, but are relied on less when other information is available. We saw, however, that because much of that other information implies gender identification, stereotypes continue to serve their questionable social functions.

Gender is a concept that clearly reveals the importance of the sociohistorical perspective. Both scientists and lay people argue that it is obvious and natural that men and women have different characteristics and are suited for different types of work. As we have seen in this chapter, however, gender is a social construction in the guise of a natural division of the world. As important as biological sex differences might be, they are eclipsed by the ways society uses gender to maintain inequalities and biases.

The story of gender is one of power, domination, oppression, and violence. These are not biological inevitabilities but social conventions created and enforced by the dominant gender. Recall that several investigators (for example, Broverman et al., 1972; Dimitrovsky, Singer, and Yinon, 1989; Taylor & Hall, 1982) found evidence for a strong masculinity bias in relating gender schema to healthful outcomes. In addition, as we previously noted, others (for example, Hyde & Linn, 1988) present data indicating that even though men and women are equally talented in those abilities necessary for economic and social advancement, men continue to far outdistance women for reasons unrelated to natural skills, abilities, or work efforts. The case for patriarchical domination, as we have seen, is based on these and related materials (for example, Scott, 1988; Kitzinger, 1987; Hare-Mustin & Marecek, 1988).

It is important that students studying social psychology understand the relationship between gender, self, and society. This is not simply an academic issue, but a social dilemma calling for a revolution in public attitudes. We must study the current framework and observe how demeaning, restrictive social arrangements are maintained. We must be adventuresome enough to consider alternative possibilities and to map their qualities. Here we should follow Scott's advice by taking care not to make a new map that is merely the mirror image of the one we hope to replace (see also Hare-Mustin & Marecek, 1988). The alternative is not a *gender-free* society, where no differences exist or are recognized, but a *genderful* society, where the male–female divide is much more variable and complex, where diversity makes the use of such simple categories obsolete.

PART FIVE

Helping and Harming:
The Social Psychology of
Altruism and Aggression

15

· ·

Understanding Aggression and Altruism

EVERYDAY LIFE SEEMS filled with instances of people harming themselves and others: "With the exception of the police and the military, the family is perhaps the most violent social group, and the home the most violent social setting in our society" (Gelles & Straus, 1979, p. 15). "According to recent studies, about one quarter of North American women have been raped or sexually assaulted at some point in their lives . . . and about one half of all female college students have experienced some form of male sexual aggression in a given year" (Malamuth & Briere, 1986, p. 75). "According to a recent report . . . 3% of Americans each year are victims of violent crime, the equivalent of approximately 6 million people. During 1984, a violent crime . . . occurred every 25 seconds" (Widom, 1989, p. 3). "Content analyses since 1968 have demonstrated that there are 5 or 6 incidents of violence per hour in prime time television and from 15 to 25 incidents per hour in cartoons" (Friedrich-Cofer & Huston, 1986, p. 365). Reflecting on the millions who have died in the twentieth century from war, genocide, terrorism, and other forms of human-made violence, the psychiatrist R. D.

Laing (1967) equated the pathological condition of schizophrenia with our normal life experiences. If that is the standard of normalcy, then perhaps those we consider abnormal are on the side of the angels!

Even as headlines remind us of our aggressive behavior, however, we are also aware of those moments when people perform extraordinary acts of heroism or selflessly help the needy victims of natural and human-made disasters. Although there appears to be less interest among media analysts in the incidence of altruistic rather than aggressive, violent acts on prime time television, real-life reports and dramatizations of people giving aid and comfort to others are by no means rare or unusual. The story of humanity's evolution has often been characterized as one of tooth-and-claw competition, but there is a growing awareness of the high levels of cooperation and mutual assistance that must have existed even in humanity's earliest years (Hoffman, 1981; Krebs & Miller, 1985).

There is little doubt that we are capable of both helping and harming others, and that these two possibilities have framed innumerable debates about which is our "real" nature. Are we self-seeking creatures with destructive instincts, as thinkers like Hobbes and Freud have suggested? If so, then our aggression is natural and society must be organized, as Hobbes (1651/1929) recommended, to restrain people's most violent impulses. Or, as Rousseau (1762/1950) claimed, are we fundamentally good and helpful by nature? In that case, society has corrupted us, and we can only regain our altruistic nature by returning to a more primitive form of communal living with fewer social restrictions. It is not *we* who must change, but *society.*

Most discussions of altruism and aggression question which form of behavior is more natural to humanity and whether they are genetically or socially determined (for example, see Campbell, 1972, 1975; Cohen, 1972; Hoffmann, 1981; Krebs & Miller, 1985). Is aggression a survival instinct of all living things, protecting the individual, the family, and the species as a whole? Are people likewise born with an altruistic instinct? For whom would this instinct have survival value? Is altruism learned behavior, designed to promote collective solidarity by curbing potentially destructive impulses? The debate over the biological versus the cultural basis for altruism and aggression seems unlikely ever to be settled by empirical data. Reasonable arguments have been made supporting a biological component to nearly every facet of human behavior; yet, even if such a component could be determined, we are nevertheless social beings whose activities are organized and regulated by formal and informal rules (Averill, 1982, 1983).

The hand of the social world appears the very moment we try to define the behavioral referent for altruism or aggression. Let us then turn to this interesting and complex issue. What do we mean when we refer to some act as altruistic or aggressive?

It would seem to be a relatively simple matter to identify a given action as either altruistic or aggressive: for example, if I help an old woman cross the street, I am behaving altruistically; if I push her out of the way, I am acting aggressively. As we will see, however, reality is not so clear-cut. What if I helped the woman to cross the street so I could get a firm grip on her purse, which I hoped to snatch? On the other hand, what if I pushed her aside to pursue a purse-snatcher? Obviously, motives and circumstances are factors in just what constitutes an altruistic or aggressive action.

Aggression

Whether I accidently or intentionally bump into you, causing you to fall and hurt yourself, my overt behavior (I bump you) and the outcome (you fall and hurt yourself) are the same. Most of us undoubtedly would consider the intentional, but not the accidental, event to be aggressive. Some investigators, however, have eschewed any references to intention in defining aggression. Rather, they speak of aggression in terms of a noxious stimulus delivered from one person to another (for example, see Buss, 1963). Others, however, have argued that we cannot understand aggression without some reference to the intention to do harm (Berkowitz, 1984, 1989; Tedeschi, Gaes, & Rivera, 1977; Tedeschi, Smith, & Brown, 1974). For example, Berkowitz considers an act to be aggressive if it involves the deliberate injury of another. The term *deliberate* indicates intentionality, a factor missing from definitions of aggression that exclusively refer to overt behavior. The emphasis on intentionality to harm another is also part of the frustration-aggression hypothesis proposed in the classic work by Dollard and his colleagues (1939), which we will consider in Chapter 16.

In a study by Blumenthal and his colleagues (cited in Tedeschi, Smith, & Brown, 1974, p. 557) subjects indicated that student demonstrators and ghetto rioters behaved agggressively, but police using force did not. Another study by Brown and Tedeschi (cited in Tedeschi, Smith, & Brown, 1974) found that people who defend themselves from another's attack are not considered aggressive, even if their defense does more harm to the attacker than was done to them in the first place. These studies suggest that aggression cannot be defined entirely in terms of intentionality. We must also consider the social context in which a so-called aggressive act takes place. This is precisely the point made by advocates of the sociohistorical perspective who argue that an act can be meaningfully understood only when social circumstances are taken into consideration.

Averill (1982, 1983), for example, conducted a series of studies in which he simply asked people to give a detailed description of a recent experience of anger. Their responses supported his view that anger and aggression are *socially* defined concepts that cannot be understood in terms of an individual's intentions or motivations. For instance, a victim involved in an otherwise avoidable accident would use anger to accuse the person responsible for that accident of behaving recklessly and irresponsibly. In this case, the subject's anger serves the social purpose of justifying the punishment that the careless person should receive.

Lutz's (1988) examination of emotions among the Ifaluk adds to this sociohistorical view of aggression. The Ifaluk term *song* suggests justifiable anger. The term, however, is not used to describe an internal state that a person experiences, as though emotions were "natural bodily events." Rather, as Lutz notes, "Each time a person declares 'I am *song*' is a gambit or bid in an effort to install a particular interpretation of events as the definition of that situation to be accepted by others" (p. 162). In other words, and paralleling Averill's view, the very concepts of anger and aggression can only be understood by examining their particular social uses—for example, to convince others of the appropriateness of the "victim's" response.

Leyens and Fraczek (1984) expand on the sociohistorical approach to aggression by reminding us of the role dominating groups play in defining certain acts as aggressive or nonaggressive. For example, what is terrorism? To the nation subjected to unprovoked attacks directed toward innocent civilians, terrorism is clearly aggression—intentional actions whose goal is to harm others. On the other hand, reprisals taken against terrorist acts, which may also harm innocent people, are generally considered less aggressive because they are justifiable self-defense. These understandings are facilitated by the dominant group's ability to manage the ways we define and understand aggression. The military operation mounted in Panama by the United States in late December 1989 was code-named "Just Cause." Who can argue against the justifiability of violence if it is just?

Types of Aggression

Those interested in defining aggression primarily from the conventionalist perspective—that is, minimizing the importance of the social context—have sought to distinguish among different types of aggressive behavior. Feshbach (1964) identified at least three different types. People demonstrate *instrumental* aggression when they harm someone incidentally while trying to achieve some goal. For example, I am eager to get tickets for tonight's concert so I vigorously push you out of my way because you are blocking my access to the ticket booth. I do not really want to injure you; I only want my tickets. *Hostile* aggression involves intentionally injuring other people. This type comes closest to the usual meaning of aggression as defined by Dollard, Berkowitz, and others. People may also use *expressive* aggression as a mode of communication, like making threats at the stranger on your lawn or shaking your fist as a sign of solidarity at a political rally.

Active and Passive Aggression

Is an act considered aggressive if it harms someone psychologically rather than physically? Is intimidation as aggressive as physical violence? Most of us would respond in the affirmative. People can clearly be aggressive without being physically violent. Ridiculing another student in front of the class or calling someone "fatty" or "nigger" can be more damaging to that person than a slap across the face. The wounds to self-esteem and pride can be much slower to heal than physical injuries.

Consider another possibility. Jim is always very friendly, perhaps overly friendly, and compliant to the extreme. He is always available, the first to pitch in and help out. We find it very easy to abuse this relationship, calling Jim away from his own activities to do just one more little favor for us. Good old Jim smilingly complies with our every wish and drops what he's doing to give us a hand. We might be prepared to claim that since we are abusing Jim, we are behaving in an aggressive manner. But would we ever consider Jim's behavior to be aggressive?

Because we tend to think of aggression as an *active* behavior, we would probably respond in the negative. Clinical psychologists, however, have been aware of a pattern of what they term *passive* aggression. Jim's overly compliant and self-sacrificing manner, for example, may reveal a kind of passive aggression in which he is "killing us with kindness." Other forms of passive aggression include sulking, withholding, and even provocative behaviors (Averill, 1983). Those who go around sulking may be communicating more than dissatisfaction; making us miserable may be the aggressive intent behind the behavior. People who withhold their affection, as in marital disputes, are also demonstrating passive aggressive behavior. People may also passively provoke others into behaving aggressively toward them, thereby revealing the other people's lack of maturity and self-control and putting them to shame.

Many instances of passive aggression appear among people with little power or influence who have no other way of retaliating against their oppressors. Direct aggression is too dangerous; passive aggression is their only defense against active aggression directed at them. Although clinical psychologists working with patient populations have been the most prominent analysts of passive aggression, it should be clear that many victims of social oppression, without power to directly express anger toward their oppressors, may also reflect this pattern of passive aggression for reasons having little to do with clinical pathology.

The Measure of Aggression

What do social psychologists actually study when they do research on aggression? Whereas the definitional problem offers us some confusing options and unresolved questions, most social psychologists have neatly solved the operational problem for purposes of research: aggression involves the administration of electric shocks to another person! Averill (1983) reports the findings from a study by Lubek in which about 65% of the research on aggression used electric shock as the main index. Fortunately, for the sake of achieving some ecological validity to the so richly defined concept of aggression, other measurement approaches have also been used—hitting, shoving, kicking, beating, and so on in game and in play situations; denigrating someone's performance on a task; responding with fantasy stories to ambiguous pictures; self-ratings, teacher-ratings, and peer ratings of aggression.

Those who hoped to ultimately find a viable definition of aggression through such investigations must be disappointed. The ethical demands of laboratory control, however, have established stringent limitations on the kinds of behaviors considered aggressive, leaving us with an incomplete picture of reality. We are still left with as many unresolved questions as we had before embarking on this brief methodological tour. Are aggressive acts intentional or accidental, active or passive, instrumental or hostile, to be understood by looking inside the individual or society? As we work through later chapters, however, a more complete understanding of the meaning of aggression will emerge.

Altruism

As we will see, it is no easier to define altruism than aggression. The list of behaviors usually considered altruistic include: rescuing (helping someone in distress); donating (giving money to a charitable cause); aiding (helping someone complete a task); sharing (giving parts of one's own reward to someone who may also be deserving). While some of these activities have a quality considered by some to be the essence of altruism—giving without expectation of any personal benefit—others do not. This has led some to distinguish between truly altruistic behaviors and prosocial behaviors performed for personal or selfish reasons.

Egoism Versus Altruism

Am I acting altruistically if I help you out of personal motives—for example, to gain a reputation of courage, selflessness, or heroism? This question opens the door to the complex debate of egoism versus altruism as the motivation for so-called altruistic acts. The egoistic thesis suggests that, despite pretensions to the contrary, we *always* act selfishly. This reasoning led thinkers like Hobbes to justify the need for a state that would regulate individuals' otherwise conflicting egoistic impulses.

In contrast with egoism, altruism implies benefitting another without regard for personal self-interest. Even if an act is prosocial, it should be considered egoistic if it is tainted by self-interest (Staub, 1978). The man who dives into the frozen lake to rescue a skater who fell through the ice is behaving egoistically if he does it to impress his girlfriend, get on the evening news, or win some kind of reward or community service medal—even if he risks his life doing so. But do people *ever* behave in an altruistic way? Can we think of any circumstances in which personal motives are not somehow involved in a seemingly altruistic act?

If we begin with the presumption of egoism, we will cynically see its hand everywhere, even in spectacular acts of heroism. On the philosophical front, the raging debate between altruism and egoism has usually resulted in the triumph of the egoist point of view. Social psychologists, however, have explored the problem empirically, looking for experimental evidence of whether altruism can exist without egoism. In a typical laboratory experiment, subjects are placed in a situation where another person needs their help. Do the subjects offer to help that person or not? And, if they do, are their motives egoistic (benefit self) or altruistic (benefit other)? The problem for the experimenter is how to determine the subjects' true motives given only the evidence of their help-giving behavior. Let us first consider some of the reasons why we might help another person for egoistic reasons. At least three different possibilities have been suggested.

First, we may offer to help others in distress because we identify with their suffering; thus, by helping them we actually help ourselves. In other words, we want to rid ourselves of the distress we feel from identifying with those in trouble.

Second, we help others to receive specific rewards or avoid specific punishments for ourselves. For example, by helping someone in need we may win the respect of our friends and neighbors, coming away with a feeling of great pride in being such a good human being. Similarly, if we help others because we fear the repercussions of failing to do so—censure, shame, or guilt—we are behaving egoistically. In both instances, while those we help benefit from our actions, we also benefit, thus precluding any characterization of our behavior as altruistic.

A third egoistic motivation for helping others has been termed *negative-state relief* (Bauman, Cialdini, & Kenrick, 1981; Cialdini et al., 1987). According to this theory, whenever we experience a negative mood state—for example, sadness over another's distress—we try to relieve that state by engaging in mood-elevating activities. Most of us have learned that helping someone else helps us feel better. In contrast with the first type of egoistic helping we considered, there is no identification with others' distress relieved by our act of helping; we simply feel sad and help them to elevate our mood.

THE EXPERIMENTAL TESTS   In an ingenious series of studies, Batson and his colleagues sought to establish an altruistic alternative to these three versions of egoism (1981, 1983, 1986, 1988, 1989). One of their first efforts challenged the personal distress interpretation of the egoistic perspective. Batson and his group first distinguished between personal distress and pure empathy: while personal distress involves an egoistic motivation—helping others to relieve one's own distress at seeing their suffering—empathy reflects an altruistic motivation—acting out of one's desire to minimize others' distress.

If this distinction is meaningful, it should be revealed in how sensitive people react when others need help. If they focus on the other person's pain and suffering, then they are predominantly concerned with personal distress. They are thus more likely to intervene and provide help to reduce their own anxiety and discomfort. On the other hand, if they focus on their feelings of compassion for the other person, they are predominantly making an empathic response and are likely to provide help to alleviate the other person's suffering. The usefulness of this motivational distinction has been demonstrated in several of the Batson studies.

Having established that personal distress and empathy could be reliably assessed, the Batson group tried to determine if they influenced people's helping behavior by presenting subjects a situation in which they could respond egoistically or altruistically. They reasoned that if people's motivation to help others is primarily oriented toward alleviating their own distress, they should be *less* likely to help if they can easily escape the distressing situation. On the other hand, if the primary motivation is empathic, they should help regardless of the ease or difficulty of escape. Results generally supported the expectation that altruism, defined as the unselfish desire to help another without self-regard, was a viable concept. This left two other contenders for the egoistic rather than the altrusitic view—specific rewards and punishments, and negative-state relief.

In 1988, Batson and his associates reported a series of five studies on whether people help others for altruistic reasons or for egoistic reasons involving rewards and punishments. They concluded from their data that the altruistic alternative was more tenable. In 1989, Batson and his colleagues reported the results of three studies pitting altruism against the egoistic alternative of negative-state relief, again concluding that altruism was a better characterization of people's helping behavior. They concluded that people do, in fact, perform acts altruistically, without apparent regard for self-interest. Because Batson's group followed the same general approach in each series of studies, we will focus on one to see just how they arrived at their conclusion.

In one design, subjects are given the role of observers; on a television monitor, they see another subject, Elaine or Charlie (an accomplice), experience distress. For example, they observe Elaine receive mild electric shocks and are told it is part of a study of the effects of aversive stimuli on task performance. At an early point in the study, Elaine appears to be bothered by the shocks. The study is stopped and she is asked if she is okay. Although she indicates that she is, she confesses to a traumatic childhood experience with electric shocks. On learning of this, the experimenter suggests that the experiment be stopped. Elaine insists that she is committed to completing the contract she made when signing on as a subject.

At this point, the experimenter has a bright idea. Since the observers have also signed on for the same study, would they (female subjects for Elaine and male subjects for Charlie) agree to help Elaine?

Subjects are reminded that their assistance is purely voluntary; thus, they can continue as observers, but if they choose to help Elaine, they should change places with her and finish the experiment. Their agreement to help provides the measure of altruism.

To test the various versions of egoism against the altrusitic alternative, Batson and his colleagues systematically varied certain features of the situation. For example, if a person helps someone in distress to avoid experiencing the punishments of censure, guilt, or shame, providing them with a way to justify not helping alleviates these punishments, thereby decreasing their egoistically based motive to help. Justifications of this sort, however, should not have a comparable effect on those who are genuinely motivated by altruism. Examination of data from just such a study led Batson and his associates to conclude that people can be, and indeed are, motivated by a genuine desire to help others without any regard for the benefits of such behavior to themselves.

To test negative-state relief theory, the Batson team (1989) created conditions in which those who helped primarily for mood-elevating reasons would help only when those conditions could be met, whereas those who helped primarily for altruistic reasons would help regardless of the effect on their mood. Batson and his associates compared subjects for whom distress was predominant (egoistic motivation) with those for whom empathy was predominant (altruistic motivation) in the stressful situation involving Elaine or Charlie. Subjects were led to expect participation in two brief studies during their assigned hour. The first involved Elaine or Charlie in the situation we just examined; the other allowed the experimenters to create two experimental conditions involving the anticipation of mood elevation. All subjects were told that for the second brief study, they would be shown a film that produced well-known effects on their mood. Half were led to believe that the film would not significantly change their current mood, while the other half believed that it would significantly elevate their mood.

According to negative-state relief theory, subjects saddened by Elaine's plight should be *less* helpful when anticipating an enhancement of their mood than when not anticipating any mood change. Why? If people's moods can be elevated without having to be helpful, they will presumably choose this less costly route (remember that being helpful involves agreeing to sit in for Elaine and receiving the mild electric shocks). In contrast, the altruism hypothesis predicts that, regardless of whether or not people anticipated having their mood elevated by the film, empathic people should agree to help Elaine.

Overall, data supported the altruism hypothesis. Empathic subjects did not decrease their helping behavior when they expected to have their mood elevated by the film. As many agreed to help when anticipating as when not anticipating mood elevation. This finding does not conform to the negative-state relief expectations.

Conclusions

The debate over whether altruism or egoism more accurately characterizes people's helping behavior is not yet resolved. Batson's work suggests, however, that we may need to revise some of our ideas about "human nature." Obviously, people help others for a variety of egoistic reasons; but, as Batson's work demonstrates, people also help others for altruistic reasons. Although Batson frames his understanding in terms of "human nature"—a conventionalist way of thinking—the issue of altruism versus egoism can also be understood in sociohistorical terms. Some years ago, for example, Titmuss (1971) examined various blood-donor systems, comparing those rewarding the blood donor with money or some other personal benefit with those offering no compensation. Titmuss concluded that any system that pays for blood inhibits donating blood as a gift.

The sociohistorical perspective, then, focuses on whether or not social arrangements interfere with altruism not, as in the conventionalist approach, whether humans are by nature egoistic or altruistic. In a blood-donating system that offers payment, it is difficult to determine when self-interest is not involved. People cannot give freely; motives are always suspect because they are framed in egoistic terms. Titmuss' implication is that altruism vanishes entirely under such conditions, compelling the use of rewards or threats to elicit help from the public.

As Batson and his associates point out, people can act both altruistically and egoistically. What motivates people to help others is determined more by the social system in which they live than their basic nature. The conspicuous absence of genuine altruism in the United States should not be attributed to a fundamentally egoistic human nature, but rather to the highly individualistic, competitive, and success-oriented nature of our social system. Under those conditions, truly selfless behavior loses on two counts. First, people have learned to be suspicious about those who proclaim that they have acted without their own self-interest clearly in mind. Second, most situations are like those Titmuss noted, so confounding personal benefit with giving help or assistance to others that it is virtually impossible to behave selflessly. Altruism therefore tends to wither away from lack of use, like a muscle that has not been exercised. Eventually people cannot act altruistically even if they want to—the social "muscle" has atrophied too much.

16

Factors Influencing Aggression and Altruism

I N THIS CHAPTER we will examine seven different factors that have been identified as being important in understanding aggression and altruism: (1) frustration and aggression; (2) empathy; (3) gender; (4) mood; (5) the recipient's response; (6) personality; and (7) the situation.

Frustration and Aggression

In 1939, a distinguished group of psychologists—Dollard, Doob, Miller, Mowrer, and Sears—authored a pioneering work on the study of aggression. It introduced the simple, persuasive idea that aggression—the intent to harm or injure another—is always a consequence of frustration—having one's movement toward a goal interrupted. People will thus try to injure anyone who interferes with their attainment of a goal. Dollard and his colleagues were quite aware that aggressing against a frustrator is not always possible. Thus, they added the notion of *displacement* to their understanding of how frustration operates to trigger aggression. If people are unable to aggress directly against the frustrator, they displace their anger and aggress against someone or something else. Displacement could include kicking the dog, throwing a book, yelling at the children, or cutting someone off on the road.

Critics of the hypothesis originally proposed by Dollard and his colleagues objected to its insistence both that aggression was the only response to frustration and that it was only triggered by frustration. For example, people might respond to frustration by withdrawal and passivity rather than aggression. Many factors have since been suggested as alternative triggering mechanisms for aggression. Investigators have demonstrated that the imitation of unpunished aggressive models is involved in children's learning of aggression (Bandura, 1973); that being insulted or having one's self-esteem challenged are more likely to lead to aggression than simply being frustrated (Maslow, 1941); that other features of the situation are important determinants of whether or not aggression will be expressed after a person is made angry (Berkowitz, 1984, 1989). The study by Averill (1983) that we previously considered (see p. 268) concluded that none of the above factors are primary determinants of aggression. According to Averill, people become angry when they believe someone has acted improperly or in an unjustified manner. As a cause of aggression, this again is a far cry from frustration.

Recently, Berkowitz (1989) sought to resurrect Dollard's original frustration-aggression hypothesis. He argued that a frustrating situation will produce aggression only insofar as the person who is frustrated experiences the frustrating event as unpleasant and aversive. We obviously will not experience these aversive negative feelings on every occasion that we are frustrated, and thus should respond with anger and aggression only when negative feelings are aroused. For example, while it may be frustrating not to win the lottery, it is unlikely that most people will respond with rage. On the other hand, if we are busy trying to complete a major project at the office to have the weekend free and a colleague continually interferes with that goal, we are likely to experience fairly strong negative feelings, perhaps even responding aggressively: "Don't you have any work to do?", you ask him with an angry gleam in your eye and slapping your pen down on your desk.

Berkowitz presents an impressive array of evidence that aversive stimuli create negative affects, which in turn evoke aggression. Read the following list of aversive stimuli and consider your own feelings and responses: "irritable cigarette smoke, foul odors, high room temperatures, and even disgusting scenes" (p. 69). Although none of these aversive stimuli fits the original definition of frustration as thwarted goal attainment, Berkowitz's position is that they illustrate the potency of aversive events in motivating aggressive responses. And, as Berkowitz notes, any frustration that becomes aversive will evoke aggression.

. . . .

Empathy

In Chapter 15 we considered one view of the role of empathy—that is, compassion for another—in altruistic behavior in the series of studies undertaken by Batson and his associates (see pp. 272–75). As we saw, his group distinguished between two kinds of response to seeing someone in trouble, personal distress and pure empathy. While personal distress is egoistically focused, empathy is characterized by a disregard for personal self-interest.

As Batson's work suggests, empathy does not appear to be a unitary quality: in his view there are two types of "empathy" with different relationships to altruistic behavior. The distinction between personal distress and empathy that Batson has proposed is but one of several formulations of the factors that might be involved in altruistic behavior (for example, see Davis, 1983; Underwood & Moore, 1982). For example, Underwood and Moore found it useful to distinguish between various kinds of what they term *perspective-taking*. In general, perspective taking refers to the ability to adopt the other person's point of view; it is usually contrasted with egocentrism, or adopting one's own point of view.

Underwood and Moore identified three main types of perspective-taking. *Perceptual* perspective-taking involves literally perceiving things through the visual standpoint of the other person. *Affective* perspective-taking refers to a person's ability to experience the feelings that another person has. *Social* or *cognitive* perspective-taking emphasizes the ability to experience the other person's thoughts, intentions, and so on. Of these three types, affective perspective-taking comes closest to the usual meaning of empathy as experiencing the other person's feelings.

Underwood and Moore's review of the literature relating perspective-taking to altruistic behavior reveals mixed, but nevertheless interesting, findings. Perceptual perspective-taking seems to be related positively to altruistic behavior—being helpful to another person, comforting them and showing generosity towards them, and so on.

Social or cognitive perspective-taking is also positively related to altruistic behavior. On the other hand, affective perspective-taking is not consistently related to altruism.

For example, if affective perspective-taking involves directly experiencing the other person's pain and suffering, there may not be a relation to altruism if another avenue is available for individuals to reduce the parallel suffering they experience. Still, if perspective-taking leads to feeling compassion for the other person, then there should be a relationship to altruism. Until these two meanings of affective perspective-taking are disentangled—for example, by using Batson's distinction between distress and empathy—discouraging results seem likely. Eisenberg and Miller's (1987) review of the literature finds a consistent, but limited relationship between empathy and altruism, which varies as a function of how empathy was assessed. Assessments based on people's responses to hypothetical situations yielded a weaker relationship than assessments based on their responses to actual situations.

Empathy has been considered relevant to aggression as well as to altruism. Presumably, people who are *less* empathic should be more likely to be aggressive toward others. Miller and Eisenberg (1988) examined the research literature on the relationship between empathy and various kinds of physical and verbal aggressive behavior. They report an overall negative relationship between empathy and aggression; in other words, the less empathic people are, the more aggressive they become. They also found that abusive parents had less empathy than nonabusive parents. In their review, and relevant to our next topic, Miller and Eisenberg found no sex differences in the correlations between empathy and aggression.

. . . .

Gender

Cultural stereotypes guide our beliefs that men and women must differ with respect to both altruism and aggression. We are told, implicitly if not explicitly, that women are more likely to need help than men, and that men are much more aggressive than women. As we just noted, however, Miller and Eisenberg demonstrated that men and women reveal little, if any, differences at least with respect to empathy and aggression. What about more direct tests?

Eagly and Crowley (1986) reviewed some 172 studies examining gender and helping, while Eagly and Steffen (1986) similarly considered some 63 studies on gender and aggression. We first encountered some of Eagly's ideas in an analysis of social influence (see pp. 133–35). Briefly, Eagly helped to debunk the stereotype that women are more easily influenced than men, pointing out that that conclusion may be more a result of the methodology used in most of the research—conformity situations—than any real differences between men and women. She also commented that, because men and women are in different positions of power and influence in society, we should expect to find men exhibiting more qualities of leadership and women more of submission. Again, this has less to do with fundamental biological differences between men and women than the nature of gender-opportunities and gender discrimination in society.

Eagly and Crowley adopted this same position in considering the gender-helping relationship. Role differences between men and women would incline them toward different kinds of helping behaviors—men in more heroic roles involving short-term forms of helping and women in roles involving more long-term, nurturant kinds of helping. Unfortunately, since the vast majority of studies on helping behavior involve short-term, heroic kinds of intervention (for example, rescuing someone in distress), the research is already biased in favor of showing men to be more helpful than women. Empirical differences thus say little about fundamental differences between men and women. The data do tell us a great deal both about the methodologies by which helping is studied (which favor men over women) as well as the social roles that men and women are currently more likely to occupy. As Eagly and Crowley suggest, if investigators are really interested in the whole range of altruistic behaviors, they may have to abandon the experimental laboratory for more natural and nurturant settings that will give women a fair chance to prove themselves to be as or more helpful than men.

Eagly and Crowley also examined the possibility, first reported by Eagly and Carli (1981), that the sex of the investigator colors research findings. In their study of social influence, Early and Carli found that male authors tended to report findings more flattering to males than to females. Eagly and Crowley were pleased to report, however, that despite the predominance of male investigators, there was no indication of a male favorability bias in the area of helping behavior.

But what about sex differences in aggression? Findings here are likewise shaped by the methodologies employed in the research. Male and female aggression may vary for any number of reasons. For example, differential placement in the status and power hierarchies of society may lead women to be less direct in expressing aggression. It may also be true, as Gilligan (1982) has suggested, that women are more concerned with not harming others, and so avoid or restrain aggressive impulses more than men.

Eagly and Steffen's review reveals some trends in the data, but also a great deal of inconsistency. Men do appear to be more aggressive overall than women; men also receive more aggression overall than women. However, these results may be a feature of the methodology that defines aggression as physically injuring another person (for example, via electric shocks), something women seem less inclined to do than men. For example, male–female differences appear to be less evident when aggression involves harm-doing of a more psychological nature. Eagly and Steffen conclude that "men and women think differently about aggression . . . women reported more guilt and anxiety as a consequence of aggression, more vigilence about the harm that aggression causes its victims, and more concern about the danger that their aggression might bring to themselves" (p. 325).

Remember that these ideas about female aggression may be based on the fact that women occupy less powerful positions in society than men. Given minimal biological differences between men and women, we would expect that as women move upwards to positions of power, they too might adopt as aggressive an outlook as men. Margaret Thatcher, the "Iron Lady", might be a case in point. It may be true, however, that those whose social roles primarily involve caretaking, as has been typical for women, might have a qualitatively distinct orientation towards many things in the world, including aggression.

Mood

Both positive and negative moods have been linked with helping. We saw earlier how the negative-state relief theory argued that, because we have learned that helping others can improve our own moods, our sadness at another person's situation might motivate us to provide help as a way to elevate our own mood. In their review of 44 studies linking negative mood with helping, Carlson and Miller (1987) found a relationship less consistent than the negative-state relief model suggests. For example, negative moods facilitate altruistic behavior when other's feelings are taken into consideration. If you are asked to imagine that a good friend is dying of cancer and to focus on how he or she feels, you are more likely to be helpful in other circumstances (for example, helping complete questionnaires for a graduate student) than if you focus on your own feelings. In other words, while you may feel distress in both cases, you are more likely to be altruistic in the former (see Thompson, Cowan, & Rosenhan, 1980). Carlson and Miller suggest that this result supports an attentional focus model more than a negative-state relief model.

Other investigations have also found evidence for a positive relationship between mood and helping behavior. Isen's (1970; Isen, Clark, & Schwartz, 1976) program of research demonstrates what she terms "the warm glow of success": people whose mood is good tend to be more generous and helpful to others. Carlson, Charlin, and Miller (1988) examined some 34 studies linking subjects' positive moods (induced through succeeding on a task, finding money, viewing enjoyable slides, and so on) and altruistic-like behavior (donating to a charity, mailing a lost letter, agreeing to solicit for a charity, and so on). Their findings demonstrate once again that people with positive moods are indeed more likely than those with negative moods to behave in generally altruistic ways. They suggested a somewhat egoistic explanation for this relationship: a good mood increases helpfulness because the mind is more attuned to positive feedback and rewards for such behavior.

. . . .

The Recipient's Response

Most of us have an intuitive sense of how the response of the target or recipient of aggression can affect the aggressor. The parallel case for altruism, however, is not as well understood. If I anticipate that my aggression against you will be met with equal but opposite force, I might withhold aggressing, preferring some other tactic. This is the idea behind mutual deterrence: if we have the power to destroy each other, we will presumably refrain from aggressive actions to avoid provoking the use of that power. Some analyses of deterrence, however, suggest that it may not always work as intended. Having examined cases in which deterrence failed as often as it worked, Lebow and Stein (1987) recommend an alternative strategy of "reassurance." While deterrence assumes that adversaries are motivated by aggression, which is checked only through opposing strength, reassurance assumes that adversaries are driven by a fear of their own vulnerability. Therefore, "reassurance dictates that defenders try to communicate to their adversaries their benign intentions" (p. 40).

Although the examples and analyses presented by Lebow and Stein primarily involve international relations, their ideas apply equally well to instances of interpersonal aggression. If aggression is driven by a sense of conquest, then a firm counterresponse might mitigate such ambition. However, if Lebow and Stein are right and aggression is driven by fears of vulnerability, then reassurances of benign intentions might serve the purpose of undoing the threatened aggression. Needless to say, there are critics of this analysis of international relations (see the 1987 *Journal of Social Issues* [#4] for a discussion). We saw earlier a related theme reported in Eagly and Steffen's examination of sex differences in aggression (see pp. 280–82). They argue that women are more likely than men to think that, by withholding aggression, they will avoid causing pain and suffering.

Apologizing might also be effective in the management of aggression. In one of two studies reported by Ohbuchi, Kameda, and Agarie (1989), female students were harmed by another female student (an accomplice) they were told was a senior psychology major. Some subjects received an apology from her while others did not. Subjects were asked to rate the accomplice's personality and their own emotions, as well as their desire to harm the accomplice. Subjects were told that these skill ratings would be used by the experimenter to grade her performance. Results demonstrated that when the accomplice apologized for harming the subjects, she received higher ratings than when she did not. Her apology effectively changed the subjects' perceptions of her, casting her in a more favorable light than when she failed to apologize for the harm she caused the subjects.

So what is the relationship between the recipient's response and altruism? Since you benefit from my helpfulness, isn't your response likely to be gratitude? The research literature in social psychology suggests that it's not quite that simple. There are several reasons why people might not take your help so kindly. Consider the effect on the recipient's sense of self-worth. Who hasn't read in the paper or seen on television accounts of destitute people who refuse legitimate aid? They often say that accepting help makes them feel and appear to others as incapable of functioning on their own. They would rather remain down-and-out and retain their dignity and sense of self-worth.

Receiving help can also engage the process of *reactance* we considered earlier (see pp. 136–37). I may suspect that there are strings attached to receiving help from another person which limit my freedom to act. My reaction is thus to reject the help to restore my threatened freedom. There is also a sense of indebtedness often associated with receiving help from others: they help you today but expect you to help them tomorrow. Some people not only feel that this restricts their freedom (reactance) but also that they cannot afford to repay the debt. Some investigators (for example, Fisher, Nadler, & Whitcher-Alagna, 1982) point out that incurring an indebtedness that can never be repaid violates several social norms, including reciprocity and equity. We will consider these norms later in the chapter.

Another possible recipient concern, related to the norm of equity, is illustrated by the following, not uncommon occurrence. Those with "good connections" who quickly move up the company ladder often find themselves deeply resented by colleagues who have been around much longer and "paid their dues." Anticipating such negative reactions, some people might be reluctant to accept this kind of career-boost. In this case, it is not future indebtedness that cannot be repaid but rather a sense that such help is undeserved and unfair to others.

While the cultural proverb tells us not to look a gift horse in the mouth, it seems that there are many reasons for doing just that. Fisher, Nadler, and Whitcher-Alagna's (1982) review of some of the research examining the reactions of recipients to receiving aid clearly confirms the importance of all of the factors we have considered, especially the threat to self-esteem occasioned by giving help to needy people.

Personality

We intuitively insist that we be able to differentiate those people who are helpful and benevolent from those who are uncooperative and inhumane. Since most social psychologists have been shaped by these same cultural beliefs, they too have searched extensively for consistent altruistic or aggressive individual tendencies. By now, we should be well aware of the difficulties involved in searching for something embedded within the individual—be it an attitude, motive, or, in this case, a personality trait—that marks his or her behavior consistently across a wide variety of situations and circumstances. We already know, for example, that it is unwise to use a simplistic measure of either traits or behaviors.

In the case of altruism and aggression, we also know that it is difficult to even agree upon a clear understanding of either concept. What consistent behaviors do we look for people to make? If we simply observe them engage in rescuing behaviors, for example, we may overlook a range of other altruistic activities. The same problem occurs with respect to aggression. Must a person physically assault others consistently for us to consider his or her behavior aggressive? Is a verbal insult sufficient? What about sarcasm or "killing with kindness"? Do we need to measure intent to injure another or focus only on behavior? As you can see, determining a personality trait for either altruism or aggression is not an easy matter. Data from a variety of research studies are, in fact, inconsistent and at times confusing. Krebs and Miller (1985), for example, conclude that the difficulties in defining altruism, establishing the criteria for the behavior, and developing assessments have yielded a set of inconsistent findings. Granting the legitimacy of this conclusion, let us nevertheless examine several studies and draw our own conclusions.

We have already encountered one effort to assess the trait of altruism in the research program conducted by Batson and his associates (see pp. 272–75). Recall that his group was intent on distinguishing between egoistic and selfless behavior, considering only the latter to represent genuine altruism. Batson and his colleagues (1986) took exception to previous research demonstrating a correspondence between altruistic behavior and several personality traits—for example, social responsibility, moral reasoning, empathy, and self-esteem (Rushton, 1981; Staub, 1974). They were concerned that such correlations did not distinguish between genuine altruism and egoistic helpful behavior, thereby creating the challenge for his own study. Would people who scored high on this clustering of traits and placed into a situation designed to distinguish genuine altruism from egoism reveal the pattern reported by both Staub and Rushton? To test this possibility, Batson's group employed the same easy versus difficult escape manipulation they had used so successfully in their other research.

Recall Batson's reasoning: a person whose helping is egoistically motivated—that is, designed to gain some personal benefit—should be more likely to help when it is difficult to escape the distressing situation than when it is relatively easy. Batson and his colleagues thus expected positive correlations between the several so-called altruistic personality traits and helping behavior under difficult, but not easy, escape conditions for egoistically motivated people. On the other hand, a person whose helping is altruistically motivated—that is, designed to relieve the other person's suffering—should help even when escape is easy. This led Batson's group to expect positive correlations between the altruistic personality traits and helping behavior under the easy escape conditions for altruistically motivated people. The researchers also expected positive correlations for these people when escape was difficult, but predicted that they would be lower than those under the easy escape conditions.

In short, Batson and his colleagues expected one pattern of correlations to emerge if the traits measured egoism and a different pattern to emerge if the traits measured altruism. For the most part, *none* of the personality traits they evaluated—all of which had been based on the previous findings reported by Staub and by Rushton—confirmed the pattern of helping expected if genuine altruism were involved. The results, however, did support the egoistic alternative. Batson's group thus did not find support for the existence of an altruistic personality if altruism is understood as helping another person without regard for self-interest. However, if altruism means helping another person in order to achieve some personal benefit, then they did find several significant correlations indicative of an egoistically motivated helpful personality.

In Batson's view, then, while there are personality traits that can reliably distinguish between individuals who are more or less likely to help another person in distress, such individuals are motivated by egoistic self-interest and not altruism. If we are willing to have our altruistic personality be self-interested, then we have support for a trait of egoistic altruism; if, however, we insist on the kind of purity Batson demands, then we do not yet have a genuine altruistic personality. If our goals are purely pragmatic—that is, we do not really care about the underlying motives of those who help, but only that they help—then we might be comfortable with Batson's conclusions. If, however, we claim that real altruism exists only when personal interest is absent, our quest for a saint has disappointingly found only an egoist.

Gergen, Gergen, and Meter (1972) have contributed to our understanding of the difficulties involved in finding the altruistic personality. In one of their own studies they evaluated the trait of altruism using a variety of well-known personality measures—self-esteem, nurturance, autonomy, self-consistency, and so on. They assessed altruistic behavior through five separate measures of a person's tendency to help, including counseling students from a nearby high school, carrying out a faculty research project, and preparing classroom materials for future use. Because they did not expect to find altruism without egoistic motivations, they were not concerned as Batson's group with distinguishing genuine altruism from egoistic altruism; helping behavior, however motivated, was sufficient for Gergen's group.

Gergen and his associates found a number of significant correlations between the trait measures and altruistic behavior; however, there were no correlational patterns that would permit them to establish a law of human behavior. To illustrate this point, they report a positive correlation between nurturance and agreeing to help counsel others, but no relationship between nurturance and any of the other measurements of helping behavior. This suggests that, rather than search for the personality of the altruist, we might examine situational factors involved in the decision to help or not to help (see the next section in this chapter). Gergen, Gergen, and Meter also report that personality traits that predict for males do not predict for females. Overall, then, they paint a somewhat discouraging picture for those seeking the altruistic personality.

An interesting and important exception to this dismal picture is reported by Oliner and Oliner (1988) in their study of those who rescued Jews in Nazi Europe. Using the records maintained and documented by Israel's Yad Vashem memorial to both the victims of the Holocaust and those who risked their lives to rescue Jews from the Nazi horror, the Oliners selected a sample of some 406 rescuers to interview some forty years after the events had taken place. A rescuer was defined as someone who took an active part in helping Jews— hiding, housing, feeding, and clothing them as well as helping them escape—at great risk to themselves and often their own families and without remuneration of any kind. In the Oliners' view, this behavior—providing assistance to others in need without consideration for personal gain—was evidence of true altruism.

Unlike the typical acts of altruism that social psychologists have studied in the laboratory, the Oliners' research examines behavior that occurs over a period of time in a real-life setting and in a dangerous and highly risky context, in which official support for such behavior is forbidden. Governmental policy promulgated by the Nazis in Germany and in the nations they occupied demanded that all Jews be turned in or surrender to authorities to purify each nation of this human blight. Few, if any of us, would consider heroism under such conditions to be anything other than altruistic in the purest sense of the term.

Although the richness and complexity of their findings cannot be readily summarized in a few pithy statements, perhaps the most striking conclusions are captured in the Oliner's analysis of the rescuers' orientations towards caring, attachment, and personal responsibility, and the enduring quality of these personal characteristics. In comparing the qualities of the rescuers with those of people they termed "bystanders" (that is, those who helped neither the Jews nor the Nazis), the Oliners concluded that a unique configuration of personal traits described the rescuers: "What distinguished rescuers was not their lack of concern with self, external approval, or achievement, but rather their capacity for extensive relationships—their stronger sense of attachment to others and their feeling of responsibility for the welfare of others, including those outside their immediate familial or communal circles" (p. 249).

Furthermore, these personal qualities appeared to be enduring characteristics of the individuals based on early experiences in the home. In other words, the Oliners believe that they have found some of the familial and personal roots of a truly altruistic personality. Being reared in a loving home in which parents behaved in a selfless, caring manner and communicated those values to their children—a home in which reasoning predominated and physical punishment was rare—is likely to produce the sense of inclusiveness that characterizes those who later in their lives reached out to help others in trouble. The Oliners claim that rescuing Jews was not especially unique in the lives of those people who performed such heroic acts; rather, it was consistent with an ethic of caring, attachment, and responsibility inculcated in them since birth.

An Aggressive Personality?

Have social psychologists found an aggressive personality? Studies have noted some impressive consistencies in people's tendency to be overtly aggressive. The picture is somewhat less clear, however, if aggression refers to the possibly normal tendency to get upset and want to hurt someone, whether we carry it out or not. In other words, when aggression is defined narrowly, there is evidence that some individuals have an underlying tendency to behave in more violent, antisocial ways than others; if aggression is defined loosely (for example, to include an occasional outburst), the evidence is less clear.

Longitudinal studies tend to support the view that there is a personality trait of aggressiveness. In an extensive review of several major longitudinal studies, including his own, Olweus (1979) found consistent support for stable aggressive behavior across a considerable span of time. A longitudinal study examines a phenomenon—in this case aggression—in the same person over various time periods, which may be relatively short (for example, three months) or relatively long (for example, 35 years). The investigator looks for a correlation between assessments made at these different time periods. If there is a positive correlation, the case for a trait of aggressiveness is more plausible. On the other hand, if inconsistency emerges—such that someone who was aggressive at one point in time is not found to be aggressive at another—the arguments on behalf of an aggressive trait are much weaker.

Olweus' review of the longitudinal research on aggression uncovered some impressive short- and long-term stabilities in aggressiveness among males. (Females were not included in the research he examined.) For example, aggressive 8- and 9-year olds were more aggressive when studied again some 10–12 years later; aggressive teenagers were more aggressive some 15–18 years later when they were adults in their mid-30s.

Olweus also examined the possibility that these stabilities could be accounted for by the environment in which the individuals lived. Such a relationship would weaken any inference that the data are the result of some personality trait of aggressiveness since a stable environment could create stable patterns of aggression. After careful evaluation—noting, for example, how much the environment had changed over the lives of many of those studied as well as how much pressure most aggressive children received to change their behavior—Olweus concluded that the results "strongly suggest that the observed stability over time of aggressive reaction patterns is . . . determined by relatively stable . . . motive systems within individuals" (p. 872).

A similar conclusion was reached by Eron and Huesmann (1987) after a review of their longitudinal data. They found that early assessments of aggression in childhood were very good predictors of aggression some 22 years later when individuals were adults. Another three-year longitudinal study found a similar pattern of stability in the United States, Australia, Finland, Poland, and Israel. Unlike Olweus' research, which reported aggression for men, Eron and Huesmann's data included both men and women, finding comparable stability for both.

As Krebs and Miller (1985) point out, research on the altruistic personality has usually been restricted to brief encounters, while that on the aggressive personality has been longitudinal. Does this difference in approaches account for the discrepancy in investigators' success at locating personality traits for altruism and aggression? Perhaps. It may be that investigators must conduct longitudinal studies to uncover genuine stabilities in individuals. Only in this way will genuine behavioral consistencies (if any exist) emerge over time in a variety of situations and circumstances.

· · · · · · · · · · · · · · · ·

The Situation

In a time when investigators are generally disillusioned with finding a correlation between personality traits and behavior, it is only natural to find a major body of work concentrating on situational determinants. A similar pattern exists with respect to the study of both altruism and aggression. The question is not whether there are some people who are more or less altruistic or aggressive, but rather what are the characteristics of situations that elicit or inhibit helping and harming behavior. We will consider several situational variables that have been examined.

Helping by the Numbers

Kitty Genovese's name first made the news in 1964. The shocking exposé of the apparent unwillingness of 38 bystanders to come to the aid of a woman screaming for help while being brutally stabbed to death by an assailant motivated a spate of studies, led in particular by Darley and Latané (1968; Latané & Darley, 1970). The theory behind their research was that a bystander's decision whether or not to intervene is the outcome of a mulitphase decision process:

1. The person must first notice the event. (In the Genovese case, although it was 3 a.m., her neighbors had been awakened by her screams and stood by watching. Clearly, they noticed her distress.)

2. Having noticed the event, the person must interpret it either as an emergency or as something relatively benign.

3. If the situation is seen as an emergency, bystanders must next decide if they have a responsibility to intervene. (We will soon see some factors that apparently influence this part of the process.)

4. If the person decides to intervene, he or she must consider the kind of assistance to offer—calling the police, directly intervening, rushing to find others, and so on.

5. Finally, the person must act or not, based on the preceding phases of the decision process.

Darley and Latané proposed that people are less likely to intervene if they believe that others are available to provide help, what they referred to as a *diffusion of responsibility.* The presence of others diffuses the responsibility that any one person faces, thereby reducing the likelihood that they will intervene (phase 3). It was later suggested that the presence of a group of nonreacting bystanders may not diffuse responsibility, but help define the situation as something other than an emergency (phase 2). In either case, however, the argument is that a person alone is more likely to act than a person among others.

Reporting in 1981, Latané noted that 56 studies had so far appeared examining the hypothesis that people are more likely to intervene when they are alone than when others are around. "In 48 of these 56 comparisons involving a total of more than 2,000 people, there was less helping in the group condition" (p. 349). The presence of others can inhibit an individual's decision to intervene: if others are nonresponsive, the person can define the situation as one not involving anything very serious; if others are available to help, the individual need not take the first step. This inhibition has been found in both laboratory and field studies.

Having just arrived in New York on a flight from London and still disoriented from the time-zone change, my wife and I awakened about 4 a.m. in a friend's house and watched what appeared to be a household burglary across the street. We watched for two hours, convincing ourselves that it was not really a burglary after all. We saw several people wander by, unconcerned about the movement of furniture out of the house and into a waiting van and reasoned that perhaps they were using the windows rather than the front door because they had lost their key or the door was stuck. That morning over breakfast, we casually mentioned the event to our friends. They knew the people who lived in the house and called them up, learning that, indeed, their friends had been cleaned out of nearly everything of value, while they slept peacefully and we watched peacefully.

The Costs of Helping

Other investigators of the bystander effect have examined the situation using a kind of cost-benefit analysis (for example, Piliavin & Piliavin, 1972; Piliavin, Rodin, & Piliavin, 1969; Piliavin et al., 1981). In these terms, the desire to intervene and help might be offset if characteristics of the person to be helped are perceived as proving costly to the potential helper (for example, the victim is drunk and dirty). In their 1969 study, Piliavin and his colleagues did their research on the New York subways, observing the reactions of bystanders when an accomplice, displaying various conditions, collapsed. Would people intervene if the victim were black or only if he were white? Would people intervene if the victim were obviously drunk or only if he were ill? Data suggested that illness is more likely than drunkenness to produce helping interventions and that race has little effect when the victim is ill. Race does have an effect, however, when the victim is drunk: people of the same race as the victim are more likely to help when the person is drunk.

The 1972 study by Piliavin and Piliavin, again using the New York subway as their research site, found that people were both slower to help and less likely to help when a victim fell down and began bleeding from the mouth than when he fell down but no blood appeared. A somewhat different interpretation of this reluctance to help a bleeding victim, however, was proposed by Shotland and Heinold

(1985). They reasoned that one of the important determinants of bystanders' decision to offer help is their actual ability to be helpful.

In a realistic examination of this and related possibilities, Shotland and Heinhold used students taking a course dealing with various kinds of trauma as their research subjects; completing the course earned the student a Red Cross Advanced First Aid and Emergency Care certificate. A realistic, but simulated, emergency involving an injury with arterial bleeding was created—for example, an obviously visible wound, blood pulsating as it would if an artery were severed, a six-inch diameter pool of blood surrounding the victim, shards of glass around the puddle.

Results confirmed Latané and Darley's assertion that there is less tendency to help someone in trouble when others are present. Shotland and Heinold also found, however, that help provided by lone bystanders was less effective than help provided when others were also involved. Expertise, evaluated according to the student's level of training, did not influence the person's decision to help, but only the kind of help given. Trained personnel and untrained personnel both intervened, but only the former provided help that would have been effective if the bleeding were really arterial, "saving" about 40% of the victims. The intervention provided by the untrained students was considerably less effective, "saving" only about 5% of the victims!

This study suggests some of the complex meanings of bystander intervention. Unlike the field situations studied by the Piliavin group—in which blood, for example, discouraged helping—in the context of a Red Cross trauma training course people are perhaps less discouraged by such sights and move forward to intervene. While other studies focus on the helping response itself rather than its quality, Shotland and Heinnold's research suggests that help given by a bystander may not be truly helpful to the recipient, especially if the help-giver lacks the requisite skills. With the current public concern over AIDS, we might expect that the presence of blood might discourage the direct intervention even of trained health personnel unless they are prepared with the proper protective clothing.

Norms and Helping

Social norms provide another situational factor that affects helping behavior. Two major norms have been identified: the norm of reciprocity and the norm of social responsibility. The norm of reciprocity, originally proposed by Gouldner (1960), is based on the assumption that, in most societies, there is an obligation to help those who have given you help and not to injure those who have been helpful to you. The norm establishes reciprocal obligations that, if followed, help stabilize a society. Likewise, these obligations establish some of the conditions under which a person is likely to help another: if you have helped me, I am presumably under a normative obligation to return that help, if not now then in the future.

The *social responsibility* norm was originally suggested by Berkowitz and Daniels (1964). Unlike reciprocity, this norm obliges people to help others who are needy or dependent (for example, children), without regard for compensation. This norm clearly comes much closer than that of reciprocity to describing genuine altruism—helping someone without consideration of benefits to one's self. Various investigations have provided general support for the operation of both of these norms in altrusitic situations (see Staub, 1972, and Sampson, 1976, pp. 427–35 for a summary of some of this research).

It should be apparent that when we turn to norms to explain helping behavior, we are calling upon a situational explanation for altruism rather than something inherent in the personality. Presumably, everyone properly socialized will have learned these norms and so will experience the obligations that they describe. Normative violations should arouse concern in the person obliged to provide help, the person expecting to receive help, and interested third parties observing the situation. Indeed, many of the inducements to follow normative obligations derive from both these self-generated concerns as well as the messages that others communicate: "share your candy with your friends" or "she helped you, now it's your turn to help her."

Norms and Aggression

Norms influence aggressive as well as altruistic behavior. The norm of *reciprocity*, for example, suggests that a favor should not be returned with an injury. This establishes an obligation constraining aggression toward those who have just provided us with a benefit: "don't bite the hand that feeds you." Likewise, the majority of social situations we encounter in our daily lives have expectations that encourage polite, rather than aggressive behavior. Despite the many impulses people may feel to harm another person, the social pressures against doing so are usually sufficient to keep most of us reasonably well in line.

Similarly, the *eye-for-an-eye* norm requires that we retaliate against wrongdoers only in proportion to the harm they have done us. There is some interesting research that demonstrates this effect (for example, see Tedeschi, Smith, & Brown, 1974). Consider your own reaction to the following situation. You learn that Bob and Harry have been asked to write an essay and to use electric shocks as the way to evaluate each other's essays! Bob reads Harry's essay and gives him one shock as his evaluation; on reading Bob's essay, however, Harry gives Bob six shocks. What would you think of Harry?

If you are like the experimental subjects who faced this situation, you would undoubtedly think that, because he exceeded the eye-for-an-eye norm, Harry is being aggressive. On the other hand, if you learned that Bob had originally given Harry seven shocks, you would probably judge Harry, whether he gave two or six shocks, as being relatively unaggressive. A parallel principle operates in legal appeals of self-defense. If a criminal attacks you with a rubber band and you strike back with a cannon, your response, though made in self-defense, exceeds normal retaliatory limits. Judgments are made about the level of aggression, therefore, that evaluate its proportionality to the provocation.

Imitation and Aggression

One of the major programs of research on aggression has examined the important situational variable known as *imitation* or *modeling* (for example, see Bandura, 1973). Modeling refers to the effects on the individual of seeing another person act aggressively and either get away without punishment or be punished for such behavior. Clearly, someone who models aggressiveness with impunity could encourage an imitative response in those who see this behavior; someone whose aggression is punished, however, is likely to inhibit the observer's own aggressive behavior under similar circumstances.

Bandura has been one of the major proponents of this perspective, finding it especially useful in understanding how children learn aggression. Much of the work employing this approach uses the infamous "bobo doll," an inflated toy doll that can be hit, shoved, kicked, and so on. In a typical laboratory study, children observe an adult model run through an aggressive routine with the bobo doll by hitting it and yelling at it. The children are then put through some aggression-arousing experience—for example, they are not allowed to play with a toy after having been told earlier that they could. They are then faced off against bobo to observe their behavior. Typically, the children learned to imitate the model (at least one not punished for acting aggressively) and so act aggressively against bobo in the same manner they observed in the adult. What will children do when the model is punished for acting aggressively toward bobo? The evidence suggests that they become fearful of expressing their aggression unless they are given a strong incentive for doing so. For example, children who observed the model being punished acted aggressively only when given a reward for imitating the model's behavior. This suggests that learning by imitation did take place, but had been inhibited by the punishment they observed. We will consider research on the impact of television violence on aggressive modeling in Chapter 17.

Priming and Aggression

Priming is another situational variable that has been implicated in both aggression and altruism. For example, the individual observes a violent action or sees a violence-associated stimulus (a gun). Berkowitz (1984), whose work has centered on the priming model, asserts that the current stimulus primes or triggers an associative network of thoughts, memories, feelings, and even action tendencies that have been previously associated with the original stimulus. In other words, a collection of associated aggressive elements is activated when one of those elements has been primed by something in the current situation. Although one stimulus might not push the individual into behaving aggressively, the network of associations primed by that stimulus might be extensive enough and provide sufficient intensity to drive aggressive behavior. A movie depicting gang violence like *Colors*, for example, might trigger an angry response in a person by focusing his or her awareness; this thought, in turn, spreads along a network of associatively connected thoughts, images, and action tendencies that leaves the individual in a state of higher arousal and might actually translate into aggression outside the theater.

Berkowitz reviews several studies demonstrating the priming effect. For example, children who read a comic book depicting images of war were more likely to complete sentences with words having an aggressive connotation than those who had just read a more neutral comic book. Other research more directly demonstrates this same effect. People who were presented with hostile words and later asked to evaluate an ambiguous target tended to make more hostile evaluations of that target than those not primed to think about hostility.

Research suggests that there are a wide variety of priming possibilities including reading comic books, thinking of hostile words, seeing a violent film, noting the presence of weapons, reading news reports of violent occurrences, and so on. Each of these stimuli can prime an associative network and lead to other thoughts and images of violence—even to violent action. For example, Berkowitz reports studies in which people primed to have aggressive thoughts gave more intense electric shocks than those not primed to another person who made errors (for example, see Turner & Layton, 1976). We will return to these ideas again in Chapter 17.

Priming and Altruism

Priming can stimulate altruistic as well as aggressive behavior. Berkowitz (1984) suggests that some of the research reported by Hornstein and his associates is consistent with a priming interpretation (Hornstein et al., 1975; Holloway, Tucker, & Hornstein, 1977). For example, subjects who heard a broadcast containing good news were more likely to act cooperatively and expect cooperation in return than those who heard a bad-news broadcast. Bad news was also shown to create a discouraging view of the world. We can surmise along with Berkowitz that the news broadcast (the stimulus) primed a network of other associations that intensified its effects on the individual and even generalized well beyond the substance of the newscast itself (for example, affecting the subject's overall view of the world).

Broader Situational Factors

A broader view of the meaning of situational factors is also possible to consider including, for example, rural versus urban living, climate, and the economy. These are situational factors, but clearly much broader in scope than those we have thus far examined.

RURAL VERSUS URBAN LIVING   Steblay (1987) reviewed some 65 sets of data, encompassing over 14,000 subjects, that examined the effects of rural versus urban living circumstances on helping. She concluded that there is a significantly greater tendency to be helpful in rural than in urban contexts, supporting our intuitions and everyday impressions that city life can be alienating and desensitizing.

What about these two contexts, however, seems to produce this effect? We commonly believe that city life hardens individuals and makes them indifferent to the claims of strangers (for example, see Milgram, 1970). Steblay also refers to Fisher's ideas about urban life. Because of the greater diversity we find in cities and our discomfort with people who are not like us, we may feel insecure and so shun the appeals of strangers. Although Steblay was unable to examine these and other interpretations that might account for rural–urban differences, they do provide some interesting future research opportunities.

CLIMATE   People also commonly believe that there is a relationship between temperature and aggression. Our common sense tells us that people are more irritable in hot weather than in cooler temperatures; of course, people tend to mingle together more in warm than in cold weather, which in itself may be partly responsible for provoking aggressive behavior. Recently, Anderson (1989) reported the results of his examination of an extensive array of both field and laboratory studies relating temperature to a variety of aggressions including violent crime, spousal abuse, honking one's horn, and delivering electric shocks in laboratory studies. Let us begin with his conclusion:

> The massive body of work . . . demonstrates two main points. First, temperature effects are direct; they operate at the individual level. Second, temperature effects are important; they influence the most antisocial behaviors imaginable (p. 94).

Anderson finds that the field studies relating temperature and aggression are especially impressive in showing, for example, how the hotter places in the world tend to have higher rates of aggression and how hotter years or periods within a given year are associated with higher incidences of murders, rapes, riots, wife beatings, and so on. While laboratory research provides a much less consistent picture, Anderson argues that such inconsistencies are far outweighed by the impressive consistencies of the field research. Like Steblay, Anderson also considered several different theoretical explanations for the temperature–aggression correlation. The data, however, do not yet support a cogent theory, and the precise mechanisms involved remain unclear.

ECONOMY   Economic circumstances have always been a fascinating source of information and speculation on aggression toward others (homicide) and the self (suicide). Early research reported by Henry and Short (1954) indicated that during periods of economic depression the suicide rate among the upper class increased, as did lynchings of blacks by poor whites. To interpret these findings, they combined the frustration-aggression hypothesis (see pp. 277–79) with the concept of *relative deprivation*.

For those used to an affluent life-style, the sudden loss of wealth and social prestige produced by an economic depression can be very frustrating. If they have been socialized to direct their anger inwards, they may commit suicide. Poor people, struggling to maintain their respectability and pride, also find economic depression frustrating because it closes the gap between them and those beneath them. These people turn their anger outwards, manifesting it in violent acts, like lynchings, against those from whom they are trying to distance themselves.

More recently, Hepworth and West (1988) used sophisticated statistical techniques to reanalyze data on lynchings and the economy originally reported in 1940 by Hovland and Sears. The data covered the period from 1882 to 1930. Hovland and Sears found strong negative correlations between economic indices and the lynchings of blacks in 14 southern states—that is, economic downturn correlated with an upturn in lynchings. This fits Henry and Short's findings and also verifies the displacement interpretation of the frustration-aggression hypothesis: aggression is displaced from the distant sources of economic failures and toward immediate targets.

Hepworth and West's reanalysis of these data suggested that the original correlations were much higher than warranted, but that even with the sophisticated statistical techniques unavailable when Hovland and Sears conducted their work, modest negative relationships were still found. As noted, Hovland and Sears originally viewed the relation between the economy and lynchings to be an example of displacement: whites, suffering from an economic downturn and being unable to get back at those truly responsible for their fate, displaced their anger and lynched poor blacks. Hepworth and West's data confirm this as a reasonable interpretation of the data.

Hepworth and West were also able to evaluate a somewhat different version of the relative deprivation thesis. In Henry and Short's study, one's own deprivation is considered relative to another person's status—for example, I compare myself to others and see myself to be relatively well or poorly off. Hepworth and West suggest that another kind of relative deprivation involves a comparison with one's own standing at a previous point in time. They refer to this as *temporal relative deprivation.* For example, if my economic standing today is lower than it was last year, I should be more frustrated than if my standing today is the same as it was last year. Analyses of data support a temporal relative deprivation effect. Economic measures of temporal deprivation correlated significantly with the number of black lynchings covering the 49-year period of the original research by Hovland and Sears. In other words, economic decline not only led to more lynchings as people, frustrated with their circumstances, compared themselves to others, but also as they compared their current condition with a relatively more prosperous one in the past.

It is important to point out that these data involve broad statistical correlations; they should not be interpreted as telling us much about the likelihood any given person will deal with frustration by lynching, or suicide, or any other violent act. However, the data do suggest the importance of economics as a situational factor in aggression, and also suggest how economic equality might mitigate violent behaviors within a population.

17

· ·

Aggression and the Media

HE STAKES ARE extremely high, involving both a multi-billion-dollar industry and the reputation of a scientific discipline that claims to be unbiased and politically neutral. The questions are complex, the methodologies difficult, the mechanisms often elusive, and the conclusions sometimes confusing. The ubiquitous presence and easy availability of television has made the media's role in promoting aggression and violence a more critical and controversial issue than ever before. Given the potential political, economic, and social repercussions of the outcome of the debate, it should come as no surprise that social psychology does not speak on the link between aggression and the media with one voice.

While not arguing that violence on television is unrelated to aggression, Kaplan and Singer (1976) find "that no such link has been demonstrated to date" (p. 63). They also suggest that if we are interested in the real causes of violence, "the effects of television violence on aggressive behavior may be minor" (p. 63). Freedman (1984) also concludes "that the available literature does not support the hypothesis that viewing violence on television causes an increase in subsequent aggression in the real world" (p. 244; see also Freedman, 1986). Most social psychologists, however, do see a causal link between televised violence and aggression, especially in children. Eron and his colleagues (1972) argue that "there is a probable causative influence of watching violent television programs in early formative years on aggression" (p. 263). Similarly, Friedrich-Cofer and Huston (1986) claim that "the weight of the evidence from different methods of investigation supports the hypothesis that television violence affects aggression" (p. 368).

Testifying before a House subcommittee, Brian Wilcox, representing the position of the American Psychological Association, enumerated the many ways that television violence has serious impacts on both children and adults noting, for example, how it desensitizes children to the effects of violence, shapes the values and opinions of both adults and children, can induce imitative acts of violence in disposed persons, and can remove or relax inhibitions to violence among viewers (Lander, 1989). In 1972, a surgeon general's report concluded that television violence has a causal effect on violent behavior in children and adolescents. In 1982, a report commissioned by the National Institute of Mental Health confirmed this causal effect in even stronger terms (see Pearl, Bouthilet, & Lazar, 1982). Several consumer groups insist, despite the fact that all the evidence is not in, that programming be less violent.

The debate divides many social psychologists who otherwise would agree on most issues. It is difficult to find fault with the critics of the causal position (televised violence causes aggression) who insist that the evidence remains inconclusive. By withholding judgment until more studies have been done, they are defending the integrity of their discipline. But it is equally difficult to fault those who believe that enough is now known to at least criticize excesses of the media.

First Amendment rights are also clearly at issue in this debate. On one hand are those who claim that the media is sufficiently implicated in promoting aggression, especially in children, that changes in social policies and legal precedent are needed (for example, Linz, Penrod, & Donnerstein, 1986). This is essentially the argument of the American Psychological Association, testifying before Congressional subcommittees on behalf of proposed legislative controls on the media. On the other hand, those urging the field to move more slowly have also raised questions about supporting legislation without carefully evaluating both the evidence and its implications for important constitutional matters (for example, see Singer & Kaplan, 1976). Should television programming be accompanied with a warning that "Viewing may be dangerous to your children's health"? Or is this an infringement on freedom of speech and expression? The American Civil Liberties Union has urged more caution in carving out exceptions from First Amendment rights, expressing concern about where it will end (for example, see Lander, 1989).

It should now be clear why, given the complexity of the issue, social psychologists and other social scientists can disagree so vehemently on policy matters. And it doesn't appear that things will change much in the near future. There is an extensive body of knowledge from both laboratory and field settings and, as Huesmann (1986) comments, "it is implausible to believe at this point that any single new study is going to change the balance much" (p. 126). He notes that believers in the causal interpretation are already convinced and so need no further persuading; those who believe that the causal effects have not yet been demonstrated, in turn, are unlikely to change their opinion even if confronted by a lot of contradictory new data.

We will now explore the research that has divided opinion so strongly to better appreciate what the debate is all about, the most likely effects of the media, especially television, and the kinds of mechanisms that seem to be involved.

Some Effects and Possible Mechanisms

Following the lead of Huesmann and Malamuth (1986), we will first consider three possible effects of the media on the individual: acquisition, maintenance, and emission of aggressive or violent behavior. *Acquisition* calls our attention to the possible role of the media in teaching people about the form and social functions of aggression. For example, in our early years we learn what is involved in acting aggressively in our culture and even when it is considered appropriate to be aggressive—when we have a conflict or disagreement with someone; when we feel upset, anxious, angry, frustrated, and so on. The media might thus serve as one of our many cultural models. In Huesmann's (1986) terms, the media may be involved in teaching us aggressive *scripts* that we call upon under certain circumstances later in our lives.

The second possible role of the media involves the *maintenance* of an aggressive style of behavior or an acceptance of aggressive values and beliefs. It is assumed that unless there is some ongoing process of encouragement or reinforcement, early lessons will simply fade away. The media might provide helpful reminders that trigger aggressive scripts and even elaborate them for us.

A third possible media effect involves its role in the *emission* of aggressive behavior. The focus here is on its triggering or, to use the term we encountered in Chapter 16, its *priming* function: it is possible that the violence we see on television and in films, hear on the radio, or read in newspapers might prime people to act aggressively. The assumption is made that even if someone has learned about aggression, without the trigger to call it forth and make that kind of response preeminent aggression is unlikely to occur.

Notice that all three effects emphasize aggression as something that people learn, rather than something innate. This focus does not require that we ignore any innate possibilities. Rather, it suggests that much of what we consider to be aggression is less an instinctive behavior than a culturally learned, organized, and regulated family of behaviors. The clear implication is that under the proper cultural conditions, we might expect to see little aggressive behavior occurring.

Possible Mechanisms

In Chapter 16 we introduced two mechanisms, imitation and priming, considered to be central to the role of the media in promoting aggression. Recall that the imitation of unpunished aggressive models proved to be an effective teacher of aggressive behavior in children. When we consider that the media often portray the hero as a violent character rewarded rather than punished for his or her aggressive conduct, we can see how potent imitation might be in teaching and in maintaining aggressive behaviors, especially in children. As we also noted, while not denying the importance of imitation Berkowitz (1984, 1989) has increasingly come to favor the priming function. Media violence can prime a network of aggressive associations in individuals who have learned those associations.

In addition to the research we considered in Chapter 16, Josephson's (1987) study helps complete the picture with respect to the media's priming function. Josephson created a naturalistic situation in which boys of varying degrees of characteristic aggression saw either a violent or a nonviolent television program before playing a game of floor hockey. In the violent film, the heroes spoke to one another over walkie-talkies just before embarking on one of the most violent episodes. The walkie-talkie was chosen by Josephson as the priming stimulus. A brief pregame interview held with each boy was conducted either by using a walkie-talkie or a microphone. It was assumed that the walkie-talkie would be the cue that would prime aggressive thoughts and images in the boys.

If the walkie-talkie served this function, boys interviewed with a walkie-talkie who had seen the violent film would behave more aggressively in the hockey game than those who had not seen the film or been similarly primed by the walkie-talkie. Josephson's data generally confirm this effect. In particular, boys judged to be characteristically aggressive who had seen the violent program and received the walkie-talkie cue revealed more aggressive behavior during the hockey game than those who saw the violent film but were not given the priming cue of the walkie-talkie. Boys who had not been exposed to the violent program showed least aggression during the game.

This study illustrates how the media can trigger an aggressive response, in this case in people who already have high levels of characteristic aggressiveness and who have learned to associate a given cue with violent feelings and actions. It is also clear that the cue need not be one typically associated with violent behavior, even though other research reported by Berkowitz suggests that such cues—weapons, for example—are especially effective in provoking aggressive responses. It seems, however, that even relatively innocuous stimuli could become aggression-triggers if given aggression associations by the media. News accounts of rapes using a cola bottle, for example, can transform the bottle from a neutral stimulus to an aggressive priming cue, triggering young men to commit sexual violence under the right circumstances.

Research on priming also suggests people do not respond equally to media violence. For example, in Josephson's study, characteristically aggressive boys were more affected by the violence they watched on the television program. Thus, the claim that violence in the media induces violence in the viewer is especially applicable to vulnerable people, including most young children. On the other hand, the priming or cue function suggests that anyone who has previously associated a given stimulus with violent thoughts, feelings, or behaviors might react violently to a given media depiction containing that stimulus; those not having these associations would show minimal impact. Because weapons are so characteristically associated with violence, they are very likely to serve this priming function for nearly anyone familiar with weapons.

INFORMATION   Another possible explanation for media effects involves its informational function. In this context, information refers to knowledge about aggression—how and when it is used to resolve conflicts and its legitimacy as a problem-solving response. Obviously, events outside the media per se provide people with information about aggression and its legitimacy for conflict resolution. For example, Archer and Gartner (1976) found a direct relationship between external aggression and domestic violence, suggesting that a nation that turns to war to solve its problems abroad encourages aggression at home as well.

Sexual Violence and Desensitization Effects

What are some of the long-term consequences of being reared on a diet of violence and aggression? Do people become desensitized and more tolerant, or disgusted and less tolerant of the aggression that they see repeatedly? A review of sexual violence in the media leads to several important conclusions (for example, see Malamuth & Briere, 1986). In the vast majority of depictions of sexual violence, women are the targets; when nonsexual violence is depicted, men are primarily the targets. Although the total amount of sexual violence depicted in the media is high, it remains generally lower than nonsexual violence. Furthermore, whereas victims of nonsexual violence usually actively resist, victims of sexual violence often resist passively, secretly enjoying or at least tolerating the violence inflicted on them.

Given these portrayals of sexual violence, we might very well expect an impact on men's attitudes towards women. Indeed, as Malamuth and Briere's review suggests, "exposure to media sexual violence can result in thought patterns more supportive of violence against women" (p. 83). In particular, men are encouraged to view women as acceptable objects of their anger, to become generally callous and insensitive in sexual matters, and to accept some of the prevailing cultural myths about rape—for example, women "ask for it" and secretly enjoy it even if they don't appear to. But do these thought patterns lead to violent behavior? Laboratory studies confirm that they do, in fact, encourage violence against women, especially sexual violence. This does not mean that media depictions lead men to immediately go out and abuse or rape women. The findings do suggest, however, that the media portrayals join with other cultural themes that denigrate women to create a general climate conducive to aggression against women (for example, see Burt, 1980).

What happens to people frequently exposed to sexually violent and degrading portrayals? Experimental studies of the numbing or desensitizing effects of sexual violence have turned up some inconsistent findings. Linz, Donnerstein, and Penrod (1988), for example, presented male viewers with one of three different types of films over a period of several days: gratuitously violent "slasher" films (for example, *Friday the 13th, Part 2*); nonviolent teenage sex movies (for example, *Porky's*); and sexually explicit but generally nonviolent movies (for example, *Debbie Does Dallas*). Subjects were presented with either two films or five films. At the conclusion of their viewing, they were later contacted to view a final film dealing with jury decision making about a rape trial involving the allegation by a woman that she had been raped during a fraternity party by one of the members. Two different versions of this film were made, with half of the subjects receiving each version: in one, the woman and her assailant had been friends for several months; in the other, they had just met that evening.

This design permitted Linz and his colleagues to examine several possible media effects. For example, does the graphic depiction of violence lead to a desensitization and numbing reaction to violence? If any desensitization occurs, does it influence the person's feelings and thoughts about the woman in the rape trial? What is the impact on the male subjects of prolonged exposure to women as sexual objects?

On the one hand, the results of the study did confirm the *numbing* effect of repeated exposure: "Sexually violent material that was originally anxiety provoking and depressing became less so with prolonged exposure" (p. 765). The authors note that this numbing effect appears rather rapidly and is apparent after viewing only two films. In addition, films that the subjects initially found to be degrading to women were reported to be less so with continued exposure to such films. There was a tendency for those repeatedly exposed to violent films to be less sympathetic to the woman in the rape trial as well as to rape victims in general when compared both with subjects in the control condition (no exposure to films) as well as those who saw the other types of films. This confirms findings reported by several other investigators.

On the other hand, Linz and his colleagues did not find that their subjects' subsequent attitudes and beliefs about women were affected by exposure to the films. This failure not only differs from the authors' expectations, but other studies demonstrating the impact of sexually explicit films on people's general attitudes about women. In speculating on why the effect did not appear in the present study, the authors suggest that one possibility is that the commercial films they used presented women in a greater variety of roles as compared with previous research which only emphasized the sexual degradation of women.

. . . .

Catharsis and Aggression

Rather than promote aggression, is it possible that media depictions of violence serve a cathartic function, purging people of their violent emotions? After watching a Sylvester Stallone or Arnold Schwarzenegger film, do you feel exhilarated and highly emotional or calm and self-possessed, your aggressive urges vicariously satisfied in the pummeling fists, flying bullets, and explosions? We will examine two alternative theories of catharsis, one advocating the effectiveness of media violence in producing a cathartic effect in the viewer, the other arguing that only actual expressions of aggression can induce true catharsis.

Feshbach (1976) argues that, whereas depictions of *real* violence (for example, news broadcasts) do not serve a cathartic function, *simulated* or fantasy depictions do. He proposes several reasons that fantasy might have this effect. It may, for example, provide an alternative way to express anger. Since I cannot actually hit you, I will imagine myself hurting you. In effect, our imagination discharges pent-up feelings of aggression. Watching simulated violence might similarly discharge our violent urges by stimulating our imagination. Another possible explanation for the cathartic effect of media violence is that action and thought are inversely related; that is, thought supersedes the impulse to action. Experiencing simulated violence is akin to thinking that substitutes for direct action. Whatever the mechanisms involved, Feshbach's position suggests that clear fantasy portrayals of aggression may actually inhibit rather than trigger aggressive behavior.

To examine this possibility, Feshbach presented children with one of three experimental conditions: reality, fantasy, or control. In the reality condition, children were informed that they would be shown a newsreel of a student riot. In the fantasy condition, they were told that they would see a Hollywood film of a student riot. Both groups were shown the same brief segment, while the control group was not shown the film at all. At the conclusion of the viewing, the children were given an opportunity to aggress against the experimenter in a game-like situation. Aggression involved subjecting the experimenter to various levels of noise, from soft to highly bothersome. Results indicated that the average level of aggression shown by the reality group was nearly twice that of the fantasy group, even though both groups had seen the same film and had been randomly assigned to one condition or the other. Feshbach interpreted these data as supporting his version of the catharsis hypothesis: whereas real aggression instigated further aggression, fantasy aggression reduced it.

But, you ask, is this really evidence of catharsis? Is it not possible that, while the reality group was driven to aggression, the fantasy group had no significant reaction at all? To test this possibility, Feshbach compared the two experimental groups against the control group's level of aggression. While the reality group's aggressive response (4.30) was significantly greater than that of the control group (3.40), the fantasy group's was significantly lower (2.29).

Feshbach's controversial view of catharsis has won few converts. Further research has consistently failed to link a cathartic response to media violence. Obviously, if there were such a demonstrable link it would prove to be an important counterargument to the hypothesis that media violence causes aggression. It simply does not seem to be the case, however, that people who, for example, view a great deal of violent television are less aggressive. There in fact appears to be much more support for the opposite view, that media depictions of violence—real or simulated—promote aggression.

A very different understanding of catharsis has been proposed by Konecni and his colleagues (Konecni & Doob, 1972; Konecni & Ebbesen, 1976). In this formulation, the opportunity to *actually* hurt someone reduces subsequent aggression. There are several essential conditions that must be met for this effect to work—for example, a person who is angry or frustrated must have the opportunity to actually harm another person. Once that person has vented his or her aggression, there is a feeling of catharsis that inhibits continued aggression. In this version of catharsis, the key is the actual aggressive behavior that drains off the anger; simulated aggression will not be effective. Konecni and his associates report the results of several studies supporting this view.

The connection between the media and Feshbach's version of catharsis is much more obvious than that between the media and Konecni's version. For Konecni people actually have to act out their aggression to successfully purge their violent emotions; simply watching and imagining violence as Feshbach argues is not sufficient. What is relevant about this second version of catharsis, however, is its claim that aggression does not beget further aggression, but rather breaks the cycle and diminishes future hostility. This claim runs counter to the position of those who argue that a cycle of violence is instigated by the media—in other words, that violence begets violence.

A Cycle of Violence?

Widom (1989) reviewed a variety of studies examining whether violence begets violence. While her concern extends much farther than our current focus on the role of the media, media effects are an integral part of her investigation. For example, Widom reports research on the impact of witnessing violence, either in the home or depicted by the media, on the observer's own likelihood of engaging in violence. Data from several studies that she examined suggest an intergenerational transmission of violence: there is a tendency for those who have been abused as children to be abusive as adults; children model abusive behaviors that they have witnessed in the family, even if the abuse is not directed towards them. When this finding is combined with the modeling of television violence and the findings relating wars and violence, a pattern emerges that confirms the thesis that violence does in fact beget violence.

. . . .

Long-term Effects of the Media:
The Bidirectional Model

There is an intriguing paradox in the debate over the effects of the media on violence. Supporters of a causal connection argue that *both* laboratory research and field studies confirm their position. Critics of the causal view agree that laboratory studies support a causal connection, but consider laboratory work to be irrelevant to understanding media effects. In addition, these critics view the field studies with suspicion and do not believe that they have been persuasive in the claims they make (for example, see Freedman, 1984, 1986). The paradox is that experimental social psychologists, usually so reliant on the laboratory, have denied the relevance of findings using this method while others, undoubtedly including some for whom field studies are a more preferred approach, find themselves calling upon the laboratory research to support their contentions.

One central difference between the laboratory and the field approaches that have thus far been conducted involves the kind of causal link they demonstrate. For the most part, laboratory research has demonstrated a one-way version of causality: events in the media cause behavior in the person. Increasingly, those who have adopted the field methods to investigate the relationship between the media and aggression have turned to a *bidirectional model* of causality: "television violence influences aggression, and aggressive predispositions influence the preference for television violence" (Friedrich-Cofer & Huston, 1986, p. 367; see also Eron, 1982; Huesmann, 1986). Bidirectional causality tells us that exposure to television violence is likely to make people more violent and that people who are more violent prefer frequent exposure to television violence. Longitudinal studies have been especially helpful in understanding how this bidirectional process operates.

Both Eron and Huesmann summarize several studies they conducted that examined the relationship between television and aggression. In one of the early studies, which they term the *Rip Van Winkle Study* (named for its location in upstate New York), for example, 875 eight-year-old children were evaluated for their characteristic levels of aggression and their television viewing habits; some 10 years later, 475 of the original sample were again evaluated. Data from this study indicated a clear positive relationship between aggressiveness and watching violent television; aggressive children watched more violent television. They also suggested that the relationship between viewing television violence and levels of aggressiveness might differ for children and for adults: young children use television violence to learn aggressiveness; adults use television violence to cue what they have already learned as children.

The *Chicago Circle Study*, a second longitudinal study covering a three-year period and conducted in a suburb of Chicago, more closely examined the intervening factors that may be involved. Both child and parent variables were assessed at three different points in time. The following child variables were examined: peer-nominated aggressiveness and peer-nominated popularity; self-ratings of own aggressiveness; aggressive and heroic fantasies; preference for sex-typed toys and games; and viewing habits, including information about favorite shows, tendency to identify with television characters, frequency of viewing, and so on. Parental behaviors that were assessed included parental rejection, use of physical punishment for aggression, and the violence of the programs watched by the parents. The Chicago Circle Study clearly confirmed (for boys as well as girls) the Rip Van Winkle Study's conclusion that there is a clear-cut, positive relationship between viewing violence on television and aggressiveness in the child.

The Chicago study examined other potential variables in that relationship. Measures of intellectual or academic achievement were related to both viewing habits and overall aggressiveness. Not surprisingly, children with low academic achievement watched more tele-

vision (and were thus exposed to more violent programming) and behaved more aggressively than children with higher levels of academic
achievement. In addition, low achieving children tended to believe
that the violence they watched on television was real and to identify
with aggressive television characters. Huesmann speculates that children with difficulties in school may turn to a world of fantasy where
they can identify with heroic figures and vicariously experience the
successes they are otherwise missing.

In addition to intellectual achievement, popularity appears to
be another significant intervening factor. In the United States—but
apparently *not* in the other western nations studied—aggressive children were less popular and spent more time viewing violent television
than popular children. Although the relationship between aggression
and low popularity was found in all the nations studied, only in the
United States are aggression and lower popularity linked to viewing
violent television as well (Eron & Huesmann, 1987). Findings congruent with these have also been reported by Himmelweit and Swift
(1976) in their 20-year longitudinal study of television viewing habits
in Great Britain. What they term a "retreat into the media" (p. 155)
appears among some of the less popular children with lower academic standing.

Measures of the children's fantasies in the Chicago study clearly
contradict the pattern we would expect if simulated violence served a
cathartic function: children who fantasize about aggression do not purge
violent impulses but instead are both more aggressive and tend to
watch more television. An examination of the several parent variables
helps complete the emerging picture. For example, parents who use
physical punishment to quell aggression or who reject their children's
accomplishments are more likely to have aggressive children. On the
other hand, there is no clear relation between parent's own viewing
habits and their children's level of aggressiveness.

The data from these several studies seem to support the bidirectional model. A child who views a great deal of television today in
the United States is likely to be treated to a rather steady diet of
violence. Exposure to such violence teaches the child a great deal
about aggression and about its appropriateness as a response to a variety of issues and problems. As Huesmann puts it, the child acquires
a repertoire of aggressive scripts. If this child is also in a home where
physical punishment and parental rejection predominate, he or she is
likely to move further into a pattern of viewing violent television,
identifying with its heroic aggressors, and losing sight of where fantasy
ends and reality begins. Lowered popularity and difficulty in school
may exacerbate these trends.

Critics like Freedman, of course, do not believe that this pessimistic scenario has been demonstrated. As persuasive as the bidirectional model is to many, Freedman remains unconvinced: "the field studies are extremely weak and there is very little evidence from the longitudinal studies to support the causal hypothesis" (Freedman, 1986, p. 377). And Freedman is not alone. The National Broadcasting Company commissioned a rather extensive study designed to examine the effects of televised violence on youngsters aged 7–19. The study and its findings were reported in 1982 by Milavsky and several colleagues. Undoubtedly to the relief of NBC executives, they concluded that there was no consistent relationship between television violence and aggressiveness among the youngsters in the study. Those skeptical of the causal link between television and violence see this study as confirming their doubts. Those who believe that a connection not only exists but has been consistently demonstrated have reexamined Milavsky's data, suggesting that its findings may actually support a conclusion consistent with the causal hypothesis!

In reviewing these data and the contradictions they contain, I sometimes feel like the Rabbi who had a reputation for being especially good in dealing with people's problems. In watching how the Rabbi worked his magic, a young man noticed something that puzzled him. The Rabbi first gave advice to the wife that she found reasonable. When the husband came in, he too received reasonable advice. The only problem was that the advice to the wife contradicted the advice given to the husband. Boldly approaching the Rabbi, the young man asked, "Rabbi, how is it that you can tell the wife that A is the right thing to do and the husband that not-A is the right thing? Isn't this inconsistent?" The Rabbi replied, "You're right too."

Altruism and the Media

In this chapter we have concentrated almost exclusively on the link between violence in the media and aggression. Is there evidence that the media can also contribute to altruism? Eron's (1986) summary of some of the relevant research on altruism suggests that viewing altruistic relationships can indeed have a positive effect, at least immediately afterward, on young children. However, he also cites studies suggesting that, since helpful behavior is less salient to people than aggressive behavior, follow-up coaching and even role playing are required if the media are to become effective altruistic models. Rosenhan and White's (1967) study of altruistic behavior in young children reached a similar conclusion. They found that both the observation of an altruistic model and rehearsal—that is, behaving in a similarly altruistic manner in the presence of the model—are critical for inducing altruistic behavior, whereas observation alone is sufficient to trigger aggression. The reasons for this discrepancy need further exploration.

A Final Word

In debating the effects of the media on aggression and altruism, few investigators have examined the issue from a sociohistorical perspective (see Herman & Chomsky, 1988, for an exception). Whereas most social psychologists have been concerned with what the media represents, we need to be equally concerned with what the media chooses *not* to represent. By selecting what is newsworthy and the angle from which to view events, the media subtly influences our view of the world with its own institutional biases.

For example, what we have learned to consider as violence may have been crafted by the media's manner of selecting issues and themes to call violent. In turn, the scripts we learn as children and apply later as adults support a particular theory of violence and aggression; this is primarily a cultural theory in which violence involves a personal or interpersonal aggressive act. By representing these cultural beliefs about violence, the media ensures that we will continue to define a certain set of behaviors as violent or aggressive while excluding other behaviors from that judgment.

We all agree that images depicted in films like *Taxi Driver, Halloween,* and *The Terminator* are violent, even if some consider the violence to be acceptable or artistically justifiable. But would we all agree that corporate or governmental acts that hurt others are also violent? Is it not an aggressive act to knowingly sell carcinogenic chemical products to a Third World people without notifying them of its dangers? Is not dumping pollutants into lakes and streams a kind of violence against the innocent people who die or become sick as a consequence of such social irresponsibility? Recall the definition of instrumental aggression: harm is the by-product of behaviors designed to accomplish a nonaggressive goal (for example, profit making). Most of us probably do not think of these kinds of events as "violent" or "aggressive" because the media exclude many highly destructive behaviors when defining those terms. In short, when evaluating the effects of the media on violence and aggression, we need to consider the ways that the media influence our thinking and our behavior, not simply by the images they present to us, but also by the images they fail to present to us. We are encouraged to focus our attention on individual and interpersonal acts as demonstrations of aggression and to ignore corporate or governmental acts that would very closely fit the definition of aggression: action that harms others.

18

· ·

Sanctions for Violence and Hopes for Altruism

O N MARCH 16, 1968, about 7:30 a.m., a company of American soldiers entered the village of My Lai with orders to clear the area of Viet Cong. Two and one-half hours later, little was left of the village. Vietnamese civilians had been raped, murdered, mutilated; a platoon leader, Lt. William Calley, was alleged to have personally ordered or carried out the killing of over 100 innocent people. In 1944, with the goal of breaking the will of the Nazi enemy, Allied planes fire-bombed the city of Dresden, killing some 135,000 civilians. In 1945, over twice that number of Japanese were obliterated in America's bombing of Hiroshima. Despite social and economic progress, the twentieth century is full of such socially sanctioned atrocities perpetrated against innocent noncombatants— the systematic destruction of millions of Jews and other "undesirables" by Nazi Germany; the starvation of millions of Ukranian peasants by Stalin's Russia; the genocide in Armenia; the destruction of Native American life and culture; brutalities in the Middle East, Asia, Africa, and Latin America.

Some social psychologists (for example, Kelman, 1973; Sanford & Comstock, 1973) insist that no understanding of aggression can be complete without first examining socially sanctioned violence—that is, those destructive acts that occur with the officially granted or clearly implied permission of society. These are not the indiscriminate, un-principled killings of criminals or madmen, but acts that reasonable and normal people agree to carry out personally or at least condone in younger, more able representatives (for example, the police or military). They may even occur as we go about the routines of our daily work lives, focused narrowly on our tasks, never seeing (or wanting to see) how our surrogates participate in a horror that later generations will discover. "And where were you?" they ask. "At work," we reply, "just following orders and doing my job."

Where do we search for an answer to the nagging question of why society often sanctions crimes of which it is later ashamed? Our first impulse is to probe the minds of those in authority who make the policies and issue the orders. We are also likely to scrutinize the personalities of those who, despite reservations, carry out their orders even if they feel they are immoral or illegal. However, social psychologists and others who have tried to understand socially sanctioned violence have eschewed this approach. As Kelman notes, "the occurrence of sanctioned massacres cannot be adequately explained by the existence of psychological forces" (p. 38). Where then do we look? We will follow Kelman's lead and consider three intertwined processes that operate under conditions of socially sanctioned violence: authorization, routinization, and dehumanization. As we will see, his analysis conforms closely to the analyses others have provided (for example, Sanford & Comstock).

Authorization

Authorization refers to the investment or empowering of legal authority to another. By delegating authority, those ordering violent acts are distanced from the consequences; because they do not personally commit the acts or necessarily even witness the horror, the acts are easier to sanction. Similarly, those who are authorized to commit violence do not have to bear responsibility for their actions. We saw this effect earlier in Milgram's studies of obedience (see Chapter 8, pp. 147–50). Recall that the experimenter, representing the legitimate institution of science, instructed subjects to knowingly apply what appeared to be dangerously painful electric shocks to another person; the subjects complied, rationalizing that the experimenter had accepted responsibility for whatever injuries they might inflict.

Redl (1973) notes how Hitler authorized his nation's aggression by declaring that he would personally assume full responsibility. Many

Germans later blamed Hitler for starting World War II, but he could not have done so without the support of a sizable portion of the German public. Because Hitler had sanctioned violence, however, they did not feel personally responsible. Accepting personal responsibility for our actions puts restraints on our impulses; when we are relieved of that responsibility by an authority we recognize as legitimate, the basis for those constraints is gone. Authorization also removes our fear of being punished for any wrongdoing. If fear once restrained us, removal of that fear may launch us on an unpredictable course of behavior.

Kelman and his associates (Kelman & Hamilton, 1988; Kelman & Lawrence, 1972) give us some further insights about the authorization process in their study of public reactions to the trial of Lt. Calley. Two distinctive patterns of public response were observed in their national sample. One group, called the AR group, approved of bringing Calley to trial and believed that people are always responsible for their actions regardless of the context of authorization in which they occur. A second group, referred to as the DR group, disapproved of bringing Calley to trial and believed that people have a duty to follow the orders of their superior officers.

Assuming that Lt. Calley was simply following orders, the DR group felt betrayed by the government's bringing him to trial. After all, they reasoned, when legitimate authority relieves people of their personal responsibility their only duty is to follow orders. Since the government authorized Calley's actions, *they* were responsible. In contrast, the AR group argued that nobody be absolved of personal responsibility under any circumstances; "I was simply following orders" is no excuse for immoral behavior. We are accountable for all of our acts and no sanction—no matter how official—can excuse us from that accountability. Calley may have committed his crimes under orders, but he disobeyed a higher, moral injunction in doing so. Justice thus demanded that Calley be brought to trial. We need not return to the Vietnam era, however, in order to find instances of DR-like behavior: claims of "I was merely following orders" have echoed throughout most societies, with the Watergate break-in and cover-up of the Nixon era and the Iran-Contra affair of Reagan's administration also revealing instances of this familiar pattern.

Many times, of course, superiors do not specifically order a destructive act; nor do they always clearly assume full responsibility for the actions of subordinates, especially when they involve the application of deadly force. This is often understood without the need for articulation. When we take a job, for example, we quickly learn our place in the organization, knowing who tells us what to do and those over whom we have some authority. If we are interested in advancing our careers, we also quickly learn what is expected of us and what the organization believes to be important; we use our initiative to go beyond specific orders or requirements always, however, remaining within organizational parameters.

Groupthink

Janis' (1972, 1982) research on decision making at high governmental levels helps illustrate another aspect of authorization. He used archival materials to compare the nature of those decision processes that led to defective outcomes (for example, the failed Bay of Pigs invasion; the decision to invade North Korea, strategic errors at Pearl Harbor and in the Vietnam War, and the Watergate cover-up) with those that led to successful outcomes (for example, the Cuban missile crisis and the Marshall Plan). As a result, Janis formulated some ideas about a decision-making process he termed *groupthink:* seeking concurrence within the group at the expense of carefully examining decision alternatives. When groupthink operates people press toward agreement within the group, and so are more likely to ignore a range of alternative courses of action.

One of the key factors involved in groupthink is a promotional style of leadership. After making up his mind and announcing his decision, for example, the president may use the group process to promote his goals rather than to question them. Under these conditions, many of the president's high-level advisors consider it disloyal to challenge him. For example, during the decision-making process that led to the Bay of Pigs fiasco, President Kennedy permitted advocates of the invasion like the CIA greater opportunity to present their case and to refute opposing arguments, while cutting off debate generated by dissenters like Senator Fulbright. The president's message was clear; his advisors closed ranks around him, choosing loyalty over a reasoned examination of some of the pitfalls of his decision. President Kennedy and his advisors operated very differently without the dynamics of groupthink in the Cuban missile crisis. Janis noted that under these conditions, the president invited dissent, neither announcing or promoting his own decision. Without groupthink, alternatives emerged and were thoughtfully evaluated without concerns of disloyalty. Consequently, the outcome was far more successful.

Both Janis' original analysis and a subsequent analysis reported by McCauley (1989) are directly relevant to our concern with authorization. When groupthink appears, are we dealing with a situation of compliance, internalization, or some complex combination of the two?

Recall from our discussion in Chapter 7 (see pp. 135–36) that compliance appears if advisors publicly agree with a decision with which they privately disagree. Internalization indicates both private and public acceptance of a decision. Janis considers groupthink to involve internalization, while McCauley's reexamination of the data suggests to him that there is also evidence for compliance; for example, some top advisors privately expressed doubts about a decision which they had publicly supported.

McCauley suggests that a combination of compliance and internalization are likely when the decision-making occurs with promotional leadership among a group of people who are generally like-minded to begin with and the group itself is relatively insulated from contradictory opinion. Under these conditions, it appears that some people comply publicly, stifling any private doubts they might have, while others internalize the decision, accepting it both publicly and privately. In either case, the outcome is a poor decision authorizing a detrimental course of action.

Situational Authorization

Situations often authorize our behavior. In his pioneering work in psychological ecology, Barker (1965) suggested that social environments have an internal logic that leads people to behave in particular ways. A baseball game and a restaurant, for example, compel different kinds of behavior by the very nature of the setting, the activities taking place, the number of people present, and so on. At a restaurant you wouldn't cheer on the chef to get your eggs just right, just as at a baseball game you probably wouldn't use silverware to eat your hot dog. Most major social institutions similarly have a compelling logic to the way they function that organizes and regulates people's actions within those systems, including top leaders. This behavior is to some extent unconscious; people act in certain ways without giving much thought to what they are doing.

If a system is highly competitive and if success is measured in terms of profits and losses, participants have a fairly clear set of behavioral directives to follow. No one at the top has to say very much about what is expected; the system is its own authorization. Milgram made a similar point when he argued that if people are not to hurt others (as subjects believed they did in his experiments), they should avoid situations that make those kinds of demands. Unfortunately, when situations like economic competition or obedience to authority permeate an entire social system, people might be induced to commit destructive or harmful actions even while carrying on the normal routines of everyday life.

Transcendent Authorization

As suggested by both Kelman and Bellah (1973), authorization may also take the form of a transcendent vision or mission that captures the public's imagination, inspiring behavior on behalf of or in defense of that ideal without regard for the consequences. Defending the world against the "Red menace," for example, led many people to abandon normal restraints and long-held principles in the cause of combating what they believed were the insidious evils of communism. During the Crusades in the eleventh through the thirteenth centuries, Christians committed untold barbaric acts against "infidels" in a fanatical effort to reconquer the Holy Land. And we are all too familiar with the crimes of Hitler, Stalin, Mao Zedong, Pol Pot, and other dictators who authorized millions of murders in the pursuit of utopian ideals.

. . . .

Routinization

According to Kelman, the second process that operates under conditions of socially sanctioned violence is *routinization*. Routinization mitigates the feelings of guilt associated with violence by making it commonplace, repetitive, and redundant. People who continuously engage in violence become inured to its horrors. This is what Hannah Arendt (1963) called the "banality of evil."

Although it did not involve violent behavior, some of Langer's research on mindless compliance illustrates one relevant characteristic of routinization (for example, see Langer, Blank, & Chanowitz, 1978). Her research demonstrated that people often comply with various requests without giving much thought to the meaning involved in the request. For example, people waiting in line to use a copying machine were asked by someone if they could use it first. The form that the request took varied. In some instances, there was hardly any rationale offered by the person making the request to be permitted to go first— "I want to use the machine because I have some copies to make." Langer and her colleagues often found people complying mindlessly to such requests without thoughtfully considering whether any legitimate rationale for letting the other person go first was offered.

A second aspect of routinization involves the everyday routinization of work that occurs in most bureaucracies; people simply perform their own work, never pausing to consider how their small role is integrated into the operation of the organization as a whole. Most bureaucracies are so highly differentiated that the overall function is obscured to most individuals concentrated on fulfilling the specific requirements of their own department, team, or subsection. Consider, for example, the complex tasks involved in the Nazi death camps: someone had to produce the gas; someone had to build the camps; someone had to operate the trains that brought the prisoners; someone had to handle the everyday camp wastes; someone had to feed and clothe the military personnel; and so on. No one person did it all; the task was divided and routinized. The result was beyond belief.

A third aspect of routinization involves *normalization*, the treatment of something extraordinary as though it were normal. Routinization helps people normalize even the most horrible of deeds and so avoid consciously encountering both what they are doing and its broader implications for humanity. Everyday we normalize events that otherwise might overwhelm us. Someone arrives at work and seems not quite themselves. They act in a confused and inattentive manner; they slur their speech a little; when we get close to them, we think we smell alcohol on their breath. This happens repeatedly. We can approach this as a situation involving an alcohol problem or we can normalize it: their behavior really isn't that unusual; that isn't alcohol we smell, it's mouthwash; they are no less attentive then they ever have been.

Now apply this same idea to violence. People not only do their routine jobs, oblivious to the larger context of which they are a part, but also transform the unusual into the usual to make it more palatable or easier to deal with. Our language helps us. We are not involved in killing people; we are involved in a "selection process." We are not harming civilians; we are involved in "pacification." We are not uprooting people and destroying their lives; we are merely in the "moving and transport" business. Euphemisms like this were often cynically employed by the United States government in the Vietnam War to deceive the public about operations that would certainly invite criticism if not condemnation.

. . . .

Dehumanization

Perhaps the most important process involved in socially sanctioned violence, pointed out by Kelman, Sanford, Comstock and many others, is that of *dehumanization*. By making the objects of our violence less than human, we do not experience the guilt associated with killing or harming fellow human beings. The following study reported by Zimbardo and his colleagues (1973) reveals just how easy it is to dehumanize another person.

The year was 1971; the place Palo Alto, California. About 70 men responded to an ad in the local paper seeking paid volunteers for a study to be done at Stanford University. Interviews reduced the number to 24 subjects who were judged to be reasonably healthy both physically and mentally. By the flip of a coin, half were assigned to be prisoners in a mock, but realistic "prison" created in the basement of the Psychology Department's building on the campus; the other half were to be "prison guards."

By prior arrangement, a city police car conducted a surprise arrest of the prisoners on Sunday morning, charging each with armed robbery and burglary, handcuffing them, bringing them in for booking, and then turning them over to the prison, where they were stripped, deloused, and issued uniforms—in this case, dresses, sandals, and stocking caps—to humiliate them. The prisoners were somewhat in a state of shock; this was just an experiment, wasn't it?

The guards, all of whom had been provided with appropriate police uniforms and reflective sun glasses, had not been given any specific instructions about what they were to do other than to maintain law and order. Remember that being a prisoner or a guard was merely a matter of a coin flip; one could as easily have been one as the other.

The guards soon began to treat the prisoners with some brutality; they punished rule infractions or the expression of disrespectful attitudes by demanding push-ups. On the second day, when the prisoners staged a mini-rebellion, the guards retaliated by using a fire extinguisher to douse the prisoners with chilling carbon dioxide. Once they had forced them back into their cells, they entered each cell, stripped the prisoners naked, removed the beds from each room, and placed the ring leaders into solitary confinement.

As time passed, the guards became increasingly adept in controlling the prisoners by promising rewards for good behavior (for example, visits to the toilet) and by punishing noncompliant behavior. In time, the prisoners became sullen and withdrawn, some even insisting that serious medical reasons demanded their release from the study. For example, one prisoner showed signs of serious emotional distress—disorganized thinking, uncontrollable crying, rage, and so on. He was eventually released. The study was so much a success that it had to be stopped early. It demonstrated that under the right circumstances people can quickly dehumanize others, disregarding their shared humanity even as they brutalize them.

Objectification is an integral part of the dehumanizing process. To treat people as objects is to implicitly make them less than human and, thus, easier to harm. Language can greatly facilitate dehumanization; the use of slang, idiom, and technical jargon to categorize people effectively depersonalizes them. By calling someone a "nigger," "fag," or "commie," you avoid having to address him or her as an equal. Dehumanization is by no means harmful only to the victim. In 1958, the philosopher Martin Buber noted how those who treat other people as objects, thereby denying them their humanity, in time come to think of themselves as mere objects as well; in effect, dehumanization denies humanity to both victim and victimizer.

Undoing Socially Sanctioned Violence

We have just considered three interrelated forces—authorization, routinization, and dehumanization—underlying socially sanctioned violence. If our goal is to prevent or minimize such violence, we might look for a way to counter these processes with forces that restore normal constraints to aggressive behavior. For example, if authorization induces people to abdicate personal responsibility for their actions, counteractive processes in society that encourage personal accountability should be actively promoted. Kelman's analysis of the differences between AR and DR types illustrates just what form these social counterforces might take.

Kelman and his associates discovered that the AR and DR groups in their national sample fundamentally differed in their perceived relationship to society. Whereas the AR group thought of themselves as "owners" responsible for the maintenance of the state, the DR group felt themselves to be more like "tenants" obligated to follow the laws but otherwise bearing little or no responsibility for the state as a whole; this was the concern, they felt, of their duly elected representatives. Kelman and his colleagues correlated these two perspectives with educational and economic levels; in general, they found that the sense of ownership increased with higher education and financial standing. Other investigators have confirmed that poverty and ignorance distance people from a sense of societal ownership (for example, see Kahn, 1972). Given this relationship, one way to counteract the effects of authorization with respect to socially sanctioned violence might be to provide better education and economic opportunities to the poor and disadvantaged, groups traditionally recruited by the state to carry out its dirty work.

Kelman also raises questions about cultural practices, some of which we considered in earlier chapters, that help to both legitimize and normalize violence. As we have seen, for example, a steady diet of violence in the media desensitizes people to violence, teaches children how aggression is an acceptable way to resolve their problems, and encourages adults to follow these violent scripts in their own lives. Providing alternative models in the media for problem solving can offset the dehumanizing circumstances people seem to increasingly find themselves in today's world. By emphasizing the commonalities among people rather than the differences, the media can promote understanding and respect rather than hostility and suspicion.

Research conducted in a naturalistic setting by Sherif and Sherif (1953) provides some instructive lessons about how we can effectively counteract processes underlying socially sanctioned violence. The Sherifs ran a summer camp for young boys, and were thus able to create and evaluate certain scenarios virtually impossible to stage in the limited confines of a laboratory. One of these scenarios was to divide the boys into different groups and have them compete with one other. Over time, each group established a unique identity and narrowly defined boundaries that effectively dehumanized its opponents, thereby facilitating a growing hostility between the different groups. Noting the intensity of the conflicts that now divided the camp, the Sherifs wondered if there were some way to restore harmony.

They reasoned that if the divided and hostile groups in the camp were forced to work together to deal with a common emergency—for example, a disruption to the camp's water supply—this shared experience might bridge the divisions that had grown between them. Happily, results confirmed their expectations; the larger requirements of the camp as a whole overcame the relatively narrow goals of the warring factions, cutting into the dynamics of competition, conflict, and dehumanization that had set in.

Sherifs' strategy of inducing cooperation among competing factions calls to mind the intergroup biasing effect that we first considered in Chapter 4 (see pp. 69–73). We saw that once people have organized their world into in-groups and out-groups, they tend to increasingly value the former at the expense of the latter. This suggests that one way to inhibit the process of dehumanization is to help people recategorize their respective in-groups and out-groups. This approach was employed by Gaertner and his associates (1989) with some success.

They reasoned that two different strategies might help people recategorize others. One strategy, somewhat similar to that used by the Sherifs, involves replacing the in-group–out-group division with one superordinate group. Presumably, if in-group and out-group members are all seen as members of the same group, then the out-group biasing effect would be diminished and with it the tendency to dehumanize out-group members. A single group can be experimentally created by various means—for example, by referring to the new group by a single name or by having everyone work together to solve a problem (as in the Sherifs' study).

The second strategy that Gaertner and his colleagues explored involved what they termed a separate–individuals approach. They reasoned that the more individuated people become, the less they will be seen as members of either an in-group or out-group. In effect, group membership would be broken up by viewing all people as unique individuals. It is possible to create a condition of high individuation experimentally—for example, by having each individual refer to him- or herself by a separate name or by seating each individual in a unique position.

Gaertner and his colleagues hypothesized that both strategies would effectively reduce the usual out-group biasing effect. Data from their study generally confirmed this hypothesis, but the strategies worked somewhat differently to equalize in-group and out-group attitudes. The one-group approach seemed to reduce out-group bias by increasing the attractiveness of people who were formerly *out-group* members. The individuated approach reduced out-group bias primarily by decreasing the attractiveness of people who were formerly members of the *in-group*.

The Oliners' study of the altruistic personality, which we considered earlier (see Chapter 16, pp. 288–89), suggested that some people who engage in the process of recategorization described by Gaertner and his colleagues, among others, do so without any special prompting. These people are characterized by their capacity to include out-group members in their overall sense of humanity. Many of those who rescued Jews during World War II, for example, did not differentiate between themselves and Jews. Some rescuers even helped injured German soldiers, judging that their responsibility was to care for *all* people in need of help. In contrast, bystanders tended to have a more narrow conception of their social world. They were exclusively oriented toward their in-group and their own interests, expressing little generalized concern or responsibility for out-group members who might be in need. In effect, the rescuers were more disposed to see others as part of one group, while bystanders tended to retain the sharply drawn in-group–out-group boundaries that invite dehumanization.

Hopes for Altruism

We have seen how, by counteracting the pressures of authorization, routinization, and dehumanization, restraints on aggressive behavior can be restored. Is there, however, no alternative than restraining violence? What about promoting altruism? Is it not possible that socially sanctioned acts of violence can be superseded by socially sanctioned acts of goodness and helpfulness?

I realize that human history to date is primarily a story of war, conquest, and destruction. The news seems to reinforce the impression that little has changed. For every altruistic act there are an untold number of barbarities. I believe that aggression, rather than altruism, continues to prevail because it is fundamental to the dynamic of our socioeconomic system. Where competition reigns; where success is the measure of social worth; where winning is everything; where force and strength are the only guarantees of humanity's superiority—herein lie the forces that keep altruism in check. Under these conditions, is it any wonder that altruism can be only a whispered hope?

Quite simply, altruism cannot emerge as long as social systems operate according to fundamentally antihuman rather life-affirming principles [see Maccoby's (1972) discussion of Fromm on this theme]. While countering the forces that encourage socially sanctioned acts of violence may lessen their impact, the course of human history will not be transformed until we excise the entire framework that nurtures the sanctioning of human destructiveness. When we find altruism we applaud it, but then we return to business as usual. It is that kind of inertia that stands in the way, not human biology or our good intentions. I return here to a theme that has appeared in several other places in this book. There is really no way to play the current societal game in an altruistic manner; we can only play it in a less aggressive form. True altruism requires that we learn to play another, more life-affirming game.

Conclusions

In this chapter we have examined aggression and altruism in the context of society at large. We explored three interrelated processes—authorization, routinization, and dehumanization—linked to socially sanctioned violence, and how they might be effectively challenged through proper social responses once the dynamics are fully understood. We saw however, that simply opposing these negative influences does not necessarily result in genuine altruism, but merely limits the destructive consequences of aggression. Genuine altruism is not simply the absence of harmful intent, but the affirmation of kindness.

The achievement of socially sanctioned altruism requires more than eliminating aggression; it demands that the very nature of the game we are playing be radically changed. There is no way to achieve sanctioned kindness in a game in which some always win and others always lose, in which some are always on top and others are always on the bottom, in which some always lead and others always follow. Sanctioned violence in some form will invariably occur under such antagonistic conditions. While we may be able to minimize aggression, we can never remove the fundamental basis for its existence in the first place. This requires a very different understanding, a virtual transformation in our value system. It is for this reason that we can only speak of altruism as a *hope*.

The ethics of caring outlined by the Oliners illustrates the kind of transformation in values needed to promote a true spirit of altruism. They make a special point of contrasting their view of heroism with the conventional understanding of psychology and social psychology. In most western cultures the mythical hero is imagined as solitary and detached, the "masked man" who performs good deeds for the community but always remains outside of it. He is also virtually superhuman, observing abstract principles of justice beyond most people's moral awareness. To the Oliners, however, heroes are rather ordinary people—bakers, farmers, teachers, factory workers—who help those in need not because of abstract principles but because of their commitments to others as members of the same community.

The Oliners conclude that the roots of altruism are available to all of us, not simply a few; and those roots appear by virtue of our attachments to other people, not by virtue of our distance and separation from them. While a society that insistently trains people to distrust others, to make no commitments or attachments, to see other people as potential threats to one's own achievements, may produce a few isolated altruistic heroes, it is unlikely to prove fertile soil for a widespread ethic of caring and kindness to others. If our heroes are ordinary people, we still need to create the conditions that permit them to act in ordinary, decent ways toward their fellow human beings.

References

Abramson, L. Y., Seligman, M. E. P., & Teasdale, J. D. (1978). Learned helplessness in humans: Critique and reformulation. *Journal of Abnormal Psychology, 87,* 49–74.

Adorno, T. W., Frenkel-Brunswik, E., Levinson, D. J., & Sanford, R. N. (1950). *The authoritarian personality.* New York: Harper.

Ajzen, I. (1977). Intuitive theories of events and the effects of base-rate information on prediction. *Journal of Personality and Social Psychology, 35,* 303–314.

Ajzen, I. (1988). *Attitudes, personality and behavior.* Chicago, IL: Dorsey Press.

Ajzen, I., & Fishbein, M. (1980). *Understanding attitudes and predicting social behavior.* Englewood Cliffs, NJ: Prentice-Hall.

Alexander, C. N., & Knight, G. W. (1971). Situated identities and social psychological experimentation. *Sociometry, 34,* 65–82.

Alexander, C. N., & Weil, H. G. (1969). Players, persons and purposes: Situational meaning and the prisoner's dilemma game. *Sociometry, 32,* 121–144.

Allen, J. L., Walker, L. D., Schroeder, D. A., & Johnson, D. E. (1987). Attributions and attribution-behavior relations: The effect of level of cognitive development. *Journal of Personality and Social Psychology, 52,* 1099–1109.

Allport, G. W. (1954). The historical background of modern social psychology. In G. Lindezy (Ed.), *Handbook of social psychology: Vol. 1.* Cambridge, MA: Addison-Wesley.

Anderson, C. A. (1989). Temperature and aggression: Ubiquitous effects of heat on occurrences of human violence. *Psychological Bulletin, 106,* 74–96.

Archer, D., & Gartner, R. (1976). Violent acts and violent times: A comparative approach to postwar homicide rates. *American Sociological Review, 41,* 937–963.

Arendt, H. (1963). *Eichmann in Jerusalem: A report on the banality of evil.* New York: Viking.

Ariès, P., & Duby, G. (1988). *A history of private life: Vol. 2. Revelations of the Medieval world.* Cambridge, MA: Belknap.

Arkin, R. M., & Duval, S. (1975). Focus of attention and causal attributions of actors and observers. *Journal of Experimental Social Psychology, 11,* 427–438.

Asch, S. E. (1956). Studies of independence and conformity, a minority of one against a unanimous majority. *Psychological Monographs, 70,* (9, Whole No. 416).

Asch, S. E. (1958). Effects of group pressure upon the modification and distortion of judgments. In E. E. Maccoby, T. M. Newcomb, & E. L. Hartley (Eds.), *Readings in social psychology* (3rd ed.). New York: Holt, Rinehart & Winston.

Averill, J. R. (1982). *Anger and aggression: An essay on emotion.* New York: Springer-Verlag.

Averill, J. R. (1983). Studies on anger and aggression: Implications for theories of emotion. *American Psychologist, 38,* 1145–1160.

Axom, D., Yates, S., & Chaiken, S. (1987). Audience response as a heuristic cue in persuasion. *Journal of Personality and Social Psychology, 53,* 30–40.

Baer, R., Hinkle, S., Smith, K., & Fenton, M. (1980). Reactance as a function of actual versus projected autonomy. *Journal of Personality and Social Psychology, 38,* 416–422.

Bandura, A. (1973). *Aggression: A social learning analysis.* Englewood Cliffs, NJ: Prentice-Hall.

Barker, R. G. (1965). Explorations in ecological psychology. *American Psychologist, 20,* 1–14.

Basgall, J. A., & Snyder, C. R. (1988). Excuses in waiting: External locus of control and reactions to success-failure feedback. *Journal of Personality and Social Psychology, 54,* 656–662.

Batson, C. D., Batson, J. G., Griffitt, C. A., Barrientos, S., Brandt, J. R., Sprengelmeyer, P., & Bayly, M. J. (1989). Negative-state relief and the empathy-altruism hypothesis. *Journal of Personality and Social Psychology, 56,* 922–933.

Batson, C. D., Bolen, M. H., Cross, J. A., & Neuringer-Benefiel, H. E. (1986). Where is the altruism in the altruistic personality? *Journal of Personality and Social Psychology, 50,* 212–220.

Batson, C. D., Duncan, B. D., Ackerman, P., Buckley, T., & Birch, K. (1981). Is empathic emotion a source of altruistic motivation? *Journal of Personality and Social Psychology, 40,* 290–302.

Batson, C. D., Dyck, J. L., Brandt, J. R., Batson, J. G., Powell, A. L., McMaster, M. R., & Griffitt, C. (1988). Five studies testing two new egoistic alternatives to the empathy-altruism hypothesis. *Journal of Personality and Social Psychology,* *55,* 52–77.

Batson, C. D., O'Quin, K., Fultz, J., Vanderplas, M., & Isen, A. M. (1983). Influence of self-reported distress and empathy on egoistic versus altruistic motivation to help. *Journal of Personality and Social Psychology, 45,* 706–718.

Bauman, D. J., Cialdini, R. B., & Kenrick, D. T. (1981). Altruism as hedonism: Helping and self-gratification as equivalent responses. *Journal of Personality and Social Psychology, 40,* 1039–1046.

Baumeister, R. F. (1982). A self-presentational view of social phenomena. *Psychological Bulletin, 91,* 3–26.

Baumeister, R. F. (1987). How the self became a problem: A psychological review of historical research. *Journal of Personality and Social Psychology, 52,* 163–176.

Becker, E. (1973). *The denial of death.* New York: Free Press.

Bellah, R. N. (1973). Evil and the American ethos. In N. Sanford & C. Comstock (Eds.), *Sanctions for evil.* San Francisco: Jossey-Bass.

Bem, S. L. (1974). The measurement of psychological androgyny. *Journal of Consulting and Clinical Psychology, 42,* 155–162.

Bem, S. L. (1975). Sex role adaptability: One consequence of psychological androgyny. *Journal of Personality and Social Psychology, 31,* 634–643.

Bem, S. L. (1981). Gender schema theory: A cognitive account of sex typing. *Psychological Review, 88,* 354–364.

Bem, S. L. (1982). Gender schema theory and self-schema theory compared: A comment on Markus, Crane, Bernstein & Siladi's "self-schemas and gender". *Journal of Personality and Social Psychology, 43,* 1192–1194.

Bem, S. L., & Lenney, E. (1976). Sex typing and the avoidance of cross-sex behavior. *Journal of Personality and Social Psychology, 33,* 48–54.

Bem, S. L., Martyna, W., & Watson, C. (1976). Sex typing and androgyny: Further explorations of the expressive domain. *Journal of Personality and Social Psychology, 34,* 1016–1023.

Berger, J. M. (1981). Motivational biases in the attribution of responsibility for an accident: A meta-analysis of the defensive-attribution hypothesis. *Psychological Bulletin, 90,* 496–512.

Berglas, S., & Jones, E. E. (1978). Drug choice as a self-handicapping strategy in response to noncontingent success. *Journal of Personality and Social Psychology, 36,* 405–417.

Berkowitz, L. (1984). Some effects of thoughts on anti- and prosocial influence of media events: A cognitive neoassociation analysis. *Psychological Bulletin, 95,* 410–427.

Berkowitz, L. (1989). Frustration-aggression hypothesis: Examination and reformulation. *Psychological Bulletin, 106,* 59–73.

Berkowitz, L., & Daniels, L. (1964). Affecting the salience of the social responsibility norm: Effects of past help on the response to dependency relationships. *Journal of Abnormal and Social Psychology, 68,* 275–281.

Bernstein, R. J. (1983). *Beyond objectivism and relativism: Science, hermeneutics and praxis.* Philadelphia, PA: University of Pennsylvania Press.

Bernstein, W. M., Stephan, W. G., & Davis, M. H. (1979). Explaining attributions for achievement: A path analytic approach. *Journal of Personality and Social Psychology, 37,* 1810–1821.

Bettelheim, B. (1958). Individual and mass behavior in extreme situations. In E. E. Maccoby, T. M. Newcomb, & E. L. Hartley (Eds.), *Readings in social psychology* (3rd ed.). New York: Holt, Rinehart & Winston.

Billig, M. (1976). *Social psychology and intergroup relations.* London: Academic Press.

Billig, M. (1987). *Arguing and thinking: A rhetorical approach to social psychology.* Cambridge: Cambridge University Press.

Block, J., & Block, J. H. (1952). An interpersonal experiment on reactions to authority. *Human Relations, 5,* 91–98.

Block, J., & Funder, D. C. (1986). Social roles and social perception: Individual differences in attribution and error. *Journal of Personality and Social Psychology, 51,* 1200–1207.

Bradley, G. W. (1978). Self-serving biases in the attribution process: A reexamination of the fact or fiction question. *Journal of Personality and Social Psychology, 36,* 56–71.

Bramel, D. (1963). Selection of a target for defensive projection. *Journal of Abnormal and Social Psychology, 66,* 318–324.

Bramel, D., & Friend, R. (1981). Hawthorne, the myth of the docile worker, and class bias in psychology. *American Psychologist, 36,* 867–878.

Bray, R. M., Johnson, D., & Chilstrom, J. T. (1982). Social influence by group members with minority opinions: A comparison of Hollander and Moscovici. *Journal of Personality and Social Psychology, 43,* 78–88.

Breckler, S. J. (1984). Empirical validation of affect, behavior and cognition as distinct components of attitudes. *Journal of Personality and Social Psychology, 47,* 1191–1205.

Brehm, J. W. (1966). *A theory of psychological reactance.* New York: Academic Press.

Brehm, S. S., & Brehm, J. W. (1981). *Psychological reactance: A theory of freedom and control.* New York: Academic Press.

Brekke, N., & Borgida, E. (1988). Expert psychological testimony in rape trials: A social-cognitive analysis. *Journal of Personality and Social Psychology, 55,* 372–386.

Brickman, P., Rabinowitz, V. C., Karuza, J., Coates, D., Cohn, E., & Kidder, L. (1982). Models of helping and coping. *American Psychologist, 37,* 368–384.

Brislin, R. W. (1974). The Ponzo illusion: Additional cues, age, orientation and culture. *Journal of Cross-cultural Psychology, 5,* 139–161.

Brislin, R. W., & Keating, C. F. (1976). Cultural differences in the perception of a three-dimensional Ponzo illusion. *Journal of Cross-cultural Psychology, 7,* 397–412.

Brodt, S. E., & Zimbardo, P. G. (1981). Modifying shyness-related social behavior through symptom misattribution. *Journal of Personality and Social Psychology, 41,* 437–449.

Broverman, I. K., Vogel, S. R., Broverman, D. M., Clarkson, F. E., & Rosenkrantz, P. S. (1972). Sex role stereotypes: A current appraisal. *Journal of Social Issues, 28,* 59–78.

Brown, J. D., Collins, R. L., & Schmidt, G. W. (1988). Self-esteem and direct versus indirect forms of self-enhancement. *Journal of Personality and Social Psychology, 55,* 445–453.

Buber, M. (1958). *I and thou.* New York: Scribners.

Burns, M. O., & Seligman, M. E. P. (1989). Explanatory style across the lifespan: Evidence for stability over 52 years. *Journal of Personality and Social Psychology, 56,* 471–477.

Burt, M. R. (1980). Cultural myths and support for rape. *Journal of Personality and Social Psychology, 38,* 217–230.

Buss, A. H. (1963). Physical aggression in relation to different frustrations. *Journal of Abnormal and Social Psychology, 67,* 1–7.

Cacioppo, J. T., Petty, R. E., & Morris, K. J. (1983). Effects of need for cognition on message evaluation, recall and persuasion. *Journal of Personality and Social Psychology, 45,* 805–818.

Campbell, D. T. (1972). On the genetics of altruism and the counter-hedonic components in human culture. *Journal of Social Issues, 28,* 21–37.

Campbell, D. T. (1975). On the conflicts between biological and social evolution and between psychology and moral tradition. *American Psychologist, 30,* 1103–1126.

Campbell, J. (1968). *The hero with a thousand faces.* Princeton, NJ: Princeton University Press.

Caplan, N., & Nelson, S. D. (1973). On being useful: The nature and consequences of psychological research on social problems. *American Psychologist, 28,* 199–211.

Carlson, A. (1988, October) Chromosome count. Ms, pp. 40, 42–44.

Carlson, M., Charlin, V., & Miller, N. (1988). Positive mood and helping behavior: A test of six hypotheses. *Journal of Personality and Social Psychology, 55,* 211–229.

Carlson, M., & Miller, N. (1987). Explanation of the relationship between negative mood and helping. *Psychological Bulletin, 102,* 91–108.

Chaiken, S. (1980). Heuristic versus systematic information processing and the use of source versus message cues in persuasion. *Journal of Personality and Social Psychology, 39,* 752–766.

Chapman, L. J., & Chapman, J. P. (1967). Genesis of popular but erroneous psycho-diagnostic observations. *Journal of Abnormal Psychology, 72,* 193–204.

Christ, C. P. (1980). *Diving deep and surfacing.* Boston: Beacon.

Cialdini, R. B., Schaller, M., Houlihan, D., Arps, K., Futz, J., & Beaman, A. L. (1987). Empathy-based helping: Is it selflessly or selfishly motivated? *Journal of Personality and Social Psychology, 52,* 749–758.

Cohen, R. (1972). Altruism: Human, cultural or what? *Journal of Social Issues, 28,* 39–57.

Colby, A., & Damon, W. (1983). Listening to a different voice: A review of Gilligan's *In a different voice. Merrill-Palmer Quarterly, 29,* 473–481.

Constantinople, A. (1973). Masculinity-femininity: An exception to the famous dictum? *Psychological Bulletin, 80,* 389–407.

Cooley, C. H. (1902). *Human nature and the social order.* New York: Scribners.

Cousins, S. D. (1989). Culture and self-perception in Japan and the United States. *Journal of Personality and Social Psychology, 56,* 124–131.

Crane, M., & Markus, H. (1982). Gender identity: The benefits of a self-schema approach. *Journal of Personality and Social Psychology, 43,* 1195–1197.

Crocker, J. (1981). Judgment of covariation by social perceivers. *Psychological Bulletin, 90,* 272–292.

Crutchfield, R. S. (1955). Conformity and character. *American Psychologist, 10,* 195–198.

Dahl, R. A. (1989). *Democracy and its critics.* New Haven: Yale University Press.

Darley, J. M., & Latané, B. (1968). Bystander intervention in emergencies: Diffusion of responsibility. *Journal of Personality and Social Psychology, 8,* 377–383.

Davis, M. H. (1983). Measuring individual differences in empathy: Evidence for a multidimensional approach. *Journal of Personality and Social Psychology, 44,* 113–126.

Deaux, K. (1984). From individual differences to social categories: Analysis of a decade's research on gender. *American Psychologist, 39,* 105–116.

Deaux, K., & Lewis, L. L. (1984). Structure of gender stereotypes: Interrelationships among components and gender label. *Journal of Personality and Social Psychology, 46,* 991–1004.

De Bono, K. G. (1987). Investigating the social-adjustive and value-expressive functions of attitudes: Implications for persuasion processes. *Journal of Personality and Social Psychology, 52,* 279–287.

De Gree, C. E., & Snyder, C. R. (1985). Adler's psychology (of use) today: Personal history of traumatic life events as a self-handicapping strategy. *Journal of Personality and Social Psychology, 48,* 1512–1519.

De Paulo, B. M., Kenny, D. A., Hoover, C. W., Webb, W., & Oliver, P. V. (1987). Accuracy of person perception: Do people know what kinds of impressions they convey? *Journal of Personality and Social Psychology, 52,* 303–315.

Deutsch, M., & Gerard, H. B. (1955). A study of normative and informational social influences upon individual judgment. *Journal of Abnormal and Social Psychology, 51,* 629–636.

Dimitrovsky, L., Singer, J., & Yinon, Y. (1989). Masculine and feminine traits: Their relation to suitedness for and success in training for traditionally masculine and feminine army functions. *Journal of Personality and Social Psychology, 57,* 839–847.

Dollard, J., Doob, L., Miller, N., Mowrer, O., & Sears, R. (1939). *Frustration and aggression.* New Haven: Yale University Press.

Dreyfus, H. L., & Rabinow, P. (1982). *Michel Foucault: Beyond structuralism and hermeneutics.* Chicago: University of Chicago Press.

Duncan, B. L. (1976). Differential social perception and attribution of intergroup violence: Testing the lower limits of stereotyping of Blacks. *Journal of Personality and Social Psychology, 34,* 590–598.

Duval, S., & Wicklund, R. A. (1972). *A theory of objective self-awareness.* San Diego: Academic Press.

Eagly, A. H. (1978). Sex differences in influenceability. *Psychological Bulletin, 85,* 86–116.

Eagly, A. H. (1983). Gender and social influence: A social psychological analysis. *American Psychologist, 38,* 971–981.

Eagly, A. H., & Carli, L. L. (1981). Sex of researchers and sex-typed communications as determinants of sex differences in influenceability: A meta-analysis of social influence studies.s *Psychological Bulletin, 90,* 1–20.

Eagly, A. H., & Crowley, M. (1986). Gender and helping behavior: A meta-analytic review of the social psychological literature. *Psychological Bulletin, 100,* 283–308.

Eagly, A. H., & Kite, M. E. (1987). Are stereotypes of nationalities applied to both women and men? *Journal of Personality and Social Psychology, 53,* 451–462.

Eagly, A. H., & Steffen, V. J. (1984). Gender stereotypes stem from the distribution of women and men into social roles. *Journal of Personality and Social Psychology, 46,* 735–754.

Eagly, A. H., & Steffen, V. J. (1986). Gender and aggressive behavior: A meta-analytic review of the social psychological literature. *Psychological Bulletin, 100,* 309–330.

Edwards, V. J., & Spence, J. T. (1987). Gender-related traits, stereotypes and schemata. *Journal of Personality and Social Psychology, 53,* 146–154.

Eisenberg, N., & Miller, P. A. (1987). The relation of empathy to prosocial and related behaviors. *Psychological Bulletin, 101,* 91–119.

Ellison, R. (1952). *Invisible man.* New York: Random House.

Emerson, J. (1975). Behavior in private places: Sustaining definitions of reality in gynecological examinations. In D. Brissett & C. Edgley (Eds.), *Life as theater.* Chicago: Aldine.

Epstein, S. (1973). The self-concept revisited: Or a theory of a theory. *American Psychologist, 28,* 404–416.

Epstein, S. (1979). The stability of behavior: 1. On predicting most of the people much of the time. *Journal of Personality and Social Psychology, 37,* 1097–1126.

Epstein, S. (1985). The implications of cognitive-experimental self-theory for research in social psychology and personality. *Journal for the Theory of Social Behavior, 15,* 283–310.

Erikson, E. H. (1959). *Identity and the life cycle.* New York: International Universities Press.

Eron, L. D. (1982). Parent-child interaction, television violence, and aggression of children. *American Psychologist, 37,* 197–211.

Eron, L. D. (1986). Interventions to mitigate the psychological effects of media violence on aggressive behavior. *Journal of Social Issues, 42,* 155–169.

Eron, L. D., & Huesmann, L. R. (1987). The stability of aggressive behavior in cross-national comparison. In C. Kagitacibasi (Ed.), *Growth and progress in cross-cultural psychology.* Lisse: Swets & Zeitlinger.

Eron, L. D., Huesmann, L. R., Lefkowitz, M. M., & Walder, L. O. (1972). Does television violence cause aggression? *American Psychologist, 27,* 253–263.

Fajans, J. (1985). The person in social context: The social character of Baining "psychology". In G. M. White & J. Kirkpatrick (Eds.), *Person, self and experience.* Berkeley: University of California Press.

Fazio, R. H., Powell, M. C., & Herr, P. M. (1983). Toward a process model of the attitude-behavior relation: Accessing one's attitude upon mere observation of the attitude object. *Journal of Personality and Social Psychology, 44,* 723–735.

Fazio, R. H., & Williams, C. J. (1986). Attitude accessibility as a moderator of the attitude-perception and attitude-behavior relations: An investigation of the 1984 presidential election. *Journal of Personality and Social Psychology, 51,* 505–514.

Feather, N. T. (1985). Attitudes, values and attributions: Explanations of unemployment. *Journal of Personality and Social Psychology, 48,* 876–889.

Feather, N. T., & Davenport, P. R. (1981). Unemployment and depressive affect: A motivational and attributional analysis. *Journal of Personality and Social Psychology, 41,* 422–436.

Felson, R. B. (1989). Parents and the reflected appraisal process: A longitudinal analysis. *Journal of Personality and Social Psychology, 56,* 965–971.

Feshbach, S. (1964). The function of aggression and the regulation of aggressive drive. *Psychological Review, 71,* 257–272.

Feshbach, S. (1976). The role of fantasy in the response to television. *Journal of Social Issues, 32,* 71–85.

Festinger, L. (1957). *A theory of cognitive dissonance.* Evanston, IL: Row-Peterson.

Festinger, L., & Carlsmith, J. M. (1959). Cognitive consequences of forced compliance. *Journal of Abnormal and Social Psychology, 58,* 203–210.

Field, H. S. (1978). Attitudes toward rape: A comparative analysis of police, rapists, crisis counselors and citizens. *Journal of Personality and Social Psychology, 36,* 156–179.

Fisher, J. D., Nadler, A., & Whitcher-Alagna, S. (1982). Recipient reactions to aid. *Psychological Bulletin, 91,* 27–54.

Follette, V. M., & Jacobson, N. S. (1987). Importance of attributions as a prediction of how people cope with failure. *Journal of Personality and Social Psychology, 52,* 1205–1211.

Försterling, F. (1986). Attributional conceptions in clinical psychology. *American Psychologist, 41,* 275–285.

Foucault, M. (1979). *Discipline and punish: The birth of the prison.* New York: Random House.

Foucault, M. (1980). *The history of sexuality: Vol. 1. An introduction.* New York: Random House.

Foushee, H. C. (1984). Dyads and triads at 35,000 feet: Factors affecting group process and aircrew performance. *American Psychologist, 39,* 885–893.

Frable, D. E. S. (1989). Sex typing and gender ideology: Two facets of the individual's gender psychology that go together. *Journal of Personality and Social Psychology, 56,* 95–108.

Frable, D. E. S., & Bem, S. L. (1985). If you are gender schematic, all members of the opposite sex look alike. *Journal of Personality and Social Psychology, 49,* 459–468.

Frager, R. (1970). Conformity and anticonformity in Japan. *Journal of Personality and Social Psychology, 15,* 203–210.

Freedman, J. L. (1984). Effect of television violence on aggressiveness. *Psychological Bulletin, 96,* 227–246.

Freedman, J. L. (1986). Television violence and aggression: A rejoinder. *Psychological Bulletin, 100,* 372–378.

French, J. R. P., Jr., & Raven, B. (1959). The bases of social power. In D. Cartwright (Ed.), *Studies in social power.* Ann Arbor, MI: Research Center for Group Dynamics, Institute for Social Research.

Freud, S. (1924–1950). *Collected papers.* London: Hogarth Press.

Freud, S. (1954). *The interpretation of dreams.* London: Allen & Unwin.

Friedrich-Cofer, L., & Huston, A. C. (1986). Television violence and aggression: The debate continues. *Psychological Bulletin, 100,* 364–371.

Fromm, E. (1955). *The sane society.* New York: Rinehart.

Funder, D. C. (1987). Errors and mistakes: Evaluating the accuracy of social judgment. *Psychological Bulletin, 101,* 75–90.

Funder, D. C., & Colvin, C. R. (1988). Friends and strangers: Acquaintanceship, agreement and the accuracy of personality judgment. *Journal of Personality and Social Psychology, 55,* 149–158.

Funder, D. C., & Dobroth, K. M. (1987). Differences between traits: Properties associated with interjudge agreement. *Journal of Personality and Social Psychology, 52,* 409–418.

Furby, L. (1979). Individualistic bias in studies of locus of control. In A. R. Buss (Ed.), *Psychology in social context.* New York: Irvington.

Gadamer, H-G. (1960/1975). *Truth and Method.* New York: Seabury Press.

Gaertner, S. L., Mann, J., Murrell, A., & Dovidio, J. F. (1989). Reducing intergroup bias: The benefits of recategorization. *Journal of Personality and Social Psychology, 57,* 239–249.

Galotti, K. M. (1989). Approaches to studying formal and everyday reasoning. *Psychological Bulletin, 105,* 331–351.

Garfinkel, H. (1967). *Studies in ethnomethodology.* Englewood Cliffs, NJ: Prentice-Hall.

Geertz, C. (1973). *The interpretation of cultures.* New York: Basic Books.

Geertz, C. (1984). "From the native's point of view": On the nature of anthropological understanding. In R. A. Shweder & R. A. LeVine (Eds.), *Culture theory: Essays on mind, self and emotion.* Cambridge: Cambridge University Press.

Gelles, R. J., & Straus, M. A. (1979). Violence in the American family. *Journal of Social Issues, 35,* 15–39.

Gergen, K. J. (1967). Multiple identity: The healthy, happy human being wears many masks. *Psychology Today, 5,* 31–35; 64–66.

Gergen, K. J. (1973). Social psychology as history. *Journal of Personality and Social Psychology, 26,* 309–320.

Gergen, K. J. (1982). *Toward transformation in social knowledge.* New York: Springer-Verlag.

Gergen, K. J. (1985). The social constructionist movement in modern psychology. *American Psychologist, 40,* 266–275.

Gergen, K. J. (1987). The language of psychological understanding. In H. J. Stamm, T. B. Rogers, & K. J. Gergen (Eds), *The analysis of psychological theory: Metapsychological perspectives.* Washington, DC: Hemisphere.

Gergen, K. J. (1989). Warranting voice and the elaboration of the self. In J. Shotter & K. J. Gergen (Eds), *Texts of identity*. London: Sage Publications.

Gergen, K. J., Gergen, M. M., & Meter, K. (1972). Individual orientations to prosocial behavior. *Journal of Social Issues, 28*, 105–130.

Gerth, H., & Mills, C. W. (1953). *Character and social structure*. New York: Harcourt Brace Jovanovich.

Gilligan, C. (1982). *In a different voice: Psychological theory and women's development*. Cambridge, MA: Harvard University Press.

Ginossar, Z., & Trope, Y. (1987). Problem solving in judgment under uncertainty. *Journal of Personality and Social Psychology, 52*, 464–474.

Goffman, E. (1955). On face-work: An analysis of ritual elements in social interaction. *Psychiatry, 18*, 213–231.

Goffman, E. (1959). *The presentation of self in everyday life*. New York: Doubleday Anchor Books.

Goldberg, L. R. (1981). Unconfounding situational attributions from uncertain, neutral and ambiguous ones: A psychometric analysis of descriptions of oneself and various types of others. *Journal of Personality and Social Psychology, 41*, 517–552.

Goldberg, P. (1968). Are women prejudiced against women? *Transaction, 5*, 28–30.

Gould, C. C., & Wartofsky, M. W. (1976). *Women and philosophy*. New York: Putnam.

Gouldner, A. (1960). The norm of reciprocity: A preliminary statement. *American Sociological Review, 25*, 161–178.

Greeno, J. G. (1989). A perspective on thinking. *American Psychologist, 44*, 134–141.

Greenpeace (1989, January/February) The economic facts. *Greenpeace*, p. 18.

Greenwald, A. G. (1980). The totalitarian ego: Fabrication and revision of personal history. *American Psychologist, 35*, 603–618.

Greenwald, A. G., & Pratkanis, A. R. (1984). The self. In R. S. Weyer & T. K. Srull (Eds.), *The handbook of social cognition: Vol. 3*. Hillsdale, NJ: Erlbaum.

Gruder, C. L., Cook, T. D., Hennigan, K. M., Flay, B. R., Alessis, C., & Halamaj, J. (1978). Empirical tests of the absolute sleeper effect predicted from the discounting cue hypothesis. *Journal of Personality and Social Psychology, 36*, 1061–1074.

Gusfield, J. (1976). The literary rhetoric of science: Comedy and pathos in drinking driver research. *American Sociological Review, 41*, 16–34.

Hales, S. (1985). The inadvertent rediscovery of self in social psychology. *Journal for the Theory of Social Behavior, 15*, 237–282.

Hare-Mustin, R. T., & Marecek, J. (1988). The meaning of difference: Gender theory, postmodernism and psychology. *American Psychologist, 43*, 455–464.

Harré, R. (1984). *Personal being.* Cambridge, MA: Harvard University Press.

Harré, R. (1985). The language game of self-ascription: A note. In K. J. Gergen & K. E. Davis (Eds.), *The social construction of the person.* New York: Springer-Verlag.

Harris, M. J., & Rosenthal, R. (1985). Mediation of interpersonal expectancy effects: 31 meta-analyses. *Psychological Bulletin, 97,* 363–386.

Harthshorne, H., & May, M. A. (1928–1930). *Studies in the nature of character* (Vols. 1–3). New York: Macmillan.

Harvey, O. J., Hunt, D. E., & Schroder, H. M. (1961). *Conceptual systems and personality organization.* New York: Wiley.

Hastie, R. (1984). Causes and effects of causal attribution. *Journal of Personality and Social Psychology, 46,* 44–56.

Heelas, P., & Lock, A. (1981). *Indigenous psychologies: The anthropology of the self.* London: Academic Press.

Heider, F. (1958). *The psychology of interpersonal relations.* New York: Wiley.

Hellman, M. E., & Toffler, B. L. (1976). Reacting to reactance: An interpersonal interpretation of the need for freedom. *Journal of Experimental Social Psychology, 12,* 519–529.

Henry, A. F., & Short, J. F. (1954). *Suicide and homicide: Some economic, sociological and psychological aspects of aggression.* New York: Free Press.

Hepworth, J. T., & West, S. G. (1988). Lynchings and the economy: A time-series reanalysis of Hovland and Sears (1940). *Journal of Personality and Social Psychology, 55,* 239–247.

Herman, E. S., & Chomsky, N. (1988). *Manufacturing consent: The political economy of the mass media.* New York: Pantheon.

Hewlett, S. A. (1986). *A lesser life: The myth of women's liberation in America.* New York: William Morrow.

Hewstone, M., & Ward, C. (1985). Ethnocentrism and causal attribution in Southeast Asia. *Journal of Personality and Social Psychology, 48,* 614–623.

Higgins, E. T. (1987). Self-discrepancy: A theory relating self and affect. *Psychological Review, 94,* 319–340.

Hilton, D. J., Smith, R. H., & Alicke, M. D. (1988). Knowledge-based information acquisition: Norms and the functions of consensus information. *Journal of Personality and Social Psychology, 55,* 534–540.

Himmelweit, H., & Swift, B. (1976). Continuities and discontinuities in media usage and taste: A longitudinal study. *Journal of Social Issues, 32,* 133–156.

Hobbes, T. (1651/1929). *Leviathan.* Oxford: Pogson Smith.

Hoch, S. J. (1987). Perceived consensus and predictive accuracy: The pros and cons of projection. *Journal of Personality and Social Psychology, 53,* 221–234.

Hoffer, E. (1951). *The true believer.* New York: Harper & Row.

Hoffman, M. L. (1981). Is altruism part of human nature? *Journal of Personality and Social Psychology, 40,* 121–137.

Hollander, E. P. (1958). Conformity, status and idiosyncracy credit. *Psychological Review, 65,* 117–127.

Hollander, E. P. (1964). *Leaders, groups and influence.* New York: Oxford University Press.

Holloway, S., Tucker, L., & Hornstein, H. A. (1977). The effects of social and non-social information on interpersonal behavior of males: The news makes news. *Journal of Personality and Social Psychology, 35,* 514–522.

Holtzworth-Munroe, A., & Jacobson, N. S. (1985). Causal attributions of married couples: When do they search for causes? What do they conclude when they do? *Journal of Personality and Social Psychology, 48,* 1398–1412.

Hornstein, H. A., Lakind, E., Frankel, G., & Manne, S. (1975). Effects of knowledge about remote social events on prosocial behavior, social conception and mood. *Journal of Personality and Social Psychology, 32,* 1038–1046.

Hovland, C. I., Lumsdaine, A. A., & Sheffield, F. D. (1949). *Experiments on mass communication.* Princeton, NJ: Princeton University Press.

Hovland, C. I., & Sears, R. R. (1940). Minor studies in aggression: 6. Correlation of lynchings with economic indices. *Journal of Psychology, 9,* 301–310.

Howard, J. A. (1984). Societal influences on attribution: Blaming some victims more than others. *Journal of Personality and Social Psychology, 47,* 494–505.

Huesmann, L. R. (1986). Psychological processes promoting the relation between exposure to media violence and aggressive behavior by the viewer. *Journal of Social Issues, 42,* 125–139.

Huesmann, L. R. & Malamuth, N. M. (1986). Media violence and antisocial behavior: An overview. *Journal of Social Issues, 42,* 1–6.

Hyde, J. S., & Linn, M. C. (1988). Gender differences in verbal ability: A meta-analysis. *Psychological Bulletin, 104,* 53–69.

Hymes, R. W. (1986). Political attitudes as social categories: A new look at selective memory. *Journal of Personality and Social Psychology, 51,* 233–241.

Isen, A. M. (1970). Success, failure, attention and reaction to others. *Journal of Personality and Social Psychology, 15,* 294–301.

Isen, A. M., Clark, M., & Schwartz, M. F. (1976). Duration of the effect of good mood on helping: "Footprints on the sands of time". *Journal of Personality and Social Psychology, 34,* 385–393.

Jacobs, R. C., & Campbell, D. T. (1961). The perpetuation of an arbitrary tradition through several generations of a laboratory micro-culture. *Journal of Abnormal and Social Psychology, 62,* 649–658.

Jahoda, M. (1959). Conformity and independence. *Human Relations, 12,* 99–120.

James, W. (1910). *Psychology: The brief course*. New York: Holt.

Janis, I. L. (1972). *Victims of groupthink*. Boston: Houghton Mifflin.

Janis, I. L. (1982). *Groupthink* (2nd ed.). Boston: Houghton Mifflin.

Janoff-Bulman, R. (1979). Characterological versus behavioral self-blame: Inquiries into depression and rape. *Journal of Personality and Social Psychology, 37*, 1798–1809.

Jellison, J. M. & Green, J. (1981). A self-presentation approach to the fundamental attribution error: The norm of internality. *Journal of Personality and Social Psychology, 40*, 643–649.

Jones, E. E., & Davis, K. (1965). From acts to dispositions: The attribution process in person perception. In L. Berkowitz (Ed.), *Advances in experimental social psychology: Vol. 2*. New York: Academic Press.

Jones, E. E., & Nisbett, R. E. (1971). *The actor and the observer: Divergent perceptions of the causes of behavior*. Morristown, NJ: General Learning Press.

Jones, S. (1973). Self- and interpersonal evaluations: Esteem theories vs. consistency theories. *Psychological Bulletin, 79*, 185–199.

Josephson, W. L. (1987). Television violence and children's aggression: Testing the priming, social script, and disinhibition predictions. *Journal of Personality and Social Psychology, 53*, 882–890.

Jussim, L. (1989). Teacher expectations: Self-fulfilling prophecies, perceptual biases and accuracy. *Journal of Personality and Social Psychology, 57*, 469–480.

Kahn, R. L. (1972). The justification of violence: Social problems and social solutions. *Journal of Social Issues, 28*, 155–175.

Kahneman, D., Slovic, P., & Tversky, A. (1982). *Judgment under uncertainty: Heuristics and biases*. Cambridge: Cambridge University Press.

Kahneman, D., & Tversky, A. (1984). Choices, values and frames, *American Psychologist, 39*, 341–350.

Kaplan, R. M., & Singer, R. D. (1976). Television violence and viewer aggression: A reexamination of the evidence. *Journal of Social Issues, 32*, 35–70.

Karinol, R., & Ross, M. (1976). The development of causal attributions in social perception. *Journal of Personality and Social Psychology, 34*, 455–464.

Kassin, S. M., Lowe, C. A., & Gibbons, F. X. (1980). Children's use of the discounting principle: A perceptual approach. *Journal of Personality and Social Psychology, 39*, 719–728.

Katz, D. (1960). The functional approach to the study of attitudes. *Public Opinion Quarterly, 24*, 163–204.

Katz, D., & Stotland, E. (1959). A preliminary statement of a theory of attitude structure and change. In S. Koch (Ed.), *Psychology: A study of a science: Vol. 3. Formulations of the person and the social context*. New York: McGraw-Hill.

Kelley, H. H. (1973). The processes of causal attribution. *American Psychologist, 28,* 107–128.

Kelley, H. H., & Stahelski, A. J. (1970). Social interaction basis of cooperators' and competitors' beliefs about others. *Journal of Personality and Social Psychology, 16,* 66–91.

Kelman, H. C. (1958). Compliance, identification and internalization: Three processes of attitude change. *Journal of Conflict Resolution, 2,* 51–60.

Kelman, H. C. (1973). Violence without moral restraint: Reflections on the dehumanization of victims and victimizers. *Journal of Social Issues, 29,* 25–61.

Kelman, H. C., & Barclay, J. (1963). The F-scale as a measure of breadth of perspective. *Journal of Abnormal and Social Psychology, 67,* 608–615.

Kelman, H. C., & Hamilton, V. L. (1988). *Crimes of obedience.* New Haven: Yale University Press.

Kelman, H. C., & Lawrence, L. H. (1972). Assignment of responsibility in the case of Lt. Calley: Preliminary report on a national survey. *Journal of Social Issues, 28,* 177–212.

Kemp, R. (1985). Planning, public hearings and the politics of discourse. In J. Forester (Ed.), *Critical theory and public life.* Cambridge, MA: The MIT Press.

Kessen, W. (1979). The American child and other cultural inventions. *American Psychologist, 34,* 815–820.

Kimble, G. A. (1989). Psychology from the standpoint of a generalist. *American Psychologist, 44,* 491–499.

Kinder, D. R. (1978). Political person perception: The asymmetrical influence of sentiment and choice on perceptions of presidential candidates. *Journal of Personality and Social Psychology, 36,* 859–871.

Kitzinger, C. (1987). *The social construction of lesbianism.* London: Sage.

Kohlberg, L. (1969). Stage and sequence: The cognitive-developmental approach to socialization. In D. A. Goslin (Ed.), *Handbook of socialization theory and research.* Chicago: Rand McNally.

Kohlberg, L. (1981). *The philosophy of moral development: Vol. 1.* New York: Harper & Row.

Kohlberg, L. (1984). *The psychology of moral development: Vol. 2.* New York: Harper & Row.

Kojima, H. (1984). A significant stride toward the comparative study of control. *American Psychologist, 39,* 972–973.

Kolditz, T. A. & Arkin, R. M. (1982). An impression management interpretation of self-handicapping. *Journal of Personality and Social Psychology, 43,* 492–502.

Konecni, V. J. & Doob, A. N. (1972). Catharsis through displacement of aggression. *Journal of Personality and Social Psychology, 23,* 379–387.

Konecni, V. J., & Ebbesen, E. B. (1976). Disinhibition versus the cathartic effect: Artifact and substance. *Journal of Personality and Social Psychology, 34,* 352–365.

Krebs, D. L., & Miller, D. T. (1985). Altruism and aggression. In G. Lindzey & E. Aronson (Eds.), *Handbook of social psychology: Vol 2.* (3rd ed.). New York: Random House.

Krosnick, J. A., & Alwin, D. F. (1989). Aging and susceptibility to attitude change. *Journal of Personality and Social Psychology, 57,* 416–425.

Kuhn, T. S. (1962). *The structure of scientific revolutions.* Chicago: University of Chicago Press.

Laing, R. D. (1967). *The politics of experience.* New York: Ballantine.

Lander, S. (1989, July) Watching TV violence shapes people's values. *APA Monitor,* p. 33.

Langer, E., Blank, A., & Chanowitz, B. (1978). The mindlessness of ostensibly thoughtful action: The role of "placebic" information in interpersonal interaction. *Journal of Personality and Social Psychology, 36,* 635–642.

La Piere, R. T. (1934). Attitudes vs. actions. *Social Forces, 13,* 230–337.

Latané, B. (1981). The psychology of social impact. *American Psychologist, 36,* 343–356.

Latané, B., & Darley, J. M. (1970). *The unresponsive bystander: Why doesn't he help?.* New York: Appleton-Century-Crofts.

Latané, B., & Wolf, S. (1981). The social impact of majorities and minorities. *Psychological Review, 88,* 438–453.

Lave, J., Murtaugh, M., & de la Rocha, O. (1984). The dialectic of arithmetic in grocery shopping. In B. Rogoff & J. Lave (Eds.), *Everyday cognition: Its development in social context.* Cambridge, MA: Harvard University Press.

Le Bon, G. (1895/1960). *The crowd.* New York: Viking Press.

Lebow, R. N., & Stein, J. G. (1987). Beyond deterrence. *Journal of Social Issues, 43,* 5–71.

Leippe, M. R., & Elkin, R. A. (1987). When motives clash: Issue involvement and response involvement as determinants of persuasion. *Journal of Personality and Social Psychology, 52,* 269–278.

Leon, G. R., Butcher, J. N., Kleinman, M., Goldberg, A., & Almagor, M. (1981). Survivors of the holocaust and their children: Current status and adjustment. *Journal of Personality and Social Psychology, 41,* 503–516.

Lerner, M. (1985). *Occupational stress groups and the psychodynamics of the world of work.* Oakland, CA: The Institute for Labor and Mental Health.

Lerner, M. J. (1965). Evaluation of performance as a function of performer's reward and attractiveness. *Journal of Personality and Social Psychology, 1,* 355–360.

Lerner, M. J., & Miller, D. T. (1978). Just world research and the attribution process: Looking back and ahead. *Psychological Bulletin, 85,* 1030–1051.

Lewin, K. (1947a). Frontiers in group dynamics: 1. Concept, method and reality in social science: Social equilibrium and social change. *Human Relations, 1,* 5–41.

Lewin, K. (1947b). Frontiers in group dynamics: 2. Channels of group life, social planning and action research. *Human Relations, 1,* 143–153.

Lewin, K. (1958). Group decision and social change. In E. E. Maccoby, T. M. Newcomb, & E. L. Hartley (Eds.), *Readings in social psychology* (3rd ed.). New York: Holt, Rinehart & Winston.

Leyens, J-P, & Fraczek, A. (1984). Aggression as an interpersonal phenomenon. In H. Tajfel (Ed.), *The social dimension: European developments in social psychology: Vol. 1.* Cambridge: Cambridge University Press.

Lifton, R. J. (1961). *Thought reform and the psychology of totalism: A study of "brainwashing" in China.* New York: Norton.

Lindzey, G., & Aronson, E. (1985). *Handbook of social psychology.* New York: Random House.

Linz, D., Penrod, S., & Donnerstein, E. (1986). Issues bearing on the legal regulation of violent and sexually violent media. *Journal of Social Issues, 42,* 171–193.

Linz, D. G., Donnerstein, E., & Penrod, S. (1988). Effects of long-term exposure to violent and sexually degrading depictions of women. *Journal of Personality and Social Psychology, 55,* 758–768.

Locksley, A., Borgida, E., Brekke, N., & Hepburn, C. (1980). Sex stereotypes and social judgment. *Journal of Personality and Social Psychology, 39,* 821–831.

Luria, A. R. (1976). *Cognitive development: Its cultural and social foundations.* Cambridge, MA: Harvard University Press.

Lutz, C. (1985). Ethnopsychology compared to what? Explaining behavior and consciousness among the Ifaluk. In G. M. White & J. Kirkpatrick (Eds.), *Person, self and experience.* Berkeley: University of California Press.

Lutz, C. (1988). *Unnatural emotions.* Chicago: University of Chicago Press.

Maass, A., & Clark, R. D. (1984). Hidden impact of minorities: Fifteen years of minority influence research. *Psychological Bulletin, 95,* 428–450.

Maccoby, M. (1972). Emotional attitudes and political choices. *Politics and Society,* 209–239.

MacIntyre, A. (1988). *Whose justice? Which rationality?* Notre Dame, Indiana: University of Notre Dame Press.

Macpherson, C. B. (1962). *The political theory of possessive individualism.* London: Oxford University Press.

Mahler, M., Pine, F., & Bergman, A. (1975). *The psychological birth of the human infant: Symbiosis and individuation.* New York: Basic Books.

Major, B. (1980). Information acquisition and attribution processes. *Journal of Personality and Social Psychology, 39,* 1010–1023.

Malamuth, N. M., & Briere, J. (1986). Sexual violence in the media: Indirect effects on aggression against women. *Journal of Social Issues, 42,* 75–92.

Manuel, F. E., & Manuel, F. P. (1979). *Utopian thought in the western world.* Cambridge, MA: Belknap Press of Harvard University Press.

Marks, G., & Miller, N. (1987). Ten years of research on the false-consensus effect: An empirical and theoretical review. *Psychological Bulletin, 102,* 72–90.

Markus, H. (1977). Self-schemata and processing information about the self. *Journal of Personality and Social Psychology, 35,* 63–78.

Markus, H., Crane, M., Bernstein, S., & Siladi, M. (1982). Self-schemas and gender. *Journal of Personality and Social Psychology, 42,* 38–50.

Markus, H., & Kunda, Z. (1986). Stability and malleability of the self-concept. *Journal of Personality and Social Psychology, 51,* 858–866.

Markus, H., & Nurius, P. (1986). Possible selves. *American Psychologist, 41,* 954–969.

Markus, H., Smith, J., & Moreland, R. L. (1985). Role of the self-concept in the perception of others. *Journal of Personality and Social Psychology, 49,* 1494–1512.

Markus, H., & Zajonc, R. B. (1985). The cognitive perspective in social psychology. In G. Lindzey & E. Aronson (Eds.), *Handbook of social psychology: Vol. 1* (3rd ed.). New York: Random House.

Maslow, A. H. (1941). Deprivation, threat and frustration. *Psychological Review, 48,* 364–366.

Matthews, K. A., & Rodin, J. (1989). Women's changing work roles. *American Psychologist, 44,* 1389–1393.

Mayo, E. (1933). *The human problems of an industrial civilization.* Cambridge, MA: Harvard University Press.

McArthur, L. A. (1972). The how and what of why: Some determinants and consequences of causal attribution. *Journal of Personality and Social Psychology, 22,* 171–193.

McCauley, C. (1989). The nature of social influence in groupthink: Compliance and internalization. *Journal of Personality and Social Psychology, 57,* 250–260.

McClintock, C. G., & Liebrand, W. B. G. (1988). Role of interdependence structure, individual value orientation and another's strategy in social decision making: A transformational analysis. *Journal of Personality and Social Psychology, 55,* 396–409.

McClure, J. (1985). The social parameter of "learned" helplessness: Its recognition and implications. *Journal of Personality and Social Psychology, 48,* 1534–1539.

McGuire, W. J. (1964). Inducing resistance to persuasion: Some contemporary approaches. In L. Berkowitz (Ed.), *Advances in experimental social psychology: Vol. 1.* New York: Academic Press.

McGuire, W. J. (1985). Attitudes and attitude change. In G. Lindzey & E. Aronson (Eds.), *Handbook of social psychology: Vol. 2.* New York: Random House.

Mead, G. H. (1934). *Mind, self and society.* Chicago: University of Chicago Press.

Mednick, M. T. (1989). On the politics of psychological constructs: Stop the bandwagon, I want to get off. *American Psychologist, 44,* 1118–1123.

Mehan, H. (1984). Institutional decision making. In B. Rogoff & J. Lave (Eds.), *Everyday cognition: Its development in social context.* Cambridge, MA: Harvard University Press.

Mehlman, R. C., & Snyder, C. R. (1985). Excuse theory: A test of the self-protective role of attributions. *Journal of Personality and Social Psychology, 49,* 994–1001.

Memmi, A. (1967). *The colonizer and the colonized.* Boston: Beacon Press.

Meyerowitz, B. E., & Chaiken, S. (1987). The effect of message framing on breast self-examination attitudes, intentions and behavior. *Journal of Personality and Social Psychology, 52,* 500–510.

Mikulincer, M. (1988). Reactance and helplessness following exposure to unsolvable problems: The effects of attributional style. *Journal of Personality and Social Psychology, 54,* 679–686.

Milavsky, J. R., Stipp, H. H., Kessler, R. C., & Rubens, W. S. (1982). *Television and aggression: A panel study.* New York: Academic Press.

Milgram, S. (1965a). Some conditions of obedience and disobedience to authority. *Human Relations, 18,* 57–75.

Milgram, S. (1965b). Liberating effects of group pressure. *Journal of Personality and Social Psychology, 1,* 127–134.

Milgram, S. (1970). The experience of living in cities. *Science, 167,* 1461–1468.

Millar, M. G., & Tesser, A. (1986). Effects of affective and cognitive focus on the attitude-behavior relation. *Journal of Personality and Social Psychology, 51,* 270–276.

Miller, J. G. (1984). Culture and the development of everyday social explanation. *Journal of Personality and Social Psychology, 46,* 961–978.

Miller, P. A., & Eisenberg, N. (1988). The relation of empathy to aggression and externalizing/antisocial behavior. *Psychological Bulletin, 103,* 324–344.

Mills, C. W. (1963). *Power, politics and people: Collected essays.* New York: Ballantine.

Minard, R. D. (1952). Race relations in the Pochontas coal field. *Journal of Social Issues, 8,* 29–44.

Money, J. (1987). Sin, sickness or status? Homosexual gender identity and psychoneuroendocrinology. *American Psychologist, 42,* 384–399.

Moscovici, S. (1985). Social influence and conformity. In G. Lindzey & E. Aronson (Eds.), *Handbook of social psychology: Vol. 2* (3rd ed.). New York: Random House.

Moscovici, S., & Lage, E. (1978). Studies in social influence: IV. Minority influence in a context of original judgments. *European Journal of Social Psychology, 8,* 349–365.

Moscovici, S., Lage, E., & Naffrechoux, M. (1969). Influence of a consistent minority on the responses of a majority in a color perception task. *Sociometry, 32,* 365–379.

Mugny, G. (1984). The influence of minorities: Ten years later. In H. Tajfel (Ed.), *The social dimension: European developments in social psychology: Vol. 2.* Cambridge: Cambridge University Press.

Nail, P. R. (1986). Toward an integration of some models and theories of social response. *Psychological Bulletin, 100,* 190–206.

Nemeth, C., Swedlund, M., & Kanki, B. (1974). Patterning of the minority's responses and their influence on the majority. *European Journal of Social Psychology, 4,* 53–64.

Nemeth, C., & Wachtler, J. (1974). Creating the perceptions of consistency and confidence: A necessary condition for minority influence. *Sociometry, 37,* 529–540.

Newcomb, T. M. (1943). *Personality and social change: Attitude formation in a student community.* New York: Dryden Press.

Newcomb, T. M. (1961). *The acquaintance process.* New York: Holt, Rinehart & Winston.

Newcomb, T. M., Koenig, K. E., Flacks, R., & Warwick, D. P. (1967). *Persistence and change: Bennington College and its students after twenty-five years.* New York: Wiley.

Ochs, E., & Schieffelin, B. B. (1984). Language acquisition and socialization. In R. A. Shweder & R. A. Levine (Eds.), *Culture theory: Essays on mind, self and emotion.* Cambridge: Cambridge University Press.

Ogilvie, D. M. (1987). The undesired self: A neglected variable in personality research. *Journal of Personality and Social Psychology, 52,* 379–385.

Ohbuchi, K., Kameda, M., & Agarie, N. (1989). Apology as aggression control: Its role in mediating appraisal of and response to harm. *Journal of Personality and Social Psychology, 56,* 219–227.

Oliner, S. P., & Oliner, P. M. (1988). *The altruistic personality.* New York: Free Press.

Olson, J. M. (1988). Misattribution, preparatory information and speech anxiety. *Journal of Personality and Social Psychology, 54,* 758–767.

Olweus, P. (1979). Stability of aggressive reaction patterns in males: A review. *Psychological Bulletin, 86,* 853–875.

Orvis, B. R., Cunningham, J. D., & Kelley, H. H. (1975). A closer examination of causal inference: The roles of consensus, distinctiveness and consistency information. *Journal of Personality and Social Psychology, 32,* 605–616.

Ottati, V., Fishbein, M., & Middlestadt, S. E. (1988). Determinants of voters' beliefs about the candidates' stands on the issues: The role of evaluative bias heuristics and the candidates' expressed message. *Journal of Personality and Social Psychology, 55,* 527–529.

Paicheler, G. (1976). Norms and attitude change: I. Polarization and styles of behavior. *European Journal of Social Psychology, 6,* 405–427.

Paicheler, G. (1977). Norms and attitude change: II. The phenomenon of bipolarization. *European Journal of Social Psychology, 7,* 5–14.

Passell, P. (1989a, May 8). The American sense of peril: A stifling cost of modern life. *New York Times,* pp. 1, 8.

Passell, P. (1989b, May 9). Making a risky life bearable: Better data, clearer choices. *New York Times,* pp. B5, B7.

Pearl, D., Bouthilet, L., & Lazar, J. (1982). *Television and Behavior: Ten years of scientific progress and implications for the eighties* (Vols. 1–2). Washington, DC: U.S. Government Printing Office.

Perlez, J. (1990, January 15). Puberty rite for girls is bitter issue across Africa. *New York Times,* p. A4.

Peters, R. S. (1958). *The concept of motivation.* London: Routledge & Kegan Paul.

Peterson, C., & Barrett, L. C. (1987). Explanatory styles and academic performance among university freshman. *Journal of Personality and Social Psychology, 53,* 603–607.

Peterson, C., & Seligman, M. E. P. (1984). Causal explanations as a risk factor for depression: Theory and evidence. *Psychological Review, 91,* 347–374.

Peterson, C., Seligman, M. E. P., & Vaillant, G. (1988). Pessimistic explanatory style is a risk factor for physical illness: A thirty-five year longitudinal study. *Journal of Personality and Social Psychology, 55,* 23–27.

Petty, R. E., & Cacioppo, J. T. (1981). *Attitudes and persuasion: Classic and contemporary approaches.* Dubuque, Iowa: William C. Brown.

Petty, R. E., Cacioppo, J. T., & Goldman, R. (1981). Personal involvement as a determinant of argument-based persuasion. *Journal of Personality and Social Psychology, 41,* 847–855.

Piaget, J. (1965). *The moral judgment of the child.* Glencoe, IL: Free Press.

Piliavin, J. A., Dovidio, J. F., Gaertner, S. L., & Clark, R. D. (1981). *Emergency intervention.* New York: Academic Press.

Piliavin, J. A., & Piliavin, I. M. (1972). Effect of blood on reactions to a victim. *Journal of Personality and Social Psychology, 23,* 353–361.

Piliavin, I. M., Rodin, J., & Piliavin, J. A. (1969). Good samaritanism: An underground phenomenon? *Journal of Personality and Social Psychology, 13,* 289–299.

Powers, T. A., & Zuroff, D. C. (1988). Interpersonal consequences of overt self-criticism: A comparison with neutral and self-enhancing presentations of self. *Journal of Personality and Social Psychology, 54,* 1054–1062.

Pratkanis, A. R., & Greenwald, A. G. (1985). How shall the self be conceived? *Journal for the Theory of Social Behavior, 15,* 311–329.

Pratkanis, A. R., Greenwald, A. G., Leippe, M. R., & Baumgardner, M. H. (1988). In search of reliable persuasion effects: 3. The sleeper effect is dead. Long live the sleeper effect. *Journal of Personality and Social Psychology, 54,* 203–218.

Prince, M. (1920). Miss Beauchamp: The theory of the psychogenesis of multiple personality. *Journal of Abnormal Psychology, 15,* 67–135.

Pryor, J. B., Gibbons, F. X., Wicklund, R. A., Fazio, R. H., & Hood, R. (1977). Self-focused attention and self-report validity. *Journal of Personality, 45,* 514–527.

Rank, O. (1936). *Will therapy and truth and reality.* New York: Knopf.

Read, S. J. (1987). Constructing causal scenarios: A knowledge structure approach to causal reasoning. *Journal of Personality and Social Psychology, 52,* 288–302.

Redl, F. (1973). The superego in uniform. In N. Sanford & C. Comstock (Eds.), *Sanctions for evil.* San Francisco: Jossey-Bass.

Reisenzein, R. (1983). The Schachter theory of emotions: Two decades later. *Psychological Bulletin, 94,* 239–264.

Richie, D. (1984). *The films of Akira Kurosawa.* Berkeley: University of California Press.

Riesman, D. (1950). *The lonely crowd.* New Haven: Yale University Press.

Riskin, J. H., Rhodes, R. C., Brannon, A. M., & Burdick, C. A. (1987). Attribution and expectations: A confluence of vulnerabilities in mild depression in a college student population. *Journal of Personality and Social Psychology, 53,* 349–354.

Roethlisberger, F. J., & Dickson, W. J. (1939). *Management and the worker.* New York: Wiley.

Rokeach, M. (1960). *The open and closed mind.* New York: Basic Books.

Rokeach, M. (1973). *The nature of human values.* New York: Free Press.

Rorty, R. (1979). *Philosophy and the mirror of nature.* Princeton, NJ: Princeton University Press.

Rorty, R. (1989). *Contingency, irony and solidarity.* Cambridge: Cambridge University Press.

Rosaldo, M. (1984). Toward an anthropology of self and feeling. In R. A. Shweder & R. A. LeVine (Eds.), *Culture theory: Essays on mind, self and emotion.* Cambridge: Cambridge University Press.

Rosaldo, R. (1989). *Culture and truth.* Boston: Beacon Press.

Rosenberg, M. J. (1960). An analysis of affective-cognitive consistency. In C. I. Hovland & M. J. Rosenberg (Eds.), *Attitude organization and change.* New Haven: Yale University Press.

Rosenberg, M. J. & Hovland, C. I. (1960). Cognitive, affective and behavioral components of attitudes. In C. I. Hovland & M. J. Rosenberg (Eds.), *Attitude organization and change*. New Haven: Yale University Press.

Rosenhan, D., & White, G. M. (1967). Observation and rehearsal as determinants of prosocial behavior. *Journal of Personality and Social Psychology, 5,* 424–431.

Rosenthal, R., & Jacobson, L. (1968). *Pygmalion in the classroom*. New York: Holt, Rinehart & Winston.

Ross, L. (1977). The intuitive psychologist and his shortcomings: Distortions in the attribution process. In L. Berkowitz (Ed.), *Advances in experimental social psychology: Vol. 10*. New York: Academic Press.

Ross, L. D., Amabile, T. M., & Steinmetz, J. L. (1977). Social roles, social control and biases in social perception processes. *Journal of Personality and Social Psychology, 35,* 485–494.

Ross, L., Bierbrauer, G., & Hoffman, S. (1976). The role of attribution processes in conformity and dissent. *American Psychologist, 31,* 148–157.

Ross, M., & Olson, J. M. (1981). An expectancy-attribution model of the effects of placebos. *Psychological Review, 88,* 408–437.

Rotenberg, M. (1977). "Alienating-individualism" and "reciprocal-individualism": A cross-cultural conceptualization. *Journal of Humanistic Psychology, 17,* 3–17.

Rousseau, J. J. (1762/1950). *The social contract and discourses*. New York: Dutton.

Rushton, J. P. (1981). The altruistic personality. In J. P. Rushton & R. M. Sorrentino (Eds.), *Altruism and helping behavior: Social, personality and developmental perspective*. Hillsdale, NJ: Erlbaum.

Ryan, B. (1971). *Blaming the victim*. New York: Pantheon Books.

Salter, S. (1989, July 9). Male-dominated abortions. *San Francisco Examiner*, p. A17.

Samelson, F. (1976). From "race psychology" to "studies in prejudice": Some observations on the thematic reversal in social psychology. Paper presented at the Eighth Annual Meeting of the International Society for the History of the Behavioral and Social Sciences. Washington, DC.

Sampson, E. E. (1963). Status congruence and cognitive consistency. *Sociometry, 26,* 146–162.

Sampson, E. E. (1976). *Social psychology and contemporary society*. New York: Wiley.

Sampson, E. E. (1983). *Justice and the critique of pure psychology*. New York: Plenum.

Sampson, E. E. (1989). The challenge of social change for psychology: Globalization and psychology's theory of the person. *American Psychologist, 44,* 914–921.

Sanford, N., & Comstock, C. (1973). *Sanctions for evil*. San Francisco: Jossey-Bass.

Sartre, J. P. (1954). *No exit*. New York: Knopf.

Scarr, S., Phillips, D., & McCartney, K. (1989). Working mothers and their families. *American Psychologist, 44,* 1402–1409.

Schachter, S. (1951). Deviation, rejection and communication. *Journal of Abnormal and Social Psychology, 46,* 190–207.

Schank, R. C., & Abelson, R. P. (1977). *Scripts, plans, goals and understanding.* Hillsdale, NJ: Erlbaum.

Schaufeli, W. D. (1988). Perceiving the causes of unemployment: An evaluation of the causal dimensions scale in a real-life situation. *Journal of Personality and Social Psychology, 54,* 347–356.

Schein, E. H. (1958). The Chinese indoctrination program for prisoners of war: A study of attempted "brainwashing". In E. E. Maccoby, T. M. Newcomb, & E. L. Hartley (Eds.), *Readings in social psychology* (3rd ed.). New York: Holt, Rinehart & Winston.

Schlenker, B. R. (1980). *Impression management: The self-concept, social identity, and interpersonal relations.* Belmont, CA: Brooks/Cole.

Schlenker, B. R., & Leary, M. R. (1982). Social anxiety and self-presentation: A conceptualization and model. *Psychological Bulletin, 92,* 641–669.

Schroder, H. M., Driver, M. J., & Streufert, S. (1967). *Human information processing.* New York: Holt, Rinehart & Winston.

Scott, J. W. (1988). *Gender and the politics of history.* New York: Columbia University Press.

Scott, M. B., & Lyman, S. (1968). Accounts. *American Sociological Review, 33,* 46–62.

Scribner, S. (1984). Studying working intelligence. In B. Rogoff and J. Lave (Eds.), *Everyday cognition: Its development in social context.* Cambridge, MA: Harvard University Press.

Sears, D. O. (1986). College sophomores in the laboratory: Influences of a narrow database on social psychology's view of human nature. *Journal of Personality and Social Psychology, 51,* 515–530.

Seligman, M. E. P. (1981). A learned helplessness point of view. In L. P. Rehm (Ed.), *Behavior therapy for depression: Present status and future directions.* New York: Academic Press.

Shaver, K. G. (1970). Defensive attribution: Effects of severity and relevance on the responsibility assigned for an accident. *Journal of Personality and Social Psychology, 14,* 101–113.

Sherif, M. (1935). A study of some social factors in perception. *Archives of Psychology, 27,* 1–60.

Sherif, M., & Sherif, C. W. (1953). *Groups in harmony and tension.* New York: Harper.

Sherwood, G. G. (1981). Self-serving biases in person perception: A reexamination of projection as a mechanism of defense. *Psychological Bulletin, 90,* 445–459.

Shields, S. A. (1975a). Functionalism, Darwinism, and the psychology of women: A study in social myth. *American Psychologist, 30,* 739–754.

Shields, S. A. (1975b). Ms. Pilgram's progress: The contributions of Leta Stetter Hollingsworth to the psychology of women. *American Psychologist, 30,* 853–857.

Shils, E. A. (1954). Authoritarianism "right" and "left". In R. Christie & M. Jahoda (Eds.), *Studies in the scope and method of the authoritarian personality.* New York: Free Press.

Shotland, R. L., & Heinold, W. D. (1985). Bystander response to arterial bleeding: Helping skills, the decision-making process and differentiating the helping response. *Journal of Personality and Social Psychology, 49,* 347–356.

Shotter, J. (1984). *Social accountability and selfhood.* Oxford: Basil Blackwell.

Shotter, J. (1985). Social accountability and self specification. In K. J. Gergen & K. E. Davis (Eds.), *The social construction of the person.* New York: Springer-Verlag.

Shotter, J. (1989). Social accountability and the social construction of "you". In J. Shotter & K. J. Gergen (Eds.), *Texts of identity.* London: Sage.

Shotter, J., & Gergen, K. J. (1989). *Texts of identity.* London: Sage.

Shrauger, J. S., & Schoeneman, T. J. (1979). Symbolic interactionist view of self-concept: Through the looking glass darkly. *Psychological Bulletin, 86,* 549–573.

Shweder, R. A., & Bourne, E. (1982). Does the concept of the person vary cross-culturally? In A. J. Marsalla & G. White (Eds.), *Cultural concepts of mental health and therapy.* Boston: Reidel.

Singer, R. D., & Kaplan, R. M. (1976). Introduction. *Journal of Social Issues, 32,* 1–7.

Sivacek, J., & Crano, W. D. (1982). Vested interest as a moderator of attitude-behavior consistency. *Journal of Personality and Social Psychology, 43,* 210–221.

Slugoski, B. R., & Ginsberg, G. P. (1989). Ego identity and explanatory speech. In J. Shotter & K. J. Gergen (Eds.), *Texts of identity.* London: Sage.

Smith, M. B., Bruner, J. S., & White, R. W. (1956). *Opinions and personality.* New York: Wiley.

Snyder, C. R., & Higgins, R. L. (1988). Excuses: Their effective role in the negotiation of reality. *Psychological Bulletin, 104,* 23–35.

Snyder, M. (1976). Attribution and behavior: Social perception and social causation. In J. H. Harvey, W. J. Ickes, & R. F. Kidd (Eds.), *New directions in attribution research.* Hillsdale, NJ: Erlbaum.

Snyder, M. (1979). Self-monitoring processes. In L. Berkowitz (Ed.), *Advances in experimental social psychology: Vol. 12.* New York: Academic Press.

Sorrentino, R. M., Bobocel, D. R., Gitta, M. Z., Olson, J. M., & Hewitt, E. C. (1988). Uncertainty orientation and persuasion: Individual differences in the effects of personal relevance on social judgments. *Journal of Personality and Social Psychology, 55,* 357–371.

Spence, J. T., & Helmreich, R. L. (1978). *Masculinity and femininity: Their psychological dimensions, correlates and antecedents.* Austin: University of Texas Press.

Spence, J. T., Helmreich, R., & Stapp, J. (1975). Ratings of self and peers on sex role attributes and their relation to self-esteem and conceptions of masculinity and femininity. *Journal of Personality and Social Psychology, 32,* 29–39.

Stam, H. J. (1987). The psychology of control: A textual critique. In H. J. Stam, T. B. Rogers, & K. J. Gergen (Eds.), *The analysis of psychological theory.* Washington, DC: Hemisphere.

Staub, E. (1972). Instigation to goodness: The role of social norms and interpersonal influence. *Journal of Social Issues, 28,* 131–150.

Staub, E. (1974). Helping a distressed person: Social, personality and stimulus determinants. In L. Berkowitz (Ed.), *Advances in experimental social psychology: Vol. 7.* New York: Academic Press.

Staub, E. (1978). *Positive social behavior and morality: Vol. 1. Social and personal influences.* New York: Academic Press.

Steblay, N. M. (1987). Helping behavior in rural and urban environments: A meta-analysis. *Psychological Bulletin, 102,* 346–356.

Strauman, T. J., & Higgins, E. T. (1987). Automatic activation of self-discrepancies and emotional syndromes: When cognitive structures influence affect. *Journal of Personality and Social Psychology, 53,* 1004–1014.

Swann, W. B. (1987). Identity negotiations: Where two roads meet. *Journal of Personality and Social Psychology, 53,* 1038–1051.

Swann, W. B., & Ely, R. J. (1984). A battle of wills: Self-verification versus behavioral confirmation. *Journal of Personality and Social Psychology, 46,* 1287–1302.

Swann, W. B., & Hill, C. A. (1982). When our identities are mistaken: Reaffirming self-conceptions through social interaction. *Journal of Personality and Social Psychology, 43,* 59–66.

Swim, J., Borgida, E., Maruyama, G., & Meyers, D. G. (1989). Joan McKay versus John McKay: Do gender stereotypes bias evaluations? *Psychological Bulletin, 105,* 409–429.

Surgeon General's Scientific Advisory Committee on Television and Social Behavior (1972). *Television and growing up: The impact of televised violence.* Washington, DC: U.S. Government Printing Office.

Tajfel, H. (1978). *Differentiation between social groups: Studies in the social psychology of intergroup relations.* London: Academic Press.

Tajfel, H. (1982). Social psychology of intergroup relations. *Annual Review of Psychology, 33,* 1–39.

Tanford, S., & Penrod, S. (1984). Social influence model: A formal integration of research on majority and minority influence processes. *Psychological Bulletin, 95,* 189–225.

Taylor, D. M., & Jaggi, V. (1974). Ethnocentrism in a South Indian context. *Journal of Cross-cultural Psychology, 5,* 162–172.

Taylor, D. M., & Moghaddam, F. M. (1987). *Theories of intergroup relations.* New York: Praeger.

Taylor, M. C., & Hall, J. A. (1982). Psychological androgyny: Theories, methods and conclusions. *Psychological Bulletin, 92,* 347–366.

Taylor, S. E. (1989). *Positive illusions.* New York: Basic Books.

Taylor, S. E., & Brown, J. D. (1988). Illusion and well-being: A social psychological perspective on mental health. *Psychological Bulletin, 103,* 193–210.

Tedeschi, J. T., Gaes, G. G., & Rivera, A. N. (1977). Aggression and the use of coercive power. *Journal of Social Issues, 33,* 101–125.

Tedeschi, J. T., Schlenker, B. R., & Bonoma, T. V. (1971). Cognitive dissonance: Private ratiocination or public spectacle? *American Psychologist, 26,* 685–695.

Tedeschi, J. T., Smith, R. B., & Brown, R. C. (1974). A reinterpretation of research on aggression. *Psychological Bulletin, 81,* 540–563.

Tetlock, P. E. (1981a). Pre- to post-election shifts in presidential rhetoric: Impression management or cognitive adjustment? *Journal of Personality and Social Psychology, 41,* 207–212.

Tetlock, P. E. (1981b). Personality and isolationism: Content analysis of senatorial speeches. *Journal of Personality and Social Psychology, 41,* 737–743.

Tetlock, P. E. (1983). Cognitive style and political ideology. *Journal of Personality and Social Psychology, 45,* 118–126.

Tetlock, P. E. (1984). Cognitive style and political belief systems in the British House of Commons. *Journal of Personality and Social Psychology, 46,* 365–375.

Tetlock, P. E. (1986). A value pluralism model of ideological reasoning. *Journal of Personality and Social Psychology, 50,* 819–827.

Tetlock, P. E. (1988). Monitoring the integrative complexity of American and Soviet policy rhetoric: What can be learned? *Journal of Social Issues, 44,* 101–131.

Tetlock, P. E., & Boettger, R. (1989). Accountability: A social magnifier of the dilution effect. *Journal of Personality and Social Psychology, 57,* 388–398.

Thompson, W. C., Cowan, C. L., & Rosenhan, D. L. (1980). Focus of attention mediates the impact of negative affect on altruism. *Journal of Personality and Social Psychology, 38,* 291–300.

Titmuss, R. M. (1971). *The gift relationship: From human blood to social policy.* New York: Random House/Vintage.

Tuan, Y. (1982). *Segmented worlds and self.* Minneapolis: University of Minnesota Press.

Turner, C. W., & Layton, J. F. (1976). Verbal imagery and connation as memory-induced mediators of aggressive behavior. *Journal of Personality and Social Psychology, 33,* 755–763.

Tversky, A., & Kahneman, D. (1974). Judgment under uncertainty: Heuristics and biases. *Science, 185,* 1124–1131.

Underwood, B., & Moore, B. (1982). Perspective-taking and altruism. *Psychological Bulletin, 91,* 143–173.

Van Hook, E., & Higgins, T. (1988). Self-related problems behind the self-concept: Motivational consequences of discrepant self-guides. *Journal of Personality and Social Psychology, 55,* 625–633.

Veitch, R., & Piccione, A. (1978). The role of attitude similarity in the attribution process. *Social Psychology, 41,* 165–169.

Vygotsky, L. S. (1978). *Mind in society.* Cambridge, MA: Harvard University Press.

Walker, L. E. A. (1989). Psychology and violence against women. *American Psychologist, 44,* 695–702.

Watson, D. (1982). The actor and the observer: How are their perceptions of causality divergent? *Psychological Bulletin, 92,* 682–700.

Weiner, B. (1985). Spontaneous causal thinking. *Psychological Bulletin, 97,* 74–84.

Weiner, B., Frieze, I., Kukla, A., Reed, L., Rest, S., & Rosenbaum, R. M. (1971). *Perceiving the causes of success and failure.* Morristown, NJ: General Learning Press.

Weiner, B., Perry, R. P., & Magnusson, J. (1988). An attributional analysis of reactions to stigmas. *Journal of Personality and Social Psychology, 55,* 738–748.

Weiner, B., Russell, D., & Lerman, D. (1979). The cognition-emotion process in achievement-related contexts. *Journal of Personality and Social Psychology, 37,* 1211–1220.

Weiner, B. A. (1979). A theory of motivation for some classroom experiences. *Journal of Educational Psychology, 71,* 3–25.

Weinstein, E. A., & Deutschberger, P. (1963). Some dimensions of altercasting. *Sociometry, 26,* 454–466.

Wertsch, J. V., Minick, N., & Arns, F. J. (1984). The creation of context in joint problem solving. In B. Rogoff & J. Lave (Eds.), *Everyday cognition: Its development in social context.* Cambridge, MA: Harvard University Press.

White, G. M., & Kirkpatrick, J. (1985). *Person, self and experience.* Berkeley: University of California Press.

Wicker, A. W. (1969). Attitudes versus actions: The relation of verbal and overt behavioral responses to attitude objects. *Journal of Social Issues, 25,* 41–78.

Wicklund, R. A. (1975). Objective self awareness. In L. Berkowitz (Ed.), *Advances in experimental social psychology: Vol. 8.* San Diego: Academic Press.

Wicklund, R. A. (1982). Self-focused attention and the validity of self-reports. In M. P. Zanna, E. T. Higgins, & C. P. Herman (Eds.), *Consistency in social behavior: The Ontario Symposium: Vol. 2.* Hillsdale, NJ: Erlbaum.

Widiger, T. A., & Settle, S. A. (1987). Broverman et al. revisited: An artifactual sex bias. *Journal of Personality and Social Psychology, 53,* 463–469.

Widom, C. S. (1989). Does violence beget violence? A critical examination of the literature. *Psychological Bulletin, 106,* 3–28.

Wilden, A. (1980). *System and structure* (2nd ed.). London: Tavistock.

Wilder, D. A. (1984). Perception of belief homogeneity and similarity following social categorization. *British Journal of Social Psychology, 23,* 323–333.

Wilson, T. D., Dunn, D. S., Bybee, J. A., Hyman, D. B., & Rotondo, J. A. (1984). Effects of analyzing reasons on attitude-behavior consistency. *Journal of Personality and Social Psychology, 47,* 5–16.

Wilson, T. D., & Linville, P. W. (1985). Improving the performance of college freshmen with attributional techniques. *Journal of Personality and Social Psychology, 49,* 287–293.

Winch, P. (1958). *The idea of a social science and its relation to philosophy.* London: Routledge & Kegan Paul

Wong, P. T. P., & Weiner, B. (1981). When people ask "why" questions and the heuristics of attributional search. *Journal of Personality and Social Psychology, 40,* 650–663.

Woodruffe, C. (1985). Consensual validation of personality traits: Additional evidence and individual differences. *Journal of Personality and Social Psychology, 48,* 1240–1252.

Wright, J. C., & Dawson, V. L. (1988). Person perception and the bounded rationality of social judgment. *Journal of Personality and Social Psychology, 55,* 780–794.

Wright, R. A., & Brehm, S. S. (1982). Reactance as impression management: A critical review. *Journal of Personality and Social Psychology, 42,* 608–618.

Wyer, R. S., Bodenhausen, G. V., & Gorman, T. F. (1985). Cognitive mediators of reactions to rape. *Journal of Personality and Social Psychology, 48,* 324–338.

Young, K. (1989). Narrative embodiments: Enclaves of the self in the realm of medicine. In J. Shotter & K. J. Gergen (Eds.), *Texts of identity.* London: Sage.

Zimbardo, P. G., Haney, C., Banks, W. C., & Jaffe, D. (1973, April 8). A Pirandellian prison: The mind is a formidable jailer. *New York Times Magazine,* pp. 38–60.

Zimbardo, P. G., Weisenberg, M., Firestone, I., & Levy, B. (1965). Communicator effectiveness in producing public conformity and private attitude change. *Journal of Personality, 33,* 233–255.

Index